The Rich Neighbor Policy

The Rich Neighbor Policy
Rockefeller and Kaiser in Brazil
Elizabeth Anne Cobbs

Yale University Press   New Haven and London

Published with assistance from the Kingsley Trust
Association Publication Fund established by the Scroll and
Key Society of Yale College.

Designed by Sonia L. Scanlon
Set in Sabon type by The Composing Room of Michigan,
Inc., Grand Rapids, Michigan.
Printed in the United States of America by Book Crafters,
Inc., Chelsea, Michigan

Library of Congress Cataloging-in-Publication Data

Cobbs, Elizabeth A.
    The rich neighbor policy : Rockefeller and Kaiser in
Brazil / Elizabeth A. Cobbs.
        p.   cm.
    Includes bibliographical references and index.
    ISBN 0-300-05179-4 (alk. paper)
    1. United States—Foreign economic relations—
Brazil.   2. Brazil—Foreign economic relations—United
States.   3. Investments, American—Brazil.
4. Rockefeller, Nelson A. (Nelson Aldrich),
1908–1979.   5. Kaiser, Henry J., 1882–   .   I. Title.
HF1456.5.B7C6   1992
337.73081—dc20   92-3939
                        CIP

A catalogue record for this book is available from the
British Library.

The paper in this book meets the guidelines for
permanence and durability of the Committee on
Production Guidelines for Book Longevity of the
Council on Library Resources.

10 9 8 7 6 5 4 3 2 1

For the Collective, past and present
—and for my mother

Contents

Illustrations

Acknowledgments

For their friendly, generous help, I would like to thank the staffs of the following archives and libraries: the Bancroft Library of the University of California, Berkeley; the Centro de Pesquisa e Documentação de História Contemporánea do Brasil; the Diplomatic Branch of the National Archives and Records Administration; the Ford Foundation Archives; the archives of Itamaraty in Rio de Janeiro; the John F. Kennedy Library and Archives; and the Rockefeller Archive Center. I would also like to thank the library of the University of California, San Diego, for extending special use privileges to me while I was writing my dissertation there. Special thanks go to Thomas E. Rosenbaum of the Rockefeller Archive Center for his continuing interest and assistance.

This research is based on oral histories as well as on manuscripts, and I owe a special debt to the individuals who gave generously of their time in interviews. I would like to thank Richard S. Aldrich, Euclydes Aranha Netto, Oswaldo Gudolle Aranha, Henry W. Bagley, Ney Bittencourt de Araújo, Roberto Campos, J. Burke Knapp, Sidney Latini, Cleantho de Paiva Leite, Paulo Pereira Lira, Lucas Lopes, Admiral Lúcio Meira, Max Pearce, David Rockefeller, Rodman C. Rockefeller, Walther Moreira Salles, Eugene E. Trefethen, and Alzira Vargas.

I received financial support for this research from a variety of institutions, without whose help the project would not have been feasible. I would like to thank the Mellon Fellowships in the Humanities for help during the year I was writing my dissertation and Stanford University for its assistance during two years of research. For funds to travel to archives in the United States and Brazil I would like to thank the American Philosophical Society, the Organization of American States, the Rockefeller Archive Center, the Stanford Center for Research in International Studies, the Stanford Center for Latin American Studies, the Stanford Office of Graduate Studies, and the University of San Diego. For financial assistance with preparing the final manuscript I thank the Society of Historians of American Foreign Relations for a grant from the Stuart L. Bernath Dissertation Fund.

The late Professor Armin Rappaport of the University of California, San Diego, inspired me to pursue the study of foreign relations. I owe much to his kindness, generosity, sharp wit, good humor, and, above all, friendship. At Stanford I received helpful insights and constructive criticism from Barton J.

Bernstein, Robert A. Packenham, and John D. Wirth. I would like to express my deep appreciation to David M. Kennedy, who guided me constantly toward the larger meanings of this study and whose meticulous editing and own deft, vivid prose were a constant inspiration to me to write better.

For assistance in Brazil, without which I would have literally been lost on many occasions, I would like to thank Cristiane Pires Pestana, Elayre Pires Pestana, Alexandre Vereza, and Norma and Manoel Valente Barbas. Their friendship made my stays in that country as enriching as I had hoped they would be. I would also like to express my appreciation to Barbara and Alan Finberg and to Lois and Colonel Cliff Mansfield for their kind hospitality during numerous research trips to New York and Washington. Leon Nower, my first and best editor as well as dear friend, merits sainthood for his willingness to listen to endless drafts. Simple thanks can only approximate my debt. Lastly, to my family, immediate and extended, I owe everything. Their love, support, encouragement, and faith made this work possible.

Abbreviations

ABCAR	Associação Brasileiro de Crédito e Assistência Rural
ACAR	Associação de Crédito e Assistência Rural
AIA	American International Association for Economic and Social Development
AID	Agency for International Development
ANCAR	Associação Nordestina de Crédito e Assistência Rural
BEW	Board of Economic Warfare
BL	Bancroft Library, University of California, Berkeley
BNDE	National Bank for Economic Development
CPDOC	Centro de Pesquisa e Documentação de História Contemporânea do Brasil
ECLA	Economic Commission on Latin America
FGV	Fundação Getúlio Vargas, Rio de Janeiro
FRUS	*Foreign Relations of the United States*. Washington: Government Printing Office.
FSA	Farm Security Administration
GATT	General Agreement on Tariffs and Trade
GEIA	Executive Group for the Automobile Industry
GPO	Government Printing Office
IBEC	International Basic Economy Corporation
ICA	International Cooperation Agency
IRI	Ibec Research Institute
JFK	John F. Kennedy Library and Archives, Boston
NA	National Archives of the United States, Washington, D.C.

OIAA	Office of Inter-American Affairs
RAC	Rockefeller Archive Center, Pocantico Hills, North Tarrytown, New York
SASA	Sementes Agroceres, Sociedade Anónima
SUMOC	Superintendency of Money and Credit
VBEC	Venezuelan Basic Economy Corporation
WOB	Willys-Overland do Brasil

The Rich Neighbor Policy

Introduction

The extraordinary faith of Americans in their nation and its institutions dates back to the earliest settlements on the North American continent. We see it in the confident superiority of the Puritans, in the righteous declarations and written constitutions of the American revolutionaries, in the calm certainty of those men who made the American system of manufactures into the world symbol of efficiency and wealth, and in the ambitious globalism of a post–World War II leadership ready to accept the definition of the twentieth century as "the American Century."[1] Many historians have drawn a picture of Americans as unusually susceptible to their illusions of continuous progress and sense of being "the chosen people."[2] Yet, as confident as Americans have been in their nation as a model for the world, twentieth-century his-

1. Henry R. Luce, *The American Century* (New York: Farrar and Rinehart, 1941).
2. See especially Louis Hartz, *The Liberal Tradition in America* (New York: Harcourt, Brace, and World, 1955), and David M. Potter, *People of Plenty: Economic Abundance and the American Character* (Chicago: University of Chicago Press, 1954).

tory shows a country frequently divided (or at least confused) about whether or how to exhort the rest of the world to follow.

The 1920s and 1930s saw the most sustained period of isolationism in modern U.S. history, as evidenced by the Nye Hearings on the U.S. entry into World War I and the Neutrality Acts of 1935, 1936, and 1937. But ever since the United States joined the Second World War, an internationalism characterized by an eagerness to dominate all levels of global politics has shaped foreign policy. It has not been easy for Americans to find a middle way between ignoring the rest of the world and trying to control it. "We may not get 100 percent of what we want in the postwar world," President Harry S Truman optimistically told his advisers, "but I think we can get 85 percent."[3] Two wars and several armed interventions later, Americans awoke to the fact that no nation has the resources and power to get its way among all the other nations of the world even 85 percent of the time. The war in Vietnam dispelled the myth that money and might could realize any military objective the United States sought, and the post-1971 era (when the United States abandoned the gold standard) showed that not even the almighty dollar was safe from the onslaught of global competition.

Yet in the early postwar period, roughly 1945 to 1960, both American leaders and the American public exhibited confidence that not only would U.S. predominance be sustained, but that its effect on world development and peace would be beneficial. Foreign aid, as a relatively new tool of international relations, played a significant role in bolstering these assumptions. Bryce Wood has shown how the Roosevelt administration experimented with foreign aid as a corollary to the Good Neighbor policy in order to bring Latin American nations into alignment with the United States in anticipation of World War II. Beginning with Export-Import Bank (also known as Eximbank) loans in 1939 and under the well-funded auspices of the Office of the Coordinator of Inter-American Affairs during World War II, the administration explored the possibilities and limitations of a system of economic rewards for managing hemispheric relations, given the fact that the United States had forsworn (at least temporarily) military intervention in the internal affairs of the other republics.[4]

Latin America thus became a test area for the development of policies that the United States put into practice on a greatly amplified scale in the

3. Quoted in *An American Portrait: A History of the United States*, ed. David Burner et al., 2d ed. (New York: Charles Scribner's Sons, 1985), 2:691.
4. Wood, *The Making of the Good Neighbor Policy* (New York: Columbia University Press, 1961), 334.

postwar period. An idea that was novel in the 1930s—a government contributing funds in order to raise living standards outside its borders as a matter of foreign economic policy—became an ad hoc but increasingly utilized tool of international relations after 1945. Bitter enemies were brought into enduring alliances by postwar reconstruction; allies were enabled to rebuild; and, beginning with the announcement of Truman's Point Four program in 1949, impoverished areas were given promises (in many cases never to be fulfilled) of a better future under Pax Americana. In the early 1950s, social scientists like Walt Rostow and Max Millikan began articulating the theories of development which laid the basis for aid programs as a permanent component of U.S. government policy. Early foreign aid cemented U.S. international leadership, while providing Americans with a comforting sense that globalism was, at least in part, an extension of America's centuries-old role as self-appointed model for a benighted world.

Ironically, while foreign aid was helping to pave the way for U.S. expansion over the rest of the globe and providing cover for military intervention in places like Indochina, American leaders virtually did away with foreign aid as a policy or practice in the region where it was first developed. At the Mexico City Conference in 1945, Nelson A. Rockefeller, as assistant secretary of state for Latin America, called for a return to normalcy in inter-American relations, in which economic development would be based primarily on private investment and made possible by Latin American safeguards to protect foreign capital and free trade. Increasingly over the next ten years, American officials, telling Latin Americans that U.S. private investment would have to fill the gap between their development goals and postwar reality, spurned economic aid to the southern republics as being statist.

This turning away from the economic aspects of the Good Neighbor policy reflected both the preoccupation of U.S. leaders with their new global role as well as the lack of a domestic consensus supporting foreign aid except when it could be clearly rationalized as being in the direct strategic interest of the United States. Far from the primary fronts of Cold War battle in Europe and Asia, Latin America witnessed the other side of anti-Communist fervor: the pervasive lack of interest in an area considered deep within the U.S. line of defense. The general unwillingness to extend economic aid to Latin America during this period reflected as well the desire of U.S. officials to place inter-American relations on a more "normal," permanent footing. As President Dwight D. Eisenhower wrote his brother Milton, who was also his adviser on Latin American questions, "In the case of the Americas, I do believe that loans are more

appropriate than grants. . . . [W]e want to establish a healthy relationship that will be characterized by mutual cooperation and which will
permanently endure. This will apply whether or not the Communist
menace seems to increase or decrease in intensity. In Asia we are primarily
concerned with meeting a crisis."[5]

Latin Americans, in view of a history of dominance by foreign corporations engaged in extractive enterprises, were highly suspicious of any
attempt to put forth private investment as the solution to underdevelopment and resented strongly the postwar lack of interest of U.S. leaders. Yet
among some Americans interest in Latin America had never waned. Interestingly, in light of his famous role in Mexico City, one of these people was
Nelson Rockefeller, who believed both in the viability of government-
supported development in some sectors as well as in the possibility of
development as an outgrowth of private investment. A person who later
joined him in this point of view was Henry J. Kaiser, who thought that, for
their own sake, American investors had to respond to the development
goals of the countries into which they ventured.

Today it is difficult to believe that anyone could have had faith in the
power of private investment or even of the U.S. government to bring about
significant positive change in the economies and social structures of Latin
America. Over the years foreign aid policy has suffered a mercurial fortune, viewed alternately with suspicion, approval, interest, bewilder-
ment, and finally with tired resignation by both the public and its representatives. Criticisms of cultural and economic intervention have filtered
down to the most basic levels of pop culture; for example, "Star Trek: The
Next Generation" spouts as its popular television characters' "prime
directive" the requirement of letting other worlds, no matter how primitive or miserable, find their own way. At the scholarly level, researchers
have documented in great detail the frequently dangerous economic and
cultural consequences of capitalist industrial development in third world
countries, while criticizing equally the political motivations and doubtful
benefits of U.S. government aid.[6] Perhaps no region better exemplifies

5. Dwight Eisenhower to Milton Eisenhower, December 1, 1954, p. 1. FGV, CPDOC,
Eisenhower Library Documents, Code 3, 54.12.01.
6. See, for example, Sylvia Hewlett, *The Cruel Dilemmas of Development* (New York: Basic
Books, 1980); Andre Gunder Frank, *Capitalism and Underdevelopment in Latin America:
Historical Studies of Chile and Brazil* (New York: Monthly Review Press, 1967); Robert I.
Rhodes, ed., *Imperialism and Underdevelopment* (London: Monthly Review Press, 1970);
Jerome Levinson and Juan de Onis, *The Alliance That Lost Its Way: A Critical Report on
the Alliance for Progress* (Chicago: Quadrangle, 1970); Riordan Roett, *The Politics of
Foreign Aid in the Brazilian Northeast* (Nashville: Vanderbilt University Press, 1972). For a
criticism of the role of foundations in the developing world see Robert F. Arnove, *Philan-*

the mixed, often negative results brought about by private investment and foreign aid than Latin America, where such activities and anti-Americanism have long flourished side by side. Yet there have been some significant, though nearly forgotten experiences of foreign aid and investment with useful outcomes. This book examines a little-known part of the story of U.S. assistance to Latin America following World War II: that is, the role of certain private individuals and organizations in promoting economic development through the transfer of American techniques, technology, and financial resources—as contrasted with the role of the U.S. government in doing the same. The setting of this story is Brazil. The main characters are the governments of the United States and Brazil, Nelson A. Rockefeller, and Henry J. Kaiser.

The United States and Brazil had enjoyed a special friendship (touted more by Brazil than by the United States) since the turn of the century. At that time, under the guidance of the Brazilian foreign minister, Baron Rio Branco, the Brazilian government actively cultivated this special relationship. Linguistically isolated in Hispanic America, in competition with powerful Argentina, and desirous of attaining a political and economic eminence among the other South American nations commensurate with its overwhelming geographical presence, Brazil consciously shifted its axis of alliance from Europe to the United States in a bid for partnership with the emerging world power.[7] In 1905 the U.S. embassy became the first foreign embassy in Brazil, and the only U.S. embassy in South America. Brazil exercised leadership in obtaining Latin American recognition of Panamanian "independence" after the United States took the isthmus from Colombia, and U.S. support—or at least its neutrality—was crucial on several occasions in enabling Brazil to solve its boundary disputes on advantageous terms. During World War I, Brazil was the only South American nation to declare war against the Central Powers. World War II forged this friendship into a strong, active, and mutually desired alliance. Brazil sent troops to Italy and was the only Latin American nation to have soldiers on the front lines in the war. To its leaders in 1945, the nation seemed poised on the brink of full-scale economic development and entry into the exclusive club of powerful nations—perhaps even as one of the five permanent members of the United Nations Security Council.

Brazilian leaders thus entered the postwar era eager to cooperate with

---

thropy and Cultural Imperialism: The Foundations at Home and Abroad (Boston: G. K. Hall, 1980).

7. E. Bradford Burns, *The Unwritten Alliance: Rio Branco and Brazilian-American Relations* (New York: Columbia University Press, 1966)

the United States, confident that they could Brazilianize American technology and thereby advance their nation toward the full sovereignty which they knew only economic power could bring.[8] But after 1945 the relationship with Brazil slipped further and further out of the range of American interests. A world divided and closed off by war had seen the United States practice an intense regionalism through the Good Neighbor policy and the Office of Inter-American Affairs. The world at peace, in which the United States could expect, at least for awhile, to dictate its terms "85 percent" of the time, saw the United States turn to a globalism which diminished the need to renew or even examine the traditional friendship with Brazil. Whereas the United States closely cultivated its prewar relationships in Latin America, its postwar attitude was "Don't call us, we'll call you." Stephen Rabe notes that after the war it took Latin Americans ten *years* to get the United States to keep its promise even to talk about economic issues.[9] While Brazilians in particular fully expected to be rewarded and recognized as the preeminent U.S. ally in South America, U.S. government officials slowly but unmistakably distanced themselves from the special relationship and the expectations it generated. As Frank McCann succinctly notes, "The closer Brazil drew to the United States the more its importance declined."[10] After 1945, the U.S. government sought to reduce the claims of all Latin America to economic "good neighborship," and especially Brazil, whose claim was the strongest.

And yet the process was gradual. For several years following World War II, Brazil remained somewhat of an exception to the rule of no foreign aid for Latin America. In this as in so many other critical matters, Roosevelt left no guide as to how he might handle this special relationship in the postwar era, and Brazilian leaders played on American ambivalence and sense of obligation to push for special assistance with development. What resulted was a series of commissions which, among other things, tested

8. Each of the elected Brazilian governments between 1945 and 1961 was supportive of development and eager to cooperate with the United States in its own way. The ideology of development was perhaps most fully articulated by President Juscelino Kubitschek, who believed, as Miriam Limoeiro Cardoso notes, that "only prosperous countries can be sovereign and wealth is a condition of sovereignty. . . . International cooperation which helps to promote development does not interfere with the sovereignty of the country or its self-direction, but, to the contrary, contributes positively so that the nation succeeds." Cardoso, *Ideologia do Desenvolvimento, Brasil: JK-JQ* (Rio de Janeiro: Paz e Terra, 1978), 98.

9. *Eisenhower and Latin America: The Foreign Policy of Anti-Communism* (Chapel Hill: University of North Carolina Press, 1988), 76.

10. "Brazil, the United States, and World War II: A Commentary," *Diplomatic History* 3, no. 1 (Winter 1979): 67.

and defined the outer limits of U.S. government willingness to cooperate with Latin American goals. These commissions also tested and ultimately exhausted Brazilian faith in the special relationship. On the brink of attaining membership in the club of Western powers, Brazil found its chief sponsor unreliable and so began to look for power—military, economic, and eventually nuclear—on its own terms. As I show in chapters 1 and 2, this is a story of a general, progressive disengagement, in which starts and stops in foreign aid played a large role in eventually leading Brazil to adopt a more independent, nationalistic foreign policy in the 1960s and 1970s.[11]

But there is a whole other story, untold until now, and the rest of this book is concerned with it. Interest in relief and later in development reached across the spectrum of American life, from government to philanthropic foundations to local churches and even to some corporations. The provision of aid was by no means the sole province of the president and Congress, whose policies have been analyzed by scholars such as Robert Packenham, Burton Kaufman, and Stephen Rabe.[12] The Cooperative for American Remittances to Europe (CARE), which began as a relief effort to coordinate packages of food and clothing to war-devastated Europe, evolved into a multimillion dollar development organization during the 1950s and eventually changed its name to the Cooperative for American Relief Everywhere. Local and national church groups started the Heifer Project and World Neighbors, two smaller grassroots organizations which are active in Latin America to this day. And the Ford Foundation, with probably the largest program of private aid in the world, adopted in 1951 its first comprehensive plan for an Overseas Development Program.[13]

Perhaps even more striking, some leaders within the corporate, profit-making wing of the private sector evidenced nearly as much cognizance of development issues as the nonprofit wing comprised of churches and foundations. Nelson Rockefeller and Henry Kaiser represent a strain of American business thought after World War II which recognized that U.S.

---

11. Stanley E. Hilton offers a clear, concise overview of Brazil's turn toward neutralism in "The United States, Brazil, and the Cold War, 1945–1960: End of the Special Relationship," *Journal of American History* 68, no. 3 (December 1981): 599–624.
12. Robert Packenham, *Liberal America and the Third World: Political Development Ideas and Social Science* (Princeton: Princeton University Press, 1973); Burton Kaufman, *Trade and Aid: Eisenhower's Foreign Economic Policy* (Baltimore: Johns Hopkins University Press, 1982).
13. Merle Curti, *American Philanthropy Abroad* (New Brunswick, N.J.: Rutgers University Press, 1963), 578, 580, 601–02.

capitalism, in view of the U.S. government's growing propensity to subordinate individual business interests to its larger Cold War strategy, had to work out its own modus vivendi with third world nationalism. Over the course of the twentieth century, first on the domestic front and then internationally, government had put business on notice that it had to achieve some compromises with its critics and could not expect unquestioning, automatic state support, whether in dealing with the United Auto Workers or Mexican nationalists. Rockefeller, Kaiser, and a number of other private sector leaders who had come of age in the era of welfare capitalism held the view that business and third world nationalism did not have to be incompatible and sought to prove that U.S.–style democratic capitalism could be a fair, constructive basis for regional development and international relations. They were convinced that it was possible to make money, good money, while contributing to national development and that not to do so was both to risk one's investment and compromise America's postwar leadership. Of course it suited their interests, but they also genuinely believed, as they had to, being ethically driven men, that there was no inherent conflict between profits and good works.

Within the context of government relations, private enterprise, and foreign philanthropy, this book investigates the activities of Nelson Rockefeller in Brazilian agriculture (chapters 3 and 4) and Henry Kaiser in the automobile industry (chapter 5) to determine why they were undertaken, how they related to U.S. foreign policy, whether or not they distributed the benefits of development to more than just the elite, and in what ways they reflected Americans' view of themselves, their culture, and their nation's role in the world between 1945 and 1960. I chose these particular individuals because of the scale and diversity of their activities in Brazil and because, in addition, each in his own arena was a leader of opinion. Rockefeller also appears in chapter 1 because of his significant role in shaping U.S. policy toward Latin America during World War II. In many ways this book is his story. Rockefeller remained an important public and private expert on Latin America from World War II until his death in 1979, and his ideas and career mirrored many of the changes that U.S.–Latin American relations underwent during the mid-twentieth century. For this reason he is of interest in his own right. Although Kaiser and Rockefeller did not directly collaborate, their projects overlapped and at times were mutually supportive. Indeed, the lack of collaboration itself points to an interesting fact: that two U.S. leaders of such different class backgrounds and geographical affiliations operated from remarkably similar assumptions about business ethics and foreign relations.

I wrote this book for several reasons. In recent years scholars of diplomatic (or, as some prefer, international) history have come to recognize that relations between foreign countries are far broader, more complex, and above all, far more interesting than simply matters of government policy. The nature of the relationship between any two countries is often determined as much by the presence or absence of historical and cultural ties, by immigration patterns, and by private economic relationships as it is by the official discourse of the respective governments.[14] In this case, Brazil and the United States have minimal historical ties to each other when compared with their ties to Europe. Both countries were populated largely by east-to-west immigration from Europe and Africa, and there is little history of cross-immigration (north or south). Although one of the United States' strongest relationships in Latin America has long been with Brazil, the extent of government-to-government cooperation or dialogue has also been minimal compared to U.S. contacts with many of the countries of Europe, the Middle East, and Asia. Yet today Brazilians follow American culture and politics closely, and at the end of the 1980s U.S. business accounted for about one-third of foreign investment in Brazil. The relationship of the United States to Brazil has been a private affair as much as, if not more than, it has been a function of government relations. Thus, a study of private interest in the economic development of Brazil should add to our knowledge of the consequences of U.S. technical assistance for the shaping of Brazil in the postwar period and to our understanding of the relationship between the two nations generally.

This book should also contribute to our understanding of the extent to which the United States attempted, following World War II, to export to the rest of the world its own domestic model of government-business-labor collaboration. This model got its start in the Progressive period when American reformers, Republican and Democrat alike, sought to channel the power of big business for social ends by placing government in the role of referee between business and labor, and business and the consumer. To an important extent, what historians have called the corporatist model of society replaced the pluralistic model as the American dream became ever more rooted in material betterment rather than in political ideals. While in the nineteenth century the vote was a primary means of social control, in the twentieth century the relatively fat paycheck convinced workers that business-government-labor cooperation was in their best interests. Ultimately, a limited share in wealth was more

14. Alexander DeConde, *American Diplomatic History in Transformation* (Washington: American Historical Assn., 1976), 46–48

satisfactory than a limited share in power. Corporatism promised an ever-expanding pie for all classes of society and a virtual guarantee of middle-class status for whites who persisted long enough in one locale or occupation.[15] Economic growth was the sine qua non of the corporatist model and, thus, although aspects of Progressive ideology warred against the idea of permanent giant corporations, from the 1920s through the 1940s—from boom to bust to war—Americans gradually came to accept the idea that mass production required advanced industrial organization, albeit under the eye of government. Bigness became a way of life in the new, immensely prosperous America.[16]

A warning should be sounded here about the word *corporatism*. Any term which can encompass the social systems of Nazi Germany, authoritarian Latin America, and the liberal United States is in need of more precise definition. Corporatism refers to a form of political and economic organization, traceable to the philosophy of Aristotle, in which the interests of the commonwealth are viewed as unitary and in which the state plays a strong role in compartmentalizing and directing competing interests to achieve the common good. The mild variant of corporatism found in the United States is a largely nonviolent, democratic

15. For a good overview of the literature on corporatism in the United States and its application to foreign policy see Thomas J. McCormick,"Drift or Mastery: A Corporatist Synthesis for American Diplomatic History," in *The Promise of American History: Progress and Prospects*, ed. Stanley I. Kutler and Stanley N. Katz (Baltimore: Johns Hopkins University Press, 1982), 318–30. In his work on the Lynn shoemakers of the nineteenth century, Alan Dawley concludes that manhood suffrage and popular sovereignty of the Jacksonian stripe gave white wage earners "a vested interest in the existing political system" which continuously tempered labor radicalism. Alan Dawley, *Class and Community: The Industrial Revolution in Lynn* (Cambridge: Harvard University Press, 1976), 235. On the overall upward mobility of American workers see Stephan Thernstrom, *The Other Bostonians: Poverty and Progress in the American Metropolis, 1880–1970* (Cambridge: Harvard University Press, 1973). Lawrence Goodwyn's book on populism seeks, in part, to document the transition from a culture of political democracy to one in which hopes for the future rested on an accommodation with corporate power. Lawrence Goodwyn, *The Populist Moment: A Short History of the Agrarian Revolt in America* (Oxford: Oxford University Press, 1978).

16. Louis Brandeis was perhaps the most prominent, most articulate spokesman for a version of Progressivism which rejected the entrenchment of giant corporations, and his influence can be see in both the Wilson administration and in the rhetoric and approach of the "second" New Deal. See, for example, Louis D. Brandeis, *Other Peoples' Money and How the Bankers Use It* (Fairfield, N.J.: Augustus Kelley, 1986), and William E. Leuchtenburg, *Franklin D. Roosevelt and the New Deal: 1932–1940* (New York: Harper and Row, 1963), 148–56. Interestingly, even some of the robber barons did not envision permanent monopolies. See Andrew Carnegie, *The Gospel of Wealth and Other Timely Essays* (Garden City, N.Y.: Doubleday 1933), 90–91. On the final acceptance of "bigness," see John M. Blum, *V Was For Victory: Politics and American Culture During World War II* (New York: Harcourt, Brace, Jovanovich, 1976), 145.

social system in which government acts as a mediating force to rationalize business, facilitate self-regulation, stimulate economic growth, and
prevent a forced redistribution of wealth while protecting the interests of
the working class to an extent just sufficient to maintain a healthy level
of consumption and political harmony. The result in the 1930s, according to the historian Ellis Hawley, was a unique synthesis of public and
private power-sharing which avoided the extremes of an abdication to
private interests and a rigid, European-style (or Latin American–style)
statism.[17]

American corporatism to this day exists in a context in which pluralist
processes still operate to some extent and in which pluralist ideology
retains a hold on legitimacy in the public eye. Indeed, the enduring legitimacy of pluralism, at odds with the reality of an increasingly centralized
society, reflects the failure of Progressivism and the New Deal to advance,
in Robert Dallek's words, "a new national self-image to replace the old
ideology of self-help and free enterprise."[18] The results are periodic
bursts of organized demand for less government at home and an enduring
suspicion of statism abroad.

Still, as Michael Hogan has shown in his study of the Marshall Plan, the
essence of the European Recovery Program was its attempt to refashion
Europe in the image of the United States by exporting this particular
corporatist model, and especially the unique, characteristic emphasis
on private sector participation and on growth rather than redistribution.
By 1947, the U.S. model reflected what Hogan calls the "New Deal
Synthesis"—the blending of government initiative and regulation with
private enterprise and a free market system through a careful delineation
of government prerogatives, an expanded arena for government-business
discussion and cooperation, and public-private power sharing. Keynes-
ianism provided ideological justification for the new synthesis. Domestically, this meant multilateral cooperation to ensure growth and
consumption; internationally, it meant multilateral, multinational cooperation to ensure monetary convertibility and free trade.

And this was what the Marshall Plan was about—increasing the prosperity of individual countries by getting them to adopt aspects of the
American production and distribution model and increasing the prosperity of the international system by cutting the web of tariffs, exchange

17. "The Corporate Ideal as Liberal Philosophy in the New Deal," in *The Roosevelt New
Deal: A Program Assessment Fifty Years Later*, ed. Wilbur J. Cohen (Austin: University of
Texas Press), 85–103.
18. *The American Style of Foreign Policy: Cultural Politics and Foreign Affairs* (Oxford:
Oxford University Press, 1983), xvii.

controls, quotas, and bilateral agreements that inhibited trade and generated international rivalries. Economic growth was not only a goal in its
own right, as Hogan says, but was seen as "the key to social harmony, to
the survival of private-enterprise capitalism, and to the preservation of
political democracy."[19] Behind the New Deal synthesis stood the great
investment banks and many capital-intensive firms, along with allies in
labor, liberal academia, foundations, and business associations. For these
groups, "one world" was not an idealistic slogan but an economic reality:
they saw the health of the United States as being inextricably linked to the
health of its trading partners—or at least its trading partners in the first
world.

For the nations that joined the Organization of American States in
1948 with the hope of entering a new era in inter-American relations, the
great question of the late 1940s and the 1950s—the question that eventually came to seem a cry in the wilderness—was, Why no Marshall Plan
for Latin America? Of course, above all what Latin Americans meant was
why were there no grants on the scale of the Marshall Plan, but almost
equally important to them was the failure of the United States to take as
active an interest in the reform and reconstruction of Latin America as it
did in the reconstruction of Europe and later Asia. Proposals and initiatives that the United States met with enthusiasm in Europe drew blank
stares when proposed by Latin Americans. Until 1960, in contrast to its
behavior in Europe and at home, the U.S. government did little to cooperate with Latin American elites in strengthening national economies, stabilizing democratic political systems, or coopting the appeal of the Left
(or the threat of the Right) through government-manipulated economic
growth. Indeed, while countries like Brazil moved closer to a democratic
corporatist development model of state activism in the economy, justice
through growth, international monitoring of trade restrictions reduction,
public-private coordination, and labor-government collaboration, the
United States steadfastly refused to recognize these moves as legitimate in
the western hemisphere, insisting instead on the maintenance of a
nineteenth-century-style liberal economic order.

Statism was allowable only on North American terms and in regions
deemed vulnerable by the United States. Latin America was expected to

19. Michael J. Hogan, *The Marshall Plan: America, Britain, and the Reconstruction of
Europe, 1947–1952* (Cambridge: Cambridge University Press, 1987), 18, 428 (quote). For
a complete and insightful discussion of liberal, corporatist business support for the New
Deal and its world view, see Robert M. Collins, *The Business Response to Keynes, 1929–
1964* (New York: Columbia University Press, 1981), esp. 56–62, and Hawley, "The Corporate Ideal as Liberal Philosophy."

observe the normal liberal trade policies which the U.S. government recognized as too risky for Western Europe and Japan but thought desirable for those "backward" southern countries which were supposed to follow in the developmental footsteps of the northern patriarch. Indeed, it may be, as Robert Dallek has suggested for the interwar years, that U.S. policy toward Latin America ("the 'ole back yard") was to some extent rooted in the "mass nostalgia" for an earlier, pluralist era in the nation's development.[20] Where else could the United States afford, economically or strategically, to act out such fantasies about its own history and role in the world?

What I suggest in this book is that, in its foreign policy, the U.S. government resisted exporting its form of corporatism because it was too expensive and too innovative—perhaps even too dangerous—for those parts of the world which were neither of paramount economic importance nor directly threatened by the Cold War. Wherever trade was limited to a discrete number of products (Europe was far more important to the world trade system than Latin America) and wherever communism was but a distant threat, broad government-to-government coordination of trade and growth was deemed unnecessary. Latin America finally got its short-lived Marshall Plan, the Alliance for Progress, only when Cuba proved that Communists could sustain a beachhead in the western hemisphere. It was allowed to lapse when it became clear that the Cuban threat could be quarantined indefinitely.

What this book also finds is that, notably, some members of the private sector were more favorable to a U.S.-style corporatist reworking of Latin America than was the American government. Indeed, in implementing the Marshall Plan the U.S. government actively recruited the support of internationalist, capital-intensive firms. In Latin America the shoe was on the other foot: business recruited government support for a coherent, activist Latin American economic policy or went its own way when such a policy was not forthcoming. Indeed, as we shall see from the Rockefeller and Kaiser case studies, there were times when international businessmen had more collaborative links to Latin American governments than to their own. And, ironically, when the United States finally adopted government-to-government planning through the Alliance for Progress, the first impulse of liberal policymakers was to eliminate the business participation which had been so crucial to the success of the Marshall Plan. In other words, for reasons having to do with left-of-center perceptions of business in the 1960s, the Kennedy administration failed to heed

20. *The American Style of Foreign Policy*, 102-05.

the successful strategy of the Marshall Plan implementers, who immediately engaged the support of the internationalist business community to overcome conservative opposition in Congress.[21]

But the Alliance for Progress is beyond the scope of this book. Here I am concerned with the process by which some members of the private sector did endeavor during the 1940s and 1950s to carry the corporatist principles of American industrial and agricultural organization to Latin America—even without much interest or support from their government. This endeavor should not be mistaken for a crusade, however. Rockefeller, like his father before him, was an advocate of the corporatist system, and Kaiser was a product of it: corporatist compromises among government, business, and labor were the system they knew best and naturally sought to apply to ventures in Latin America. However, they did also think that the American system would be of benefit to Latin America. What frustrated them, especially Rockefeller, was the failure of the U.S. government to join in the international corporatist triad by actively encouraging growth.

Yet, for the Latin American countries in which they operated, the relatively mild form of corporatist collaboration represented by entrepreneurs like Rockefeller and Kaiser fit harmoniously with the existing cultural and political organization of society. Although historians do not agree on the *extent* to which corporatism defines Latin American society, it is nonetheless obvious that the Catholic, Iberian tradition is strongly hierarchical and paternalistic, especially compared with more impersonal, pluralistic Protestant cultures.[22] The state in Latin America has long had a directive, regulatory role, working closely with landed elites, business, and (since the 1930s to an important extent) labor to maintain national stability and achieve development. State intervention that was greeted with dismay as a necessary evil in the United States created barely a ripple to the south. *How* the state has comported itself, oppressively or in an enlightened fashion, has been generally seen as more relevant than the fact of its strong role. Indeed, Rockefeller's and Kaiser's successes may

21. *The Marshall Plan*, 140. On the Alliance for Progress see Daniel Sharp, "The Private Sector and the Alliance," in *The Alliance for Progress: A Retrospective*, ed. L. Ronald Scheman (New York: Praeger, 1988), 185–90, and Elizabeth A. Cobbs, "U.S. Business: Self-Interest and Neutrality," in *Exporting Democracy: The United States and Latin America*, ed. Abraham F. Lowenthal (Baltimore: Johns Hopkins University Press, 1991).
22. See Peter F. Klarén, "Lost Promise: Explaining Latin American Underdevelopment," and Howard J. Wiarda, "Social Change, Political Development, and the Latin American Tradition," in Peter F. Klarén and Thomas J. Bossert, eds. *Promise of Development: Theories of Change in Latin America*, 26–31 and 197–218, respectively (Boulder: Westview Press, 1986).

have been due in large part to their bridging the gap between the unrealistic laissez-faire expectations that the United States, even when it did not follow such practices at home, persisted in applying to Latin America and the strongly corporatist heritage of the southern nations. The tradition of the Rockefeller family itself was highly personalistic and paternalistic, and both Nelson Rockefeller and Henry Kaiser were strongly influenced by the collaborative, corporatist style and structure of the New Deal. Although the pluralistic and democratic dimensions of North American corporatism may not have fit nearly as well with Latin American culture as Kaiser and Rockefeller might have liked, the characteristic U.S. emphasis on growth rather than redistribution to achieve social justice and economic development dovetailed with the goals of reformist elites anxious to hold onto their own wealth while building a more prosperous nation for all.

Last, the story of how certain American citizens worked in foreign countries to promote economic development provides the opportunity to study the public-private dualism of American politics and life. In the United States, on the one hand, the competition of private interests has long been glorified as the key to the overall good. Postwar governments from Eisenhower to Reagan have trumpeted their fidelity to free enterprise and laissez-faire as both the best economic system and the surest antidote to creeping socialism. No other wealthy industrialized country offers so few public services to its citizenry as the United States in the name of avoiding big government and giving free play to private competition. On the other hand, precisely because the private sector is self-interested, there is a strong tendency across political lines to assume that disinterestedness, to the extent that it exists, is concentrated in the public sector. Government is an extension of the people, and thus, albeit flawed, is accountable to a standard of virtue which goes beyond self-interest. Foreign policy is entrusted to the government precisely because it supposedly does not have a specific, selfish interest to protect, other than the integrity and general welfare of the nation. Reduced to the most simplistic paradigm, these assumptions suggest that there would be a greater attempt to do good in the policy of the U.S. government than in the actions of private companies or citizens. And yet, as I argue, the private sector has sometimes evidenced a stronger commitment to consistent, constructive relations with Latin America than has the U.S. government.

Though ostensibly disinterested, the U.S. government followed a narrow policy during the postwar period in which Latin America occupied a place of low priority in the scheme of world relationships and by extension a place of low esteem in the eyes of many officials. While reconstructing the European and Japanese economies and eventually developing large aid programs in Asia and Africa, this policy rejected constructive economic intervention in Latin America and relied on ad hoc political or military pressure to maintain the status quo. Private groups filled the vacuum. Neither as ideologically rigid nor as preoccupied with the Cold War as the government, private Americans developed much broader interests in Latin America than their government and occasionally more flexible, varied approaches to dealing with local governments.

One reason for this may be that business had an economic stake in Latin America which was far more tangible, immediate, and fragile than the strategic stake of the government. U.S. diplomats from Sumner Welles to Nelson Rockefeller to Cyrus Vance have long fought a losing battle to convince the U.S. government and public that Latin America is important. Yet few political crises south of the Rio Grande have managed to generate interest by North Americans for more than a year or two. It is precisely this lack of sustained interest in Latin America, combined with the relative weakness of those nations vis-à-vis the United States, which has allowed each administration to reinvent Latin American policy virtually anew, constrained little by history, by domestic constituencies, or by any effective threat of retaliation from abroad. As Joseph Tulchin once noted about the interwar period, "This insulation from outside forces gives the process of formulating policy [toward Latin America] an academic quality."[23] One might add that insulation tends to give policy a unilateral quality as well or, as Robert Dallek would note, a sometimes irrational quality.

But for businessmen invested in Latin America the relationship was different in kind, especially after World War II. While the U.S. government became increasingly impervious to Latin American criticism in its role as global hegemon, U.S. business became increasingly vulnerable to foreign critics. Before the war, as part of the Good Neighbor Policy, the U.S. government developed a much more selective policy of intervention than it had previously had. In the late nineteenth and early twentieth centuries, the United States had been relatively willing to shell shores or threaten a landing of troops whenever companies or individuals suffered damage at the hands of local governments. This commitment to intervention on behalf of business had been weakening throughout the 1920s,[24] and

23. *The Aftermath of War: World War I and United States Policy Toward Latin America* (New York: New York University Press, 1971), vi.
24. Ibid., 242–44; also see Joan Hoff Wilson, *American Business and Foreign Policy, 1920–1933* (Lexington: University of Kentucky Press, 1971), 165–66.

following the nationalization of Mexican oil in 1938 the U.S. government told business decisively and publicly that it would use force to defend corporate interests only when the executive branch deemed it necessary for broader security reasons (e.g., Guatemala, 1954). Since business confidence is predicated on the reliability and predictability of environmental factors over years, if not decades, the on-again, off-again interventionism of the government forced most U.S. companies to find their own accommodation with local regimes.

After World War II, U.S. investors entered manufacturing in Latin America in significant numbers for the first time, especially in large-market countries like Brazil. This trend further increased the vulnerability of business in several ways: production for consumption (import substitution) instead of for export made local perceptions and sensibilities more relevant (Kaiser's automobile investments are a good example); investments in manufacturing were more susceptible to both indigenous and foreign competition than were investments in extractive industries of the type that U.S. investors had previously preferred; and, by investing in larger countries rather than in the small countries of the Caribbean or Central America, companies automatically had less influence on national policy and direction. In addition, the anti-imperialism and third world nationalism unleashed by World War II heightened the perils to U.S. investors, just as many of them were exploring foreign opportunities for the first time.

These developments meant not only that Latin American policy held the interest of capital-intensive firms, but that the displeasure of foreign governments, local political upsets, debt crises, and hostility toward Americans could have an immediate, direct effect on their economic well-being. It was precisely this sustained self-interest that at times erupted in blatant, coercive interventionism—by United Fruit in Guatemala, International Petroleum Company in Peru, and International Telephone and Telegraph in Chile, for example—but that also made much private sector diplomacy in Latin America gradually more pragmatic and reciprocal than that of the government.[25] Corporatist compromises had more relevance to U.S. business than to the U.S. government, which had to accept

---

25. Stephen Schlesinger and Stephen Kinzer, *Bitter Fruit: The Untold Story of the American Coup in Guatemala* (New York: Doubleday, 1982); Adalberto J. Pinelo, *The Multinational Corporation as a Force in Latin American Politics: A Case Study of the International Petroleum Company in Peru* (New York: Praeger, 1973); and "Multinational Corporations and United States Foreign Policy, Hearings on the International Telephone and Telegraph Company and Chile, 1970–1971," parts 1 and 2, U.S. Senate Committee on Foreign Relations (Washington: GPO, 1973).

few compromises in dealing with Latin America. The oppressive actions of certain U.S. corporations have been well documented; what I seek to understand is *other* aspects of the complex relationship of private Americans to Latin American development. The contrast between the approaches of certain private groups and those of the U.S. government in attempting to transfer American know-how to Brazil forms a central theme of this book.

At the same time, because the negative consequences of imperialism and many types of foreign investment, especially in extractive industries, were so well known to American leaders both before and after World War II, this book also gives us the opportunity to explore the peculiarly American confidence in private solutions to problems of equity, distribution, and development. Why did people like Rockefeller and Kaiser think that postwar foreign enterprise would be any different from prewar extractive monopolies, fostering rather than retarding development? As the trend toward privatization of socialized industry gains momentum throughout the world today (rushing headlong in Eastern Europe and the former Soviet Union), it is worth questioning whether this American cultural trait bears any relationship to real possibilities, under certain circumstances, for reconciling the efficiency of private ownership with the needs and goals of the general population in developing nations.

Some scholars may view such an endeavor as an attempt to apologize for a relationship which often seems essentially and overwhelmingly oppressive toward Latin America. Indeed, I myself have questioned whether or not I wish to be the bearer of good news about the role of the U.S. private sector in Latin America, and this research has provoked continuous self-examination in the face of earlier convictions. But a number of considerations motivate this attempt to move beyond anti-*yanqui* feeling. First, immense regional and national differences demand that we not lump all the countries between the Rio Grande and Tierra del Fuego into one Latin mass. True, U.S. presidents have on occasion been unable to tell these countries apart; but the rest of us have a responsibility to try. (When Ronald Reagan visited Brazil in 1984, he opened his speech to businessmen in São Paulo by saying, "It's a pleasure to be in Bolivia." The following morning a São Paulo newspaper came back with a half-page ad announcing, "The people of Bolivia welcome the President of Canada.")[26] Proximity to or distance from the United States does make a difference. Mexico and Central America, for example, have traditionally been far more constrained by the nearness of their powerful

26. *Christian Science Monitor,* March 16, 1987, 16.

neighbor to the north than Brazil by its distant North American ally. In the words of a Mexican adage, "So far from God; so close to the United States."

Criticisms of dependency theory also caution scholars to treat Latin American nations as actors, not simply as objects, in their relations with the United States and in the choices they make about domestic and foreign policy.[27] This book has been influenced in part by authors such as Stanley Hilton, who emphasizes how Brazil maneuvered among the great powers in the interwar period, and Robert Packenham, who advocates an "analytic dependency" perspective which "assumes that dependency is not dichotomous but a matter of degree; [and] that nations are seldom if ever wholly dependent or wholly independent."[28] It has also been informed by the recent work of Paul Drake, whose book on the Andes, while acknowledging the basically unequal, dependent relationship of south to north, found a compatibility, even if short-lived, between the efforts of Progressive reformers from the United States and the development strategies of elites and workers in Latin America.[29] Indeed, these and many other authors in the past twenty years have done much to transform the bold, stark outlines of early dependency theory into a more realistic portrait of human and international relations, and this book continues the effort.[30] Specifically, as a historian of the United States first and foremost, I endeavor to shed light on North American activities and intent, which have sometimes been lost in the emphasis on the structural consequences of foreign investment. How did leaders of the private sector intermesh with the governments and entrepreneurial forces of the devel-

---

27. One book which explores the variability of choices by local actors, and the correspondingly contingent nature of U.S. influence, is Michael J. Francis, *The Limits of Hegemony: United States Relations with Argentina and Chile During World War II* (Notre Dame: University of Notre Dame Press, 1977).
28. Packenham, "Holistic Dependency: Two Approaches to Dependency and Dependency Reversal," *Occasional Papers in Latin American Studies,* no. 6 (Stanford: Stanford-Berkeley Joint Center for Latin American Studies, 1984), 6. Also see Stanley Hilton, *Brazil and the Great Powers, 1930–1939: The Politics of Trade Rivalry* (Austin: University of Texas Press, 1973).
29. *The Money Doctor in the Andes: The Kemmerer Missions, 1923–1933* (Durham: Duke University Press, 1989).
30. For the classic statement of Dependency Theory see Fernando Henrique Cardoso and Enzo Faletto, *Dependency and Development in Latin America* (Berkeley: University of California, 1979). An excellent, extremely useful overview of how Dependency Theory has been reshaped and modified (as well as the theories of Modernization, Corporatism, and Bureaucratic Authoritarianism) can also be found in Klarén and Bossert, eds., *Promise of Development.* Also see Peter Evans, "After Dependency: Recent Studies of Class, State, and Industrialization," *Latin American Research Review* 20, no. 2 (1985): 149–60.

oping world? How did they shape their nation's role in the world and their own role in the nation? How did they come to terms with the contingent nature of U.S. government support and their own vulnerability to third world nationalism? Also, by working through several case studies, I look at the question of how and when local elites are able to "nationalize" development, believing that even a modified dependency theory does not adequately account for this phenomenon and that further empirical data on North-South interactions are needed. If nothing else, the speed of Brazilian industrialization since the 1950s under democratic and, later, military regimes and its consistently large trade surplus with the United States preclude any automatic conclusions about the entirely negative impact of U.S. involvement in the Brazilian economy.

The fundamental goal of this book is to lend insight into Americans' views of themselves and the genuinely mixed regard that the U.S. encounters in Brazil as well as in the other countries of South America. I hope to increase our understanding of the role of the private sector in foreign relations—and especially in the design of postwar strategies for the management of North-South development issues—while bringing into relief the complexity of America's relationship to the southern republics with which it shares a hemisphere and from which it preempted a name. Understanding is the least we owe to those Latin Americans who endeavored to build their countries under tremendous economic and political constraints and to those North Americans who never succumbed to the prevailing chauvinism and indifference of their own society toward that effort.

Chapter 1

The Rich Neighbor and
the Good Neighbor

Nelson Aldrich Rockefeller, born in 1908 on the birthday of his grandfather John D. Rockefeller, was probably the most enduring and most influential advocate of a stronger U.S. relationship with Brazil between 1945 and 1960. To an important extent he represents the continuity of Good Neighbor economic policies and thus the policy alternatives that were not chosen after World War II. Called upon for advice by both governments as a kind of impresario of American interest in Brazilian development, Rockefeller was a perpetual advocate for regionalism within a context of globalism or "universalism." Rockefeller's philosophy and programs incorporated elements of both the conservative Republican appeal for a Fortress America made by Taft and Hoover and the Roosevelt and Truman insistence on global security. In other words, then, as throughout his life, Rockefeller fell between parties.

Nevertheless, in 1945, Rockefeller's influence among both Republicans and Democrats was considerable for a young, wealthy man, and he used this influence—forged in five years as Franklin D. Roosevelt's special coordinator for inter-American affairs—to push through approval of regional defense arrangements at the opening conference of the United Nations. Against the express position of the State Department but with the unanimous support of the Latin American representatives, Rockefeller convinced the conservative head of the U.S. delegation, Republican senator Arthur Vandenberg, to adopt the proviso (Article 51 of the U.N. Constitution) allowing for regional treaty organizations which ultimately formed the legal basis for the Rio Pact and the North Atlantic Treaty Organization as well as the Warsaw Pact.

It is highly doubtful that Nelson Rockefeller anticipated that Article 51 would help to spur a cold war between the United States and the Union of Soviet Socialist Republics by legitimizing the existence of competing blocs. But it is very clear that Rockefeller was both in favor of explicit spheres of influence and extremely aware of the "responsibilities" to its "clients" which he believed the United States had to assume in exchange for their allegiance. When he could not convince the Truman administration to sustain a committed alliance with Brazil by assuming these responsibilities, he undertook his own program of aid to further Brazilian development. One result was to help mitigate the deterioration of U.S.–Brazil relations that occurred after World War II. Another was to sustain and broaden a precedent for the involvement of private citizens in world development that would be heeded by other Americans in subsequent decades. A final result was to illuminate the infidelity of the Good Neighbor as contrasted with the surprising constancy of the Rich Neighbor, providing a model for the development of "business diplomacy" in the 1950s and 1960s.

The Rich Neighbor and the Good Neighbor

Nelson Rockefeller loved the dash of politics and the chances it offered for solving problems, organizing people, and having new and exciting experiences. The third child of Abigail Aldrich and John D. Rockefeller, Jr., Nelson was an exuberant ringleader in adventures with his four brothers and one sister. Later, as a student at Dartmouth College in the 1920s, he was known for his easy humor, crumpled informality, and willingness to jump into sports, interclass rivalries and pranks, and committee activities of every sort. He played on the soccer team, edited the college photography magazine, and headed an arts committee which brought Carl Sandburg, Bertrand Russell, Edna St. Vincent Millay, and Thornton Wilder to the campus. Making friends came naturally to him, and he was elected sophomore vice president at the end of his freshman year. He also enjoyed parties and the jazz bands that became popular in the mid-1920s. As one classmate recalled, "He enjoyed dancing. . . and at such parties as we had Nelson usually tried to dance with every girl there before the evening ended."[1]

As a young man Nelson also displayed a serious side which reflected the careful, religious upbringing given by his parents. Unusually for a wealthy American family, the Rockefellers were devout Baptists.[2] Each day started with prayers before breakfast, and Sundays were spent going to church in the morning and singing hymns as a family in the evening. In college, Nelson was on the Chapel Committee and for two years taught Sunday School for a class of eight- to ten-year-old girls. He did not drink or smoke, and in spite of being dyslexic made Phi Beta Kappa as a junior.

Nelson's parents, Abigail and John, Jr., were especially concerned about teaching thrift to their children, a lesson made important by the

1. Quoted in *Nelson Rockefeller: A Biography*, by Joe Alex Morris (New York: Harper and Brothers, 1960), 36. There is presently not a comprehensive, scholarly biography of Nelson Rockefeller. However, the several accounts of Rockefeller's life, ranging from laudatory to damning, are fairly consistent with one another in their basic facts, if not in their interpretations. For biographical information on Nelson Rockefeller I have relied primarily on Morris's campaign biography and on Peter Collier and David Horowitz's highly critical work, *The Rockefellers: An American Dynasty* (New York: Holt, Rinehart, and Winston, 1976). The authors of both books had access to many of Rockefeller's personal papers, which were closed after his death. For further information on various aspects of Nelson Rockefeller's life and career also see Stewart Alsop, *Nixon and Rockefeller: A Double Portrait* (Garden City, N.Y.: Doubleday, 1960); Robert H. Connery and Gerald Benjamin, *Rockefeller of New York: Executive Power in the Statehouse* (Ithaca: Cornell University Press, 1979); James Desmond, *Nelson Rockefeller: A Political Biography* (New York: Macmillan, 1964); Therese Hess et al., *The Disability of Wealth: An Inquiry into the Nomination of Nelson Rockefeller as Vice-President* (Washington: Institute for Policy Studies, 1974); Michael Kramer and Sam Roberts, *"I Never Wanted To Be Vice-President of Anything!"* (New York: Basic Books, 1976); Joseph E. Persico, *The Imperial Rockefeller: A Biography of Nelson A. Rockefeller* (New York: Simon and Schuster, 1982); Michael Turner, *The Vice-President as Policy Maker: Rockefeller in the Ford White House* (Westport, Conn.: Greenwood Press, 1982); and James E. Underwood and William Daniels, *Governor Rockefeller in New York: The Apex of Pragmatic Liberalism in the United States* (Westport: Greenwood Press, 1982).

2. As H. L. Mencken once wrote, "Most Americans when they accumulate money climb the golden ramparts of the nearest Episcopal Church. . . . But the Rockefellers cling to the primeval rain-God of the American hinterland and show no sign of being ashamed of him." Quoted in Collier and Horowitz, *The Rockefellers*, 37.

family's religious and cultural values yet made difficult by its enormous wealth. Like their father before them, the Rockefeller children were taught the strict system of personal accounting which their dime-conscious grandfather had begun in 1855 with his "Ledger A," when he got his first job as a clerk accountant at four dollars a week. But while frugality and financial exactitude may have been paving stones on the road to riches for Rockefeller Sr., for his heirs, elaborate homilies to thrift were a compensation for wealth. While enjoying the luxury of servants, summer homes, and elegant surroundings, the children earned small allowances by killing flies for pennies, shining shoes, and hoeing the garden. In the family tradition, they set aside 10 percent for charity. John, Jr., went over the children's ledgers personally to make sure the accounts were straight and the tradition carried on. Any child whose books were out of balance was fined five cents; those with perfect records earned a five-cent bonus.[3]

Philanthropy was a way of life in the Rockefeller household. While working to maintain the family fortune, John, Jr., had slowly carved out philanthropy as his way of making a mark different from his father and at the same time defusing public anger toward the name that was a synonym for callous wealth. Junior, as he was called by family associates through-out his lifetime, was a devoted son who spent the better part of his life trying to create the conditions for a favorable appraisal of his father's role in the evolution of corporate capitalism and modern America. Philan-thropy served this very practical goal as well as the family's religious values.

Early in his own working life, Junior had also felt the bitter hatred of those wronged and sometimes crushed by Rockefeller power. In the fall of 1913, as a major stockholder and board member of the Colorado Fuel and Iron Company, Junior had supported company management in their violent responses to miners who were striking for better hours and wages and union recognition. Insisting he knew too little to intervene in the company's operations, Rockefeller refused to inform himself better in spite of national protest, the calling out of the state militia, and a congres-sional investigation. When twenty-five people, including two women and eleven children, died in a pitched battle and resulting fire at the miners' tent camp at Ludlow, Colorado, "Rockefeller" was the name cried out in anger and horror across the nation. A Cleveland newspaper opened its lead story with the statement, "The charred bodies of two dozen women

3. Ibid., 12–13, 182–83.

and children show that ROCKEFELLER KNOWS HOW TO WIN!"[4] When Rockefeller appeared before the Industrial Relations Commission an audience member shouted, "Murderer!," and the chairman's outrage was palpable in seven days of relentless questioning. In their speeches angry labor organizers made threats against his life, and there was at least one bomb plot against him.

For Junior, the rigid distinction which John D. Rockefeller, Sr., had made between wielding great power and having any responsibility for its human consequences gave way under the pressure. He began looking beyond the circle of advisers he had inherited from his father, and with the help of a liberal Canadian (and later prime minister), William Lyon Mackenzie King, came up with a plan which allowed workers to elect recognized representatives by secret ballot. The "company union" which resulted, while it proved a new means for social control, was a controversial compromise for a businessman of Rockefeller's stature. With a courage rare in an age when most industrialists remained smugly positioned behind the clubs of Pinkerton agents, Rockefeller went to Ludlow in 1915 to visit the site of the massacre and to talk at length with the miners over a period of two weeks. Finally willing to hear their claims, he not only arranged for improved conditions, but instituted sweeping labor reforms in all companies controlled by the family.

Anathema to organized labor in 1913, the Rockefeller name became a symbol for cooperation in following decades. When Nelson Rockefeller appeared as a guest of honor at an Urban League awards dinner in the 1950s alongside Jacob Potofsky of the Amalgamated Clothing Workers Union and David Dubinsky of the International Ladies Garment Workers Union, Potofsky joked in reference to past collaboration, "I am glad to see a reunion of that fine firm with that good old American name of Dubinsky, Potofsky, and Rockefeller!"[5] While "10 percent to charity" was a legacy of the Christian Baptist values of John D. Rockefeller, Sr., corporate social responsibility (or welfare capitalism, as historians would name it) was the lesson which John D. Rockefeller, Jr., instilled in his children out of his own experiences in trying to shape a future as the son of a so-called robber baron father.

Nelson Rockefeller came of age in an era which presented yet new issues for a person of wealth. He did not question the morality of great wealth in a world of limited resources (this was the torment of the next

4. Cited in ibid., 116.
5. Morris, *Nelson Rockefeller*, 6.

Rockefeller generation);[6] he was too much of a believer in the American Dream of success, money, and power for that. Campaigning in 1960, he bumped into a Republican supporter on the New York subway. "How does it feel to be rich?" the attractive young woman asked. "Fine," Rockefeller replied with gusto. "How's it feel to be good-looking?"[7] After graduating from Dartmouth in 1930, Nelson Rockefeller found himself entering a business world changed by the Depression. The economic and social trauma seemed to confirm on a national scale the lesson his father had taught about corporate social responsibility. Although a confirmed Republican, Nelson supported the thrust of New Deal reforms, as did a number of other progressive business leaders.[8] "When the collapse came in 1929, industry was not sufficiently established in the good will of the country . . . and it became a target for public indignation," he told a gathering of Standard Oil executives in 1937. "President Roosevelt and his administration have taken advantage of this opportunity to enact measures to correct some of the situations which industry should never have permitted to develop."[9]

The 1930s were also a time of world travel for Rockefeller, first on a honeymoon tour of the Orient and India with his young bride, Mary Clark, in 1930 and then on a twenty-nation business tour of South America in 1937. On the first trip, Rockefeller wrote to his family frequently about the disdain for national peoples he observed among most of the Europeans and Americans living in Japan, Burma, and India. A Japanese friend from Dartmouth recounted to Rockefeller how, after he returned from eight years in the United States, he was refused admittance to American and European social events and clubs in Japan. In Burma, the European elite treated the Burmese as subhuman, and ostracized even the young American couple as colonials. Nelson wrote home, "All of these things left a very strong impression and one which we felt boded little good for future relations [of the West] with those countries. It was evident we were not handling ourselves as a people abroad in a way that developed confidence or respect."[10] While in India, Rockefeller and his wife

---

6. For an account of the difficulties of the fourth generation in reconciling the legacy of their great-grandfather with the spirit of the 1960s and 1970s, see Collier and Horowitz, *The Rockefellers*, 503–621.
7. Quoted in Kramer and Roberts, *"I Never Wanted to Be Vice-President,"* 68–69.
8. Collins, *The Business Response to Keynes*, 53–73; and Hawley, "The Corporate Ideal as Liberal Philosophy," 85–103.
9. "Importance of Community Efforts as Distinguished from Employees Welfare Work on the Part of Executives," 1937 speech to Standard Oil executives, p. 2. RAC, RFA, R.G. 2, Business Interests, "Standard Oil (N.J.)—Standard Club," Box 135.
10. Letter cited in Morris, *Nelson Rockefeller*, 87.

went to the home of Gandhi three times in the hope of talking with him. On the last occasion the great leader told them about his vision of independence from the British Empire. In a letter to his family, the twenty-two-year-old Rockefeller gushed, "He is a remarkable man—terribly nice, too."[11]

Nelson Rockefeller's early sensitivity to ethnocentrism and just plain snobbishness had a number of sources. The family had been interested in race relations since before the Civil War, when the mother of John D. Rockefeller, Sr., had been an ardent supporter of abolition. One of Junior's first and primary philanthropies was the General Education Board, which promoted tax-supported public schools in the South and contributed to Negro colleges. Nelson Rockefeller's mother, with whom he had a close relationship, shared her husband's interest in questions of prejudice and gently but with deep feeling cautioned her sons against "the feeling of dislike that a person or a nation has against another person or nation without just cause." As her three oldest sons entered adulthood she wrote them, "I want to make an appeal to your sense of fair play and to beseech you to begin your lives as young men by giving the other fellow, be he Jew or Negro or of whatever race, a fair chance and a square deal. It is to the disgrace of America that horrible lynchings and race riots frequently occur in our midst. . . . What I would like you always to do is what I try humbly to do myself; that is, never to say or to do anything which would wound the feelings or the self-respect of any human being, and to give special consideration to all who are in any way repressed."[12] The Rockefeller children attended an experimental high school run by Columbia Teachers College because, as Junior once put it, he above all wanted his children to "learn neither to scorn nor fear the common man."[13] Nelson learned this lesson, which was to prove invaluable in his later career as a politician. It also enabled him to be comfortable both with wealth and with people who did not share in it. He knew how to be a rich neighbor, whether in Queens or Caracas, without either parading his wealth or denying it. It was a useful skill, especially for an American in the postwar world when all Americans (from the perspective of other peoples) seemed rich.

After working for several years in the family business—during which time he managed the leasing and opening of Rockefeller Center in the midst of the Depression—Nelson went on his first trip to South America

---

11. Letter cited in ibid., 90.
12. Letter cited in ibid., 77.
13. Quoted in Collier and Horowitz, *The Rockefellers*, 187.

in the spring of 1937. His primary goal was to visit the Venezuela operations of Creole Petroleum Company, a subsidiary of Standard Oil of New Jersey. Rockefeller had become a major stockholder and member of the board of directors of Creole several years earlier, when he had asked his father to exchange the shares of Standard that had been put into a trust fund for him in 1934 for shares of Creole. Rockefeller became fascinated with the tropical beauty of South America ("The trees are full of monkeys and birds of all descriptions and colors, big and small") as well as with its potential as an area for investment ("there's certainly plenty of oil here").[14]

He was also struck, once again, by the disdain for the national people that hung like a plush curtain around the lives of the Americans living in Venezuela, blocking the view of those outside. In one city he met the wife of a manager of a large American company who had lived in Venezuela for twelve years and in Mexico for eight, yet could not speak Spanish. When he asked her why she had never learned, she replied "Why should I? Who would I talk to in Spanish?"[15] But his visit to South America differed from that to Asia, for this time Nelson Rockefeller was in a country where he personally had a large investment and thus, so he thought, an opportunity to do something.

Recent political changes in Venezuela undoubtedly influenced Rockefeller's sense of opportunity as well. The death of dictator Juan Vicente Gómez in 1935 had inaugurated a movement toward social reform, which included the passage in 1936 of new labor legislation providing for collective bargaining and an eight-hour day. Although there was no indication that the successor government of Eleázar López Contreras contemplated revoking the long-standing concessions of the oil companies (even the expropriation of oil investments in more volatile Mexico two years later came as a surprise to companies and the State Department), the foreign corporations were clearly less secure than before.[16] With Venezuelans demanding higher living standards and in the face of the general public's resentment of the oil companies, Rockefeller must have sensed the opportunity not only to protect his own long-term investment but, more important, to play the innovative mediator who adapts corporate practice to changing conditions, such as Mackenzie King had done for his father years before during the Colorado labor conflict.

---

14. Rockefeller in a letter to his parents written in 1937, cited by Morris, *Nelson Rockefeller*, 111–12.
15. Ibid., 117.
16. Wood, *The Making of the Good Neighbor Policy*, 204, 260–61.

Rockefeller returned to the United States with a new purpose. One of the first things he did was to enroll in a Berlitz language school crash course in Spanish. He also gave a speech before executives at the Standard Club of Standard Oil (New Jersey) in which he challenged them to become more involved in social issues and laid down the outline of a new personal philosophy and blueprint for action. Corporate responsibility for social conditions, Nelson told his audience, should extend beyond the lives of employees (his father's innovation) to the communities and even to the countries in which those employees lived. Executives should be models of active participation in the "social, spiritual, and cultural life" of the community. Rockefeller emphasized that executives and employees working abroad "should learn to speak the language and develop an understanding of the customs, habits, and psychology of the people."[17]

By advocating that corporations, specifically, the corporation over which his family had greatest (if limited) control, undertake responsibility "for the advancement of the educational, social and economic development of the community or country in which they are working," Rockefeller placed himself at the forefront of internationalism, both in terms of the business community and the U.S. government.[18] As the historian David Kennedy has noted, the government had found it challenging to persuade American companies even to invest abroad, considering the attractions of the home market. After World War I, the "parochialism of American businessmen" had led them to use profits from the war years "to fuel a spectacular expansion of the home economy, rather than extending still farther their position in the world economy."[19] With the crash in 1929, simple parochialism deepened into an economic nationalism that gripped hearts from Washington State to Washington, D.C. To advocate, in the midst of a worldwide depression and a fever of domestic isolationism, that American corporations undertake responsibility for the educational, social, and economic development of the countries in which they invested seemed visionary—or laughable. For their part, the Standard Oil executives were apparently neither inspired nor amused.

Rockefeller labored to show that his novel recommendations were not

17. Rockefeller, "Importance of Community Efforts," 3.
18. Ibid. See Wood for a description of the State Department's growing recognition, especially after the Mexican crisis of 1938, of the imperative for companies to bring their profits and labor policies more in line with the social aims of local peoples and thus in line with the tone and intent of the Good Neighbor policy (The Making of the Good Neighbor Policy, 277–78, 299–300, 330–33).
19. Over Here: The First World War and American Society (New York: Oxford University Press, 1980), 345–46.

sheer idealism but rather were anchored by that great American, and Rockefeller, institution, self-interest. As Alexis de Tocqueville had observed a century earlier in 1835, "The American moralists do not profess that men ought to sacrifice themselves for their fellow creatures because it is noble to make such sacrifices; but they boldly aver that such sacrifices are as necessary to him who imposes them upon himself as to him for whose sake they are made. . . . The Americans . . . are fond of explaining almost all the actions of their lives by the principle of interest rightly understood."[20] Rockefeller began his speech essentially by reiterating the right of revolution (and invoking the threat of socialism): "When the people become convinced—rightly or wrongly—that the owners have disregarded the responsibilities of their stewardship, they can withdraw through legislative action or otherwise these privileges of private ownership." Time and money spent to advance the general welfare of society and build goodwill toward industry was not "evidence of emotionalism," he insisted, but "a sound investment," "a long range gamble . . . [with] much at stake," and "good business from the dollars and cents point of view."[21]

Yet the overall tone of the speech was highly idealistic, with references to the Declaration of Independence and to the leadership of Thomas Jefferson and Alexander Hamilton. Rockefeller's words echoed the criticisms made five years earlier by Adolf A. Berle, Jr., who became a close colleague, and Gardiner C. Means in the influential book *The Modern Corporation and Private Property*. Berle and Means described the twentieth-century organization of wealth into giant corporations led by managers who had only symbolic responsibilities to stockholders and none toward workers and the community at large.[22] The corporation, the twenty-nine-year-old Rockefeller told his audience of executives, is "without a soul or any of the human qualities which give man a sense of balance and feeling of social responsibility and interest in his fellow man."[23]

A final point Rockefeller made in this seminal speech concerned leadership. Although he aimed his prescriptions at the executives of Standard Oil, it is clear he was also thinking through his own goals and developing leadership style. The impersonality of the giant corporation—and its remoteness from the strong-willed men whose nineteenth-century exploits made it possible, Rockefeller implied—had diminished the role of

20. *Democracy in America*, trans. Henry Reeve (New York: Oxford University Press, 1947), 333–34.
21. "Importance of Community Efforts," 1, 3.
22. *The Modern Corporation and Private Property* (New York: Macmillan, 1932).
23. "Importance of Community Efforts," 2.

"free acting individuals" in American life. The way to overcome this problem was for the executives of these corporations to become the Renaissance men that the American forefathers had been and then to apply these qualities through active participation in the life of the nation. The directors and executives of the corporation, Rockefeller pleaded, must "have a fundamental sense of integrity, an awareness and understanding of the inter-relation of their company's affairs with our economic and social life, and a sensitiveness to the gradual evolution of social thought."[24] Above all, they should not hold themselves aloof from social issues but exercise their citizenship with energy. Years later Nelson Rockefeller would comment that one of the greatest dangers to democratic government was "the scorn or scepticism toward practical, partisan politics."[25]

After giving his speech to the unenthusiastic audience, Rockefeller set out to make his words good. Using his position as a Creole director, he went back to Venezuela in 1939 with twelve Berlitz instructors in tow. Company representatives and their wives would no longer have an excuse for not speaking the local language. Creole took down the barbed wire which had surrounded its compounds in the Maracaibo Basin, set up a public health program to combat malaria, hookworm, and other tropical diseases which plagued the workers, and paved streets and installed sewers in the surrounding shantytowns. Rockefeller also met with local leaders who had expressed concern about the nation's dependence on oil as virtually the only source of revenue, and together with local partners formed a company to consider projects which would promote economic diversification. The Compañía de Fomento Venezolano (Venezuelan Development Company) was capitalized at $3 million dollars, one million each coming from Rockefeller's family, local partners, and the three oil companies (Creole, Shell, and Gulf) operating in Venezuela.[26]

The American experts Rockefeller sent to Venezuela to advise him on what directions the new company should take came up with a variety of possible ventures, including a construction company devoted to low cost housing and a project for low cost food distribution. But with war in

24. Ibid.
25. *The Future of Federalism: The Godkin Lectures* (Cambridge: Harvard University Press, 1962), 19. Although it is doubtful that Rockefeller wrote the Godkin lectures himself since he employed a full-time speechwriter, it is evident that he would not have given them if they had not expressed his views. In addition, Rockefeller's own activism and partisanship over the years attest clearly to his belief in the statement quoted.
26. See Collier and Horowitz, *The Rockefellers*, 211–12, and Morris, *Nelson Rockefellers*, 126–27.

Europe looming ever larger in the background, most projects had to be postponed. The one project the new company did undertake in 1940, at the suggestion of President López Contreras, was to build a hotel in Caracas. The capital had only one run down hotel at the time, which the government thought an embarrassment. Rockefeller apparently recognized that the hotel project would be primarily of benefit to the upper class of Venezuela but undertook it as a good faith gesture toward the president and with the intent of following through with more socially useful projects after the war was over. Carl Spaeth, an adviser, wrote to Rockefeller from Caracas in early 1940, "After all, our hotel, if successful, is going to benefit—both from a social and investment standpoint—a class of people which has little need for 'benefitting' either socially or economically." Nelson wrote back a week later, "I . . . am in complete agreement with your point of view."[27] Still, the hotel was step one of the plan and its success was critical to building Venezuelan confidence. Unfortunately, construction was started on the premise that foreign tourists would make up 73 percent of the clientele, but by the time the building was completed, the United States was in the war and tourist trade was closed off.

Nelson's younger brother Laurance was a partner in the venture, and John D. Rockefeller, Jr., watched his sons' efforts with a careful eye from New York. As always, Junior was extremely concerned that a Rockefeller activity appear responsible, and when it seemed for a time that it might be necessary to delay completion of the project, he cautioned against postponement and offered to help with financing if "the boys" agreed to hold off on any further business forays into Latin America for the duration of the war and would consider eventually selling off their interest in the hotel. Because of Nelson's "assurances to the people of Venezuela" and his commitments to the other partners, the hotel project should be completed as expeditiously as possible, Junior wrote to his sons. "If that is done," he advised, "it would seem to me that there could be no just cause for criticism of Nelson or a charge of bad faith."[28] At the point when prospects for the project appeared the most bleak, Junior offered to buy back at par value all of the stock sold to Venezuelans so they would not suffer a loss. A number of investors took him up on the offer. The hotel was completed on schedule and, to the surprise of many, was an immediate financial success.

27. Carl Spaeth to Nelson Rockefeller, March 18, 1940, p. 3, and Rockefeller to Spaeth, March 25, 1940, p. 2. RAC, R.G. 2, Business Interests, Box 109, Folder 3C.
28. Memorandum from John D. Rockefeller, Jr., March 25, 1941, p. 2. RAC, R.G. 2, Business Interests, Box 110, Folder 3.

But Nelson Rockefeller regarded the investments in Venezuela as more than just a business opportunity or a chance to rectify American ethnocentrism. In his world travels during the Depression and in the friendships he had already made with leaders such as the journalist Rómulo Betancourt of Venezuela (who later became president) and President Lázaro Cárdenas of Mexico, Rockefeller had developed a compelling interest in international relations and the political position of the United States in the western hemisphere. The approaching war intensified this interest, and Rockefeller began to conceive of the Compañía's development efforts as an extension not only of responsible capitalism, but also of the national preparedness effort. As he wrote to one of his men at Fomento Venezolano, "Great changes are taking place in the world today, and the United States will not easily maintain its position of pre-eminence. Our relations with Latin-America are of vital importance and the job which you are doing is of no small importance in this connection."[29]

Around the time he was founding the Compañía, Rockefeller started meeting regularly with a small group of acquaintances who shared his interest in Latin America and world politics. The circle included Joseph Rovensky, the head of Chase National Bank's foreign department; Jay Crane of Standard Oil of New Jersey; Wallace Harrison, the young architect who had designed Rockefeller Center; and the Czechoslovakian economist Beardsley Ruml. Rockefeller was the group's organizer, but Ruml, who had extensive experience in both business and philanthropy, was its main intellectual resource. On one occasion Rockefeller and Ruml traveled to Washington to talk about increased outreach to Latin America with Ben Cohen and Tommy Corcoran, two of Roosevelt's advisers, and at another point the small group tried to organize a kind of business council on Latin America. Not much came of either effort. Then, during the late spring of 1940, the group developed a position paper called "Hemisphere Economic Policy." Rockefeller obtained an appointment with President Franklin D. Roosevelt's closest adviser, Harry Hopkins, to discuss the written proposal.

On the evening of June 14, 1940, scarcely a week before France surrendered to Germany, Rockefeller and Ruml met with Hopkins at the White House. The pivot of their proposal was that U.S. support for the economic development of Latin America was in the direct interest of the nation. It also reflected American concern at that point about who would win the war and the traditional fallback position of the United States as

29. Rockefeller to Edward H. Robbins, August 2, 1940, p. 1. RAC, R.G. 2, Business Interests, Box 109, Folder 3B.

regional hegemon. "Regardless of whether the outcome of the war is a German or Allied victory, the United States must protect its international position," the document began. "If the United States is to maintain its security and its political and economic hemisphere position it must take economic measures at once to secure economic prosperity in Central and South America, and to establish this prosperity in the frame of hemisphere economic cooperation and dependence."[30] The economic measures suggested were the purchase of surplus agricultural and mineral products from Latin America to make up for markets which had been closed off to them by the war; the reduction or elimination of U.S. tariffs in order to encourage exports from Latin America; investment in Latin American raw materials needed by the United States; and the flexible rescheduling of Latin American debts to the United States. Rockefeller and Ruml also proposed the creation of "a small advisory committee of private individuals with direct access to the President" to undertake the job, along with an interdepartmental task force.[31] It was a committee that sounded remarkably like Rockefeller's working group.

Hopkins took the proposal to President Roosevelt, who sent it out the very next day to the secretaries of the departments of State, Treasury, Agriculture, and Commerce for their opinions. Three weeks later James Forrestal, a special assistant to Roosevelt who soon became under secretary of the navy, invited Rockefeller to Washington and asked him on behalf of the president to accept the position of coordinator of inter-American affairs. After a brief consultation with presidential candidate Wendell Willkie (the Rockefellers were Republicans, after all), Nelson said yes.

Roosevelt's acceptance of the Rockefeller proposal was not surprising in the context of earlier policy. In his first two terms as president, Franklin Delano Roosevelt had brought the United States into a new kind of relationship with Latin America. From the time of the War with Spain (1898)—in which the United States had "freed" Cuba, Puerto Rico, and the Philippines only to colonize them—to the taking of Panama (1903) and the twenty-two-year occupation of Nicaragua (1911–33), the United States had candidly and brutally maintained its right to invade, punish, or occupy the Central American nations whenever politics or revolution impinged on U.S. interests or sensibilities. After World War I, as Euro-

30. "Hemisphere Economic Policy," reprinted in the appendix of the *History of the Office of the Coordinator of Inter-American Affairs*, Donald W. Rowland (Washington: GPO, 1947), 279.
31. Ibid.

pean economic strength in the western hemisphere began to diminish, the United States started moving away from the policy of frequent military intervention. The Harding and Coolidge administrations negotiated their conflicts with Honduras (1923) and Mexico (1927), and President Herbert Hoover resisted sending troops to Haiti and Panama when revolutions broke out there in 1929 and 1931, respectively. Hoover also publicly denounced the policy of using force "to secure or maintain contracts between our citizens and foreign States or their citizens."[32] But it was Franklin D. Roosevelt who, with the seasoned guidance of men like Secretary of State Cordell Hull and Under Secretary Sumner Welles, elevated this trend to an established policy and international promise.

The heart of the Good Neighbor policy was nothing more than an expression of the traditional, legal right of states to respect for their sovereignty and national borders—something the United States had glorified in principle and violated in practice since its founding as a republic. In 1933, at the Inter-American Conference in Montevideo, Uruguay, the United States for the first time in its history gave conditional approval to a motion stating that "no state has the right to intervene in the internal affairs of another." Three years later, in Buenos Aires, the Roosevelt administration voted unconditionally for this principle, adding to it approval of a second motion establishing defense of the western hemisphere as a collective responsibility. Since the times of John Quincy Adams and the formulation of the Monroe Doctrine in 1823, the United States had insisted that, among other privileges, the defense of the Americas was its charge alone. The changes made by the Roosevelt administration were momentous indeed.

But any policy supported by Franklin D. Roosevelt, even when it was a matter of conforming to the first rule of international law, could never remain merely legalistic in spirit. A policy that in the mouth of Hoover might have sounded simply like the rational thing to do was a ringing appeal for humanity and justice when articulated by the buoyant, passionate Roosevelt. When he attended the Buenos Aires Conference in 1936, fresh from victory at the American polls just a month earlier, half a million Argentines jammed the streets to see him. Roosevelt's endorsement of nonintervention was hailed not only in Latin America, but also in the United States, where the idea of nonintervention was popular.

Although the Good Neighbor policy was in intent an expression of what the United States would *not* do, in the closing years of the 1930s it

32. Cited by Armin Rappaport, *A History of American Diplomacy* (New York: Macmillan, 1975), 321.

subtly became a symbol for what Latin Americans thought the United States *should* do. Because of his identification with economic justice in the United States and his apparent concern for the common person, Roosevelt had endeared himself to people the world over. He seemed the Good Neighbor personified. In case of a fire, he would lend a hose. In case of a war, he would lend a battleship. In case of extreme poverty, such as that suffered by most of Latin America, he might just lend a million. What Latin Americans wanted out of their rich and powerful Good Neighbor was not just freedom from intervention, but concrete assistance with economic development. For Roosevelt, whose whole manner spoke eloquently of generosity, it would have taken a determined effort not to allow this desire to become an expectation.

Yet even though there was initially little intent to encourage such hopes, in the ominous 1930s it must have seemed foolish to dash them entirely. Allies were too important. The result was that while U.S. policymakers did not fully endorse the economic expectations raised by the Good Neighbor policy, they found themselves drawn increasingly into using promises of economic assistance as a bargaining tool and thus into assuming responsibilities in which they had little inherent interest and for which there was little precedent either in world history or in American national culture.

In the case of Brazil, expectations of economic assistance grew slowly and to a large extent in response to attempts by the United States to secure an alliance. Brazil and the United States had enjoyed a strong diplomatic relationship since the beginning of the century, but after World War I the economic relationship gained in importance as well. Brazil began making more of its foreign purchases in the United States, and the United States gradually started to replace Great Britain as Brazil's major trading partner.[33] But in the 1930s, things changed again. Whereas in the 1910s and 1920s Britain had been the primary competitor, in the years immediately before World War II it was Germany that vied with the United States for Brazilian trade.

From 1935 to 1937, Germany slowly but perceptibly took over the lead from the United States in exports to Brazil.[34] It did so by securing a Brazilian agreement to accept so-called compensation marks as payment

33. Between 1913 and 1938, Brazil went from purchasing 15.7 percent of its foreign goods in the United States to purchasing 24.2 percent; the United States increased the percentage of Brazilian exports bought from 33 percent to 34 percent of all goods sold. *Commerce Yearbook for 1922* (Washington: GPO, 1923), 610, and *Foreign Commerce Yearbook for 1948* (Washington: GPO, 1950), 291.
34. In the period 1935 to 1937, German imports to Brazil grew from 20.4 percent of the total purchased by Brazil from foreign nations to 23.8 percent. The U.S. market share

for exports bought by the Third Reich. The enforced use of these marks, a restricted currency that could be spent only on German goods, resulted in a de facto barter system that worked against the United States in at least two ways: first, the trade in compensation marks yielded no hard currency that Brazil could use to pay debts to the United States and other countries or to buy products not provided by Germany; and second, because the United States had refused to deal in compensation marks with Germany, Brazilian exporters made tremendous gains on U.S. farmers in supplying the German market with cotton.

Yet the U.S. government refused to use its considerable leverage over the Brazilian economy to discourage bilateral trade relations with Germany. State Department officials considered remaining on good terms with Brazil as war approached a higher priority than making a stand on multilateral free trade principles. Although Brazilians feared at times that the United States might retaliate with a tax on coffee, the tariff never materialized. Instead, U.S. policy was marked by concessions. The State Department made protests but largely ignored the compensation trade. Most important, the Roosevelt administration took the first step toward meeting the desire of the Brazilian government for direct economic assistance.

President Getúlio Vargas of Brazil was determined to build a national steel plant as a key to industrial development. When it became clear in 1940 that U.S. private companies were not willing to invest in the development of Brazilian steel and that German companies were ready to do so, the United States made an Export-Import bank loan of $20 million to Brazil to build the plant. Although the loan was made primarily for reasons of geopolitical expediency, by preempting German investments in a major economic development project, the United States in effect declared itself a recourse for funds to promote development. Indeed, this was the first major loan for economic development that the United States made to a foreign country. Volta Redonda, as the steel plant was called, was to become a symbol of the type of Good Neighbor that Latin Americans wanted.[35]

---

slipped from 23.4 percent to 22.9 percent. Information cited by John Wirth in *The Politics of Brazilian Development: 1930–1954* (Stanford: Stanford University Press, 1970), 59.

35. The story of the interwar trade between the United States and Brazil is one of the most well documented topics in the history of the relationship between the two nations. Two central works, which differ primarily on the question of how skillfully Brazilian policymakers took advantage of German-American rivalry to further the nation's economic interests, are John Wirth, *Politics of Brazilian Development*, and Stanley Hilton, *Brazil and the Great Powers, 1930–1939: The Politics of Trade Rivalry* (Austin: University of Texas Press, 1973).

Around the time of the Volta Redonda deal President Roosevelt asked Nelson Rockefeller to put into action his ideas for closer hemispheric relations. Rockefeller's proposals were consistent with the larger trend of U.S.–Latin American relations, as shaped by Roosevelt, Hull, and Welles. Over the preceding months, the United States had moved significantly closer to making an explicit commitment to regional economic responsibilities. When Welles attended the Panama Conference of foreign ministers in September 1939, the main purpose of which was to discuss neutrality and security, he carried with him the authority to negotiate economic agreements and financial assistance of various types. One result was the creation of the first multilateral group on regional economic problems: the Inter-American Financial and Economic Advisory Committee. According to Bryce Wood, the establishment of the committee "amounted to a transformation of the conception of reciprocity [rather than nonintervention] as the central idea of the Good Neighbor policy."[36] In June 1940, one week after Rockefeller presented his "Hemisphere Economic Policy" to Hopkins, the name of the group was changed to the Inter-American Development Commission, and it was now given the authority to explore even broader questions concerning the "economic potentialities of the American republics."[37] Consistent with his preference for multifront assaults when it came to dealing with major problems, Roosevelt must have viewed Rockefeller's proposed interdepartmental coordinating agency as yet another way of meeting the issue of Latin American development. He may also have seen the exuberant Rockefeller as a useful young Republican to bring into his increasingly bipartisan wartime administration. In any case, he appointed him coordinator of the newly created Office of Inter-American Affairs (OIAA).

Wartime

Nelson threw himself into the new job, which, although as yet undefined, must have seemed to him appropriately big enough for a Rockefeller. Rising around 6:00 A.M. to listen to news broadcasts or write memos while having breakfast, he was off to his office by 8:00 A.M., picking up staff members on the way to discuss business in the car. He was "the Eager Beaver to end all EBs," said David Lilienthal, the future chairman of the Atomic Energy Commission.[38] Rockefeller had given a clue to the type of

---

36. *The Making of the Good Neighbor Policy,* 311–12.
37. Rowland, *History of the Office of Coordinator,* 4.
38. Quoted in Collier and Horowitz, *The Rockefellers,* 228.

leadership he would adopt in the "Hemisphere Economic Policy" proposal: "Half measures would be worse than wasted; they would subject
the United States to ridicule and contempt."[39]

Between 1940 and 1944, OIAA grew from a small staff with a projected budget of $3.5 million (plus whatever Rockefeller could wheedle
out of Congress, as Forrestal had put it) to an agency of several hundred
employees which could point to $140 million dollars' worth of pro-
grams.[40] Although obligated to coordinate with Sumner Welles of the
State Department, Rockefeller was directly responsible to the president,
to whom he submitted his reports and recommendations. As historians
have noted, Roosevelt frequently put his advisers in positions with competing jurisdictions. The Office of the Coordinator was no exception.
OIAA and the Board of Economic Warfare (BEW), signed into being on
the same day, wrestled for a full year with the question of which agency
was to have primary responsibility for economic development projects in
the hemisphere. The board eventually won major responsibility for development activities, which included sending technical missions abroad to
stimulate the provision and acquisition of strategic materials. Rockefeller's OIAA became accountable for two related but different activities:
propaganda for the United States and for hemispheric cooperation,
which was issued through the OIAA Publications and Information Division, and economic development programs focused on food and public
health, which were handled by the Food Supply and Health divisions.[41]

Francis Jamieson, a Pulitzer Prize–winning journalist who became a
close friend of Nelson, headed the information division. Under Jamieson's astute direction, it became the model for the Office of War Information and, much later, for the U.S. Information Agency.[42] Jamieson's staff
developed radio broadcasts which were beamed throughout Latin America, published a glossy picture magazine in Spanish that was modeled
after *Life* and attained a readership of half a million, and printed a weekly
Spanish edition of the *New York Times* which was distributed throughout
Latin America. Rockefeller, long a board member of the New York Mu-
seum of Modern Art, sent an exhibition of modern art to Brazil, arranged
for Mexican art to be shown in the United States, organized goodwill

39. "Hemisphere Economic Policy," Rowland, *History of the Office of Coordinator*, 279.
40. For an excellent, concise analysis of the history of OIAA see Claude C. Erb, "Prelude to
Point Four: The Institute of Inter-American Affairs," *Diplomatic History* 9, no. 3 (Summer
1985): 249–69.
41. Rowland, *History of the Office of Coordinator*, 8, 207–10.
42. Ibid., 9; U.S. Congress, House Committee on Foreign Affairs, *International Cooperation Act of 1949 (Point Four Program)*, (Washington: GPO, 1950), 84.

tours by American and Latin artists and movie stars, and commissioned American sculptor Jo Davidson to create busts of the presidents of all the Latin American countries that belonged to the Pan American Union. He even convinced Walt Disney to create new cartoon characters (like the colorful Brazilian parrot and friend of Donald Duck, Zé Carioca) to carry the propaganda of Pan-Americanism throughout the hemisphere.[43]

Although the emphasis of OIAA propaganda was always on the positive and although Rockefeller had a genuine passion for Hispanic and Luso-Brazilian culture, he defined his responsibility as one of waging "psychological warfare in the Hemisphere."[44] Given that thousands had recently died in the Bataan death march on the Pacific front and that the grim battle of Stalingrad was just beginning in Europe, Rockefeller's view of his task was understandable in the context of the siege. Another of his projects was coordinating a campaign to urge U.S. companies abroad not to advertise in newspapers with anti-American or pro-Nazi editorial policies and to fire pro-Nazi German employees working in South America. As on other fronts in the war, individual rights and freedom of the press took a distant second place to the defense effort.

The other half of OIAA activities centered on efforts to promote food development and public health programs in Latin America. Using the precedent of the Reconstruction Finance Corporation, Rockefeller persuaded Congress to allow him to set up corporations in eighteen Latin American countries; both the United States and local governments contributed funds to these *servicios,* as they were called, which created safe water systems, provided midwife services, dispensed medicines, plowed fields for planting, and traded healthy breeding animals for sickly chickens and pigs. As in strategically important Brazil, OIAA ran major health, sanitation, and disease prevention programs in a number of countries with little direct connection to the war effort, including Paraguay, Peru, Colombia, and Haiti. According to Claude Erb, to have denied "aid to any country because it was unimportant to U.S. interests would have jeopardized . . . hemispheric solidarity, the chief goal of Rockefeller's office."[45]

Besides, economic development had been at the heart of Rockefeller's

43. Monica Herz, "Zé Carioca: O Embaixador de Duas Caras" (Diss., CNPq, Rio de Janeiro, 1986).
44. Rockefeller to General George C. Marshall, August 28, 1942, p. 1. NA, R.G. 229, OIAA Department of Information, Content Planning Division, Box 1459, Folder: "Content Liaison." Document obtained by author in the archives of the Centro de Pesquisa e Documentação de História Contemporânea do Brasil (CPDOC), Rio de Janeiro, IAA 42.05.28.
45. "Prelude to Point Four," 257.

interests even before the war. Throughout the four years that he was coordinator, Rockefeller pushed the food and health programs that he hoped would outlast the wartime emergency. In 1941 he wrote to Vice President Henry Wallace (also Nelson's morning tennis partner) that "economic defense of the Hemisphere requires concrete evidence *now* that this nation is irrevocably committed to a long range, continuing program of Hemisphere economic development and cooperation. Long-range commitments are the best form of emergency economic defense in the Hemisphere."[46] In 1943 Rockefeller drafted a memo to Under Secretary Welles in which he said that programs to maximize economic development "should have a lasting effect on the relationship between the United States and the other Republics, and play a significant part in assisting this country, as well as the others, in solving some of the important post-war economic problems." He pushed for more money for Mexico and extra programs for Brazil.[47]

The reaction to Rockefeller's programs and proposals was mixed. Most of his supporters considered them primarily a wartime necessity, while his detractors considered them a waste of money under any circumstances. Laurence Duggan, the head of the Division of American Republics in the State Department and someone who did anticipate a future need for an agency "capable of carrying on a similar [development] function," was anxious to forestall so much special attention to the region; he feared that after the war the department might find itself committed to two organizations, "one operating with respect to the other American republics and the other with respect to the rest of the world."[48] Philip Bonsal, another diplomat in the American Republics Division, argued further that the OIAA "set a standard of hand-outs on a scale which we will certainly not be able to maintain in the post-war era."[49]

The Latin American nations for the most part responded well to the wartime programs, but even OIAA staffers anticipated that such acceptance might not extend to long-term programs. As one agency subcommittee noted, "Consideration for sovereignty and national prestige in the

46. Rockefeller to Henry Wallace, August 13, 1941, cited in Collier and Horowitz, *The Rockefellers*.
47. Draft memorandum by Rockefeller, p. 1, attached to a letter from Emilio G. Collado (special assistant to the under secretary) to Sumner Welles, August 18, 1943. Also see Collado to Ambassador George Messersmith (Mexico), October 20, 1943, p. 2, and "Minutes of Meeting in Dr. Berle's Office," October 14, 1943, p. 4. NA, R.G. 353, Lot File 60D665, Box 2, Folder: "Committee on Inter-American Development, Correspondence."
48. Laurence Duggan to Sumner Welles, August 3, 1943, p. 5. NA, R.G. 353, Lot File 60D665, Box 2, Folder: "Committee on Inter-American Development, Correspondence."
49. Quoted in Erb, "Prelude to Point Four," 264.

other countries promotes varying degrees of readiness to enter into cooperation which must for years to come be heavily weighted on the side of assistance from us." The committee report added that even if the other republics agreed to such arrangements and the U.S. federal government decided to undertake the "mammoth task" of supplying sustained aid, "requisite legislative authority would not be obtainable."[50]

Although Congress approved most of Rockefeller's wartime budget requests, he frequently felt the ire of conservative critics, who dubbed him a big spender. Congressional skeptics questioned whether or not the development programs really served specific wartime requirements of the United States.[51] Roosevelt's greatest asset was his personal access to Roosevelt, who appeared to enjoy the scrappy young patrician and assured him of presidential support at several key junctures. Rockefeller eventually won over many early critics with his charm and dedication to his cause. He developed a reputation as a knowledgeable, well-prepared witness in congressional hearings and an effective defender of OIAA when it came to bureaucratic infighting. As Henry Wallace once noted in his diary, "I told the President today that Nelson Rockefeller's definition of a coordinator is a man who can keep all the balls in the air without losing his own."[52]

One of the outcomes of his wartime experiences with OIAA was that Rockefeller became a well-known national and international personality. One magazine criticized Francis Jamieson for having done as much to promote Nelson Rockefeller as to promote the cause of the United States.[53] With his irrepressible penchant for visual aids such as charts, graphs, and layouts for overhead projection, Rockefeller became an enthusiastic user of Madison Avenue public relations techniques. As a member of a family that was already highly conscious of its image, Nelson was on his way to becoming an expertly packaged political personality.

While his colleagues in the U.S. government cautioned Nelson Rockefeller not to go too far in the direction of economic cooperation and aid, some Latin American nations continuously urged the coordinator to go further still. In Brazil, the war had already brought an unprecedented economic integration of the two nations, and many Brazilians looked upon this integration as representing their best chance to launch a pro-

50. "Report of Subcommittee II—Field of Agriculture," December 16, 1944, p. 3–4. NA, R.G. 353, Lot File 60D665, Box 2, Folder: "Committee on Inter-American Development, Miscellaneous Draft Papers."
51. Erb, "Prelude to Point Four," 265–67.
52. From *The Price of Vision: The Diary of Henry A. Wallace*, ed. John Morton Blum (Boston: Houghton Mifflin, 1973), 146. Diary entry for December 16, 1942.
53. *The New Republic*, July 2, 1945, cited in Collier and Horowitz, *The Rockefellers*, 232.

gram of sustained economic development. The devastation of the European economies in the war and the enormous U.S. demand for raw materials increased the value of Brazilian exports to the United States nearly sevenfold between 1939 and 1950, and the value of U.S. exports to Brazil more than tripled.[54] Brazil sent ground troops to Europe to fight in the war and supplied at reasonable cost some of the raw materials most crucial to the war effort, especially manganese.[55]

United States officials faced two main difficulties in ensuring the smooth transfer of strategic raw materials from Brazil. First of all, although the Brazilian government was willing to cooperate (Brazil agreed to sell a number of strategic substances only to the United States from 1941 to 1943, including manganese, industrial diamonds, bauxite, and rubber),[56] the quantity of raw materials Brazil could make available was limited by the rudimentary condition of mines and transportation networks. Second, the use of most merchant ships for materials transport and other wartime needs placed a severe strain on the relatively nonindustrialized Brazilian economy, which had depended on imports for many crucial commodities. Spiraling prices for the few goods available, the rationing of fuel, and import restrictions on such items as trucks and newsprint made the development of import substitutes highly desirable. At one point in 1942, the nation's large textile industry faced being shut down in four months if shipments of caustic soda from the United States could not get through.[57]

If the United States wanted to "assure the continued flow of strategic

54. In 1939 the value of U.S. exports to Brazil was $87 million. By 1950, the figure was nearly $379 million. In 1939, Brazil exported to the United States goods valued at $110 million. By 1950, these sales had jumped to $734 million. Throughout this period Brazil maintained an overwhelming trade surplus in relation to the United States. *Foreign Commerce Yearbook*, 1939 and 1951 editions (Washington: GPO, 1939 and 1951), 173 (1939 ed.), and 562 (1951 ed.).

55. Even before the war, U.S. preparedness experts had trained their sights on Brazilian manganese. In 1938 an expert in army intelligence observed, "Manganese . . . is by all odds our most serious metallic deficiency. It is absolutely essential to the manufacture of steel; during the [First] World War, when imports from Russia were cut off, there was a time when a complete shut down of our steel industry within seven months was foreseen unless additional sources of manganese could be tapped. War reserves of this item are now being maintained, but our principal war reliance will be on Brazil." George F. Eliot, *The Ramparts We Watch: A Study of the Problems of American National Defense* (New York: Reynal and Hitchcock, 1938), 91.

56. "Brazil: Background Report," Board of Economic Warfare, American Hemisphere Division, August 1942, section V, p. 3.

57. "Naval Intelligence Report (Excerpts)," Board of Economic Warfare, Document No. 31059, San Juan, Puerto Rico, April 13, 1943, p. 5. Found in the Stanford Library edition of the *Report of the American Technical Mission to Brazil* (Washington: Board of Economic Warfare, December 1942), vol. 2.

materials," a BEW report stated in 1942, "we must maintain Brazil's transportation, communication, and general trade systems in a reasonably stable condition."[58] Increasingly, the United States had a stake in making sure that Brazil's infrastructure functioned at least moderately well. At the same time that Nelson Rockefeller's cultural programs were bringing entertainers like Carmen Miranda to the United States and his food programs were trading skinny native chickens for fat Iowa fryers, the Board of Economic Warfare was trying to figure out ways to make Brazil's basic economy function better in the context of the war. Although BEW planners realized that economic assistance aimed at securing these ends might be interpreted as being motivated by "altruistic considerations," they knew that "actually any assistance which the United States is able to render . . . inadvertently derives to its own benefit."[59]

Early in the war U.S. officials began to see the development of local industry in Brazil as a way of relieving pressure on the United States to keep not only Brazil but the other major Latin American allies as well supplied with essential goods. In response to a Brazilian request for help with both war mobilization and economic development, the State Department decided to send its first technical aid mission to Brazil in 1942 under the leadership of New Deal administrator Morris L. Cooke. As justification for the Cooke mission the background report of the BEW said, "[The] present critical condition of the shipping situation, both to and from Latin American countries, makes it imperative that some solution be found to alleviate the difficulties surrounding the receipt of vital supplies in those countries. Of the two countries best suited to increased industrialization, Argentina and Brazil, the former, for obvious reasons, does not present possibilities as attractive as those of the latter."[60] In other words, it suited U.S. purposes to see at least one of the major countries of South America industrialize so that it could assist in servicing the hemisphere, and Brazil, because of its close political alliance, was to be that country. Neutral Argentina, which refused to join such emergency supply agreements as the Petroleum Pool, was largely cut off.

The United States' convenience was Brazil's necessity. For the South American nation, as for other developing countries, import substitution seemed a viable route to long-term development. Getúlio Vargas, president of Brazil from 1930 to 1937 and its dictator from 1937 to 1945 under an authoritarian regime called the Estado Novo (New State), had

58. "Brazil: Background Report," i.
59. Ibid.
60. Ibid., i-ii.

come to power at a time when the worldwide Great Depression made clear the liabilities of Brazil's traditional dependence on one or two export crops. A disastrous collapse in the price of coffee during the Depression, coupled with rapid currency devaluation in Brazil, had already reduced the nation's ability to pay for imports and thereby fueled a spurt of industrialization in light industry. But Vargas was determined to use the powers of the Estado Novo to create a genuinely diversified economy. In addition to setting protective tariffs, import quotas, and wage requirements, he was also prepared to intervene directly through public investments such as the national steel plant built at Volta Redonda with Brazilian public and private monies and with the $20 million loan from the Export-Import Bank of the United States.[61] So, for Vargas, the Cooke mission was above all another gambit for involving the Good Neighbor in the long-term implementation of economic development.

A twelve-member U.S. delegation and a Brazilian delegation of some one hundred members made up the mission.[62] The U.S. delegation spent several weeks examining Brazilian rural and industrial conditions firsthand. The widely experienced members of the U.S. team included experts on metallurgy, transportation, textile production, electric power, oil, and economics. They couched their findings in a comprehensive, sector-by-sector report on the Brazilian economy and its potential for industrialization. The report recommended projects ranging from creation of a transport system based on the use of towed glider planes to development of the São Francisco valley along the lines suggested by the experience of the Tennessee Valley Authority. Especially important, from the Brazilian point of view and from the point of view of Cooke, who was inspired by the potential he saw in Brazil, the projects had "not only an immediate usefulness but likewise a purpose to strengthen Brazil's industrial fabric permanently."[63] The members of the U.S. delegation returned highly impressed with the Brazilian determination to diversify. In the final document Cooke compared the two nations: "Brazil has the spirit which infused the United States during the development of its now great industrial strength."[64]

But the views of a representative of the BEW (or of the coordinator of OIAA, Nelson Rockefeller) were one thing and the changing priorities of

61. Thomas Skidmore, *Politics in Brazil, 1930–1964: An Experiment in Democracy* (New York: Oxford University Press, 1967), 42–44.
62. *Report of the American Technical Mission*, 1:9.
63. Ibid., 1:1, 7.
64. Ibid., 1:64.

the State Department quite another. Since the beginning of the war, the BEW had been an advocate for U.S. involvement in foreign economic development, to the extent of competing with OIAA for jurisdiction over it. Henry Wallace, whose special concern was the Board of Economic Warfare, shared Nelson Rockefeller's interest in development and warned Rockefeller in 1942 that if the United States did not help the peoples of poor nations "to read and write and improve their agriculture and become mechanically literate," the Germans and Japanese would.[65] For this reason, it was BEW policy throughout the war to write higher wages for workers, better food, and improved medicine and hygiene into contracts with foreign governments to develop raw materials, such as rubber in the Amazon Basin. Yet, ironically, the State Department opposed this policy as a form of intervention.[66]

Although the State Department had approved U.S. involvement in promoting aspects of inter-American trade and development, Hull and Welles had never worked out precisely how far the government should go in that direction, especially as the expediencies of war shifted their attention away from regional concerns. Hull especially, as well as members of the State Department whose specializations were outside of Latin America, did not warm to the idea of U.S. support for development; they viewed it as extravagant and a diversion from global issues. When Welles left the government in mid-1943, the U.S. commitment to regional development and an active involvement in inter-American issues was further weakened. Ultimately, department officials had little intention of helping Brazil do much more than develop industry directly related to the war effort and cope with immediate shortages.[67] Since the department had the final word on foreign relations, the Cooke report stayed on the shelf. Although Cooke subsequently published a popular version of the report (*Brazil on the March*) to drum up support for his ideas and the Brazilians made a Portuguese translation publicly available (*A Missão Cooke*), in the United States the report was ignored and remained classified for many years.

In addition to ambivalence within the United States on questions of economic development, another reason for the lack of interest in the Cooke report might have been the perception that Brazil was already doing pretty well for itself and had gotten enough for its wartime service.

65. Henry Wallace's record of a conversation with Nelson Rockefeller, held on August 26, 1942, in *The Price of Vision*, 110.
66. See editor's footnote in ibid., 68–69f.
67. Gerson Moura, "Brazilian Foreign Relations, 1939–1950: The Changing Nature of Brazil-United States Relations During and After the Second World War" (Diss., University College London, 1982), 110–11.

Brazilian rubber products manufacturing had boomed during the war. Reports of the BEW in 1942 and 1943 noted that Brazil was now supplying the tire and tube requirements of all of Latin America except Argentina and Uruguay. Industrial loans began to overtake agricultural loans in São Paulo banks. Most important, the development of the Volta Redonda steel plant, the Itabira iron mine, and the Victória e Minas railroad line connecting the iron mines to the port (all undertaken with wartime loans from the U.S. government) signaled a strong beginning for heavy industry in Brazil. In light of these developments and the large dollar surpluses resulting from raw materials sales, it is perhaps understandable why the United States did not undertake to do more. As one official report noted with apparent satisfaction, "In conclusion, Brazil has been the Latin American country most benefited by this war, and no doubt will emerge from the war as the most important Latin American country."[68] Also, as war surged toward the Axis heartland in 1943, defending the Brazilian "bulge" and developing its economy became less of a priority.

Although the Cooke mission was forgotten for a time, the effort was not in vain from the Brazilian point of view. The technicians had completed the first thorough examination of Brazil's economy, setting a precedent for future endeavors.[69] The mission had taken a regional approach in analyzing the economy and had emphasized the importance of moving Brazilian development away from the coastal fringe and into the rich, unexploited hinterland.[70] The concern about disparities between regions as well as that about developing the interior became hallmarks of Brazilian development in the midfifties. The mission also raised for the first time the possibility of creating "a government-controlled bank which is to be concerned with the development of industrial enterprises to meet Brazil's immediate needs and her future prosperity."[71] Just such a bank would become one of the most important accomplishments of another U.S. mission ten years later. Last, the mission helped to reinforce the idea of a U.S. commitment to Brazil's development. Brazilians would use the

68. "Naval Intelligence Report (Excerpts)," 1–2. For another favorable contemporary assessment of Brazilian gains see John C. Campbell, "Nationalism and Regionalism in South America," *Foreign Affairs* 21, no. 1 (October 1942): 145. References to the development of Brazilian rubber products industries may also be found in "Brazil: Background Report," section VII, p. 3.
69. Robert T. Daland, *Brazilian Planning: Development Politics and Administration* (Chapel Hill: University of North Carolina Press, 1967), 27–28.
70. Werner Baer, *The Brazilian Economy: Its Growth and Development* (Columbus: Grid Publishing, 1979), 51; and *Report of the American Technical Mission*, 1:63.
71. *Report of the American Technical Mission*, 1:55.

precedent established by the mission to extract more and more assistance from the U.S. government in the next decade.

Meanwhile, at the end of 1944, Cordell Hull resigned as secretary of state. Edward Stettinius, Jr., the new secretary, called Rockefeller back from a tour of the Caribbean to tell him that Roosevelt wanted him to become the assistant secretary of state in charge of Latin America—taking the position Laurence Duggan had filled and elevating it in rank. (It later became clear that Rockefeller was Roosevelt's choice, not Stettinius's.) Although confirmed by the Senate, Rockefeller spent only nine months in the State Department. Rockefeller had by this time cultivated such strong relationships with all of the Latin American ambassadors and governments that, in the face of declining State Department interest in the region, he was running almost a one-man foreign policy show. Majority sentiment in the department favored foregoing regional spheres of influence in order to strengthen the embryonic United Nations. Rockefeller was in close personal contact with Latin American diplomats who, although they did not welcome U.S. predominance in the region, wanted stronger assurances of a commitment to mutual defense and hemispheric cooperation. Together with a small group of foreign ministers from Costa Rica, Mexico, and various other countries, Rockefeller began the planning which would ultimately lead to the Chapultepec Conference in Mexico City in 1945 and the formation of the Organization of American States.

At the conference, the disagreements within the department came out in the open, with staff of the International Division vehemently opposing any regional defense arrangement. "It was their set purpose," Sumner Welles later observed from the sidelines, "to destroy entirely the inter-American structure erected during the preceding eleven years. They gave as their pretext their desire that the American Republics take no step that would make for a regional rather than a universal international order."[72] Although Secretary of State Stettinius was present, his newness and lack of familiarity with Latin America forced him to rely largely on Rockefeller, who led a smaller group in the department which, backed by members of the Senate Foreign Relations Committee, argued for regional unity.

The long-standing conflict between regionalism and universalism extended well beyond the U.S. State Department, however. Since the beginning of the wartime Grand Alliance, Roosevelt had had to balance the unapologetic realpolitik of Churchill and Stalin, who viewed regional

72. Sumner Welles, *Where Are We Heading?* (New York: Harper and Brothers, 1946), 207.

spheres of influence as unavoidable and even desirable, against the overt Wilsonian idealism of his own administration and the U.S. public, which rejected power politics and demanded a worldwide organization for maintaining the peace. In pushing for the United Nations, Roosevelt and Hull repeatedly countered British and Soviet suggestions for postwar regional councils.[73] At the same time, just as Winston Churchill swore he would not preside over the dismantling of the British Empire, so Franklin D. Roosevelt was not about to be the first American president to repudiate the Monroe Doctrine. Besides, as Secretary of War Henry Stimson justified American "fussing around" in its own sphere of influence, "I think it's not asking too much to have our little region over here which never has bothered anybody."[74] As ever, idealism in balance-of-power politics in Europe warred with realism when it came to U.S. interests in the western hemisphere. Roosevelt reconciled these tendencies, in part, by encouraging advocates of both sides in the State Department. Casualties of the resulting intradepartmental feuds included Sumner Welles and eventually Nelson Rockefeller.[75]

But at the Chapultepec Conference at least, the regional bloc within the State Department had the enthusiastic support of almost every other foreign delegation. Adolf Berle, then-ambassador to Brazil, noted in his diary a concern that the United States would be bypassed by the other republics in their determination to obtain a regional agreement. "Few people here realize the real drive behind it. It is terrific," Berle wrote. "The American nations think that Dumbarton Oaks means that any little dispute in the Hemisphere will be thrown into the proposed World Council. . . . So they propose the tightest union here. If we miss it, they will probably make that Union themselves, perhaps under European leadership."[76] As the historian Roger Trask notes, Latin Americans also hoped to use a strong regional organization as leverage to obtain continuing economic cooperation from the north as well as to hold the United States to its Good Neighbor political commitments.[77] Of course, ultimately, the

73. Robert Dallek, *Franklin D. Roosevelt and American Foreign Policy, 1932–1945* (New York: Oxford, 1979), 420, 435, 439, 479, 536.
74. Quoted in David Green, *The Containment of Latin America: A History of the Myths and Realities of the Good Neighbor Policy* (Chicago: Quadrangle Books, 1971), 230.
75. On the dismissal of Welles see Dallek, *Franklin D. Roosevelt and American Foreign Policy*, 421.
76. *Navigating the Rapids: 1918–1971*, ed. Beatrice Bishop Berle and Travis Beal Jacobs (New York: Harcourt, Brace, Jovanovich, 1973), 472.
77. "The Impact of the Cold War on United States–Latin American Relations, 1945–1949," *Diplomatic History* 1, no. 3 (Summer 1977): 272–73.

United States would endeavor to use this same organization for the opposite purpose: to endorse its dominant position in the hemisphere and reinforce, rather than transform, the status quo.[78]

Rockefeller's influence held at the Mexico City conference, and the U.S. delegation gave its consent to the Act of Chapultepec, which established the first collective security system in the western hemisphere and laid the basis for the establishment of the Organization of American States in 1948. But regionalism was not yet in the clear. Two months later the universalist leadership of the State Department, which opposed permanent regional defense agreements, was assembled in full force at the San Francisco Conference to found the United Nations. Franklin D. Roosevelt had died, and Rockefeller was not even invited. Stettinius finally gave Rockefeller permission to attend when, at the opening sessions, it became clear that he uniquely could deliver the Latin American vote as a bloc on crucial issues.

Heedless of the political consequences, Rockefeller began lobbying for the regional point of view as soon as he arrived, first pushing through admittance of profascist Argentina (a measure advocated by Mexico and several other American republics) and then meeting privately with the U.S. delegation leader, Senator Arthur Vandenberg, to persuade him to oppose the State Department position on regional defense agreements like the Act of Chapultepec. Vandenberg, with the support of Secretary of War Henry Stimson, swung around the U.S. delegation and successfully negotiated with the Allies on the inclusion of Article 51, the regional "self-defense clause," in the U.N. Constitution. Rockefeller won his point but alienated much of the Truman administration in the process.[79]

While the proposals themselves soon became an accepted part of U.S. policy, and indeed became the legal basis for the Organization of American States, the North Atlantic Treaty Organization, the Southeast Asia Treaty Organization, and other regional agreements, the method of lobbying was inherently objectionable. Dean Acheson, James Dunn, Archibald MacLeish, Charles Bohlen, and John Foster Dulles all opposed Rockefeller's individualistic maneuvers, and when James Byrnes replaced Stettinius as secretary of state a few months later, President Truman politely accepted Rockefeller's resignation. Yet there was never any indication that Rockefeller regretted his actions. Politics, he later said, were "reckless . . . real-life combat."[80]

78. R. Harrison Wagner, *United States Policy Toward Latin America* (Stanford: Stanford University Press, 1970), 62–63.
79. Trask, "The Impact of the Cold War," 273; Morris, *Nelson Rockefeller*, 215–22.
80. Rockefeller, *The Future of Federalism*, 20–21.

With Rockefeller out of the government—not to mention Roosevelt, Welles, Wallace, and other notable advocates of Pan-Americanism—and the major political issues related to Latin America conveniently solved by the events in San Francisco, the Truman administration relegated hemispheric concerns to the background, where many felt they belonged. The following few years were momentous: the United States dropped the atomic bomb on Hiroshima and Nagasaki; the Soviet Union refused to give up the sphere of control in hostile Eastern Europe which the Red Army had wrested from pro-Nazi and anti-Russian governments; Truman announced his famous doctrine appointing America as guardian of freedom in the world; General George Marshall launched a plan for the reconstruction of Europe; and Russia staged its first blockade of Berlin and developed an atomic bomb. The Cold War was well under way.

The Beginnings of Postwar Aid to Brazil: Public and Private

The end of World War II coincided with the end of the Estado Novo in Brazil. With the blessing of the United States, the military deposed Vargas when it became clear that his continuance would be an obstacle to the redemocratization of the nation. Eurico Gaspar Dutra, the popularly elected president who took over at the end of 1945, rejected state intervention in the economy in favor of a return to economic liberalism. Dutra's finance minister, Pedro Luis Correia e Castro, stated in his annual report for 1946 that bank credit must be "organized in the classical mold" and stressed that "the return to the norms of free trade" would create a "climate of confidence conducive to an increase in production." The government responded to wartime inflation resulting from high earnings and limited imports by opening the country to finished goods from abroad and turning loose the pent-up demand. Within a year and a half, Brazil's enormous foreign exchange reserves were almost gone. Recognizing (if not admitting) that these liberal practices had severe limitations, the Dutra government after 1947 implemented exchange and import controls and began looking closely at options for government investment in economic development.[81]

The United States supported the trend toward economic liberalism and away from the statism of the Estado Novo for reasons both of ideology and political expediency. In spite of diminished State Department interest

81. See Skidmore, *Politics in Brazil*, 48–53, regarding the downfall of Vargas, and 69–71 on the liberal economic practices of the Dutra government. Correia e Castro's comments are quoted by Skidmore on 69.

in regional questions, Brazil remained a strategically important country. It was a leader of Latin American support for the United States in the United Nations; it was the major military ally in South America; it was still the most important source of a number of raw materials vital to the United States, including (after World War II) atomic energy raw materials such as monazite sands and uranium. Yet for the State Department, global issues took precedence over regional ones, and for the public and Congress there seemed little reason to continue giving money away now that the war was over. Brazil's adoption of a laissez-faire approach to development would relieve the United States of the obligation to intervene in support of accelerated industrialization after the war and thereby forestall any criticisms that the United States was not doing enough for Brazil. Also, as evidenced by their common tendency to compare Brazil with the United States at an earlier point in its development, most officials expected that a normal capitalist development trajectory required an open market and a hands-off government in Brazil. Thus, North American support for a laissez-faire approach could be made to seem honorable as well as be expedient.

Officials had reason to be optimistic about continued good relations. The war had forged a strong military alliance, reinforced by accords in 1951, and established Brazil as a key export market for U.S. manufactures. An intelligence survey of the principal newspapers of Latin American republics in 1948 found that of the Brazilian papers examined 76 percent were essentially pro–United States. The next most friendly press could be found in Mexico, where only 40 percent of the newspapers had a favorable orientation.[82]

Within two years of the war's end, however, strains began to appear. Brazilians resented several developments. First, like many Latin Americans, they were disappointed by the lack of any program for Latin America comparable to the Marshall Plan for Europe. The Good Neighbor suddenly seemed decidedly uninterested in the rest of the neighborhood. In the United Nations, Argentines, Chileans, and Brazilians all pressed for equal recognition of the economic needs of Latin America. As one patronizing and peevish State Department representative put it, "They obviously want 'full value' from their [United Nations] club dues, pitifully small as these may be."[83] Brazilians also resented the tendency of

82. "Survey of the Principal Newspapers of the Other American Republics," Department of State, Office of Intelligence Research, Report No. 4600, February 9, 1948. Reprinted in *O.S.S/State Department Intelligence and Research Reports, XIV, Latin America, 1941–1961*, ed. Paul Kesaris (Washington: University Publications of America, 1982).
83. "Analysis of Policies Followed By the Other American Republics in the General Assembly of the U.N.," Department of State, Office of Intelligence Research, Report No. 4314, p.

the U.S. government to lump their country together with the Hispanic American nations, which was part of the process by which the United States began distancing itself from Brazil after the war. Aside from the significant cultural differences between Brazil and the Hispanic countries, Brazilians felt that the extent of their contributions in both world wars entitled them to special consideration. The lack of any special initiatives extended towards Brazil after the war contrasted unpleasantly with the attentive wooing of Brazil before and during the war. Last, the economic difficulties that began emerging in 1947 demonstrated the necessity for assistance if Brazil was really to experience the kind of transformation prophesied by Morris Cooke and native boosters like the industrialist Roberto Simonsen.

In 1947, while attending the closing session of the Inter-American Conference for the Maintenance of Continental Peace and Security held in Brazil, President Truman agreed to the establishment of another joint mission devoted to Brazilian development. Although spurred to make this concession perhaps by the need to convince Dutra of the United States' continued interest in its special ally, U.S. officials quickly looked to the mission as an opportunity to reinforce the Brazilian administration's tendencies toward economic liberalism.

The Joint Brazil–United States Technical Mission began its work in September 1948 under the direction of John Abbink for the U.S. delegation and Octávio Gouvêa de Bulhões for the Brazilian section. *Self-help* was the unofficial byword of the Abbink group, which endeavored to convince its Brazilian counterpart that the free enterprise development of the United States was the best model for Brazil to follow. The commission emphasized the importance of agricultural development proceeding hand in hand with industrial development (as it had in the United States) as a way of freeing up workers for industrial employment without jeopardizing the food supply and as a way of diminishing the import of items Brazil could grow for itself.[84] Abbink thought "nationalist thinking" tended to persist most among those Brazilians "unacquainted with the United States and its development."[85] The delegation also emphasized "financial stabilization," meaning the control of inflation. Another principal goal of the U.S. delegation, as Abbink stated in a report to Secretary of State Dean Acheson in 1949, "was to make it clear to Brazilian officials

21. Reprinted in Kesaris, ed., *O.S.S/State Department Intelligence and Research Reports, XIV, Latin America, 1941–1961.*
84. *Report of the Joint Brazil-United States Technical Commission* (Washington: GPO, 1949), 28–29, 65–66.
85. Herschel Johnson to Dean Acheson, November 18, 1948, in *Foreign Relations of the United States (FRUS)*, 1948 (Washington: GPO, 1972), 9:386.

with whom it came in contact that Brazil could not expect huge amounts of assistance from the United States."[86]

The Brazilian delegates accepted the premises of limited public assistance from the United States and implementation of austerity measures to ensure the balance of payments. The neo-liberal views expressed in the report reflected as much the thinking of Bulhões as of Abbink. But there was a distant little cloud in the otherwise clear sky. The mission ended with a request by the Brazilians for the establishment of an ongoing joint technical commission to aid in obtaining loans for those capital goods which Brazil could not otherwise afford. Abbink did acknowledge that it "would be unrealistic to suppose that the aims of the program can be achieved without the United States government itself making loans for specific key projects for which private capital is unavailable."[87]

Although Abbink reported the idea to Acheson, he expressed reservations about the difficulty of maintaining coherence between U.S. policy goals and the interests of an ongoing, semiautonomous joint body.[88] Acheson, he later said, instructed him to soft-pedal the idea. Abbink was also confident that private capital and project-by-project public aid would suffice to fulfill most of Brazil's needs. But he did add a caveat: "The American members of the Joint Commission . . . are fully persuaded that our present policy of reiterating our faith in the willingness of private capital to move into countries like Brazil, while taking no active steps to foster a larger movement, is not adding to United States prestige abroad."[89] Specifically, the delegation recommended that the U.S. government offer guarantees to investors that their profits in cruzeiros could be converted into dollars and give income tax concessions to Americans on their earnings from investments abroad.

As limited as these investment incentives may seem, the Brazilian government heartily supported them. Finance Minister Correia e Castro expected that the recommendations of the commission would stimulate large U.S. capital investments.[90] But the Treasury Department opposed the taxation treaty, and the proposed legal concessions were not implemented.[91] In other words, the Truman administration not only refused to give public aid to Brazil, but also declined to develop a coherent program

---

86. John Abbink to Dean Acheson, March 17, 1949, in *FRUS*, 1949 (Washington: GPO, 1975), 2:555.
87. Ibid., 2:561.
88. Ibid., 2:562–563.
89. Ibid., 2:557.
90. *New York Times*, February 12, 1949, 7.
91. *FRUS*, 1950, 2:773f.

of encouraging private investment and initiative. Within a few months tensions rose once again. President Dutra visited the United States in mid-1949, and although Brazilian representatives made it clear that they hoped some form of concrete aid would arise from the meetings, Truman essentially reiterated the recommendations of the Abbink report. The U.S. ambassador to Brazil, Herschel Johnson, cabled the State Department in May of 1949, "It is difficult to express without apparent exaggeration, feeling I have, which is shared not only by responsible members of Embassy but by responsible and representative members of American community, that amity which has characteristically prevailed in American-Brazilian relationship is in some degree of jeopardy at present time."[92]

Even though relations between the governments of Brazil and the United States seemed continuously problematic in the first few years after the war and particularly strained by 1949, the name of Rockefeller continued to represent what seemed promising in U.S.-Brazil relations, at least from the Brazilian perspective. After being fired by Truman in September of 1945, Nelson Rockefeller had returned home to New York no less determined to continue the elaborate wartime collaboration between Latin America and the United States that he had helped build under Roosevelt and Sumner Welles.

There was no one left in government with whom to play ball, so he decided to form his own team. Because Rockefeller's public and private activities were always intertwined and because his wealth enabled him to maintain an entourage, most of the top staff of OIAA left with him. For Rockefeller, the distinctions between the operations of government and those of private citizens were not rigid, inviolate, or perhaps even entirely understandable. He had come into government from private enterprise, had had direct access to President Roosevelt himself, and had little patience with functional distinctions and bureaucratic discipline, as evidenced by his maverick behavior in the State Department. He and the men around him moved easily and frequently between public and private spheres. When Rockefeller called a meeting in New York to discuss his next steps, the associates at his side included Wallace Harrison, the architect whom Nelson brought into government and then made head of the OIAA when he became assistant secretary of state; John E. Lockwood, the legal counsel for the OIAA who was to become chief attorney to the entire Rockefeller clan; and Francis Jamieson, head of the OIAA Informa-

92. Herschel Johnson to Dean Acheson, May 1, 1949, in *FRUS*, 1949, 2:566.

tion Division, who later became Rockefeller's personal director of public relations.

From the late summer of 1945 to the spring of 1946, the group developed plans for an organization which would carry on with the kind of programs OIAA had operated, minus the culture and propaganda division. Although the U.S. government had not eliminated the OIAA after the war, the State Department and Congress had trimmed its budget and scope of responsibilities to the bone. Where the government would not act, private organizations would. Since his first efforts to reform Creole Petroleum and establish the Compañía de Fomento Venezolano, Rockefeller had envisioned a role for individual enterprise in strengthening relations with Latin America. The Truman administration was missing important opportunities, he believed, but it was a situation that the private sector could do something about. "I felt," Rockefeller said later, "that if private enterprise didn't step in and get things started nobody would do anything."[93]

The use of private means to promote development was not only convenient. It was also in harmony with Rockefeller's larger goals. As he outlined in a letter to his father in the late summer of 1946, he had come to believe that "the only basis for lasting peace and security in the world rests on strong leadership from the United States." In turn, the United States could maintain its preeminence only if the world's people "increasingly have reason to feel that their best interests and opportunity for the future are identified with our country and our way of life." This meant promoting not only the country but also its economic system. And who could be better for this job than a Rockefeller? "You more than anyone have become a symbol to people throughout the world that democracy and the capitalistic system are interested in their well-being," Nelson complimented his father. "Now more than ever before it is important that we as a family carry on with the courage and vision that led you and Grandfather to pioneer new fields and blaze new trails."[94] Thus, although Rockefeller would doubtless have preferred having the resources of the U.S. government at his disposal, a private approach was one way to demonstrate explicitly a socially responsible American capitalism.

The Rockefeller solution was an organization called the American International Association for Economic and Social Development (AIA). The small planning group working out of Rockefeller Center soon de-

93. Quoted in Desmond, *Rockefeller: A Political Biography,* 56.
94. Nelson Rockefeller to John D. Rockefeller, Jr., September 6, 1946, p. 1. RAC, R.G. 2, Economic Interests—AIA, Box 1, Folder 4.

cided that the association would focus on food and agricultural problems; it would promote public health measures from time to time, but for the most part this work was left to the Rockefeller Foundation, which had long pioneered in containing yellow fever, malaria, and hookworm, first in the American South and later around the globe.[95] The Food Supply Division of OIAA had made some initial inroads into the seed, equipment, training, and credit problems facing food production in Latin America, and Rockefeller decided that it would be logical to expand on this preliminary work.

The group also decided to limit its programs initially to Brazil and Venezuela. The reasons for Venezuela were obvious. Fomento Venezolano already had a foothold, and Rockefeller's own assets gave him leverage both with American companies there and with the Venezuelan government. In Brazil, on the other hand, the Rockefeller family had no financial interests, except for the innocuous subsidiary of an American company in which they held major stock, the Corn Products Refining Company (makers of Karo syrup). The Rockefeller fortune was based on oil, though, not syrup, and the reasons for focusing on Brazil must be viewed as largely political. Brazil was America's foremost ally in South America and a nation of enormous economic potential. Any attempt to influence U.S. policy toward Latin America could find no better stage than the country which occupied first rank in that scheme. Looking beyond Latin America, Rockefeller also saw opportunities for influencing world trends. "The successful execution of this program [AIA] can set the pattern for the kind of large scale world cooperation which must come," Nelson wrote in an impassioned letter to his father.[96] A world-size precedent required a continent-size proving ground. Brazil was it.

Through the early months of 1946, planning proceeded apace. Kenneth Kadow, who had headed the wartime Food Supply Program for OIAA in Brazil, drafted a sixteen-page proposal for AIA in Brazil, ranging from the introduction of new seed and animal types, to running literacy campaigns, providing low-cost farm loans, and organizing farmers' cooperatives and 4-H Clubs. Some of the programs would be purely educational and thus require a steady source of donations; others, Kadow suggested, would be costly at first but would eventually pay their own way and even make a profit for the other programs. Rockefeller supervised the plans carefully, making notes as to cost and sources of

95. John Ettling, *The Germ of Laziness: Rockefeller Philanthropy and Public Health in the New South* (Cambridge: Harvard University Press, 1981).
96. Ibid., 3.

financing. It was assumed that the AIA would bear the greatest part of the financial burden, but that some help would come from the Brazilian government.

After incorporating the American International Association in July 1946, however, the planning group began to realize that they would have to separate those projects which might eventually make a profit from those which never would. Rockefeller at first resisted the idea of a second, profit-making corporation, but attorney John Lockwood explained that there was no real legal alternative. Besides, as Lockwood insisted in language the Baptist-raised Rockefeller understood, "One of these should be a Sunday company and one should be a weekday company. That is in the historical, puritan, and protestant tradition of this country—make money all week and tend to your eleemosynary operations on Sunday."[97] Rockefeller finally agreed, and all AIA personnel were notified that "the second corporation will probably be organized in December under a name yet to be selected. It will carry out projects of a business nature, all of which are expected to realize profit (none of which, however, will accrue to Mr. Rockefeller)."[98] On January 9, 1947, the International Basic Economy Corporation (IBEC) was launched under the laws of the State of New York.

In the year or so that it took to plan AIA and IBEC, several of Rockefeller's associates had made trips to Brazil to scout project possibilities firsthand. Once plans were firm, Rockefeller himself flew to Rio de Janeiro to call on Brazilian president Eurico Dutra and other acquaintances in government. He hosted a reception for more than three hundred people and met with numerous personal friends to obtain support and ideas for potential projects. He finagled a $25,000 grant from the Brazilian subsidiary of the Corn Products Refining Company to pay for a project to improve seed production, and in a later trip to Venezuela approached all of the American oil companies based there for funds to start the AIA in that country. In Brazil, the fledgling staff of AIA intervened in an outbreak of hog cholera during the last months of 1946, flying supplies of vaccine and a leading U.S. veterinarian to Rio. Within days, the U.S. specialist, together with Brazilian veterinarians from the Ministry of Agriculture, had worked out strict procedures for administering the vaccine and containing the epidemic. By early 1947, AIA was on the map with agricultur-

---

97. Quoted in Martha Dalrymple, *The AIA Story* (New York: American International Association, 1968), 9–10.
98. Memo to "All Personnel" from J. W. Hisle, November 27, 1946, p. 1. RAC, P.R. Files, AIA, Box 1, Folder 8.

ists, and within a few months IBEC too became a familiar name in business circles.

Nelson Rockefeller went to Brazil with the advantage of being well known and for the most part well liked because of his government role during the war. Brazilians identified Rockefeller much more with the widely admired Roosevelt administration than with the American business community. Newspaper coverage of Rockefeller's trips in 1946 and 1947 was highly complimentary, and Oswaldo Aranha, the former foreign minister, was reputed to have said, "My, it's nice to have an ambassador from the United States again."[99] Francis Jamieson, who traveled with Rockefeller, commented, "Rockefeller is probably the number one North American in the eyes of the average Brazilian, whether he is the man in the street or an influential businessman or a government leader."[100]

For Nelson Rockefeller, the next ten to fifteen years would revolve around the question he posed in 1949 for the Point Four program of the Truman administration: "How can we help get more buying power in the hands of the other peoples of the world? How can we help them get more dollars without just giving it to them?"[101] This was the essential question for a man who obviously did not believe that the rich should give their wealth away (or that the poor would really benefit from a bottomless charity or that a state-driven redistribution of wealth would produce economic growth and economic justice), but who wanted to prove that the best interests of the world lay in the American system. As the Brazilian economist Roberto Campos commented years later, "I think his idea was that if some sort of people's capitalism succeeded in the United States, why should it not be implanted abroad? And he looked to Brazil as a rather promising area for a good mission of some sort of broad based capitalism."[102]

To some extent, Rockefeller appears to have generalized from his own life experiences to those of the United States. "The United States is a rich and powerful country in a poor world; like a rich family in a poor town," he once said in relation to IBEC (and perhaps in relation to himself). "The poor don't want charity, but they would like to be helped to stand on their

99. Quoted in Dalrymple, *The AIA Story*, 31.
100. Ibid. Also see Francis Jamieson to Harry Frantz, December 6, 1946. RAC, R.G. 2, P.R., Box 13, Folder: "Francis A. Jamieson—Personal, 1959."
101. Testimony of Nelson Rockefeller, *Hearings of the Committee on Foreign Affairs, House of Representatives, International Cooperation Act of 1949 ("Point IV" Program)* (Washington: GPO, 1950), 79.
102. Author's interview with Roberto Campos, Rio de Janeiro, Brazil, October 13, 1986.

feet. Today our welfare and security depend on the welfare and security of other peoples."[103] From 1945 to 1947, during the transition from world war to Cold War, Nelson Rockefeller initiated a new kind of North American presence in Latin America. With the plans for AIA and IBEC in hand, the rich neighbor was ready to give life to his theories.

Thus in the immediate postwar period the U.S. government and Nelson Rockefeller, the "number one North American in the eyes of the average Brazilian," stood in curiously contrasting relationships to the people and government of Brazil. Whereas the goodwill between the two nations appeared to be dimming, Rockefeller's projects seemed a bright star on the horizon. With Roosevelt dead and the war over, the U.S. government was not clear on exactly what being a Good Neighbor meant either to Americans or Brazilians, and it was not yet ready either to give or withhold unequivocally the far-reaching assistance Brazil sought. The next few years would test just how far the United States was willing to go.

103. Morris, *Nelson Rockefeller*, 252.

As the thirty-two-year-old coordinator of the Office of Inter-American Affairs, Nelson Rockefeller disarmed Washington critics with an unabashed promotion of U.S.–Latin American ties. Rockefeller is shown here at an inter-American gathering in 1940. *Photo courtesy of Farris A. Flint, Famous Features Syndicate.*

The father of five, Rockefeller visited schools and spoke with neighborhood children during his private fact-finding trips to Venezuela and Brazil (1947). *Photo courtesy of Rockefeller Archive Center.*

Rockefeller (shown here [*at far right*] during a visit to Venezuela in 1948) enjoyed inspecting IBEC farm projects personally. *Photo courtesy of Rockefeller Archive Center.*

"The corn worth a million!" Sementes Agroceres promoted hybrid seed extensively to overcome farmers' resistance to the need for annual purchases. *Photo courtesy of Rockefeller Archive Center.*

Juscelino Kubitschek, then governor of Minas Gerais and later president of the republic, cutting the ribbon at the opening of an ACAR community center located in former slave quarters at Mucambeiro (1950). *Photo courtesy of Rockefeller Archive Center.*

Ever the politician, Rockefeller stops at a Rio de Janeiro coffee bar to mix with the locals. *Photo courtesy of Rockefeller Archive Center.*

Henry J. Kaiser sought the advice of influential Americans as well as Brazilians during his travels to South America in 1954. *L-R:* Former Assistant Secretary of State Edward Miller, Bob Elliott (secretary to Henry Kaiser), Oswaldo G. Aranha, Kaiser, and Brazilian Ambassador Walther Moreira Salles. *Photo courtesy of Oswaldo G. Aranha.*

Edgar Kaiser discussing the *metas* (goals) for national automobile production with President Juscelino Kubitschek. *Photo courtesy of Euclydes Aranha Netto.*

Admiral Lúcio Meira, head of Kubitschek's special group for auto production (GEIA), inspects the Willys plant with top WOB executives. *L-R:* Euclydes Aranha Netto, Hickman Price, and Lúcio Meira. *Photo courtesy of Euclydes Aranha Netto.*

The complete Willys line, from jeeps to sports cars, pictured against the São Paulo sky-line in 1966. *Photo courtesy of the Bancroft Library.*

Brazilian Ambassador Juracy Magalhaes confers the Southern Cross on Edgar Kaiser on behalf of the Brazilian government. *Photo courtesy of Eu-clydes Aranha Netto.*

Chapter 2

The Good Neighbor

Equivocates

The political leadership of Brazil entered the postwar era with a vision that must have surpassed the dearest hopes of the U.S. government or any American entrepreneur. The Brazilian elite was divided between those who believed in a moderate form of what the historian Thomas Skidmore has called "developmentalist-nationalism"[1] (roughly, Vargas and his followers) and those who advocated economic liberalism (exemplified by the Dutra government), yet it was united in an essentially capitalist view of Brazil and the world. The elite envisioned Brazil as the up-and-coming continental power of South America, based on accelerated economic development within a capitalist framework, and it looked to the United States as its best hope

---

1. See Skidmore, *Politics in Brazil*, 87-92, for a concise and helpful overview of the development debate in Brazil during this period.

for financial resources and technical know how. While Argentina, Brazil's traditional rival, viewed the United States with suspicion and hostility, Brazilian leaders greeted North Americans with confidence in themselves and high hopes for an advantageous postwar alliance. Brazil was probably the only nation in all of Latin America in which nationalism did not equal anti-Americanism. For the United States, it was an opportunity to build the kind of alliance that symbolized the best hopes of the United Nations and postwar foreign relations: one based on commonly held democratic values, mutual security guarantees, respect for sovereignty, and free trade. So many other relationships were problematic at best and fraught with danger at worst. How could this one go wrong?

Brazilians' commitment to economic diversification and development had been growing slowly but steadily since the mid-1930s. During the Great Depression, the weakness of foreign markets for coffee had cut Brazil's foreign earnings, forcing the nation to stop buying imports for which it had to pay hard currency. The result was an increase in the local manufacture of products normally imported. The light industrialization created by this import substitution was supplemented by the beginnings of heavy industry when President Getúlio Vargas negotiated the loan for the steel plant at Volta Redonda in 1940. The statism of the Estado Novo was characterized most by legislation which set minimum wages and created government-controlled unions, but Vargas also strengthened the civil service and federal financial institutions (tax collections, foreign exchange authorities, Bank of Brazil) and created the National Steel Company just before the war. During World War II, the trend toward federal intervention in the economy was heightened by the process of coordinating raw materials development and military preparedness activities as well as by planning efforts such as the Cooke mission.

After the collapse of the authoritarian Estado Novo in 1945, the return to democracy, with literacy requirements on the right to vote, brought with it the conservative presidency of Eurico Dutra and a return to the precepts of liberal economics: a balanced federal budget, a tight money supply, openness to foreign capital, and the abandonment of restrictions on the international movement of currency, capital, and goods. But this period also saw a growing public debate among Brazil's leaders over strategies for economic development, with the liberal position increasingly outflanked by developmentalist-nationalism.

Developmentalist-nationalists rejected the liberal acceptance of the international division of labor according to comparative advantage, a concept created by European economists that relegated Brazil to being a supplier of semitropical goods for industrialized northern economies.

Although they assumed a democratic-capitalist future for Brazil, developmentalist-nationalists advocated an activist approach to breaking the bottlenecks which hampered Brazil's development. This activist approach represented a kind of democratic corporatism based on government initiative within a context of largely private ownership. Specifically, the developmentalist-nationalists promoted special incentives for the private sector and the creation of mixed public-private enterprises in areas in which private enterprise was not willing to invest; the Volta Redonda steel plant is an early example of such an undertaking. Politicians who appreciated the economic orientation of the Estado Novo (though not its political structure) were joined by a younger generation of economists and intellectuals who believed that Brazil could attain a better standard of living for all of its peoples if it became a more modern, industrialized nation and by members of the nationalist Brazilian military, who saw industrialization as the key to national security and world status.

The neoliberal Dutra government, which presided over the depletion of the $708 million in foreign currency reserves which Brazil had built up in blocked credits through profitable trade during World War II, strengthened the developmentalist-nationalist position through its economic failures. In a context of few restrictions on imports and other flows of capital and goods, the funds earned from wartime production and privation were gone by the middle of 1947. The developmentalist-nationalist position was also inadvertently enhanced by advocates of radical nationalism, who, although they had little influence at the time in conservative Brazil, articulated resentment against the powerful northern nations in the popular press, giving emotional weight to the arguments of the moderate developmentalist-nationalists against liberalism.[2]

The tendency of developmentalist-nationalism to look to the federal government to stimulate economic growth reinforced an important assumption of many Brazilian politicians after the war: that outside aid from the United States was necessary to development and would eventually be made available. Government-to-government aid was a natural extension of a greater federal role in the economy: the Estado Novo had created Brazil's first really coherent national government, and thus the machinery to distribute aid and coordinate development at the national level. Also, politicians who were willing to entertain statist solutions to domestic problems were perhaps more willing to push for international aid to solve national problems.

2. Ibid., 89–90.

The United States had encouraged Brazilian expectations of a close, cooperative relationship: in personal notes from Roosevelt to Vargas during the war, in the extensive program of Rockefeller's OIAA, and in the coordinated operations of Brazilian and American soldiers on the Italian front. From 1944 to 1946, American officials discussed with Brazil ways of enhancing the southern nation's status in the fledgling United Nations, from making Brazil a permanent member of the Security Council to giving it the maximum term for a temporary member.[3] After the Yalta Conference, Secretary of State Edward Stettinius traveled to Brazil, where he reiterated to President Vargas that if France did not become one of the Big Five of the U.N. Security Council, Roosevelt would support Brazil as France's replacement.[4] Brazil would have become the first nation south of the equator to attain world power status. A few months later, Berent Friele, head of OIAA in Brazil, told Oswaldo Aranha that "Brazil will play an important part" in the rehabilitation of the postwar world and that the United States would be forever "grateful to you and President Vargas for the support which you gave us during the darkest days in our history."[5]

Yet the Brazilians soon found that the vicissitudes of peace were more unpredictable than those of war—at least when it came to an alliance with the United States. Between 1946 and 1949 it became abundantly clear not only that the "North American memory" was "very weak," as Oswaldo Aranha put it to Minister of Foreign Affairs Raúl Fernandes, but that the Americans did not "even want to hear from us."[6] A combination of domestic preoccupations and the numbing desperation of a "world reduced to material misery and moral anarchy" caused the wartime solidarity and postwar ambitions of Brazil to seem very far away indeed, according to Aranha. Yet Brazil had to find ways of inducing the United States to follow through on its implicit as well as explicit promises to help

3. Frank McCann, *The Brazilian-American Alliance, 1937–1945* (Princeton: Princeton University Press, 1973), 341, 457–58; Stanley Hilton, "Brazilian Diplomacy and the Washington-Rio de Janeiro 'Axis' During the World War II Era," *Hispanic American Historical Review* (May 1979): 224–27. Although McCann and Hilton disagree on how much priority the United States placed on creating a strong position for Brazil in the UN, their research makes it clear that it was European and Canadian opposition which eliminated the possibility of a permanent seat for Brazil.
4. Alzira Vargas attended this meeting, along with her father, President Vargas, Stettinius, and the Brazilian ambassador to the United States. Interview with Alzira Vargas, Rio de Janeiro, November 18, 1986.
5. Berent Friele to Oswaldo Aranha, June 15, 1945, p. 1. FGV, CPDOC, OA 45.06.15.
6. Oswaldo Aranha to Raúl Fernandes, March 18, 1947, pp. 1–2. FGV, CPDOC, OA 47.03.18.

accelerate Brazil's development. "If they want to cooperate with us, I have no doubt that our progress will be accelerated, inflation corrected, production developed. . . . It is this which must be obtained," Aranha wrote to his successor at Itamaraty, the Brazilian Foreign Ministry. Appealing to the United States, he argued further, "is not a policy; it is a necessity. We have no other source of help in a world drained and miserable. We must knock on this door until it opens like the door to the house of a friend, which it should be."[7]

Aranha and other observers of the United States, such as Brazilian ambassador Carlos Martins, found the nation "profoundly disturbed by world leadership," yet simultaneously preoccupied with domestic party politics and "panicked" at the possible return of a depression.[8] To knowledgeable Brazilians, domestic considerations seemed the impetus for many American foreign policy moves. As the U.S. government tightened the purse strings on Eximbank funds, loan criteria became focused on projects which would facilitate the reconversion of American wartime industries and promote the international commercial system created at Bretton Woods and sponsored by the United States.[9] Even the Marshall Plan and the heightened conflict with the Soviet Union to which it contributed appeared to Brazilian officials to be motivated primarily by American needs. Although the plan would serve to avert Soviet influence in Europe, its greatest usefulness would be to improve world economic conditions as they affected the United States. As Martins reported to Rio, the United States normally sold one-third of its exports to Europe, but after the war found that none of its European customers had money to spend. The Marshall Plan was designed, Martins thought, to turn European allies back into "paying customers," while at the same time draining off some of the excess income in the United States which threatened to send inflation soaring. The plan was humanitarian in its international implications, Martins observed, but eminently political in its domestic ones: "The increase in taxes [required by the Marshall Plan] will be like a bloodletting, relieving the public of its acquisitive power and hence of non-essential expenditures, delaying the coming of a future depression. This delay is . . . vital for the political party which would stay in

7. Ibid., 3–4.
8. See Aranha to Fernandes (ibid.) and Carlos Martins to Raúl Fernandes, November 5, 1947, p. 1. Itamaraty, *Missões Diplomáticas Brasileiras, Washington, Ofícios* (hereafter referred to as *Missões*), *Novembro-Dezembro, 1947.*
9. Carlos Martins to João Neves da Fontoura, March 20, 1946, p. 3. Itamaraty, *Missões, Março-Abril 1946.*

power."[10] It was also vital in consideration of the U.S. government's recognition that, as Martins noted in a second report, "a depression equal to or worse than that of 1929 would transform American democracy radically."[11]

But the United States' preoccupation with its own problems and with the problems of Europe and Asia as they related to the United States did not present the only obstacle to Brazilians getting the aid which they considered essential for economic development. The Brazilian Foreign Office recognized that conflicting long-range goals as well as transitory circumstances were obstacles to cooperation.

In an analytical history of inter-American economic relations prepared in 1948, Ambassador Martins charted for Foreign Minister Raúl Fernandes several basic conflicts. Martins foresaw that the United States would doubtless continue to insist that Latin America return to the principles of classical economics regarding the international division of labor. One reason for this was the strong sway of ideology, Martins thought. "According to Max Weber and Sombart," Martins wrote from the embassy in Washington, "one of the characteristics of Protestant cultures is the militant passion for moral universalisms, and the ethical idealism of this country is, without doubt, that of liberal capitalism."[12] Brazil and the rest of Latin America, Martins foresaw, would be caught in the web of North American preconceptions and preoccupations.

In addition to having different temperamental and ideological propensities, the United States was at odds with Latin American and Brazilian economic goals as a result of the experiences of the previous two world wars. While the wars had led Latin Americans to seek a system of hemispheric cooperation and unity, they had led the United States to view its interests as being intimately connected with the solution of global problems and the creation of global, as opposed to regional or hemispheric, unity. Following the wars, regional economic systems seemed "each time more inadvisable" to the United States, Martins wrote. Notwithstanding the Good Neighbor Policy, it had been the aim of the United States since 1934 to foster free international trade in the belief that economic nationalism, even economic regionalism, would abandon Asia "to economic depression and social and political instability," foster "pan-

10. Carlos Martins to Raúl Fernandes, September 29, 1947, p. 2. Itamaraty, *Missões, Setembro-Outubro, 1947.*
11. Carlos Martins to Raúl Fernandes, November 5, 1947, p. 1. Itamaraty, *Missões, Novembro-Dezembro, 1947.*
12. Carlos Martins to Raúl Fernandes, March 28, 1948, pp. 13–14. Itamaraty, *Missões, Março, 1948.*

American protectionism," result "in the economic monopoly of the United States in the rest of the hemisphere" (something Martins implied that the United States wished to avoid), and provoke "retaliatory measures by other countries not in the system." Thus, he thought, the pretensions of Latin Americans to special economic privileges or assistance from the United States would necessarily conflict with its postwar economic foreign policy in four crucial ways: "regional preferences versus the worldwide expansion of multilateral trade; national industries versus international commerce; economic nationalism versus the needs of foreign capital; controlled economies versus free-trade."[13]

A final irony Martins observed was that much of the Latin American impetus toward state promotion of economic development and away from liberal economics had been inspired by the United States and its own earlier adoption of Keynesian economics. During the 1930s and 1940s, "Latin Americans became at each turn more influenced by the experiences of the 'New Deal', like the 'Commodity Credit Corporation', 'the Reconstruction Finance Corporation', the 'Tennessee Valley Authority'." Yet just at the point that Latin American nations proposed to undertake similar economic experiments, the United States started to react against "the growing state control of economic life which characterized the Roosevelt administration."[14] Martins anticipated that in coming years, U.S. support for Latin American development would be limited not only by the trend away from regionalism, but also by American disapproval of the statist (or corporatist) approaches to development which Roosevelt had helped to inspire. Of course, many aspects of New Deal corporatism were ultimately institutionalized in the United States, but within a cultural context that continued to idealize pluralism, free enterprise, and limited government. Unable, perhaps, to accept the increased statism of their own society and determined to return to normalcy following the Depression and the war, the U.S. public, the Congress, and the presidential administration were hardly ready, Martins recognized, to accept or promote a New Deal in Latin America, their traditional backyard. Needless to say, such a policy would also have involved paying more money and greater attention to Latin America than the United States was willing to commit.

13. Ibid., 8–9.
14. Ibid., 13. Also see Joseph Tulchin, *Problems in Latin American History* (New York: Harper and Row, 1973), 502, for a brief discussion of Latin Americans' favorable response to the reforms of the New Deal and admiration of Roosevelt's "commitment to improving conditions for the poor." The Rooseveltian imagery persisted: in 1963, one of the architects of the Alliance for Progress published a book calling the Kennedy program a "New Deal for Latin America." Lincoln Gordon, *New Deal for Latin America: The Alliance for Progress* (Cambridge: Harvard University Press, 1963).

But Brazilians were by no means daunted by U.S. resistance to an innovative economic transformation of Latin America. Although Martins and many other Brazilian officials recognized the severe limitations of the U.S.–Latin American relationship, they thought of Latin America as Hispanic America and of Brazil as the third party in the hemispheric balance. For both historical and cultural reasons they could not quite believe that the United States would lump their country together with the Hispanic nations under one policy approach. They were confident that any tendencies along those lines could be countered effectively by appeals to the traditional friendship and recent wartime alliance of the United States and Brazil. To a certain extent they were right.

The Truman administration, like the administration before it, recognized Brazil as the "first nation" in its Latin American policy. At that time Latin American nations represented one-third of the votes in the United Nations, and the United States relied on Brazil to help keep other countries in line with American proposals and positions. As Abraham Lowenthal and Albert Fishlow note, "In a U.N. Assembly swollen [in the 1970s] to 150 members, a bloc of 25 votes could not compare in significance with the 20 Latin American votes which Washington could almost unanimously command on crucial political issues in the 60-member Assembly of the 1950s."[15] Because of this, U.S. policymakers considered Brazil's "determined bid for recognition as a world power" useful to the United States and operated on the policy of encouraging and supporting these aspirations "within reason." In this case, reason was defined as policies which did not overstep the bounds of international harmony by favoring Brazil beyond its role as a regional leader. Officials were concerned about giving just the right amount of weight to regional issues and no more: "The inter-American system shall become a strong pillar in the structure of world organization" read a position paper written for Secretary of State George C. Marshall in 1947. "If worse should come to worst with respect to the future of the United Nations, however, it would be more than ever important to our defense that the inter-American system survive."[16]

Regionalism was clearly a fallback, but to keep these regional options open the United States had to, "within reason," respond to the demands

15. *Latin America's Emergence: Toward a U.S. Response* (New York: Foreign Policy Association, 1979), 32.
16. All quotes from "Secret Memorandum I for the Secretary: Immediate Policy Matters," January 1947, pp. 2–3. NA, R.G. 59, Records of the Deputy Assistant Secretary of State for Inter-American Affairs, 1945–56, Lot Files 58D691, 57D598, 57D634, Box 6, Folder: "Policy-Position Papers, 1945–49."

of Brazil for a bigger political and economic role in the world. In their report for Marshall, State Department analysts took note that "Brazil realizes that its ambition in this direction can be attained only through the continued help of the United States." The report recommended an informal quid pro quo: continued support for Brazil in exchange for "Brazil's proffered support for U.S. world policies, which has already been of considerable use to us."[17] A few months later, Secretary Marshall told Oswaldo Aranha, "Brazil has always led in the conciliation of differences in international relations. . . . I count on the influence of this relationship [between the U.S. and Brazil] in the generous unification of the . . . nations of the western hemisphere."[18] Although Brazil did not become one of the Big Five of the Security Council, as a result of U.S. support Aranha became the first president of the United Nations General Assembly. So it was with a modicum of concern that American officials realized, in mid-1949, that the U.S. policy of limiting economic aid to economic advice—in the form of the short-lived Abbink mission—had finally seriously strained its relationship with the Brazilian government.

Bad feelings arose over several events. The lack of a foreign aid initiative for Latin America had been a sore point since the creation of the Marshall Plan. Although the Eximbank and the World Bank extended $130 million in loans to Brazil between January 1949 and the middle of 1950, similar amounts were loaned to Mexico and Argentina.[19] The loan to Argentina was particularly offensive, indeed insulting, to many Brazilians because Argentina had supported the Axis in World War II while Brazil had lost much of its merchant fleet in the Allied cause, had provided bases for American soldiers, and had actually fought in Europe. Many Brazilians felt, John Abbink noted with chagrin and some sympathy, that the United States "presumes on Brazilian friendship, but that we lean forward to enlist the cooperation and solve the problems of other Latin American countries."[20] As elsewhere in the world, it sometimes seemed that former enemies or competitors (Argentina in this case, but even more famously Germany and Japan) had a stronger hand than former allies in maneuvering U.S. aid in exchange for support in the Cold War. What was more, a major loan to the Brazilian state of Minas Gerais was held up for over a year during this period because of a conflict between the Eximbank

17. Ibid., 5–6.
18. Quoted in a memorandum from the U.S. embassy in Rio to Itamaraty, July 23, 1947, p. 1. Itamaraty, *Estados Unidos da América, Notas, Janeiro-Maio, 1946.*
19. *Foreign Relations of the United States* (FRUS), 1950 (Washington: GPO, 1956), 2:761.
20. John Abbink to Edward Miller, April 13, 1950, FRUS, 1950, 2:758.

and the World Bank over which was to be the bank of first recourse for development loans.

Brazilians were also concerned about growing U.S. interest in African colonial development, which Ambassador Maurício Nabuco, successor to Carlos Martins, called the complement to "European economic stabilization" under the Marshall Plan. Brazilians feared that such plans would not only "relegate to second place [once again] the economic interests of those countries previously courted under the good neighbor policy," but also stimulate the production of competitive agricultural commodities.[21] The fears of African competition were exacerbated by a U.S. Senate investigation into coffee prices in 1950, during which the combative head of the committee, Senator Guy Gillette, suggested that the United States promote coffee production in other countries to circumvent the high prices Brazil had been charging following several frosts. A press representative for Nelson Rockefeller in Brazil, Henry Bagley, reported to the Rockefeller office in New York that as upset as the Brazilian public seemed to be over the loans to Peronist Argentina, the question of agricultural competition struck an even more sensitive nerve. "The probability that we will use a lot of Point IV money to help backward areas in Africa which may become major competitors of our friend Brazil is often heard. And when Gillette suggested that we stimulate coffee production elsewhere, the Brazilians saw red."[22] Although the State Department protested the committee's rash statements, the Brazilians were not reassured.[23]

In May 1949, in the midst of this troubled period, President Dutra visited the United States at the invitation of President Truman. Although Truman and Secretary of State Dean Acheson did not intend anything beyond a good will gesture, the Brazilians hoped that the invitation signaled their opportunity to secure a stronger commitment to close relations in the form of financial assistance for economic development. The U.S. ambassador to Brazil, Herschel Johnson, was also hopeful—and worried that some tangible aid be forthcoming. "If President Dutra returns empty handed," he warned, "with nothing but oral reiteration of our ancient friendship, he will be the object of bitter political criticism."[24]

---

21. Maurício Nabuco to Itamaraty, March 3, 1950, pp. 3–4. Itamaraty, *Missões, Março 1950*. Also see Edward Miller to Acting Secretary of State Webb, "Memorandum for the President," October 5, 1950, *FRUS*, 1950, 2:766–71.
22. Henry Bagley to Francis Jamieson, June 20, 1950. RAC, R.G. 2, P.R., Box 12, Folder: "H. W. Bagley, 1950."
23. Edward Miller to James Webb, "Memorandum for the President," October 5, 1950, *FRUS*, 1950, 2:766–71.
24. *FRUS*, 1949 (Washington, D.C.: GPO, 1975), 2:566.

Yet Johnson's sense of urgency was not shared by his superiors, who planned nothing beyond the usual statements of goodwill.

At the end of the trip, Foreign Minister Fernandes met with Under Secretary of State James Webb for a routine final conversation and surprised Webb with an angry analysis of postwar relations. Fernandes criticized the equal treatment given to Argentina, the use of Marshall Plan monies by Europe to develop coffee in Africa, the inadequate amount of World Bank and Eximbank loans, and the limitations of the Abbink report. Webb, taken aback, asked Fernandes what he thought would be the best approach to solving these problems. The minister then proposed a new joint commission to design and fund development projects. Although Webb did not immediately take Fernandes up on the idea, the depth of Brazilian discontent had finally registered with the State Department.[25] A few weeks later, the State Department replaced the head of the Division of American Republics, Assistant Secretary of State Spruille Braden, with Edward G. Miller, Jr., a New York attorney and friend of Nelson Rockefeller. (Rockefeller had held the assistant secretary position before Braden.) Miller had a personal interest in Latin America, having spent part of his boyhood in Cuba, where his father was in the sugar business, and he and Rockefeller kept in frequent contact about ideas for salvaging ties to Latin America and countering U.S. indifference.[26] Rockefeller even lent Miller his Washington home for the duration of Miller's appointment, once again blurring the lines between the public and private spheres and ensuring his access to government policymakers responsible for Latin American relations.[27] In contrast to Braden, whose demeanor was often arrogant and abrasive, Miller was a congenial man, humorous and witty, and he spoke Spanish fluently.[28] Under Miller's leadership the search began for a more constructive approach to Brazil.

In responding to the concerns raised by Fernandes, U.S. officials demonstrated a strong commitment to remaining on good terms with Brazil and a sheepish recognition that American talk had been bigger than

25. For an account of this meeting and the negotiations and problems leading up to the joint commission, see W. Michael Weis, "Roots of Estrangement: The United States and Brazil, 1950–1961," (Ph.D. diss., Ohio State University 1987), 47–49.

26. Miller's files as assistant secretary contain twenty-five pieces of correspondence with Nelson Rockefeller between 1949 and 1952 (as well as a few letters between himself and David Rockefeller). In letters and meetings Miller kept Rockefeller up to date on events in U.S.–Latin American diplomacy and frequently asked for his advice and help on important matters, including the Joint Brazil-U.S. Economic Development Commission. NA, R.G. 59, Lot File 53D26, Office Files of the Assistant Secretary of State for Latin America, 1949–53, Box 11, Folder: "R."

27. Interview with Richard S. Aldrich, Burlingame, California, January 8, 1988.

28. Interview with J. Burke Knapp, Portola Valley, California, April 1, 1985.

American action. Somewhat defensively, Edward Miller placed part of the blame on the Dutra government for not being "aggressive or effective in developing a program for obtaining United States assistance for the implementation of economic development schemes."[29] The Brazilians in fact had attempted to be just that when, at the end of the Abbink mission and later during Fernandes's meeting with Webb, they had requested the creation of an ongoing joint technical commission to develop specific proposals. Both Miller and John Abbink also criticized Brazilian officials for "presenting incomplete or contradictory material" in their loan applications, in comparison with other Latin American countries.[30] But early in 1950 Abbink said that it was "unfortunate that joint United States–Brazil overall study and conversations were permitted officially to lapse"; and Miller, responding a week later to Abbink's statement, expressed his strong feeling that "something should be done by way of a more positive approach to Brazil's desire for our cooperation."[31]

By October 1950 Miller could report to President Truman that the State Department was indeed taking a "more positive" tack through "the creation of the first Joint Commission for Economic Development" under the Point Four program.[32] A short while later Truman told Ambassador Nabuco that "he would take a personal interest in their [loan] problems." Truman was interested in the commission as a means both to solve the problems with Brazil and to initiate implementation of Point Four, and he told Acheson to come to him for help if there were any further problems ironing out the jurisdictional disputes between the World Bank and Eximbank.[33]

The Dutra administration had successfully pressured the United States into responding to its desire for help with coordinated economic development. Why did the United States respond? First, the Brazilians successfully used their war record, the grievances they had over the Gillette

---

29. *FRUS*, 1950, 2:768.
30. Ibid., 2:758, 763, 776. Correspondence from John Abbink and Edward Miller.
31. Ibid., 2:758–59. Abbink to Miller, April 13, 1950.
32. Ibid., 2:771. Edward Miller to Acting Secretary of State Webb, "Memorandum for the President," October 5, 1950. In his inaugural address of January 1949, President Harry S Truman listed as his fourth point the need for "a bold new program for making the benefits of our scientific advances and industrial progress available for the improvement and growth of underdeveloped areas." Point Four, as the program came to be known, was implemented by Congress under the Act for International Development (Public Law 535). From *Partners in Progress: A Report to President Truman by the International Development Advisory Board*, foreword by Nelson Rockefeller (New York: Simon and Schuster, 1951), 91.
33. "Memorandum of Conversation by the Secretary of State," October 9, 1950, *FRUS*, 1950, 2:775, 778.

report and the loans to Perón, and, most important, the precedents established by the Cooke and Abbink missions to push the Americans into following up on their great ideas with some real help. Second, the U.S. administration was susceptible to these demands because, as a policy statement of 1950 reiterated, Brazil was "the keystone of our over-all Latin American policy."[34]

Viewing Brazil as "the keystone" meant that the United States still had an interest in developing the nation's economy as part of enhancing its usefulness as a major ally, especially since Brazilians themselves so strongly desired U.S. help. In the 1950 policy statement, the Department of State anticipated that in the event of a major war its southern ally would demand essential commodities from the United States as a quid pro quo for strategic materials. "With this in mind," the memo stated, "every possible encouragement has been given to Brazil's efforts to increase her productive capacity of those essential items, with particular attention given to steel."[35] Edward Miller, in closed congressional hearings, called the Brazilian insistence on getting adequate quantities of basic goods in wartime "almost an obsession"—and then (displaying an American obsession) described how crucial it was that the United States have access to certain vital materials such as manganese, iron ore, and monazite sands. "We want to have cooperation from them with regard to increasing strategic materials," Miller said, adding, "Our principal supply of manganese has been in the past from the Soviet Union."[36]

The United States was also still committed to strengthening Brazil's prestige vis-à-vis the other Latin American nations (especially anti-American Argentina) so as to make it a more effective leader of pro–U.S. opinion. One way of doing this was to make the Point Four program in Brazil "a model for all other countries in Latin America," as Miller put it.[37] While State Department officials and Brazilian representatives worked out the details of a bilateral agreement in the fall of 1950, Truman's Point Four advisory commission, chaired by none other than Nelson Rockefeller, was entrusted with the task of considering "the types

34. "Policy Statement for Brazil," December 18, 1950, FRUS, 1950, 2:765f.
35. Ibid., 2:760.
36. Testimony of Edward G. Miller, March 16, 1952, Committee on Foreign Affairs, House of Representatives, Historical Series, Selected Executive Session Hearings of the Committee, 1951–56, (Washington: GPO, 1980), 16:394.
37. Edward Miller to Dean Acheson, October 30, 1950, FRUS, 1950, 2:779. Also see page 765f of this volume, where the "Policy Statement for Brazil" (December 18, 1950) is quoted: "It is a policy of the United States to encourage and support all appropriate Brazilian efforts to improve that country's international position and prestige in the United Nations."

and size of programs" most likely "to accomplish with maximum dispatch and effectiveness the broad objectives of the Point Four program."[38] In its report, published a few months later, the committee called for increased private investment abroad while also pointing to the "acute" need for government-financed programs in underdeveloped areas around the world. "Joint Commissions" were the primary tool recommended by the committee to promote economic planning and development.[39] Brazil was to have the first. Thus, although once again wary of raising expectations, U.S. officials were willing by the middle of 1950 to engage in a little of the bilateralism that the Brazilians had historically pushed for and that conferred a special status on the U.S.-Brazil relationship within the Latin American context.

The Korean War also gave impetus to efforts to intensify the alliance with Brazil through economic cooperation, but the basic decision to increase the level of cooperation was made independently of wartime considerations. Not until early 1951, three months after the first notes establishing the commission had been sent from Rio, did U.S. officials began to push strongly for deployment of a Brazilian infantry division in Korea.[40] Throughout 1951 the State and Defense departments pressed the Vargas government to commit troops. Army negotiators, rather lacking in tact, told the chief of staff of the Brazilian armed forces, General Góes Monteiro, that by sending soldiers to Korea, Brazil could raise its standing in U.S. defense priorities from last place (the rank given to all South America) to first.[41]

The U.S. ambassador to Brazil at one point raised the idea of using economic leverage to coerce participation but dismissed the idea as not very good; it appears economic threats were never used. Instead, officials offered the incentives of gains in prestige and additional military equipment.[42] When Vargas emphasized that economic development was "unpostponable" and had to come before any involvement in foreign wars,

---

38. *Partners in Progress*, 89–90.

39. Ibid., 62–67.

40. Stanley Hilton gives somewhat more weight to the role of the Korean War in stimulating U.S. agreement to a new joint commission. However, discussions to establish the commission were under way before North Korean troops crossed the 38th parallel. The war nevertheless did temporarily reinforce the always conditional and fluctuating U.S. commitment to Brazilian development and strengthened the bargaining position of the incoming Vargas government. Hilton, "The United States, Brazil, and the Cold War."

41. "Memorandum of Conversation by Randolph Kidder," *FRUS*, 1951 (Washington: GPO, 1979), 2:1214–15. Present at this meeting were General Monteiro and General Edwin Silbert of the Inter-American Defense Board.

42. Ibid., 1200. Edward Miller (for Dean Acheson) to Herschel Johnson, May 28, 1951. Also see "Memorandum of Conversation," August 3, 1951, 1206.

U.S. officials could point to the recently created commission.[43] Brazil never did send troops to Korea, but the nation's repeated promises to consider doing so may have strengthened the new U.S. commitment to economic cooperation.

The Cold War probably gave more impetus to the commission's establishment than did the Korean conflict. Although U.S. officials saw Communist influence in South America as minimal at that time—reflected in the continent's "last place" defense ranking—there was nonetheless a desire to maintain strong alliances in Latin America, especially with the larger countries. J. Burke Knapp, who headed the joint commission that began work in mid-1951, later said "the Joint Commission in Brazil fit into a pattern of cultivating Latin America. In a geopolitical sense there is no doubt that it was related to the Cold War, which pressed the U.S. to look to its fences and make a greater effort to cultivate and woo Latin America."[44]

Thus, by the end of 1950, the Department of State favored the creation of an ongoing commission as much as the Brazilian government did. They saw advantages to the United States in strengthening Brazil's infrastructure and economy and in sustaining among Brazilians a sense of reciprocity in their relationship with the United States. The onset of the Korean War and the continuing Cold War heightened these perceptions. The department concluded that it might be worth actually fulfilling the promise of earlier plans through a working commission.

The Joint Commission

American officials hailed the Joint Brazil–United States Economic Development Commission as "a new departure in the conduct of economic relations between governments." In both private conversation and public pronouncements, State Department representatives spoke of the commission as "a new technique and one which involves action and not merely study." Edward Miller emphasized publicly that the commission was "an action body, the purpose of which is in the shortest possible period to vitalize the economy of the country which can be in the future one of our most powerful allies."[45] The key difference between the Abbink and

43. Ibid., 1188. Herschel Johnson to Dean Acheson, January 15, 1951, and Memorandum of the Bureau of Inter-American Affairs, 1191–94.
44. Interview with Knapp.
45. Text of a speech by Edward Miller, Department of State *Bulletin* 25, no. 650 (December 10, 1951): 951. Also see statement by Merwin Bohan, interim head of the Joint Brazil-U.S. Economic Development Commission, *FRUS*, 1951, 2:1233.

Cooke missions and the joint commission had to do with money: the two missions went in expecting to save it, the commission went in expecting to spend it. Developments in the relationship between the two countries had coincided with the introduction of Point Four to make a policy of coordinated aid (in the form of loans) a reality at last.

The start of the commission also coincided with a change in the government of Brazil. In November 1950, Brazilians elected the former dictator Getúlio Vargas to succeed Dutra. Vargas ran for office on a developmentalist-nationalist platform. In his campaign he advocated an activist approach to development as well as nationalization of Brazil's then unexplored and undetermined oil resources: "O petroleo é nosso" (The oil is ours), he claimed during the campaign. Although negotiations for the commission had taken place under Dutra, the importance of the bilateral agreement was underscored by Vargas's election. Even before his inauguration early in 1951, Vargas sent Truman a comprehensive list of projects with which Brazil desired U.S. assistance and which would represent "a policy of support for the intensive development of our economy."[46]

Although privately skeptical about how far the United States would go to help Brazil, Vargas brought to his communication with Truman the authority of a prominent wartime leader who knew specifically what the United States "owed" its ally and the tone of one who would not be deterred by liberal economic niceties when it came to "rationalizing agriculture and industrialization."[47] Development efforts would have a higher profile under Vargas, and the value of cooperation with the United States would be more keenly tested and observed. Since the Truman government had encouraged the ouster of Vargas in 1945, the United States worried it would not be on the best footing with the new government. This concern undoubtedly strengthened Brazil's bargaining position. Edward Miller told Dean Acheson it was "important that we press forward" with the program for Brazil, and Truman appointed Nelson Rockefeller as his special representative to the Vargas inaugural. Rockefeller, of course, represented the high point of cooperation under Roosevelt. Vargas thanked Truman for his choice, saying that Rockefeller "has worked always with untiring ardor for the strengthening of inter-American relations."[48]

46. Getúlio Vargas to the U.S. Government, January 11, 1951, *Impasse Na Democracia Brasileira, 1951–1955: Coletânea de Documentos* (Rio de Janeiro: Fundação Getúlio Vargas, 1983), 71.

47. Ibid.

48. Brazilian diplomat Egydio da Camara Souza tried to reassure Miller that Vargas was "coming into power without any hard feelings" toward the United States over "the Berle

The commission began operating a few months later, on July 19, 1951. Two men served actively as head of the American section: Merwin L. Bohan, economic counselor in the Department of State and American representative on the Inter-American Economic and Social Council, and J. Burke Knapp of the World Bank. Bohan was interim chairman of the delegation for the first few months and then returned to head the commission when Knapp left after one year. The head of the Brazilian section was Ary Frederico Torres, an engineer who had participated in and often presided over most of the major industrial projects in Brazil in the preceding decade, including the Eximbank-financed Volta Redonda steel plant. Valentim Bouças, IBM's representative in Brazil and a long-time booster of foreign trade and investment, assisted Torres on loan negotiations and other finance matters.[49]

The joint commission operated from July 1951 to December 1953 (although it existed in name only for the last six months). During this time it created detailed plans for forty-one projects to be funded by the Eximbank and the World Bank. The basic goal of the program was "to eliminate some of the most serious impediments to the economic development of Brazil."[50] The commission found that the fastest growing sector of the Brazilian economy between 1939 and 1951 was manufacturing, in which real output had increased nearly two and a half times. Yet the commission concluded, as had the earlier study groups, that the pace of industrialization could not be maintained unless Brazilians could break through the bottlenecks in transportation, fuel, and power.[51]

As a result, the joint group devoted almost all of the forty-one projects to the nation's infrastructure: eighteen projects were for railroad development, eight were for power plants (half of which were hydroelectric), and eight were for port improvements and shipping investments. The fuel problem was not addressed because Brazilian law prohibited foreign private investments in petroleum exploration, and American insistence on foreign private involvement precluded U.S. public loans, as Edward Mil-

episode" and kept "in his heart the strong friendship he felt for Roosevelt." (Souza to Miller, December 4, 1950, p. 1. Also see Miller to Acheson, January 24, 1951, p. 1. NA, R.G. 59, Lot File 53D26, Box 2, Folder: "Brazil: 1949–1950.") Quote taken from letter of Vargas to Truman (undated copy of letter), p. 1. FGV, CPDOC, GV 51.04.10/4.

49. Vera Alice Cardoso-Silva, "Foreign Policy and National Development: The Brazilian Experiment Under Vargas" (Ph.D. diss., University of Illinois, 1984), 281–82.

50. *The Development of Brazil: Report of the Joint Brazil-United States Economic Development Commission* (Washington: GPO, 1954), 3. Hereafter referred to as the *Joint Commission Report.*

51. Ibid., 14–15.

ler put it, "for any phase of the petroleum industry, including refining"—
in effect this constituted a political bottleneck.[52] The cost of the entire
program was estimated to be approximately $1 billion, of which more
than one-third ($387.3 million) would be provided by hard currency
loans from the World Bank and Eximbank. The rest of the budget was to
be met with local currency collected through a special tax on higher
incomes and through private investment.[53]

The commission accomplished several important things. Perhaps most
significantly, it created the Brazilian National Bank for Economic Development (BNDE). The bank both received tax funds from the Brazilian
government and channeled international loans toward various projects.
It was initially capitalized with an $18 million loan from the Eximbank in
1952, and during the rest of the decade sponsored development projects
worth hundreds of millions of dollars which fostered the rapid growth of
Brazil as a major industrialized nation.[54] The commission's work also led
to the establishment of a national railway administration which stan-
dardized gauges throughout Brazil and supervised universal conversion
to diesel fuel.[55]

On a more modest but equally vital level, the commission trained
Brazilian businessmen and government officials in the fine points of loan
negotiation. Whereas in 1949 and 1950 Brazilian loan applications had
to be returned repeatedly for clarification and additional information, by
1952 Dean Acheson was announcing publicly that Brazilian proposals
were among the world's most professional.[56] This impressive gain in
expertise did not end with the exit of American advisers in 1953; by 1960

52. "Policy Statement for Brazil," *FRUS*, 1950, 2:761f.
53. *Joint Commission Report*, iii.
54. For statistics on projects sponsored and loans obtained by the Brazilian National Bank
for Economic Development see the *Annual Report of the Export-Import Bank of Washington* for the period ending June 1962 (Washington: GPO, 1962). Also see Skidmore,
Politics in Brazil, 166, 315, for an assessment of the development bank's important role later
in the decade.
55. The conversion to diesel fuel for railways was part of a larger movement, also stimulated
by the commission, away from an economy based on wood energy sources to one based on
petroleum. At the time, when petroleum was inexpensive to import, this seemed a reasonably risk-free development strategy. It was an approach that was to have enormous consequences in the 1970s, when OPEC-led price increases would force oil-short Brazil to go into
massive debt to sustain the growth (and even the basic functioning) of its economy.
56. *New York Times*, July 11, 1952, 6. During a state visit to Rio de Janeiro, Acheson was
reported to have said, "The Export-Import Bank and the International Bank officials had
commented that the Brazilian projects were almost the only ones they had received that were
so detailed they did not need to ask for more information."

Brazilians had negotiated more credits with the Eximbank than any other country in the world.[57]

The planning process also strengthened the national commitment to industrial development and gave prominence to Brazilian economists and engineers, who were to play critical roles then and continue to do so to the present day. Burke Knapp, in retrospect, said the most significant outcomes of the commission were to introduce a "whole philosophy" of investment planning by trained experts and "to create continuing institutions like a railway management that would be competent to do . . . planning for itself in the future."[58] Brazilian economists Lucas Lopes and Roberto Campos, both of whom held significant positions with the commission and went on to assume major political roles in Brazil, agreed that the first accomplishment of the commission was to establish techniques of analysis and planning. "Previous to that," according to Campos, "you had simply market surveys rather than any attempt at interconnected economic analysis. Most of the government initiatives were really based on departmental requests to the central budget office, without any real effort at profitability analysis, cash flow, and so on."[59]

According to Lopes, who became President Juscelino Kubitschek's economic minister, the commission "had an importance equivalent, in this period of Brazilian history, to the planning board of Roosevelt in the decade of the thirties."[60] Although a number of the projects designed by the commission were not immediately implemented because of problems between Brazil and the World Bank, the plans were subsequently used as part of Kubitschek's famous program of *metas* (targets) for economic development (1956–61). Lopes later wrote, "In some cases the [Meta Coordinating] Groups had nothing more to do than to implement the studies of the Joint Brazil-U.S. Commission and the BNDE."[61]

Yet paradoxically, the commission did more to harm U.S.-Brazil relations than to improve them. Of the forty-one proposed projects, only a handful had been funded by the time the commission ended, and only fourteen by 1955. Under the terms governing the commission, it was the State Department, not the government of Brazil, that decided which of the

57. *Annual Report of the Export-Import Bank of Washington* for the period ending June 1960, xvi–xvii.
58. Interview with Burke Knapp.
59. Interview with Roberto Campos.
60. Interview with Lucas Lopes, Rio de Janeiro, October 16, 1986.
61. "JK e o Programa de Metas; Palestra do Ministro Lucas Lopes, Brasilia, 14 de Maio de 1986," 14. Copy obtained from Lucas Lopes.

two banks was to be approached on any given loan. The Eximbank approved all joint commission projects submitted to it. The World Bank, however, refused to consider the majority of loan applications ever submitted and in fact after 1954 did not make another loan to Brazil for four years.

When the commission suspended its activities in July 1953, at least one prominent Brazilian official took an optimistic view (though he asked not to be named) and said that, regardless of loans given or withheld, "for the first time in our history we have an exact and documented blueprint of what needs to be done. . . . Whether it is done now or later, we know what we need most for our development."[62] But sentiments like this were in a distinct minority. After all the talk in 1951 about action, the Brazilians in 1954 had yet another essentially unimplemented study on their hands. The conservative and frequently pro-U.S. newspaper *Correio da Manha* accused the Eisenhower administration in July of reneging on promises made by Truman, although by 1954 feelings ran so high that the Commercial Federation of São Paulo blamed the policy of the preceding five years. "Frankly speaking," the federation added in a letter directed to a U.S. Senate fact-finding committee, "we feel that the American-Brazilian friendship has so far benefited only one side."[63] The goal of maintaining some sense of reciprocity had come to naught.

The alliance had in fact profited both sides, but Brazilians had not reaped the full range of benefits they had expected or to which they felt entitled. The United States would continue to benefit from strategic materials agreements it had signed with Brazil for manganese, iron ore, and atomic raw materials. The United States could also continue to count on strong Brazilian support in the United Nations and on Brazil as its major military ally in the western hemisphere following the Second World War. The Brazilians benefited from these arrangements as well. Raw materials sales brought in foreign exchange, and Brazilian majority ownership (51 percent) in the largest mines meant that a substantial portion of the new wealth stayed in the country. Prominence in the United Nations and military cooperation with the United States heightened Brazil's international standing.

Above all, however, the Brazilians sought U.S. help with comprehensive economic development, and it was here that they found the alliance

---

62. *New York Times*, July 19, 1953, 15.
63. See the *New York Times*, July 23, 1953, 6, for the reference to *Correio da Manha* and "Study of Latin American Countries," Senate Committee on Banking and Currency (Washington: GPO, 1954), 145, for the statement of the São Paulo Commercial Federation.

lacking. Raw materials and military agreements might produce some benefits, but in a nationalistic era they had high costs as well. Help with long-term development was the only benefit the United States could offer Brazil that politicians like Vargas could point to as an inarguably good reason for cooperation. The United States under Truman was willing to offer this help as long as it was consistent with strategic objectives and not too burdensome for the State Department. Economic incentives for developing Brazil existed but did not compel attention. Foreign trade overall was still a small percentage of the U.S. gross national product, and the main U.S. import from Brazil, coffee, was not an essential good. Yet for Brazil economic development as a means to building a strong nation was the crux of the alliance and had been since the beginning of the century. The breakdown of the joint commission seemed to frustrate everything for which the Brazilians had hoped.

Why did the effort—at least in its foreign loan aspect—fail? The commission had completed its assignment: designing a range of development projects, determining their order of priority, and submitting them to the U.S. government to be forwarded to one of two funding agencies. The government did indeed forward the proposals, some of which were funded by the Eximbank but many of which sat at the World Bank. The breakdown occurred for two primary reasons. First of all, the Truman administration had trouble getting the two banks to cooperate, and the conservative leadership of the World Bank did not make this job any easier. Second, the Eisenhower administration entered the fray between the banks with a bias against the Eximbank and a Latin America policy which called for minimizing both economic cooperation and the special relationship with Brazil and for pressuring nations such as Brazil to conform to laissez-faire practices.

A Business Orientation: The World Bank

The Eximbank, which started financing Latin American purchases of U.S. goods in 1934 and first took on a developmental role with the Volta Redonda steel plant in 1940, had strong ties in Latin America well before the International Bank for Reconstruction and Development (World Bank) began making loans in 1947. Eximbank, like the World Bank later on, had negotiated a number of snags over the years in lending money to Brazil and other Latin countries. The challenges were numerous from the banks' point of view as well as from Brazil's: obtaining strong applications, weathering changes in government, accounting for economic instability and a high inflation rate, and maneuvering around the political obstacles set up by U.S. exporters who had had trouble since the 1930s collecting on their invoices promptly because of Brazilian currency shortages. Such problems were nothing new, and the pages of *Foreign Relations of the United States* for the years 1946–54 are filled with references to the loan negotiations between the banks and Brazil. Edward Miller adopted a philosophical outlook: "As of this writing," he said with regard to one sticky session, "our heroine [Brazil] is again tied to the railroad track, but I think she will be snatched from disaster next week."[64]

The joint commission took these so-called normal difficulties into account when they made their recommendations, including the endemic problems of inflation and currency shortages, which the commission referred to as "a natural accompaniment of phases of rapid economic growth financed predominantly from domestic resources." They concluded that Brazil was still an excellent credit risk and that even a conservative appraisal showed Brazil capable of assuming the debt load that would be created by full implementation of the development program. Regarding Brazil's debt-absorption capacity, the final report in December 1953 noted that the "present ratio of debt service to total exchange receipts—about 8 percent—is lower than that of most other countries that have benefited by credits from foreign public lending institutions. It is also modest in comparison with the ratios that existed for some of the now highly developed countries during earlier phases of their economic development."[65]

It is against this backdrop that one should view the World Bank's competition with the Eximbank, and its final refusal to help Brazil on the basis of a general credit unworthiness. The two institutions had been in conflict with one another almost since the inception of the World Bank. Part of the antagonism was owing to a natural confusion over jurisdiction, since the World Bank had a specific mandate to engage in development funding in Latin America while the Eximbank had been financing both trade and development since 1934. World Bank officials began pushing in 1950 for clarification on which bank was to have the major responsibility for development, suggesting that that function should go to the international institution. The president of the World Bank, Eugene Black, claimed that his institution was "the chosen instrument for long-term development lending programs and that the Eximbank should, in the case of Brazil, confine itself to short-term financing directly related to trade promotion."[66]

64. Edward Miller to Herschel Johnson, May 31, 1952, *FRUS*, 1952–54 (Washington: GPO, 1983), 4:581.
65. *Joint Commission Report*, 237, 234–35.
66. *FRUS*, 1950, 2:762. Miller to Johnson, August 23, 1950.

Fueling the dispute was the World Bank's interest in increasing its leverage vis-à-vis Brazil and other potential borrowers. The bank wanted to be able to place stringent conditions on the loans it made, in terms both of the borrowing country's general financial position and of the management of specific projects. Stringent loan conditions reflected a concern for Brazil's development mixed with a determination to establish the fiscal reputation of the newly created World Bank and an attitude of technological superiority. "We [at the Bank] were very pure about this," Burke Knapp later acknowledged. "We would say, we know how this ought to be done, and if it's not done that way it won't accomplish its purposes for the country concerned, and if it doesn't accomplish its purposes for the country concerned repayment of the loan will not be completely assured." The Eximbank, because of pressures brought to bear by the State Department and by exporters eager for markets, tended to follow a more expansive policy than the international bank and to place fewer conditions on the loans it made. This made it "a dangerous competitor," according to Knapp. Members of the World Bank knew that they would have a perennial problem establishing their own program of "tough" loans as long as Brazilians had access to the easier Eximbank.[67]

So long as the jurisdictional question went undecided, the World Bank showed itself willing to cooperate with the joint commission, as exemplified by its giving Knapp leave from the bank for a year to head the commission at Miller's request. The Eximbank, in contrast, both protested any incursions onto its traditional territory and had to be coaxed into sending a representative to Brazil even to observe the workings of the commission.[68] The World Bank's President Black also held out the temptation of up to $250 million in loans for Brazil, and as early as August 1950 told Edward Miller that he was even prepared, under certain conditions and against the bank's usual policy, "to make a public announcement to this effect."[69] Black asserted he was "bullish" on Brazil but, as Miller reported to Acheson, "unwilling to act unless the sphere of activity of the Export-Import Bank is limited and defined to his satisfaction."[70]

Secretary of State Acheson feared antagonizing the Eximbank, "on whose cooperation the Department must depend in other areas of the

67. Interview with Burke Knapp.
68. Merwin Bohan to Burke Knapp, November 9, 1951, FRUS, 1952–54, 4:1234–35. Also see FRUS, 1950, 2:762, for a brief account by Miller of Eximbank's attempt to beat out the World Bank on a loan to the Brazilian State of Minas Gerais.
69. "Memorandum of Conversation" by Dean Acheson, October 19, 1950, FRUS, 1950, 2:776.
70. Ibid., 763, Miller to Johnson, August 23, 1950, and p. 776, Memorandum by Dean Acheson.

world."[71] But the necessity of establishing some boundaries and the attractiveness of Eugene Black's repeated offers—backed by $105 million in loans even before the commission was established—eventually led the government in February 1951 to make the World Bank the institution of first recourse for development proposals.[72] Within a year, Edward Miller and Merwin Bohan were to rue the decision.

The first indication that the World Bank might not come through on its general promises was the bank's reluctance in September 1951 to announce publicly that it intended to earmark $100 million for a program of railroad and port development, conditional, of course, on receipt of properly worked out plans. This reluctance was strangely at odds with Black's earlier eagerness to get on with a bullish program for Brazil. Both the U.S. and Brazilian governments wanted the public statement in order to have something to show for the first few months of the commission's existence. Ambassador Herschel Johnson also thought the overall relationship with Brazil needed "a fillip in the very near future" if the United States was going to convince President Vargas to make a troop commitment in Korea.[73] Yet, according to Miller, only Burke Knapp's direct intervention convinced the bank to issue the kind of statement Black had shown himself willing to make in August 1950, when he was still trying to gain jurisdictional priority over the Eximbank.[74]

The next major problem surfaced when Vargas, who had relied heavily on populist and nationalist appeal to win the nation's highest office after being ousted only six years before, announced a new decree on January 3, 1952, placing tighter limits on remittances of profits made by foreign investors in Brazil and making these new limits retroactive. The State Department expressed concern about the threat this presented to U.S. investments and to the commission's goal of attracting foreign capital to Brazil.[75] Business groups in the United States, as they had done on other occasions when their interests were threatened, began calling for a ban on public loans to Brazil.[76]

---

71. Ibid., 777.
72. Edward Miller to Herschel Johnson, May 31, 1952, FRUS, 1952–54, 4:582. Also see the Annual Reports of the World Bank for the years 1949–51.
73. Johnson to Miller, August 31, 1951, FRUS, 1951, 2:1221.
74. Ibid., 1222. According to Miller, "It was extremely fortunate that Burke Knapp arrived . . . in time." Miller to Johnson, September 14, 1951.
75. FRUS, 1952–54, 4:570–72.
76. The U.S. Council of the International Chamber of Commerce called for a halt on all loans to Brazil until the remittance decree was "corrected." New York Times, January 17, 1952, 35. A typical earlier dispute demonstrating the influence of business opinion on international loans is documented in the Foreign Relations volume for 1946. At that time,

A number of Brazilian officials, including the foreign minister and the finance minister, were also disturbed by Vargas's decree and took steps (with Vargas's approval, ultimately) to secure passage of a foreign exchange bill in the Brazilian Congress that partially devalued the cruzeiro and made remittances less profitable for foreigners—instead of setting an arbitrary limit on them. The bill represented a compromise because, though it nullified the remittance decree, it got at the root of the problem, high remittances, while also improving Brazil's terms of trade through monetary devaluation.[77]

This kind of tempest and face-saving compromise was nothing new either to the State Department or to Itamaraty. Throughout the next few months of turmoil, U.S. officials judiciously waited for the Brazilians to work out their own solution. It was clear to Miller and Ambassador Johnson, and presumably to their superiors, that time and patience would solve the problem and that overt pressure on Brazil would only make it more difficult for Vargas to compromise. They also recognized that putting too much pressure on Brazil would jeopardize other U.S. policy goals, such as the concluding of military and raw materials agreements, and arouse "a deep and abiding hostility" that could only strengthen the influence of Brazilians opposed to cooperation with the United States.[78] For these reasons, the State Department urged the Eximbank and the World Bank to proceed with loans on joint commission projects in spite of business objections and the banks' apprehension about the decree on profit remittances.[79]

The World Bank was especially susceptible to pressure from private investors, since it sold its own bonds in world markets. But the bank's resistance to continuing a good will policy while the foreign exchange bill was being worked on seemed to go beyond a simple concern for maintain-

---

American investors holding bonds for a Brazilian coffee loan were highly concerned about Brazilian moves toward liquidating the stockpiles of coffee which were collateral on the loan. The State Department was considering Eximbank and World Bank loans to Brazil for other purposes but noted, "Any announcement of Brazil's intention to seek capital assistance in this country would almost certainly stimulate strong objection on the part of . . . bondholders. With a congressional election in the offing, the possibilities of such a situation are too apparent to ignore." *FRUS*, 1946, *American Republics* volume (Washington: GPO, 1969), 489.

77. *FRUS*, 1952–54, 4:578f.
78. Ibid., 4:573–75. Johnson outlined these considerations to Miller on March 11, 1952.
79. Ambassador Johnson counseled patience on several occasions (March 11, May 8, May 9, and May 22, 1952), and Miller noted on May 15 that it was "too bad that this problem has created so many difficulties that weren't really necessary but I take it that is part of diplomacy to be continually staving off disaster." Ibid., 4:578.

ing institutional credibility. Black adopted almost a punitive tone with Brazilian negotiators, emphasizing by his actions and statements the control the bank had over Brazil's development plans—and thus over the future of Brazil itself. In a conversation he had in May 1952 with Valentim Bouças, the loan negotiator for the commission and one of the most openly pro-American members of the Vargas administration, Black set an arbitrary loan ceiling of $40 million until the free market bill passed. He told Bouças further that the bank "would have to cut down" (in fact, cut in half) one of the projects most crucial to Brazil, the rehabilitation of the railroad linking Brazil's key cities of São Paulo, Belo Horizonte, and Rio de Janeiro. Later, when Bouças enthusiastically told Black about a new plan to finance Brazil's commercial arrears and thereby improve the nation's credit standing, Black dashed ice water on the discussion by replying that "Brazil had to get the Bank's consent before entering into such an operation."[80]

Edward Miller reported to Ambassador Johnson that Bouças was "infuriated" and had "exploded" over Black's arrogant approach. Miller acknowledged the bank's need "to take into account strong sentiment in U.S. financial quarters" and had earlier refused to transfer loan applications to the more amenable Eximbank,[81] but he told Johnson that he sometimes regretted ever having yielded up so much jurisdiction to the World Bank. Miller commented at the end of May that while Black "sees the point of view of the business community with all too perceptive eyes, he seems to have blinkers on when it comes to trying to understand the Brazilians. He talks to a person like Bouças just as if he were talking to a prospective borrower in the Chase National Bank, everything being on a take-it-or-leave-it basis."[82] The U.S. representative on the World Bank's board of directors was equally influenced by business interests, Miller seemed to feel, and of little help in persuading the bank's president to follow the State Department strategy. Miller told Johnson, "At times I believe that the real Executive Director of the Bank is not the Assistant Secretary of the Treasury [who was the U.S. appointee to the World Bank's governing board] but Leo Welch of Standard [Oil] of New Jersey."[83]

80. Ibid., 4:581–83. Miller to Johnson, May 31, 1952.
81. Ibid., 4:575f.
82. Ibid., 4:582. Eugene Black was senior vice president of the Chase National Bank before heading the International Bank.
83. Ibid. Leo Welch was treasurer of Standard Oil of New Jersey and well known to Miller as one of the most conservative voices of business opinion when it came to relations with Latin America. Welch sat on the State Department's Business Advisory Council (Latin American Committee) under both Truman and Eisenhower and consistently promoted hard-line

Under pressure from the State Department and from Brazilians, the World Bank grudgingly approved two loans to Brazil during the late spring of 1952, easing the pressure on the Vargas government and saving the commission's work for at least the time being. Had the bank not made the loans, the Brazilian internal financing plan would have collapsed. The plan, charging a tax on personal and corporate incomes for the projects of the joint commission and the BNDE, had been opposed in the Brazilian Congress by a number of businessmen and was scheduled to expire in June 1952 if accompanying foreign loans were not procured by that date. Thus, the prestige of the shaky Vargas government as well as the existence of the joint commission was narrowly saved.

Yet tensions between the World Bank and the Vargas government never really abated. Brazil continued to suffer extreme currency shortages even though the price of coffee, its primary export, was high at the time. A policy of stockpiling imported materials in response to the Korean War depleted Brazilian reserves once again. By the end of 1952 Brazilian commercial arrears had zoomed, and the free exchange bill, although it had some strong support in the Brazilian Congress, still had not passed because of objections raised by special interests. The State Department, the Eximbank, and ultimately the National Advisory Council agreed that a policy of continued cooperation (meaning funding) and support for pro-U.S. Brazilian ministers was the best way to help the Vargas government develop the domestic support necessary for passage of the bill. This policy, they felt, would both protect the U.S.-Brazil relationship and have the best chance of leading to an improvement in terms for American investors and exporters. Dean Acheson confirmed to the National Advisory Council that the department was "fully prepared to carry the matter through" and that he was convinced "there has not been any neglect [by the Brazilians] of the gravity of the situation."[84]

---

approaches. During the Korean War, one committee report Welch helped prepare suggested that the task of obtaining "increased supplies of strategic materials from Latin America should be approached as a business problem. . . . We cannot afford aimless and amiable generosity." On another occasion Welch criticized the State Department's overall Latin America policy for "an undue softness stemming from an underestimation of the relative bargaining strength which the United States has with the area." First quote from "Ways to Increase U.S. Imports of Strategic Materials from Latin America," February 8, 1951, pp. 3–4. NA, R.G. 59, Lot File 57D618, Folder: "Business Advisory Council-Latin American Committee, 1951." Second quote from letter of Leo Welch to Edward Miller, May 28, 1952, p. 1 of "Comments." NA, R.G. 59, Lot File 53D26, Box 3, Folder: "Business Advisory Council."

84. Dean Acheson's position was communicated by William C. Martin of the Federal Reserve at a special meeting of the National Advisory Council on October 10, 1952, to discuss the Brazilian situation. *FRUS*, 1952–1954, 4:595–99.

The World Bank disagreed with this strategy. Eugene Black was dogmatic about not giving any more funds until Brazil mended its ways, and he opposed any new loans by the U.S. government as well.[85] Even after the multiple exchange-rate system was confirmed in February 1953, nullifying the decree on profit remittances, Black kept the pressure up because by then he was concerned about passage of a railroad reorganization bill by the Brazilian Congress. Once again, the State Department and the head of the joint commission, Merwin Bohan, advocated showing good faith in the ability of their Brazilian counterparts to see the bill safely through Congress by announcing an intent to fund railroad development, subject to clearly stated terms. Not to do so, they felt—especially considering that the commission would soon be coming to an end—would be to jeopardize passage of the bill, damage U.S.-Brazil relations, and "completely wipe out the prestige of the Joint Commission."[86]

Eugene Black implacably opposed any such incentives, saying the bank could not possibly consider support for railroad development until the bill was passed and would not "compromise its principles to accommodate US political considerations." Ironically, Black then articulated the constraints he was under as a result of the economic and political interests of European members of the World Bank, who were concerned about their old debts with Brazil. True to the "take-it-or-leave-it" style of negotiation on which Miller had earlier commented, Black told U.S. officials that if "the Department or the Joint Commission cannot work with the IBRD on the above basis . . . they are free to seek other sources of financing."[87] Considering that the bank had fought hard and successfully for a nearly monopolistic lending position, such a comment can most charitably be described as cavalier, less charitably as arrogant and tightfisted. Although the State Department could, perhaps, have reversed its decision to make the World Bank the lender of choice, the joint commission had no freedom whatsoever "to seek other sources of financing."

Why did the World Bank take the positions it did? The Brazilians eventually squeezed a few more loans out of the bank, but the majority of loan applications went unheeded. From the evidence available, two major reasons emerge for the bank's behavior. The first is the personal leadership of Eugene Black who, at least in the case of Brazil, seemed to take

85. Ibid., 4:598. Minutes of the National Advisory Council, October 10, 1952.
86. Ibid., 4:603. Memorandum of conversation between representatives of the International Bank and the State Department, January 12, 1953.
87. Ibid., 4:603–05.

pride in being inflexible and above pressure from any quarter except conservative U.S. businessmen and perhaps the bank's European membership. Both Miller and Bohan commented upon the abiding bitterness this approach caused among Brazilians. In the opinion of Burke Knapp, however, Black was simply "a conservative banker" who was "very principled" and pursued the policies initially necessary "to establish the reputation of the Bank *as* a bank."[88]

The second reason had to do with the World Bank's strong commitment to fiscal orthodoxy and to its relationships in the financial community. Brazil continued to have major currency and credit problems throughout 1953 and 1954. By mid-1953, Brazilian commercial indebtedness to the United States and other creditors had reached $850 million, approximately two-thirds of the value of annual exports.[89] This situation was eased somewhat by a $300-million balance of payments loan from the Eximbank but aggravated again the next year by a U.S. consumer boycott of Brazilian coffee when frost sent prices soaring and the Brazilian government did nothing to moderate the costs and keep exports moving.

The conservativeness of the World Bank and its susceptibility to the opinion of world financial centers made loans under these conditions not necessarily unsound but highly undesirable in view of the funding guidelines the bank had sought to establish. It hardly made sense from the bank's point of view to fight so hard for the jurisdiction necessary to impose stringent conditions and then to turn around and make loans within the wildly fluctuating and inconsistently managed Brazilian economy. The bank was determined to maintain its lending standards at all costs, which is not a surprising position for a bank. On the spectrum ranging from commercial lending agency to foreign aid administration the World Bank clearly saw itself as closer to the first pole at this point in its history, while the State Department had planned a role for the bank much closer to the second pole. Brazil was caught in the middle.

The World Bank's ties to private investors also affected its response to Brazil's nationalization of oil in 1953. Although Brazil had no major known reserves of oil, the nationalization of oil was seen by many in Brazil and the United States as a step away from initiating a program of aggressive exploration. Even Vargas, who created Petrobrás, the govern-

88. Ibid., 4:601 (Miller) and 618 (Bohan). Burke Knapp's comment is taken from an interview he gave the author.
89. Ibid., National Intelligence Estimate, "Probable Developments in Brazil," December 4, 1953, 4:641.

ment oil monopoly, had originally sought to engineer a combination of public and private financing before he was convinced by nationalists, especially among the military, to come up with a wholly Brazilian solution.[90] Under Truman, the U.S. government had not made an issue out of this particular manifestation of nationalism, other than to refuse to make loans for an aspect of development they wanted left to private companies. At one point, when the Brazilians had sought to buy oil refining equipment during the Korean War (when the United States had placed tight restrictions on exports of strategic equipment), the State Department even intervened to get the machinery cleared, in recognition of the fact that oil was a special issue on which "nationalistic fervor" had to be expected and dealt with gingerly.[91] Indeed, the question of who would develop Brazil's hypothetical oil industry was perhaps the most controversial issue of the 1950s.

But the World Bank was ready to use the weight of its bargaining power to push Brazil on allowing foreign investment in oil, even after the creation of Petrobrás. The joint commission had remained relatively neutral on the issue, although it expressed concern about where Brazil would get the money and expertise to implement an effective exploration program. It was clear, the commission's final report stated, "that the balance of payments outlook of a country in the process of industrialization in which the maximum possible effort is not being made to fortify the domestic fuel basis cannot but be viewed with concern."[92] The World Bank took this further and in late 1953, in conversations with Brazilians, linked its difficulties with providing loans to the nation's unwillingness to allow for foreign investment in oil development.[93] The unremitting pressure and disapproval of the bank was undoubtedly one of the many destabilizing forces which would lead ultimately to the downfall of Vargas, who pointed to the opposition of "international groups" to Petrobrás in his last communication to the nation.[94] Again, however, as with the remit-

90. According to Cardoso-Silva (200–06), most of the Brazilian press, including O Estado de São Paulo and the Rio daily O Jornal, opposed nationalization, but in "the case of basic industries, the nationalist military's views were more weighty to the government." For an account of Vargas's willingness to negotiate with the private oil companies see the American Society of International Law, "International Investment Conference," February 24, 1956, 35–36 of the session on "Legal Incentives to Investment Abroad." Also see John Wirth's comprehensive account of the origins of Petrobrás in The Politics of Brazilian Development.
91. Embassy Counselor Sheldon Mills to the State Department officer in charge of Brazilian affairs, Randolph Kidder, May 21, 1951, FRUS, 1951, 2:1198–99.
92. Joint Commission Report, 32.
93. "Probable Developments in Brazil," FRUS, 1952–54, 4:642.
94. Skidmore, Politics in Brazil, 142.

tance decree, the commercial arrears, and the railway reorganization bill, the specific issue (in this case, oil) was not as important to the bank as the "poor management" they thought it reflected, since the nation would not have the capital for many years to pursue oil exploration vigorously. Unless Brazil played by the bank's rules of development, the bank was not willing to play.

Why did the Truman administration not place more pressure on the World Bank to cooperate than it did? In May of 1953 Merwin Bohan pronounced the decision to make the bank the primary source of financing "a major error." Bohan attributed the decision to a failure to keep in mind the political goals of the program, which would have dictated using a funding source over which the United States had political control.[95] Yet from the beginning of the jurisdictional conflict the United States had shown an awareness of the need to direct loans of "a strategic character," such as those for development of the manganese mines, to the Eximbank.[96] It may be that U.S. officials did not so much forget the program's political goals as they failed to foresee the economic and political complications that would arise in Brazil after 1951 and the difficulties of working with the World Bank under those conditions.

Edward Miller had recognized the problem by May of 1952 and felt that threatening the bank with handing over its jurisdiction to the Eximbank constituted "the one method of bringing leverage on Mr. Black." But this maneuver would have "repercussions of enormous magnitude," Miller worried, hoping he would "never have to face up to the decision."[97] Although Miller was prepared to consider risking the displeasure of the bank for the sake of U.S.-Brazilian relations, it seems that there was never a consensus within the administration on which relationship had higher priority. Willard Thorp, assistant secretary of state for economic affairs, had expressed the opinion in early 1951 that solving the jurisdictional dispute was "of greater importance to the Department" than responding to Brazilian demands for immediate assistance, so it is likely that arriving at such a consensus would have been problematic.[98] The postwar international system was still new, and although the United States wished to protect regional interests, institutions like the World Bank represented universalist goals, which were of a higher priority. The conflict which Carlos Martins had foreseen between the regional em-

95. Ibid., 617. Merwin Bohan to the Department of State, May 20, 1953.
96. *FRUS*, 1950, 2:762.
97. Miller to Johnson, May 31, 1952, *FRUS*, 1952–54, 4:582.
98. *FRUS*, 1950, 2:1190f.

phasis of Latin American foreign policy and the postwar globalism of the United States had finally claimed a casualty: the joint commission.

There was also, clearly, a simple but crucial lack of will and interest within the American government when it came to resolving important problems with Latin America. Bohan thought Miller was "the only one in Washington" who recognized the financial commitments which the United States had made to the commission, and he told Miller that "other agencies, including sections of our own Department, have the happy feeling that it is no skin off their nose and that they can sit around and criticize while ARA [American Republic Affairs] carries the load."[99] When Rockefeller's Point Four advisory committee completed its assessment of Latin American needs, the economic adviser to the State Department wrote Miller, "I believe these recommendations constitute a splendid program for Latin America. I likewise believe that Nelson will be a Houdini if he gets them through Congress."[100]

The staffing of the commission from the U.S. side, as contrasted with the high-powered Brazilian membership, had also been weak from the beginning, as was typical of missions to Latin America. The first chief, Francis Truslow, died on the way to Brazil; Burke Knapp was a temporary appointee; and Merwin Bohan was a last-minute replacement. At the outset, Simon Hanson, a prominent critic of U.S. policy, noted that "Truslow is already written off in Washington as a man who cannot possibly accomplish the terrific job of pushing a program through . . . a priority set-up [in which Latin America ranks last] that will be incredibly difficult to break. And another Cooke or Abbink is not what is needed. . . . it is probable that Nelson Rockefeller is the only person who could do the job." Interestingly, Hanson suggested that one hope for reversing the decline in U.S.-Brazil relations lay in business pressuring the government to reorient its policy.[101]

Even Edward Miller was ambivalent at times over how much and what kind of aid the United States "owed" Latin America. From Miller's point of view, the unchallenged preeminence of the United States in the hemisphere brought with it "serious national disadvantages" which were only partially offset by the "competitive advantage to American exporters." In private correspondence with the U.S. ambassador to Brazil in 1951 and in

99. Bohan to Miller, October 22, 1952, p. 1. NA, R.G. 59, Lot File 53D26, Box 3, File: "Brazil 1952."

100. Ivan B. White to Miller, February 20, 1950, p. 1. NA, R.G. 59, Lot File 53D26, File: "Point IV."

101. *Latin American Letter*, no. 314, March 31, 1952 (Washington), 2.

a report to the State Department's Business Advisory Council in 1952, Miller stated his belief that the decline of British, German, and other foreign influences in Latin America had placed a great burden on the United States to meet all of the trade and investment needs of the other American republics. "The result," Miller candidly told Herschel Johnson, "is that the Latin Americans have developed an almost obsessive feeling that the United States owes them a living and that we are responsible for all their ills." [102]

In any case, whether out of a conflict with universalist goals or a simple lack of interest and commitment, the Truman administration never did push the problem with the World Bank to a resolution, and by the time the problem became acute there was another president in the White House.

Putting Brazil in its Place: The Eisenhower Administration

Although Brazilians were not sure what to expect from the Republican government, they were at first cautiously optimistic. An important reason for this optimism was Vargas's relationship with Nelson Rockefeller and Rockefeller's relationship with the new administration. "Nelson is one of the stars of Republican Party politics and was one of the big shots in the Eisenhower victory," Foreign Minister João Neves da Fontoura wrote Getúlio Vargas after a meeting he had with Rockefeller following the November election. "Nelson told me that I could be tranquil as to the future cooperation of the American government with ours." [103] Only a few days later, Rockefeller traveled to Brazil as a private citizen and took the opportunity, as usual, to meet with a variety of influential Brazilians, including the president. At a small, private reception given for Rockefeller by officials in São Paulo, "the illustrious American personality showed himself invariably cordial and attentive to the questions raised, manifesting his own point of view with visible spontaneity." [104] The lively and pointed conversation covered a range of topics from agricultural to indus-

102. Miller to Johnson, December 6, 1951, p. 1–2. NA, R.G. 59, Lot File 53D26, File: "Brazil 1951." Also see "United States Relations with Latin America," presented for discussion at the Business Advisory Council, May 7, 1952, pp. 11–12. NA, R.G. 59, Lot File 57D618, File: "Business Advisory Council—Latin American Committee, 1952–56."
103. João Neves da Fontoura to Getúlio Vargas, November 10, 1952, in *Impasse Na Democracia Brasileira, 1951–1955: Coletânea de Documentos* (Rio de Janeiro: Fundação Getúlio Vargas, 1983), 92.
104. Report (unsigned) on conversations with Nelson Rockefeller, Sao Paulo, November 14, 1952, p. 5. FGV, CPDOC, GV 52.11.07/4.

trial production, and the Brazilians present "reaped from the talk the clear impression that, personally, the American visitor views with concern the great economic problems related to production, and appears disposed to give adequate and active collaboration." When officials pressed Rockefeller, who was rumored to be under consideration for appointment to high office under Eisenhower, on whether the new administration would supply adequate financing for Brazilian projects, Rockefeller smiled and said, "Maybe."[105]

Rockefeller's optimism as to his own prospects, however, and the Brazilians' as to theirs, was short-lived. Not only did Eisenhower not appoint Rockefeller to a post with foreign policy authority, but the State Department under John Foster Dulles notified the Brazilian government in May 1953 that the joint commission would terminate in July. Under Vargas's protestations the program was extended officially until December, but all work stopped in the summer. The commission had been planned as a temporary body from the beginning, not to last "more than 18 to 24 months,"[106] but termination at the point when the foreign financing plan was in the process of collapsing meant throwing away much of the goodwill the program had built. Although the commission actually did help Brazil by working with local people to carry out a domestic financing plan, to design strong projects, and to create enduring institutions, the component most symbolic of U.S. cooperation—foreign financing—was publicly dumped.

Policy under Eisenhower coincided much more closely with the views and interests of the World Bank. First of all, the administration entered with a bias against foreign aid and a determination to decrease the Eximbank's autonomy and scope. In a reorganization plan presented to Congress early in 1953, Eisenhower eliminated the board of directors of the bank, putting a single administrator in its place, and took away the bank's seat on the National Advisory Council.[107] To justify cutting back the bank, the administration later said it wanted to avoid stimulating competitive industries in other countries, but considering that much of the Eximbank's monies went into noncompetitive infrastructure development this was seen, even by the American business community, as a convenient excuse.[108] Development loans had been highly profitable for U.S. businesses, and bankers and exporters both strongly protested Eisenhower's policy of leaving the financing of foreign development up to

105. Ibid., pp. 2, 3, 5.
106. Notes of the Under Secretary's meeting, October 31, 1951, *FRUS*, 1951, 2:1233.
107. House of Representatives, 83rd Congress, First Session, Document No. 135, "Reorganization Plan No. 5," p. 2.
108. "The Ex-Im Bank and Mr. Humphrey," *Fortune*, November 1953, 114, 244, 246.

the World Bank. In congressional hearings in 1954 they made the point that European countries were offering better credit terms to importing nations and that Eximbank loans, unlike World Bank loans, guaranteed that purchases would be made in the United States.[109] Although Eisenhower later resurrected the Eximbank, he entered office with an ideological bias against the activist role the bank gave the United States in sponsoring economic development. When Dr. Milton Eisenhower, the president's brother, visited Brazil in 1953 as Ike's personal envoy, all he would tell Vargas was that he hoped "the misunderstandings with respect to the International Bank [could] be overcome."[110] Back in the United States, Milton suggested to his brother that the Eximbank be revitalized, which it was—but in most other respects he reinforced the idea of limited economic cooperation with Latin America.[111]

The administration was also more willing to live with the disgruntlement of Brazil because of its strong commitment to private investment and its policy of minimizing the traditional bilateral relationship. In contrast to the Truman administration's policy of providing coordinated assistance to Brazil, the policy recommendation which emerged in 1954 under Eisenhower was to extend aid to Brazil on a "piece-meal" basis only, until Brazil developed a lower pricing system for coffee "which permits coffee to move in volume, and a petroleum policy which permits the development of petroleum reserves."[112] Like the World Bank, the Republican administration was willing to use its leverage to keep the petroleum issue alive, both for the sake of private investors and as a way to ease the currency shortages that still plagued U.S. exporters to Brazil. Members of the administration maintained that the only way for Brazil to improve its exchange position significantly was to "attract large amounts of additional foreign capital for exploration in petroleum."[113] The

109. "Study of the Export-Import Bank and the World Bank," Senate Committee on Banking and Currency (Washington: GPO, 1954). Representatives of the Bank of America, the Bankers Trust Co., and the Grace National Bank of New York all presented statements opposing the curtailment of the Eximbank and the enhancement of the World Bank's role.
110. "Memorandum by Dr. Milton Eisenhower of a conversation with President Vargas," July 27, 1953, FRUS, 1952–54, 4:628.
111. Wagner, United States Policy Toward Latin America, 91–92. Also see Wagner for a useful overview of the conflict among Humphrey, Eximbank, and the U.S. Congress (ibid., 111–17).
112. FRUS, 1952–54, 4:664.
113. Ibid., 662. Memorandum of Conversation, October 7, 1954. The continuing interest of private investors in Brazilian petroleum was indicated by the president of Standard Oil of New Jersey in an interview from 1956: "The Brazilian oil industry is nationalized by law, and it's a shame, really, because Brazil is an enormous country with enormous natural resources. . . . There are some very promising basin areas in Brazil, and I feel just as sure as I can that, if free enterprise were allowed in Brazil under a proper petroleum law, they

Eisenhower administration was clearly more comfortable with "linkage" bargaining tactics than the Truman administration had been.[114]

Although Milton Eisenhower claimed during press conferences in Rio and São Paulo on his 1953 tour that U.S. policy had not changed, in fact one result of his trip was to recommend a shift away from the bilateralism that had developed during the second Truman administration. John Foster Dulles endorsed this recommendation. In response to a letter from an American citizen in Rio urging "special attention" for Brazil, Dulles told the president, "I agree with Dr. Eisenhower's analysis, in which he maintains that Mrs. Cowles [the writer of the letter] has overlooked some important considerations in our relations with Brazil and warns against offending the other Latin American countries by singling Brazil out for special attention. I believe our notice of Brazil can be effected best within our present program of increased attention to all the countries of this area."[115]

To Brazilians this meant being treated like "another one of the Latin American 'republiquetas,' " as one Brazilian businessman expressed it to an American diplomat in Rio.[116] Ambassador Maurício Nabuco said to John M. Cabot, Miller's successor, that "the use of the term 'Latin American' to include Brazil and the Spanish speaking countries seems to be very recent, [and] it is now being applied to an ever increasing area and in an even wider sense." Referring to the American Civil War, Nabuco added sharply, "Lincoln, a Republican, asked Brazil, not Latin America, to arbitrate the ALABAMA claim against England." Nabuco warned Cabot that "if the United States succeed in moulding Portuguese and Spanish America into a single block, they run the risk of seeing the block turn against it's [sic] northern neighbor."[117] Brazilians especially resented the

---

would be able to find a great deal of oil there." *U.S. News and World Report*, September 28, 1956, 70.

114. On the hardening of the U.S. position see Gerald K. Haines, *The Americanization of Brazil: A Study of U.S. Cold War Diplomacy in the Third World, 1945–1954* (Wilmington, Del.: Scholarly Resources, 1989), 76–79.

115. *Republiquetas* means "little republics" but in this context connotes something like "banana republics." John Foster Dulles to President Eisenhower, Dwight D. Eisenhower papers, Ann Whitman file, International Series, Box 4, Brazil (10), p. 1, reproduced by the Declassified Documents Reference System, Carrollton Press, Inc., 1983 (#002403).

116. Walter N. Walmsley to John M. Cabot regarding the comments of Fernando Lee, February 25, 1953, p. 2. NA, R.G. 59, Lot File 56D13, "Records of the Assistant Secretary of State for Inter-American Affairs (John M. Cabot), 1953–1954," Box 1, File: "Brazil."

117. Maurício Nabuco to John Cabot, February 25, 1953, pp. 1–2. NA, R.G. 59, Decimal File 611.32/2–255 (1955–59). Three neutral nations helped to arbitrate the *Alabama* claims in 1872: Italy, Switzerland, and Brazil. Clearly, however, that request could not have come from Lincoln.

equal and sometimes even more favorable treatment of Argentina. While Perón maintained an unfriendly, anti-American stance, U.S. officials seemed continuously solicitous of Argentine favor and unwilling to offend Perón by shows of preference for Brazil. Brazilians "could not understand why the Argentine tail should wag the American dog."[118]

The Department of State rejected a final attempt by the Brazilians to establish a new joint economic board in 1954, stating that the government could not set a precedent under which high-level U.S. officials "would be expected to participate on joint boards to examine the internal economic problems of foreign governments."[119] Of course, in reality the Eisenhower administration was not concerned with establishing a precedent but rather with breaking one. Too much contact with Brazil, such as before and during World War II, created a presumption of equality and mutual access. The more powerful partner in any human relationship is the one who controls the distance between the parties, and Eisenhower was determined to put Brazil in its place. Brazil was still a strategic country, but in the future the U.S. government would not perceive the need to cultivate a sense of reciprocity as a means of ensuring the alliance.

Merwin Bohan, Nelson Rockefeller, and others would continue to advocate implementation of the joint commission projects, but they had minimal influence in the conservative Eisenhower administration, which had little interest in Latin America and even less in supplying economic aid. It took an outbreak of open anti-Americanism in 1958 and the Cuban revolution in 1959 to change this attitude. According to Stephen Rabe, it was not until the Cold War came to Latin America in the late 1950s that Eisenhower and his advisers saw any need "to alter the basic tenets of their Latin American policy."[120] While Rabe, Kaufman, and other scholars have demonstrated the considerable extent to which the late Eisenhower administration did eventually develop an activist aid policy toward Latin America (thereby laying the basis for the Alliance for Progress), these studies should not obscure the fact that the administration began by resolutely stamping out the vestiges of the Good Neighbor

---

118. Walter N. Walmsley to John M. Cabot, quoting Fernando Lee, February 25, 1953, p. 2. NA, R.G. 59, Lot File 56D13, Box 1, File: "Brazil." Also see letter sent by Milton Eisenhower to Henry Holland regarding similar comments made by Brazilian sociologist and government official Gilberto Freyre, November 9, 1954, p. 1. NA, R.G. 59, Lot File 57D295, "Records of the Assistant Secretary of State for Inter-American Affairs (Henry Holland), 1953–1956," Box 2, File: "Brazil 1954."

119. Memorandum by the assistant secretary of state for inter-American affairs, April 16, 1954, *FRUS*, 1952–54, 4:650.

120. *Eisenhower and Latin America*, 83.

Policy, including nonintervention (Guatemala, 1954) and substantive economic cooperation (Brazil, 1953). In essence, the administration was forced to address the problems in inter-American relations that it itself had created. Ironically, Rockefeller, in spite of the two official posts he held under Eisenhower, was listened to more by Democrats than by fellow Republicans during this period. Eisenhower considered Rockefeller a spender and was reluctant to accept his advice on matters of foreign aid. Early in the administration, the Brazilian ambassador came to Rockefeller regarding his problems in obtaining a short-term foreign exchange loan because he could "get nobody" in the State Department; Rockefeller turned around and asked Adolf Berle, an important member of the earlier Roosevelt administration, if he could "get the Eisenhower Administration to do something about it." Berle noted in his diary that it was "queer" that such a prominent Republican had to ask a Democrat for help.[121]

Beginning in 1956, after Eisenhower had to some extent reversed his extreme position on the worldwide lending authority of the Eximbank, Brazilians were once again able to negotiate loans with the U.S. government. Under the strongly developmentalist Kubitschek administration (discussed in chapter 5), Brazil obtained hundreds of millions of dollars in loans from the Eximbank for port, railway, and power developments. The credit for this is due to Kubitschek's effective, activist leadership as well as to the loan expertise and precise program plans generated by the joint commission. By 1962, Brazil had received a total of $1.1 billion in disbursements from the bank, more than all of Asia and more than any other country in the world except France.[122] But what had changed was that the loans were no longer part of a coordinated planning process in which the United States participated but rather were negotiated strictly as business loans at usual rates. Brazil competed equally with other nations, not as a first-class ally. As Henry Holland, Eisenhower's second assistant secretary of state for Inter-American affairs, stated to the conservative Treasury Department, the administration's objective for Brazil was "to achieve economic stability, not economic development to be financed with U.S. grants."[123]

121. *Navigating the Rapids*, 614–15.
122. *Annual Report of the Export-Import Bank of Washington* for the period ending June 30, 1962, part II.
123. Memorandum of Conversation between members of the Treasury Department, State Department, and Eximbank, July 6, 1955, p. 2. NA, R.G. 59, Lot File 57D295, Box 2, File: "Brazil 1955." Also see the minutes of the Business Advisory Council for October 12, 1954 (p. 3), at which Henry Holland made it clear that the State Department was "unalterably

Although the United States helped launch the Brazilian industrial economy in the late 1950s by offering scarce financing for the kinds of infrastructural development recommended by the joint commission, there was little public or diplomatic recognition of this fact. The United States did not exactly neglect Brazil after 1953, but its actions communicated its determination to trade with and develop Brazil on unilateral rather than bilateral terms. The immense power disparity between Brazil and its supposed ally was a point that the Eisenhower administration did not hesitate to drive home. Brazilians would continue to knock at the door of the U.S. government, but as the decade progressed there was little sense that it was any longer the door to the house of a friend. The United States had in effect rejected the special relationship, dismissing the opportunity to sustain and foster a uniquely positive postwar alliance. The question which remained was whether Brazil would do so, too. As Argentina's experience had shown, provocateurs sometimes got more attention (positive and negative) than did team players. In other words, the United States offered few diplomatic rewards for being a good ally.

Essentially, Brazil had sought to be for the United States the kind of bridge to Latin America that Britain was to Europe and to obtain the special privileges that such a posture accorded [124] Brazilian diplomats' whole approach to foreign policy since the turn of the century had been premised on the cultural and geographic uniqueness of their nation—its individuality in Latin America and thus its special relationship to the United States. But after World War II, and especially under Eisenhower, the United States repeatedly denied this individuality, with the result that Brazilians began subtly to redefine their nation as a leader of Latin America rather than as a bridge between the United States and Hispanic America.[125] The attempts of certain private Americans during the 1940s and 1950s to carry out a more mutual relationship with Brazil and thereby to compensate for their government's arrogant attitude would complicate and temper this process.

---

opposed to 'soft' loans" and was interested in increasing noneconomic technical aid only as long as it did not represent "overselling and conforming to the wishes of the receiving country." NA, R.G. 59, Lot File 57D618, File: "Business Advisory Council-Latin American Committee, 1952–1956."

124. Hogan, *The Marshall Plan*, 441.
125. Hilton, "The United States, Brazil, and the Cold War," 622–23.

Chapter 3

The Rich Neighbor

Plunges In: The American

International Association

and the Associação de

Crédito e Assistência Rural

F rom the air, the green hills of the inland
state of Minas Gerais roll one into the
other, rust-red roads rising with the folds of the
mountains and curving down into the valleys below. Verdant pasture and forest luxuriate over
the soft landscape, framing the combed and
cultivated fields of corn, cotton, beans, and rice.
From 1949 to 1961, the American International
Association (AIA) worked with Brazilians to
bring the rural development momentum of late
American populism and the New Deal to the
outlying farms of Minas Gerais, a state bigger
than Iowa, Nebraska, and Kansas combined.
The centerpiece of the AIA effort was a project

loosely modeled after the Depression-era Farm Security Administration (FSA) in the United States and called the Associação de Crédito e Assistência Rural (Rural credit and assistance organization), or ACAR.

While the United States was surveying the wreckage of World War II and Brazil was contemplating strategies for jogging America's memory of promises made in wartime, Nelson Rockefeller was implementing his own answer to questions of postwar economic development: AIA. Like the ACAR project it later started in Minas Gerais, the association had its roots in the Roosevelt administration. As coordinator of the Office of Inter-American Affairs, Rockefeller had overseen the first multiyear, multiproject experiment in U.S. government aid to promote foreign economic development. As discussed in chapter 1, one result was the creation of the temporary program, the Food Supply Division, which provided the impetus for private Rockefeller efforts following the war.

In Brazil, the OIAA Food Supply Division had focused on increasing the yields of produce and livestock in the northeast, an area afflicted then and now by devastating poverty, starvation, and malnutrition. The region was also of strategic importance during World War II. With its easternmost shores facing across the Atlantic toward the Allied base in Dakar, Senegal, the great bulge of Brazil provided military bases that were the halfway point for U.S. planes headed to the North African front. And just as the Brazilian northeast was the jumping off point on the continent, so it was the likely point of entry in an invasion.[1] In either case, it had to be protected and was, by Brazilian and American troops.

Initially, the main goal of the food program was to provision these troops. The program was therefore of immediate use to the United States in supplying its bases at Natal and Recife, as well as part of the overall U.S. diplomatic effort to cushion the economic shock of the war on Brazil and its other South American allies.[2] But OIAA considered the food program a part of its developmentalist thrust also. Its second and third goals were "to give Brazil the benefit of North American techniques in the long time

---

1. See McCann, "Brazil, the United States and World War II," 133–34, regarding U.S. concern about the vulnerability of the Natal bulge to German forces in North Africa.
2. During World War II, the Latin American allies relied heavily on the United States to supply them with both raw and finished materials because of the impossibility of trade with Europe after 1941. OIAA and the BEW faced persistent problems with supplying the southern allies because of submarine warfare off the coast of Brazil and the diversion of most merchant shipping to European convoys.

approach to the agricultural and nutritional problems of the country"
and to further "the spirit of good will."[3]

The steps that OIAA took to encourage production were so simple as
hardly to merit the overblown title of North American techniques, but
they were nonetheless effective. The principal methods were the distribution of seeds and tools to small farmers and the granting of small cash
loans. OIAA brought seventy-five thousand ordinary gardening hoes to
area farmers, who had previously sown and cultivated their fields with
sharp sticks. This alone, OIAA estimated, quadrupled the manpower
productivity of the farmers, with the result that the region went from a
food production deficit to a surplus in two years.[4] Program administra-
tors, who later helped Nelson Rockefeller establish AIA, were also impressed by the results of the small loans (up to a maximum of $250)
granted to poor farmers. These farmers not only substantially increased
their production, but scrupulously repaid the money. On the thousands of
small loans made, OIAA had a loss rate below 1 percent, far less than the
4 percent interest which the agency collected overall. Only wealthy
farmers attempted to renege. Writing to Henry Wallace, then–secretary
of commerce, the head of the OIAA Food Supply Program in Brazil
commented that "we made six relatively large loans of the amount of
$5,000 to $6,000. These loans were made to large land owners with
excellent standing in their communities. To this date not one of them has
been repaid and we have started legal proceedings to take their lands. The
indications are that the loans will now be paid. The moral of this little
story is that evidently the honest people in Brazil are the little people, as is
so often the case among ordinary populations."[5]

At the end of the war, the OIAA was transformed into a new agency
called the Institute of Inter-American Affairs. The institute, operating on
a fraction of the budget of OIAA, continued some of the same programs,
but, as seen in the preceding chapter, whatever ill-defined commitment
there had been to Latin American development evaporated rapidly in the
heat of U.S. demobilization and European reconstruction. In Brazil,
the Food Supply Program became the Rural Education Program. Under
the wartime servicio arrangement, in which host countries contributed
increasingly to program budgets, Brazil had assumed most of the costs.

3. Memorandum from Berent Friele to Jefferson Caffrey and Nelson Rockefeller, March 2,
1944, in the *Annual Report of the Food Supply Division*, 1943, p. 38. FGV, CPDOC, CDA,
IAA 46.11.15.
4. Morris, *Nelson Rockefeller*, 179.
5. Kenneth J. Kadow to Henry A. Wallace, July 17, 1945, p. 2. RAC, John R. Camp Papers,
Box 1, Folder 1.

The operation was strongly supported by both the Brazilians involved and the North Americans who were assigned to it in that country. Yet in June of 1948, vaguely citing "financial and other limitations," the U.S. institute abruptly withdrew from the cooperative program.[6]

The former top staff of OIAA were not willing to give up on the programs they had created. Nelson Rockefeller had the personal resources to take over where federal policy left off and a constitutional tradition of limited government behind him which allowed private initiative in any realm not specifically assigned to government. Foreign aid was clearly a wide open field. Besides, Rockefeller was also unwilling to let go of the network of personal relations and policy commitments he had fostered. He had both his political ambitions and his father's code of honor to fulfill. Nelson was not just the representative of the United States, he was a Rockefeller, and according to his family's highly self-conscious definition of itself that meant strict observance of all promises and agreements. "Having been a spearhead for the administration in Latin America during the war," he later said, "and having made many speeches about our intentions as a nation to carry on wartime cooperation as a permanent thing, I felt a real personal responsibility."[7] Rockefeller was just beginning his career as a politician and entrepreneur of foreign policy ideas and likely did not want to abandon any of his well-built bridges to Latin America.

Perhaps because of the existing expertise on Brazil and on agriculture in the small group, the association proposed to begin its operations in Brazil in agriculture and then to expand almost immediately to Venezuela, where Rockefeller had gotten a start years earlier. Kenneth Kadow, the first director of AIA, wrote to his friend John Camp (later the director of AIA in Venezuela) that Brazil was to be "the proving ground" for the obvious reason that "I have the necessary facts and information to allow an immediate start there."[8] In addition to the convenience of existing expertise, Nelson Rockefeller probably chose Brazil because, as a senior staff person of the Rockefeller Brothers' Fund later articulated, "we know that one or two of the trustees feel that Brazil is a key country and a

6. U.S. Embassy to Raúl Fernandes, Minister of Foreign Relations, June 11, 1948, p. 2. Itamaraty, Estados Unidos da América, Notas, Janeiro-Junho, 1948.
7. Dalrymple, The AIA Story, 8. Martha Dalrymple was an AIA board member who wrote the only published history of the organization. This book is very useful for an overview of AIA's activities throughout Latin America as well as for an account of its beginnings in Brazil and Venezuela.
8. Kenneth Kadow to John R. Camp, May 10, 1946, p. 1. RAC, John R. Camp Papers, Box 1, Folder 2.

strategic country in the world, and the strategic country in Latin America."[9] Brazil was the outstanding member of the wartime hemispheric alliance, and Nelson Rockefeller had been both the appointed and self-appointed shepherd of that alliance. It made sense to start a new program for Latin America in strategic Brazil. The reasons for starting similar programs in Venezuela were obvious: Nelson Rockefeller's own investments in Creole Petroleum, which gave him access to corporate contributions for AIA as well as a stake in local perceptions of corporate America.

The working group chose food for local consumption, not produce for export, as the focus for AIA's work on the assumption that both the welfare of the people and the future industrialization of the country depended on an adequate, nonimported food supply. Much of the early discussion about agriculture echoed the traditional American sympathy with farmers and populist ideas for furthering the interests of the yeomanry. An OIAA report written at the end of 1944 called collaboration on agricultural development in the Americas "imperative," claiming that "the welfare of farming and farmers and the interrelated welfare of all consumers in the other Republics is our welfare."[10] In his draft of the original plan for AIA, Kadow proposed working with the Brazilian government to establish farmers' cooperatives for the purchase and marketing of crops. The goal was to eliminate unscrupulous middlemen who took advantage of the lack of silos and other storage facilities in Brazil to buy up harvests at low prices and then later import food from other regions at a high cost. The program would stabilize prices for farmers and consumers and "would eventually reach great masses of people," Kadow wrote.[11]

Two of the three most important projects Nelson Rockefeller would ultimately sponsor in Brazil were part of the AIA plan from the beginning, although it took a couple of years to get the various efforts under way.[12]

9. James N. Hyde to Dana Creel, October 12, 1964, p. 7. RAC, Rockefeller Brothers' Fund (RBF), Box 12, Folder 6.

10. "Report of Subcommittee II: Field of Agriculture," December 16, 1944, p. 3. NA, R.G. 353, Lot File 60D665, Committee on Inter-American Development, 1944–1945," Box 2, Folder: "Committee on Inter-American Economic Development (Miscellaneous Draft Papers)."

11. Kenneth J. Kadow to Nelson Rockefeller and Francis Jamieson, May 17, 1946, p. 9. RAC, R.G. 2, P.R., Box 1, Folder: "AIA—General." For a full discussion of agricultural cooperatives and "the cooperative vision" of American populism see Goodwyn, The Populist Moment.

12. Between 1946 and 1968, the association carried out a number of projects in Brazil, including a rural extension project in two small towns in the interior of the state of São Paulo which started in 1947, predating ACAR. AIA was also responsible for the introduction of

The first of these, a company to develop and promote the use of hybrid seed, was passed to AIA's profit-making counterpart, IBEC, in 1947. The second project, ACAR, was conceived as a rural credit program which would attempt to duplicate the success of the wartime Food Supply Program. Rockefeller and his team foresaw starting a new type of servicio agreement, one between a foreign nonprofit organization and a local government rather than between nations. AIA would initially provide the majority of the ideas, expertise, and money, with the Brazilians gradually adopting, adapting, and assuming financial responsibility for the program. Above all, AIA would be a catalyst for local leadership, not a substitute for it.[13]

With plans in hand, Nelson Rockefeller flew on a chartered DC-3 to Belo Horizonte, the capital of Minas Gerais, during a whirlwind tour of the country in September 1948. The only inland state of any political or economic consequence in Brazil at that time, Minas Gerais had a long history of providing leadership to the nation. In the years of the Old Republic (1889–1930), *mineiros* and *paulistas* (citizens of Minas Gerais and São Paulo, respectively) had dominated the country both politically and economically.[14] Minas was also a major agricultural producer with considerable natural resources (including the mines of gold, diamonds, iron, and manganese which had given the state its name, General Mines). Rockefeller, as usual, went straight to the top. Meeting with Governor Mílton Campos, who greeted him at the airport, Rockefeller outlined his plan for a rural credit and extension program in Minas. The program would have its own name and its own governing board composed of two Brazilians, two Americans, and a fifth person selected by AIA but approved by the state government. To prevent the Brazilians from being outvoted by the AIA representatives, all decisions would require the affirmative vote of at least four people, giving both sides a veto.[15] AIA would

---

the active, widespread 4-S Club movement in Brazil (*Saúde*—health, *Saber*—knowledge, *Sentir*—feeling, *Servir*—service), based on the 4-H movement in the United States. Of the AIA projects, I have chosen to focus on the CAR system because it was the most well known undertaking and the one activity ultimately adopted in its totality by the Brazilian federal government.

13. Kenneth Kadow to Nelson Rockefeller and Francis Jamieson, May 17, 1946, p. 1. RAC, R.G. 2, P.R., Box 1, Folder: "AIA—General." For a restatement of this "basic assumption," as Kadow called it, also see "Some Guiding Principles for AIA," by John Camp, April 15, 1953, p. 1. RAC, AIA, Box 1, Folder 1.

14. A *mineiro* is a person from Minas Gerais; a *paulista* a person from the state of São Paulo. For a brief introduction to the political history of the Old Republic see Peter Flynn, *Brazil: A Political Analysis* (London: Ernest Benn, 1978), chap. 3.

15. Dalrymple, *The AIA Story*, 199.

contribute $75,000 toward the program's cost each year for three years. The contribution of the state of Minas Gerais would grow from $25,000 the first year to $75,000 the second year to $125,000 the third year. At the end of the three years, both AIA and Minas would have paid $225,000, splitting the total cost.[16] Governor Campos approved of the idea, and on January 1, 1949, ACAR opened for business.

While Rockefeller used the OIAA servicio as the model for the project's financing and administration, he clearly based much of the content of the ACAR program on the even earlier efforts of the New Deal's Farm Security Administration (FSA).[17] Rockefeller chose Robert W. Hudgens, former associate director of the FSA and the "last of the liberals" in the agency before it was abolished in 1946, to head the overall AIA program.[18] Hudgens in turn brought on Walter Crawford, who had worked in the FSA in Arkansas in the early 1930s and had been a staff member of the wartime Food Supply Program in Paraguay, to organize the ACAR program in Minas Gerais.

The purpose of ACAR was simple: to arrange low-interest bank loans to small farmers and to provide the technical assistance and supervision necessary to ensure efficient use of the credits. While the state provided the loan funds, they were to be channeled through local banks. Initially, AIA found it difficult to interest banks in the arrangement because the low interest rates would leave little profit for the private institutions, compared with other types of loans on which they could spend staff time. But Crawford was eventually able to interest Alfonso Paulino of the Minas Gerais Savings Bank in the ACAR philosophy, and with none of the bank's own assets at stake, Paulino agreed to start the program with a commitment to thirty to forty loans for the first year.[19] Crawford mean-

16. American International Association, *Annual Report, 1948*, Chart D. RAC, AIA, Box 1, Folder 2.
17. The FSA did not provide the model for all AIA programs. In São Paulo state the AIA program was run by Dr. John B. Griffing, who used the more traditional methods of "pure extension" that went back to the Progressive Era in the United States. Like many American agriculturists, Griffing felt that credit programs such as those innovated by the FSA were unnecessary and expensive. Through Griffing and Hudgens, AIA experimented with rural education and improvement programs that used credit as well as ones that did not. As it turned out, the ACAR model gained wider recognition and acceptance in Brazil than did the purely educational programs run by Griffing. For information on pure extension versus the FSA rural credit programs see Sidney Baldwin, *Poverty and Politics: The Rise and Decline of the Farm Security Administration* (Chapel Hill: University of North Carolina Press, 1968), 31, 200–01, 287–90. On the differences between Griffing and Hudgens see Dalrymple, *The AIA Story*, 38–40.
18. Baldwin, *Poverty and Politics*, 397, 401.
19. Dalrymple, *The AIA Story*, 42–43.

while made contact with farmers by launching a campaign on how to exterminate the leaf-cutting ants which infested Minas Gerais and dotted the countryside with anthills as high as a man's waist. The staff of ACAR then helped farmers apply to the bank for money and visited the farmers regularly to help them implement the planned improvements. Every loan made that first year was paid back at the appointed time.[20]

It quickly became clear, however, that much more than simple agricultural credit was needed. In the three years that followed, ACAR grew into a multiservice rural extension organization with integrated programs for women and youth as well as adult male farmers that increasingly placed emphasis on the welfare of the entire farming family. In addition to introducing 4-S Clubs (the Brazilian equivalent of 4-H) for young people, ACAR developed a new approach to its extension work known as "the man, the girl and the jeep."[21] In spite of some local dismay over the seeming impropriety of a man and woman traveling alone over the rough backcountry roads, ACAR trained and teamed female home economists with male agricultural extensionists and sent them out to every farm which had a loan. The women instructed wives and mothers on how to improve sanitation, preserve foods, filter water, sew mattresses, and use a wider variety of fruits and vegetables for a balanced diet. ACAR published simple pamphlets in Portuguese on home care, and one of AIA's consultants started the first university-level home economics courses in 1952 at the state agricultural college at Viçosa.[22] A study by the U.S. National Planning Association in 1955 commended ACAR for its strong programs for rural women, in comparison with extension services which operated in two or three other countries of Latin America.[23]

In keeping with the traditional Rockefeller interest in sanitation and the eradication of hookworm, the construction of privies and examination for parasites was another part of the ACAR program. In three of the

20. In addition to the close supervision provided by ACAR, the honesty and industriousness for which mineiros are famous in Brazil must be considered an important factor in the loan repayment record. The ACAR successes were also made possible by the preexisting familiarity of the farming community with money and its uses. As Arthur Mosher noted in a study for the National Planning Association, "In Bolivia, Peru, and Ecuador, efforts to raise agricultural productivity among the considerable sector of the population which is Indian are hampered by the fact that many of these people know little of the use of money. . . . Brazil is not confronted by this problem." Arthur T. Mosher, *Technical Cooperation in Latin America: Case Study of the Agricultural Program of ACAR in Brazil* (National Planning Association, Washington: 1955), 5.
21. Dalrymple, *The AIA Story,* 43.
22. Ibid., 48.
23. Mosher, *Technical Cooperation in Latin America,* 37.

four typical loans described in the 1955 study of ACAR, the construction of a family outhouse was one of the supervised expenditures.[24] As one farmer described the broader services of the association, "With the help of ACAR, both through our loans and our planning, we have put in a filter for drinking water, we have all taken worm medicine, and we have planted a home garden. Now we plan to plant some coffee and some oranges for home use."[25] ACAR also instituted a cooperative arrangement with the Health Department of Minas Gerais to provide basic medical and dental care to outlying farm families, just as the FSA had made medical and dental care a component of its program in the United States.[26] In Brazil, the state of Minas agreed to set up clinics staffed with at least one doctor and a nurse in the areas in which ACAR was working, while ACAR agreed to provide transportation when necessary and to organize rural meetings for public health education. In the first year (1949), eight thousand people were seen in the clinics. By 1953, according to an ACAR estimate, this number had nearly tripled, with twenty-two thousand people receiving medical or dental treatment.

The emphasis on family welfare distinguished the ACAR program both from other American-instigated rural education projects in Latin America and from the preexisting programs of the Brazilian state agricultural agencies. On the average, families spent 13 percent of the loan money they received on home improvements such as plumbing, repairs, sewing machines, and electricity.[27] The program aimed not so much at a macroeconomic increase in the agricultural productivity of Minas Gerais as at improving the overall quality of life of small farming families. Again, this approach reflected very much the U.S. domestic program of the FSA, which had aimed its resources, in spite of opposition from groups which wanted to rationalize agriculture (such as the American Farm Bureau Federation), at poor and tenant farmers whom the agency helped through small, supervised "rural rehabilitation loans" designed to enhance family

24. Ibid., 38–42. For a history of the Rockefeller family's interest in the eradication of the hookworm, see John Ettling, *The Germ of Laziness*. Hookworms are a type of intestinal parasite spread by the lack of toilet facilities. Over the years the bare earth becomes infested with parasites, which humans then catch through their feet. The construction of privies and the wearing of shoes prevent a recurrence of hookworm disease once the parasites have been eliminated with medicine.
25. Ibid., 40–41.
26. Baldwin, *Poverty and Politics*, 208.
27. Louise Brown, "Non-Profit Group Helping Brazilian Farm Development," *Brazilian Business*, April 1961, 61. Mosher also notes that, of the rural education programs in Latin America which he studied for the National Planning Association, ACAR had the largest staff of home agents and the strongest program for rural women (Mosher, *Technical Cooperation in Latin America*, 37).

subsistence.[28] In Brazil, one local member of the ACAR governing board justified this emphasis, saying, "That is the way it should be. To start at the other end might mean a more rapid increase in production, but not much of this would result in better family living at an early date. Moreover, emphasizing agricultural production would mean working with wealthier families."[29]

But working small did not preclude thinking big. Thoughtful, carefully orchestrated publicity was a family trait of all Rockefeller efforts. From the beginning, AIA thoroughly documented and publicized ACAR's activities for the purpose of popularizing them, proving their efficacy, and encouraging the rest of the country to undertake similar ventures. Brazilian planners as well as American representatives of Point Four took note of ACAR's releases. "Without wishing to blow my own horn more than a little peep," publicist Henry Bagley wrote Francis Jamieson in New York about one public report, "I can say that the pamphlet has made quite a hit."[30]

ACAR printed its annual reports in Portuguese to underscore its Brazilian sponsorship. Not until the sixth annual report was published was an edition in English also made available. The annual reports focused on what ACAR was doing; only a few brief paragraphs were devoted to its history or to the AIA and only one line to its American sponsor, Nelson Rockefeller. The inspiration for the program was traced to the Great Depression in the United States and the Farm Security Administration. The Annual Report for 1950 adopted a slightly populist tone (ever effective in the context of Brazilian politics) in its description of the FSA, saying that "bankers in the beginning, ridiculed the idea, accusing the government of risking public money on 'unguaranteed' loans. . . . The facts proved the FSA was right: the collection rate on its loans during the [Depression] crisis was better than that of the Banks."[31]

28. Baldwin, *Poverty and Politics*, 182, 200. According to Hudgens, the difference between the FSA and the American Farm Bureau Federation was that "the Farm Bureau's political activities were based on the concept that farming is an industry, and therefore nothing should be done in a system that allowed inefficient people to stay in an industry and preempt resources like land. . . . We were saying, on the other hand, that farming must be sound from a business and technological point of view, but that for the welfare of the country as a whole, it's a good thing to keep as many people on the farms as can make a decent living there." Robert W. Hudgens Interview (1954), p. 269 (New York: Columbia University Oral History Collection).
29. Mosher, *Technical Cooperation in Latin America*, 57.
30. Henry Bagley to Francis Jamieson, September 4, 1951, p. 1. RAC, R.G. 2, P.R., Box 12, Folder: "Bagley, July-Dec. 1951."
31. *Segundo Relatório Anual da ACAR*, 1950, p. 3. RAC, AIA, Box 45, Folder 325.

The connection to the Rockefellers was clear but never emphasized. In the AIA program in Venezuela this presented a problem when Creole Petroleum complained that it was not getting enough publicity for its financial contributions to AIA activities there. With Nelson Rockefeller's approval, the director of the Venezuela program, John Camp, responded that they would identify "the oil companies more closely with AIA" in the future, but that "in general *public* information we have in the past sought to place primary emphasis on the actual operations of the various AIA programs with secondary emphasis on the individuals or organizations that have made these activities possible."[32] Camp made it clear that too close an initial identification would have inhibited public acceptance. Roberto Campos, an economist and a minister under several Brazilian presidents, commented years later that the Rockefeller sponsorship of ACAR in Minas Gerais was not well known and that "the low profile was probably useful."[33] From the self-image ACAR presented to the public, it is clear that the primary goal of AIA was to Brazilianize the project and only secondarily to identify it with the United States. Promotion of the Rockefeller name, at least in public statements, was evidently not a priority.

The Brazilianization of ACAR was not simply a matter of publicity, however. As experiences in other parts of the third world were to prove in the following decades, matching imported projects with local conditions and cultures, developing technologies which benefit more than local elites, and getting local societies to adapt and incorporate North American or European "improvements" is invariably difficult and frequently impossible. ACAR, in little more than a decade, significantly raised the incomes of small farmers, developed an all-Brazilian staff and governing board, and fostered the creation of a federal system of CARs into which it was ultimately incorporated. The program as it was designed and operated by the AIA was solid. But the only reason it succeeded was that Brazilians wanted it and were ready for it, within limits.

The AIA began its work in an environment that was highly favorable in terms of the willingness of Brazilian federal and state governments to cooperate actively in experiments to promote development, but at times frustrating in terms of the low priority given to farming. Events following World War II—the failure of Dutra's program of economic liberalism, Vargas's reelection, and the work of the joint commission—had decisively

32. John Camp to Mr. Haight of Creole Petroleum, April 22, 1951, pp. 1–2. RAC, R.G. 2, P.R., AIA, Box 1, Folder 12.
33. Interview with Roberto Campos, Rio de Janeiro, October 13, 1986.

resolved in favor of government-instigated industrialization the great political and economic debate over whether to follow in the tradition of international comparative advantage or to pursue industrial development. Because Brazil's traditional comparative advantage had been in agricultural products (first dyestuffs, then sugar, rubber, and finally coffee), the commitment to industrialize meant that agricultural development, including attempts to boost food production, came to take third or fourth place in terms of national interest. New priorities in industry combined with old stalemates in land tenure to limit support for efforts to improve agriculture.

Throughout ACAR's early history, Brazilian agriculture had one of the greatest total outputs in the world, but one of the lowest levels of productivity. Many of the best lands were held in large concentrations by wealthy families who allowed them to sit idle, while 75 percent of active farmers held lands under fifty hectares.[34] The overwhelming majority of farmers knew little about the use of fertilizers, hybrid seeds, or such basic equipment as hoes and plows. In spite of the exorbitant profits of middlemen, spoilage ruined at least 20 percent of produce because of the lack of storage facilities and adequate farm-to-market roads. While state agricultural agencies, called *fomentos,* existed to help farmers overcome some of these problems, in most states they were largely ineffective or worked only with the *fazendeiros,* who owned large tracts of land cultivated with produce for export. The fomentos provided some services to farmers, such as the distribution of seeds and breeding stock and the services of "tractor patrols," but there were no extension programs that educated farmers about how to plow, plant, cultivate, or market better. Farmers had few resources to change this situation. Most of them were poor, isolated, and illiterate. The priority on rapid industrialization, the concentration of educational opportunities in urban areas, and the electoral law, which required literacy as a basis for voter qualification, perpetuated their political impotence.[35]

Yet in spite of the obstacles, there was support for limited change on

34. In 1950, out of 2,064,484 agricultural holdings in the nation, 1,544,107 were under fifty hectares. Werner Baer, *Industrialization and Economic Development in Brazil* (Homewood, Ill.: Richard D. Irwin, 1965), 262.

35. Edward G. Schuh, *The Agricultural Development of Brazil* (New York: Praeger, 1970), 69. The political weakness and low priority of the agricultural sector during the 1950s is a truism of Brazilian economics and politics. For information on agricultural bottlenecks and politics also see the chapters on agriculture in Werner Baer's two books, *Industrialization and Economic Development in Brazil* and *The Brazilian Economy: Growth and Development,* 2d ed. (New York: Praeger, 1983).

both the federal and state level. Presidents Getúlio Vargas (1951–54) and Juscelino Kubitschek (1956–60) had reasons to oppose certain developments in agriculture and encourage others. Vargas himself was a large landowner in the state of Rio Grande do Sul, and both Vargas and Kubitschek were dependent on the political support of the wealthy fazendeiros as well as of their large popular followings. Yet Vargas, as a farmer, was personally interested in new developments in agriculture and, according to his personal secretary, "keen on the increased production of wheat to reduce Brazil's dependency on imports."[36] Kubitschek had been orphaned by his father's death at a young age, had walked his mother to her job as an ill-paid schoolteacher, and knew what it meant to be poor as well as self-made. Both men were politically wary. As the historian Thomas Skidmore notes, "Kubitschek, like Vargas before him, never raised the land question in a way other than to suggest politically innocuous measures. . . . Having been trained in the political school of Minas Gerais, Kubitschek was hardly inclined to tamper with the existing system of rural property."[37]

Room for maneuver came through proposals to increase the resources of the system, not redistribute them. Like the United States, Brazil had the land mass, natural resources, and seemingly endless frontier conducive to the "expand the pie" view of development characteristic of modern North American corporatism. This is why the proposals of ACAR, aimed at helping small farmers better utilize what they had, were appealing and nonthreatening. Kubitschek, who first became familiar with ACAR as the successor to Mílton Campos in the governorship of Minas Gerais, cited the "great success" of ACAR in his *General Directives for the National Plan of Development*, which he published as a candidate for president in 1955.[38] He promoted the program on a national level when he became president in 1956.

On the state level, Nelson Rockefeller and AIA were fortunate to encounter Mílton Campos as governor in their initial foray into the rolling green hills of Minas Gerais. Campos had come to the governorship of Minas on a ticket stressing democracy and development. A lawyer and judge, Campos had been a highly visible critic of Getúlio Vargas throughout the Estado Novo and World War II years. Campos was known for his commitment to the democratic process and his opposition to political coercion. During a long strike by railway workers in Minas early in his

36. Interview with Cleantho de Paiva Leite, Rio de Janeiro, October 24, 1986.
37. *Politics in Brazil*, 169.
38. *Diretrizes Gerais do Plano Nacional de Desenvolvimento* (Belo Horizonte, 1955), 130.

term, someone suggested to Campos that he send a train of military police to deal with the strikers. Campos replied, "Wouldn't it be better to send the train paymaster?" Campos also began an active program of rural development, creating an alphabet soup of state agricultural and rural electrification agencies that any New Dealer would have admired. In addition, the Campos administration doubled the number of primary schools and founded the state's first agricultural college, at Viçosa, which was to offer the first graduate program in agriculture and become a model for the nation. In this context, Campos's support for Nelson Rockefeller's idea of a jointly sponsored experiment in agricultural extension is quite understandable.[39]

Rockefeller's relationship with Campos testified to his ability to work with a variety of Latin American politicians and his unwillingness to take sides in what he considered domestic disputes. Rockefeller had worked closely with President Vargas during the war, was a friend of the Vargas family, and made a point of publicly demonstrating his continued affection for the family after Vargas was deposed in 1945. Alzira Vargas, daughter of the president, says that "Nelson was my friend in the good days and in the bad days." She recounts that during the family's ostracism in Rio following Vargas's downfall, Nelson came to Rio and threw a big party for several hundred people. When Alzira and her husband arrived, Nelson ran up to greet and embrace them warmly in front of the other invited guests.[40] Yet with perfect aplomb and no break in faith between him and Vargas, Rockefeller could go in 1948 to Mílton Campos, one of Vargas's political opponents, to set up a project in Minas Gerais. Rockefeller persisted in treating Brazilian politicians as he did American politicians: he was eager to work with those individuals, regardless of party, who wanted to get things done.

In Brazil between 1945 and 1964, as in most contexts, this attitude was both sensible and in accord with traditional American foreign policy. But Rockefeller also has been criticized at times—especially after his report for Richard Nixon in 1969—because he was more willing than many American politicians to carry this practice openly to its logical extreme by being unwilling to break ties with or publicly castigate even the most repressive Latin American regimes, such as those of Juan Perón in Argentina and François "Papa Doc" Duvalier in Haiti. Such men were local politicians in Rockefeller's scheme, and their tenure and fate were local

39. *Dicionário Histórico-Biográfico Brasileiro, 1930–1983* (Rio de Janeiro: Forense-Universitária Ltda., 1984), 584–85.
40. Interview with Alzira V-----

matters. Legitimacy was presumed, based on de facto power. Rockefeller was by no means alone in holding this view, but he was one of the few American politicians to make it explicit, with no apologies. Of course, socialist and communist politicians in Latin America have not been given this leeway by any segment of the American government. Here an opposite policy is traditional: legitimacy is questioned or denied, even when such a leader has been democratically elected.

Yet Rockefeller's eclectic and constantly widening circle of acquaintances in Brazil undoubtedly provided legitimacy and political support for his undertakings. A visit he made to Rio de Janeiro in November 1952 as a private citizen is instructive. On that one trip to that one city, he had meetings and conversations with nearly the entire top leadership of the country, including, among others, President Getúlio Vargas, Alzira Vargas, Governor Ernani Amaral Peixoto, Foreign Minister João Neves da Fontoura, Finance Minister Horácio Lafer, Banco do Brazil president Ricardo Jafet, Maciel Filho, director of the Superintendency of Money and Credit, Army Chief of Staff General Góes Monteiro, Gustavo Capanema, leader of the Congress, ex-president Eurico Dutra, former foreign minister Oswaldo Aranha, businessman Valentim Bouças, joint commission director Ary Torres, newspaper magnate and opposition supporter Assis Chateaubriand, and Ambassador to the U.S. Carlos Martins.[41]

Because of his ongoing outreach, Rockefeller's AIA was greeted with approval and enthusiasm across the spectrum of Brazilian politics. An analysis of the press by AIA in 1951, including radio programs and newspapers ranging from politically "independent" to "Anti-Vargas" to "Anti-U.S. Capitalism," found that "comment on AIA projects seen by this office for the period covered was 100 per cent favorable, praising aims and administration, and urging expansion throughout the country. A recurring suggestion was that AIA take over rural rehabilitation programs in Brazil of the federal and state governments and those of the Point Four program."[42] A Gazeta, in São Paulo, praised Rockefeller's efforts as

41. See RAC, Berent Friele Papers, Box 7, Folder: "Brazil General: NAR Brazil visit, November 1952."
42. "Analysis of Brazilian and Venezuelan Press Comment on AIA Programs, March to September 1951," p. 2. RAC, AIA, Box 9, Folder 75. This report is also interesting in that it underscores both the extent to which AIA benefited from traditional Brazilian friendliness (as opposed to Hispanic American suspicion) toward Americans and the difficulties caused for AIA by working in a Hispanic country in which Nelson Rockefeller had significant personal investments. The report found editorial comment "split sharply according to country of origin. Brazilian comment seen by this office was entirely favorable. Venezuelan comment was in no instance entirely favorable. From Venezuelan comment it can be inferred

having been "attempted without fanfare; without great sums of money, without worries and heavy paper work. . . . The results are extraordinary and his [Rockefeller's] staff is responsible to a great extent for what has been accomplished."[43] *O Estado de São Paulo,* one of Brazil's most widely respected newspapers, gave detailed treatment and restrained approval to the AIA. *Folha da Manha,* which Rockefeller's chief publicist characterized as "stand-offish" but influential, commented that the region which AIA had chosen to concentrate on in São Paulo state "does not present any of the conditions of economic privilege, therefore it cannot be looked upon as a place where profit motives are chiefly at play."[44] In 1954 a commercial film company in Rio, with outlets in several hundred Brazilian theaters, considered the work of AIA sufficiently popular and interesting to shoot a fifteen-minute short on ACAR in the Ubá area of Minas Gerais.[45]

Another important political test was passed in the early fifties when the opposition candidate, Juscelino Kubitschek, succeeded Governor Mílton Campos in office. ACAR had managed to sustain a reputation of political neutrality, and Director Walter Crawford was able to make a favorable impression on the new governor when he invited Kubitschek to cut the ribbon on a new community center that ACAR was opening in the isolated community of Macumbeiro. The center was located in what had been the slave quarters of a wealthy *fazenda* and was clearly designed to serve the poorest of farmers. As governor, Kubitschek not only renewed the ACAR agreement negotiated by Campos, but vastly increased the state's contribution.[46]

Within a few years of ACAR's initial successes, other Brazilian states began to ask ACAR and AIA for help in starting their own rural extension programs. Meanwhile Walter Crawford had begun to think through the long-term future of AIA's involvement with rural extension. The AIA did not have the money or staff to compete favorably with the big government organizations and private foundations in the technical assistance field, Crawford wrote in 1953 to Wallace Harrison, who was then president of the association. These organizations did not care to pool their resources to work with AIA, he said, because "they feel that they can operate just as

---

that AIA programs are valued for their overall aims. However . . . [they are also considered] propaganda for Rockefellers." (p. 1).
43. Ibid., p. 3 (translated from *A Gazeta,* August 8, 1950).
44. Francis A. Jamieson to the Boards of Directors of AIA and IBEC, March 14, 1949, p. 6. Translation from *Folha da Manha* provided.
45. *AIA Highlights,* July 8–August 16, 1954, p. 1. RAC, AIA, Box 2, Folder 17.
46. Dalrymple, *The AIA Story,* 44–46.

efficiently and cheaply as we can and do not want to share in the 'glory' of a job well done." Crawford felt that AIA had to carve out a more definite niche in the technical assistance field that would allow it to be both less expensive and more extensive. AIA was especially limited by its commitment to the servicio model, he asserted, which required substantial matching funds from AIA to get a program going. "The Brazilian states of Rio Grande do Sul, Paraná, Rio de Janeiro and Espírito Santo all have asked us to help them get 'ACAR like programs' started. . . . I would like to be given the opportunity of getting these programs into operation without repeating the expensive jointly financed AIA managed operations we have in ACAR," he wrote. With ACAR training, Crawford concluded, "they should be able to do a very creditable job for themselves."[47]

The first opportunity to start out in this new direction came in 1954 when Rómulo de Almeida, president of the Bank of the Northeast of Brazil, asked AIA for help in establishing a rural extension organization. AIA agreed to join with the Bank of the Northeast and the Bank of Brazil in setting up the Associação Nordestina de Crédito e Assistência Rural (ANCAR). Although ANCAR was to have the same structure as ACAR, AIA would put no money into the venture. The banks would have responsibility for control and direction, and AIA was to send one representative to the governing board and conduct the staff training program. Crawford wrote to the AIA board in January 1954, "This is a good opportunity to test out the effectiveness of spreading AIA work through an organization in which we are only a minor participant. . . . It will cost AIA a good deal less this way and if it is reasonably successful, we will have made a step forward in shifting responsibility to local groups."[48] The test was a success: ANCAR eventually set up local offices in all eight states of the northeast. By early 1956, AIA had concluded similar agreements with three other states, helping to set up Brazilian-run organizations in Rio Grande do Sul, Santa Catarina, and Paraná.

Throughout the 1950s, the idea of starting a national, federally operated rural extension system came up repeatedly. For awhile, AIA officials considered starting such a program with the help of the U.S. Institute of Inter-American Affairs (the descendant of OIAA) and the Brazilian Ministry of Agriculture. But Walter Crawford noted that, true to form in this

47. Walter L. Crawford to Wallace K. Harrison, August 18, 1953, pp. 2, 12. RAC, AIA, Box 2, Folder 14.
48. Dalrymple, The AIA Story, 53–54.

period, American officials were reluctant, and nothing came of the proposal.[49] Renato Costa Lima, secretary of agriculture for the state of São Paulo and a friend of Rockefeller, wrote to AIA in mid-1954 praising the work of ACAR in Minas Gerais and expressing his hope that the idea would "be extended to all Brazil."[50]

The decisive moment came when Brazilians elected Juscelino Kubitschek, who had cited the work of ACAR in his campaign proposals for agriculture, to the presidency. Berent Friele, one of the original group that had designed the AIA and widely considered by Brazilians as Nelson Rockefeller's personal representative there, wrote with enthusiasm to Wallace Harrison about Kubitschek's election. "The incoming President of the Republic Juscelino Kubitschek, former Governor of the State of Minas Gerais, is one of ACAR's greatest enthusiasts and has declared his intention to promote ACAR on a national basis during his administration," he reported. In terms of Rockefeller's overall goal of promoting Brazilian development under the mantle of U.S. capitalism, the implications were even broader, as Friele noted: "This joint venture between Brazilians and Americans was the first practical experience which Dr. Kubitschek had during his political career in working with foreigners. The happy relationships which developed therefrom may well have a bearing on his outlook and future attitude toward the United States and foreign capital generally."[51]

The next month, February 1956, Friele's predictions for ACAR were borne out when Kubitschek asked ACAR representative Walter Crawford and AIA publicist Henry Bagley, a former Associated Press reporter who had covered the Brazilian Expeditionary Force in Italy, to meet with him at Catete Palace in Rio, the presidential residence. "I want you to do the same thing for all of Brazil that we did for Minas Gerais," Kubitschek told the hurriedly summoned Americans. "Will you help me do it?" Kubitschek made it clear that the Bank of Brazil would put up the money and that the name of the project was not important, "as long as it is a CAR organization." Crawford and Bagley heard out the request but were not authorized to respond to it. Neither were they entirely sure if the proposal was sound. As Bagley later noted in a report to AIA headquarters at Rockefeller Center, "AIA would be putting all its eggs in one basket, and

49. Walter Crawford to the AIA Board of Directors, December 4, 1953, p. 1. RAC, AIA, Box 2, Folder 14.
50. *AIA Highlights*, June 24–July 7, 1954, p. 1. RAC, AIA, Box 2, Folder 17.
51. Berent Friele to Wallace K. Harrison, January 18, 1956, p. 2. RAC, RBF, Box 12, Folder 1.

that basket would not only be leaky but might be completely overturned with a change in the federal government."[52]

Nelson Rockefeller approved of the idea, however, and flew to Brazil in April to discuss it. He went first to Belo Horizonte to consult with João Napoleão de Andrade, who was then the president of ACAR and a long-time friend of Kubitschek. João Napoleão then set up a meeting between Kubitschek and Rockefeller, held over lunch at Catete Palace. Rockefeller agreed to participate in the new national organization, the Associação Brasileiro de Crédito e Assistência Rural (ABCAR).[53] ABCAR was set up as a semiautonomous organization, with its own governing board composed of a representative from each state CAR, to which AIA, the state organizations, and the National Congress all contributed funds. Rockefeller's interest in having a national impact with minimal cost and maximum Brazilian participation had coincided with Kubitschek's drive for development.

As the Brazilianization of the CAR system proceeded apace, Walter Crawford began searching for new areas in which AIA could have an impact on the development of Brazilian agriculture. He did not have to look far. In 1957 AIA merged with a nonprofit offshoot of IBEC called the Ibec Research Institute (IRI). Nelson and David Rockefeller began IRI in 1950 to do research on basic agricultural problems in Brazil. Over a period of years, IRI had made progress on a variety of fronts. For example, it devised the method of salvaging coffee trees after a frost (*decepagem*) which is still used in Brazil today; it developed a legume for the nourishment of cattle, IRI 1022, which is able to draw significant amounts of nitrogen from the air, thereby saving on chemical fertilizers; and it conducted research on how to increase the yield of such high-protein foods as milk, eggs, and meat which was published in Portuguese, Spanish, and English and distributed to agricultural colleges and extension workers throughout the world. A Ford Foundation study in 1960 found that one of IRI's greatest strengths was its approach, called American by the author, "of starting with important practical problems as the basis of selecting research objectives."[54]

---

52. Dalrymple, *The AIA Story*, 55–57. Also see Bagley's records in the file "January-June 1956," RAC, R.G. 2, P.R., Box 12.
53. Dalrymple, *The AIA Story*, 57–58.
54. William H. Nicholls, "An Appraisal of Brazilian Agricultural Economics," Vanderbilt University, July 1960, p. 14. Ford Foundation Archives, Report No. 000227. Nicholls also reported, "My general impressions of IRI's research were very favorable, and Brazilian specialists also indicated that they consider IRI's research worthwhile and of good quality." For general information on IRI also see Dalrymple, pp. 25–27, 36, and 170.

The aspect of IRI's work which especially interested Walter Crawford was its research on the *campos cerrados* (closed lands) of Brazil. The campos cerrados were millions of acres of unused savannah covering about one-fourth of the territory of Brazil. Most of these lands were in areas of low population density and had a good climate and good rainfall, but the soil was poor and had been traditionally used only for occasional grazing. IRI set up an experimental station at Brasília, which is surrounded by campos cerrados, and there demonstrated that by the addition of lime and fertilizers to the soil corn and a wide variety of other crops could be grown on these lands.[55]

Crawford saw in the campos cerrados one possible solution to the unequal and inefficient distribution of land which continued to stunt Brazilian agriculture, especially in the long-settled and poverty-stricken northeast. Like other AIA people in the field, Crawford had been perplexed for years about how to achieve any substantial progress without land reform. What was needed, he felt, was a carefully thought out plan. "For year[s] we have been working at the job by pieces, extension, supervised credit, etc., etc.," he wrote the AIA board in 1960.[56] John Camp, with the AIA in Venezuela, was similarly concerned about land reform. In a letter to another AIA board member in 1961, Camp criticized a pamphlet published in the United States which called land reform a kind of "collectivism." "The implication in this pamphlet is that government action is always bad," he observed, "yet the U.S. government had much to do with establishing our free enterprise system of farming. Our early land laws and especially the Homestead Law and the way they were administered by the government, made it possible for several million family-operated farms to be established."[57] Essentially, Camp believed that U.S. leaders should recognize Latin America's need for the same freedom of experimentation and degree of state activism that had characterized North American agriculture. Once again, it was a question of U.S. "do as I say, not as I do."

Although the Brazilian legislature had talked about reform for years, virtually nothing had been done about it. In 1961, a commission headed by former Minas Gerais governor Mílton Campos studied various possibilities for reform and came up with a plan to appropriate (with compensation) those rural lands which had been held for a period of at least ten years without any attempt by the owners to explore, improve, or

55. *Américas*, July 1963, 13–14. Also see Dalrymple, *The AIA Story*, 26–27, 169–71.
56. Walter Crawford to the AIA Board, April 26, 1960, p. 3. RAC, AIA, Box 7, Folder 57.
57. John Camp to Berent Friele, February 4, 1961, p. 1. RAC, AIA, Box 7, Folder 59.

cultivate them.[58] The volatile Brazilian Congress heavily criticized, modified, and finally tabled the plan. After twenty years of military dictatorship and the redemocratization of the mid-1980s, Brazil was still discussing reform into the 1990s. The economist Roberto Campos has characterized land reform as one of the pivotal historical achievements of the United States which placed it, economically, so far in advance of countries like Brazil. "Two advantages of the United States over the Latin American countries were, first, to have realized the need for and achieved very early on an agrarian reform . . . and second, to have developed agricultural research to a very high degree along with an excellent system of extension work."[59]

In late 1960 and early 1961 Crawford and Camp began working on a plan for a kind of land reform which would circumvent the unwillingness of large property owners to part with little-used lands and the reluctance of Brazilian politicians to make them do so. Using the research of IRI and a suggestion initially made by Camp, Crawford wrote a proposal entitled "Agriculture in Brazil" which called for the resettlement of landless *nordestinos* (northeasterners) on the campos cerrados of the west central plains (*planalto*) of Brazil. In addition to its merits, from the viewpoint of Brazilian politicians, of avoiding conflict with the interests of landowners, the proposal complemented the popular and visionary push to develop the interior of Brazil symbolized by the construction of Brasília.

Outside of the northeast, the idea was also well received in Minas Gerais and São Paulo. In April 1961, Crawford wrote to Camp that he had had a long talk with Paulo de Salvio, appointed by the governor of Minas to reorganize the state's agricultural agencies, including ACAR. "It fits perfectly into his ideas and he is 'encantado' [enchanted] with it," Crawford reported enthusiastically. "I am very confident Minas will be interested, and I already know five different areas in the western part of the state where between five and ten thousand families could be resettled on good land now completely unused."[60] *O Estado de São Paulo* expressed general support for the work of IRI in the campos cerrados, saying, "Any preoccupation with studying the reclamation of the *cerrados* might appear absurd when we have so many other problems demanding solution. But if we consider the extensiveness of the areas characterized by this type of vegetation and if we worry about the underdeveloped state of numerous settlements without the wealth that would

58. *Diccionário Histórico-Biográfico Brasileiro*, 586–87.
59. Interview with Roberto Campos.
60. Walter Crawford to John Camp, April 7, 1961, p. 2. RAC, AIA, Box 7, Folder 60.

give them life and progress, then we have to recognize the utility of these studies and their importance in Brazilian economic life."[61]

The U.S. government gave Crawford's ideas a push when President John F. Kennedy asked Merwin Bohan, who had left government after the disappointing results of the joint commission years earlier, to go back to Brazil and conduct a survey of the northeast to determine how it should be assisted under the Alliance for Progress. Among other things Bohan's report strongly recommended, at a projected cost of $150 million to the Alliance for Progress, "the permanent settlement of agricultural and industrial Northeastern immigrants . . . in the vast unoccupied areas of Goiás and Mato Grosso."[62]

There are indications that Bohan's team was aware of the AIA proposal even before visiting Brazil. Nearly a year earlier, AIA had submitted a proposal to the International Cooperation Agency (ICA, soon to be renamed the Agency for International Development [AID]) for a government grant in the amount of $110 million to begin the resettlement. At that time AIA board member Berent Friele was in frequent contact with Adolf Berle, head of the Kennedy committee which had just finished drafting the Alliance for Progress, and with Lincoln Gordon, soon to be the ambassador to Brazil. He made sure they both had a copy of Crawford's proposal. Berle also suggested to John Camp, who was then coordinating the AIA headquarters in New York, that he personally reach Berle's task force regarding the AIA plan for rural development.[63] The next month Camp reported to another AIA board member, "I believe everyone is aware of our special interest. . . . Berle is very favorable to our proposal to ICA for a rural development program in Brazil and I would expect to have his support at the appropriate time."[64] Camp and other Rockefeller associates spoke also with Richard Goodwin, John Kennedy's personal assistant in charge of the Alliance for Progress, who promised to recommend that Edward Kennedy visit ACAR in Minas Gerais when he traveled to Brazil on behalf of his brother.[65] Last, the Ford Foundation had been a contributor to IRI's work on the campos cerrados, and foundation representative Ray Carlson was a member of the Bohan commission. Carlson later communicated with Walter Crawford about the commission's decision to make the "resettlement of Northeasterners in the

61. Clipping from *O Estado de São Paulo* (no date given) attached to a letter from J. F. Harrington to Martha Dalrymple, January 4, 1961. RAC, AIA, Box 4, Folder 41.
62. *Northeast Brazil Survey Team Report*, February 1962, p. 16. RAC, AIA, Box 7, Folder 62.
63. Berent Friele to John Camp, February 10, 1961. RAC, AIA, Box 7, Folder 59.
64. John Camp to Louise Boyer, March 15, 1961, p. 1. RAC, AIA, Box 7, Folder 60.
65. Martha Dalrymple to Jimmy Apodaca, July 20, 1961, p. 1. RAC, AIA, Box 7, Folder 61.

Central Plateau . . . one of the principal points in the long-term program."[66]

For the next several years Crawford pursued funding for his resettlement vision. The Brazilian component of AIA had never had a large budget, so Crawford and Camp were depending on the U.S. government to come through with funding. For awhile the prospect was promising. Soon after the Bohan commission released its recommendations and the United States and Brazil signed an agreement for development of the northeast, the head of AID in Brazil made clear to Crawford that he was "very much in favor of the principle of using private organization[s] to the extent possible in executing the Alliance for Progress program." Several months later the same official told Crawford that there was no question about the rural development program being done under contract with AIA "because he felt AIA had the experience and competency to execute the project efficiently in a manner that 'would let him sleep nights without worrying about how it was getting along.' "[67] Yet within a short period of time Crawford began running into the variety of obstacles that would eventually make it impossible for AIA to put into action its proposal for resettling the land-poor nordestinos. As Riordan Roett has shown, the U.S. government's long-term development goals for the Brazilian northeast were rapidly subverted by its desire to have an immediate, highly visible impact in the region in the face of peasant unrest, which began to be evident in 1961, sparked in part by the Cuban Revolution. The head of AID-Brazil stalled Crawford repeatedly with statements to the effect that they were "terribly tied up right now in trying to get the emergency aspects of the NE [northeast] program rolling . . . that the Planalto Central aspect of that program is more long range and, therefore, can wait a little longer." AID and Crawford also ran into some Brazilian resistance to the project. Celso Furtado, head of the Superintendency for the Development of the Northeast, wanted resettlement to occur in other areas of the northeast rather than in the central states and eventually fought for and won a resettlement project in the northern state of Maranhão.[68] AID continued to express a commitment to the AIA proposal, but there were constant problems with negotiating a contract and sustain-

---

66. Walter Crawford to John Camp, April 18, 1962, p. 1. RAC, AIA, Box 7, Folder 62.
67. Walter Crawford to Philip M. Glick, April 30, 1962, p. 2 , and Walter Crawford to John Camp, September 24, 1962, pp. 1–2. RAC, AIA, Box 7, Folders 62 and 63.
68. Walter Crawford reported the comments from AID, as well as Celso Furtado's objections, to John Camp on June 8, 1962 (p. 2) and September 24, 1962 (p. 1). RAC, AIA, Box 7, Folders 62 and 63, respectively. For information on the Maranhão resettlement project see Roett, *The Politics of Foreign Aid*, 58–60.

ing the federal agency's interest.[69] AID eventually commissioned Crawford to conduct a study on settlement in the campos cerrados but, aside
from a final report and some initial planning by a consortium of North
American land grant colleges, nothing further came of the effort. Brazil
had yet another unimplemented report sponsored by the U.S. government. Ironically, AIA was never able to achieve with its own government
the kind of dynamic, cooperative relationship that it had had with the
Brazilian.

Nevertheless, government and private observers in the United States
maintained a watchful interest in AIA during its years in Brazil, and AIA
made consistent efforts to keep government officials posted on its work.
Rockefeller clearly viewed AIA as a bridge between the United States and
Brazil and its work as a model for both private and intergovernmental
cooperation. His goal was to stimulate an interchange between Latin
America and the United States during the long lull which followed World
War II and to keep alive the commitment to regional development which
OIAA had tried to stimulate. To do this, AIA had to be visible both north
and south.

Anticipating the State Department's fears that AIA might come to be
seen as a cost-free substitute for the Institute of Inter-American Affairs,
Rockefeller wrote in early 1947 to Spruille Braden, his successor as assistant secretary of state for Latin America. He urged Braden to persevere
with the developmental programs in public health, sanitation, agriculture, and education that OIAA had started, saying, "If the United States
Government terminates these activities, it will . . . raise the question as to
whether or not much of the war-time cooperation was not strictly one of
expediency." Rockefeller also emphasized that his private work would
not conflict with the government programs. "I want to assure you," he
wrote Braden, "that the activities of these two corporations [AIA and
IBEC] not only will not duplicate or conflict with the program of the
Institute of Inter-American Affairs, but quite to the contrary, I believe that
the two lines of activity can very effectively supplement each other." A
staff member under Braden in the State Department routed the letter to
the Department of Commerce and Bureau of the Budget with the comment that it confirmed the point made at an earlier interdepartmental

69. John Camp to Walter Crawford, March 15, 1963, p. 1. RAC, AIA, Box 7, Folder 63.
Camp reported to Crawford that negotiations with AID had been "negative" in both
Venezuela and Columbia, with AID proposing contracts that would either have caused AIA
to lose money or prevented AIA from operating "with any degree of autonomy." Camp
suggested that AIA would be better off trying to develop programs with its own resources.

meeting that Rockefeller's activities would not rival or supplant those of the government.[70]

Rockefeller and his staff meanwhile kept up a steady stream of correspondence with friends and acquaintances in the State Department. The American embassies in Rio and Caracas regularly sent the department information on what AIA was doing there, and when President Truman announced Point Four, the head of AIA wrote Under Secretary of State James Webb to say that AIA had programs "actually underway in several of the South American countries, and would welcome an opportunity to collaborate with the Department of State in the promotion of the President's plan."[71] At Webb's request Rockefeller testified in the first week of congressional hearings on Point Four, making, according to a State Department assessment, "a very impressive statement speaking from notes" which "was very well received and very effective."[72]

Although there is no indication that Webb or anyone else in the department viewed AIA as an extension of government policy or of special importance in terms of the United States's major objectives in Latin America, it is clear that officials were aware of the organization and had some sense of its value. To begin with, ACAR complemented other recommendations the United States had made to Brazil. In 1949 the Abbink mission advised Brazil to give high priority to improving agriculture in order to free up workers for industrial employment without jeopardizing the food supply or creating the need to import items which Brazil could grow for itself. Like AIA, the mission emphasized the historical precedent of the United States, where agricultural productivity had fueled industrialization.[73] Later, in 1951, when President Vargas presented President Truman with a long list of the development projects for which he hoped to obtain U.S. help, the economic adviser on Latin American affairs for the State Department drafted a point-by-point analysis of how the United States might respond. With regard to regional development of the São Francisco Valley, which the adviser ranked as "postponable" in view of the Korean War emergency, he noted that AIA, "a Rockefeller non-profit organization," was carrying on a cooperative program with the govern-

70. Nelson Rockefeller to Spruille Braden, February 10, 1947, pp. 1–2; and Andrew V. Corry of the Office of American Republic Affairs to IIAA, the Department of Commerce, and the Bureau of the Budget, February 13, 1947. NA, R.G. 59, Decimal File 180.5034/2–1047 (1945–49).

71. Robert W. Hudgens to James E. Webb, March 9, 1949, p. 1. NA, R.G. 59, Decimal File 800.50 TA/3–949 (1945–49).

72. Assistant Secretary of State Mr. Gross to James Webb, September 30, 1949, p. 1. NA, R.G. 59, Decimal File 800.50 TA/9–3049 (1945–49).

73. *Report of the Joint Brazil–United States Technical Commission*, 28–29, 65–66.

ment in Minas Gerais and would be willing to undertake similar work in the São Francisco Valley at the request of the Brazilian government and with U.S. funding.[74]

Although Rockefeller's IBEC garnered most of the headlines in the U.S. press in the 1940s and 1950s for its "enlightened capitalism," AIA was well known among U.S. experts in agriculture and technical assistance. In 1954 and 1955, ACAR was the star of a National Planning Association study coordinated by the University of Chicago with Ford Foundation funds appraising U.S. technical assistance. "The popularity of ACAR's approach, as measured by requests from other parts of the country for aid in launching similar programs, is a significant indication that ACAR has brought a ferment into a lagging national agricultural development program," the planning association told its influential American audience.[75] Merle Curti, in his pioneering history of U.S. philanthropy abroad (1963), cited the work of Rockefeller in Brazil and Venezuela as his major example of a "carefully integrated," U.S.-sponsored program in Latin America dealing with agriculture, vocational training, home care, and health.[76] ACAR was also the subject of several dissertations, theses, and scholarly articles in the United States.

By the end of the 1950s, AIA had firmly established ACAR and its other CAR affiliates both as operating entities and as strong models of technical assistance from the perspective of Americans and Brazilians alike. At the same time, AIA was also running out of money for its ACAR program and beginning to confront questions about its own long-term financial solvency.

From beginning to end, AIA was almost wholly financed by the Rockefeller family and its affiliated foundations and corporations. Nelson Rockefeller personally gave AIA an average of $100,000 a year for twenty years, and his father and brother David gave about half that, for an estimated total of $3 million dollars.[77] The Rockefeller Brothers Fund

74. Ivan B. White to Edward G. Miller, Jr., January 31, 1951, p. 1 of the section on the São Francisco Valley. NA, R.G. 59, Lot File 53D26, Papers of Edward Miller, Box 2, Folder: "Brazil 1951."

75. Mosher, *Technical Cooperation in Latin America*, 5. Even before the Mosher study was published, the chief of the overall study, Dr. Ted Schultz, communicated to AIA that ACAR would be written up as one of the four most outstanding operations in Latin America (along with the Rockefeller Foundation's Mexican Corn Program) and as the only organization whose work had been fully documented. From *AIA Highlights*, December 27, 1954, p. 1. RAC, AIA, Box 2, Folder 17.

76. *American Philanthropy Abroad*, 606.

77. It is difficult to find firm figures for the amount of money donated by the Rockefeller family to the association, although it is clear that their donations were consistent and large. Over one five-year period, 1960–65, Nelson gave $450,000 and his father $500,000. In the

was another major donor, its grants totaling somewhat over $4 million. AIA also received substantial contributions from all of Nelson's other brothers and his sister as well as from the consortium of American oil companies operating in Venezuela, which included Creole Petroleum. Between 1946 and 1968, the total AIA budget for all programs in Latin America was $11.6 million, $3.4 million of which was spent in Brazil.

The Rockefeller fortune could easily sustain the expense. Nelson spent more on one campaign for governor than he spent on AIA in twenty years.[78] But as rich as the Rockefellers were, they did not envision supporting AIA indefinitely. To be a success, the project had to stand on its own. Initially, the idea had been that IBEC would generate profits substantial enough to help AIA attain a degree of self-sufficiency. However, as will be seen, IBEC never had the profits to make this possible. In the mid-1960s, IBEC was contributing only $10,000 a year to AIA's annual budget of nearly half a million. The oil companies, which Rockefeller originally saw as a steady source of funding, were interested only in Venezuela, and even there they stopped making significant contributions after a few years. The Ford Foundation and US-AID gave AIA several grants for IRI, but the institute eventually reestablished its corporate status in 1963 (after a six-year merger) and AIA received no further funds. A number of Brazilian and American companies made ongoing contributions to the program in the range of $5,000 to $20,000 a year, but they were usually for specific programs, not for general operating expenses, which the Rockefellers continued to pick up.[79]

For ACAR and ABCAR, which were still receiving funds from the AIA general account in 1959 and 1960, the gradual move toward complete Brazilianization became a race. Under financial pressure from the Rockefeller Brothers Fund, the AIA board voted in 1959 to put Brazilian government officials "on notice" that AIA's cooperation would terminate by the end of 1961.[80] Meanwhile, the president of ABCAR, João Napoleão

next five-year period, Nelson pledged $100,000 per year, and his brother David $50,000 per year. Although I was not able to find figures for the period before 1960, it seems safe to assume that the annual level of giving to AIA during the earlier period was at least as high, if not higher. See "Agenda and Docket," Rockefeller Brothers Foundation meeting, May 19, 1960, p. 17. RAC, RBF, Box 12, Folder 3. Also, John Camp to Nelson Rockefeller, November 28, 1966, p. 1 (attached to a memo from Camp to James N. Hyde, March 23, 1967, Appendix G). RAC, RBF, Box 12, folder: "AIA, 1966–69."

78. According to Collier and Horowitz, Rockefeller's expenditures for the 1970 campaign amounted to $7.2 million. Collier and Horowitz, *The Rockefellers*, 461.

79. See memo from John Camp to Nelson Rockefeller (ibid.) for a description of AIA sources of funding as of 1967.

80. "Docket Memorandum, Rockefeller Brothers Fund, Inc., Executive Committee," September 14, 1959, p. 2. RAC, RBF, Box 12, Folder 3.

de Andrade, and Walter Crawford began a sustained campaign to get the legislation that would make ABCAR and its regional branches an official and permanent Brazilian agency. Juscelino Kubitschek promised João Napoleão that he would present such a bill to Congress with his full support, but his term ended before any action was taken.[81] The Brazilian elections again went in the favor of the CAR organizations. In Minas Gerais, a politician who had been secretary of finance for the state when ACAR began was elected governor over another politician who was "not very friendly to ACAR." To the presidency Brazilians elected Jânio Quadros, who was a personal acquaintance of Nelson Rockefeller and considered "knowledgeable and sympathetic" toward ABCAR.[82] President Quadros personally approved the ABCAR budget for 1961–62 and told João Napoleão that he would like to see the draft of a bill for Congress.[83] Although the presidency of Quadros was a disaster for Brazil, it was a boon to ABCAR. The legislation sailed through Congress, and on December 31, 1961, an important part of the New Deal, transplanted by a Rockefeller, became part of the Brazilian federal system.

Although AIA had cleared itself of all financial responsibility for ACAR, its funding problems were far from over. In the years since starting its programs in Brazil and Venezuela, AIA had expanded to twenty-three Latin American countries, sponsoring rural youth projects (4-S and 4-H clubs), nutrition information programs, and training seminars in mass communications. Its outreach in Latin America had grown phenomenally, while its funding base had remained essentially the same: the Rockefeller family.

From the beginning, project staff had had trouble raising funds for AIA as the creation of one particular, highly visible elite family. While Nelson Rockefeller's sponsorship had done much to give AIA prestige in both the United States and Brazil, according to Robert Hudgens it also "stood in the way" of outreach to other sources of support. As Rockefeller himself

---

81. Crawford reported to the AIA board in early June of 1960 that the most important recent development in ABCAR had been the "progress made on institutionalizing it officially. João Napoleão, through Santiago Dantas, obtained the promise of the President to present a bill to the Congress and support it. . . . He [Dantas] is now drafting legislation to present in the form of a presidential 'meta,' and it is hoped that approval may be obtained before the end of this year." Walter Crawford to Louise Boyer, Berent Friele, and Lawrence Levy, June 6, 1960, p. 1. RAC, AIA, Box 3, Folder 28.

82. "AIA—Brazil Quarterly Report," prepared by Walter Crawford, July–September 1960, pp. 1, 3, 4, 16. By an interesting coincidence, the politician reported as "not friendly" was Tancredo Neves, who twenty-four years later was elected as the first civilian president following the twenty-year military dictatorship.

83. "AIA Progress Report," April–June, 1961, p. 3. RAC, AIA, Box 9, Folder 78.

once observed to Hudgens after being turned down for funding by a Coca-Cola executive, "You know what that man is thinking now? He's thinking to himself, I'm not going to put my money into something that's going to prove that Nelson Rockefeller is a world-wide philanthropist."[84] Considering Rockefeller's clear political ambitions and the tendency of most Americans to feel that the Rockefellers, in general, had already gotten enough out of the system, the executive's response is understandable. From AIA's point of view, it was also unfortunate.

But AIA may have eventually overcome the obstacles associated with the Rockefeller connection if it had not developed other problems. In the early 1960s it began to experience the traditional funding dilemma of nonprofit organizations. The foundation sources which had given it seed money as an experimental program no longer wanted to continue funding it once the experiment had been proven a success. For example, the Rockefeller Brothers Fund, AIA's largest contributor, initially gave funds to ACAR and ABCAR in 1956 with the understanding that the program would be absorbed by the Brazilian government at the end of 1959. Although the foundation gave AIA two subsequent five-year grants for its existing programs, fund officials made it extremely clear to AIA staff and board members that it had no interest in supporting projects which had passed the experimental stage. As a top official put it, the fund would give AIA funds only "if it can identify pressing and new opportunities."[85] To survive, AIA would have to obtain government funding for old programs, while developing new programs with which to approach foundation sources. The fund's last grant was clearly made simply because AIA had long been a family pet. The purpose of the grant, according to AIA's contact at the fund, was to give AIA five years within which "to wind up its program," merge with government operations, or find "sources of finance outside the family."[86]

But for various reasons, AIA officials could not bring themselves to adopt either strategy—government funding or new programming—for long-term survival. Why AIA did not strike out in new directions is not entirely clear, but it seems to have been a combination of an aging staff and board (many of whom were near retirement age by the mid-1960s)[87]

---

84. Hudgens interview, pp. 217, 220.
85. James Hyde to Dana S. Creel, October 12, 1964, p. 4. RAC, RBF, Box 12, Folder 6.
86. James Hyde to RBF Files, January 6, 1965, p. 1. RAC, RBF, Box 12, Folder 6.
87. The internal documents of AIA give no indication of a self-perception of slowing down. It is in the reports of the Rockefeller Brothers Fund that this point is made, based on conversations with AIA board members and the resulting evaluations of fund staff. As early as 1964, the main AIA contact at the fund had concluded that the AIA directors were

and the unwillingness of Nelson Rockefeller to lend his talents personally to rejuvenating the organization. Rockefeller would shortly begin his third term as governor of New York and had long ago diverted most of his own time and expendable financial resources into a domestic political career.

Although Rockefeller held no office in AIA other than that of a member of its board of directors, he was still its ideological and financial anchor. All of the other members of the board were family members, staff, or friends of Nelson, as had been the case from the beginning. If the board was "out of touch," as one Rockefeller Brothers Fund official concluded in 1964, it could only have been because Nelson Rockefeller was out of touch. In the 1940s and 1950s, the dedicated staff had made the plans for AIA come alive and really work, but always with Rockefeller's enthusiastic coaching and personal intervention at key political junctures, such as in the negotiations with Governor Campos and President Kubitschek. From 1958 onward, Nelson Rockefeller threw himself completely into his career as New York governor and perpetual presidential hopeful. "This organization is for you to do with as you see fit," John Camp wrote Nelson in 1966 in a last-ditch effort to develop some new directions for the organization. "All of us in AIA are ready to follow your guidance."[88] For whatever reasons, a lack of time or a shift in interests, Rockefeller did not take up the challenge of creating a new agenda. The pitfalls of having a leadership structured around one dynamic personality—and a budget based on one purse—must have been painfully evident to those who had dedicated their lives to the organization.

What is more, AIA did not fully exploit the possibilities for government funding. Between 1946 and 1960, the association had striven to promote private involvement in foreign assistance. In the 1950s it was one of the first organizations to seek government funding to carry out technical assistance programs, and in the 1960s it participated actively in government forums to promote better working relationships between the U.S. foreign assistance administration and nonprofit subcontractors. With the

"generally not in touch with the conflicting technical questions or the general political questions which would cause them to put forward opportunities." James N. Hyde to Dana S. Creel, October 12, 1964, p. 4. In 1968, Dana Creel wrote to David Rockefeller that to have continued the AIA program "it would also have been necessary to recruit a new generation of staff, the present members all being near retirement age." Dana Creel to David Rockefeller, August 8, 1968, p. 1. RAC, RBF, Box 12, Folders 6, and "AIA, 1966–69" (unnumbered), respectively.

88. John Camp to Nelson Rockefeller, November 28, 1966, p. 3. Attached to a memo from John Camp to James Hyde, dated March 23, 1967. RAC, RBF, Box 12, folder: "AIA, 1966–69."

advent of the Kennedy administration, much of what AIA had promoted came to pass. The Agency for International Development (AID) was much more receptive to doling out bits of its budget to private subcontractors than its predecessor, ICA, had been. In 1961, the attorney who later represented AIA in its contract negotiations with the government chaired a special president's task force on private contracting. For the first time, the government had made a commitment both to dollars for Latin America and to a role for private organizations. The best strategy for any nonprofit organization seeking to work in Latin America in the 1960s was to get on the Alliance for Progress bandwagon.

AIA had grown used to its autonomy and generous budgets, however. While many other subcontractors had little choice but to rely on the government for funding—in spite of unending bureaucracy, petty regulations, and civil servant suspicion of private contractors—AIA had had the privilege of Rockefeller protection and largesse.[89] Although there was more money than ever for contractors, AIA rebelled against the confines established for the private appendages of the U.S. government, especially those which threatened to infringe on its autonomy. And, while more easily available, the money was not so good. In a discussion with the Rockefeller Brothers Fund, the treasurer of AIA articulated the organizational consensus that "in addition to all of the administrative strings attached to AID funds, the administrative money was scarcely attractive enough to lead to a major decision to increase staff and undertake a broader scale of operations."[90]

Caught between an inability to develop new programs with which it could approach other foundations and an unwillingness to accept government supervision of its budget and programs, AIA had effectively dealt itself out of business. In a meeting in early 1967, Nelson Rockefeller and some of the associates who had founded AIA decided that since there were "no prospects for large additional financing" the organization would have to develop plans for winding down.[91]

89. The President's Committee on Private Contracting by AID reported in 1961 that "the private and university contractors are bitter, almost savage, in their complaints about delays and about what they insist is a cold hostility in ICA toward contracts and contractors." From "Positive Contracting for AID," President's Task Force on Foreign Assistance, Working Group on Contracting, August 15, 1961, p. 3. RAC, AIA, Box 8, Folder 69. The chairman of this committee was Philip Glick, who became AIA's advocate in its contracting problems with the government in 1962. As noted above, AIA had encountered various difficulties in trying to arrange government contracts, both with ICA and with the more liberal AID. Glick recommended to AIA officials in 1963 that they maintain a cautious distance from AID in order to preserve autonomy.
90. James Hyde to RBF Files, January 6, 1965, p. 2. RAC, RBF, Box 12, Folder 6.
91. "Memorandum for Wallace K. Harrison," March 8, 1967, p. 1. RAC, AIA, Box 2, Folder 19.

The impact of AIA's work was felt long after the organization's demise. In Brazil, the outcomes of ACAR's work in the hilly farms of Minas Gerais and through the federal ABCAR system were, by most standards, positive and permanent. A variety of studies written between 1954 and 1970 by both Brazilian and American authors found significant achievement overall. As summarized by José Paulo Ribeiro and Clifton Wharton, Jr., there was "a consistent pattern of positive change by the borrower families in their productivity, farm income, and net worth, as well as in their levels of living. The improvements that these farm families were able to make on the consumption/social side attest to the effect of the increased income upon the quality of farm living."[92] Studies also showed that CAR programs tended to increase yields for particular crops and the total productivity of the areas where they were located, although in times of high inflation CAR-educated farmers were found to place their money into fixed assets rather than into factors which would increase production. Although it could thus be said that in periods of high inflation CAR farmers were less productive, it can also be said they were more market wise. As the researcher who reported these data noted, "In an inflationary situation such as in Brazil, larger gains and losses are to be had by the appropriate or inappropriate investments in assets. The purchase of land as a hedge against inflation is much more important than its use as a factor of production."[93] CAR families also had an enviable credit record. In Minas Gerais, for example, loan repayment was frequently 100 percent and between 1949 and 1963 never fell below 99.8 percent.[94] But the most important fact in any analysis of the program's results is that poor families were eating and living better and steadily increasing the value of their crops and lands.

ACAR and ABCAR also had an important effect on the overall agricultural policy of Brazil. In the words of Lucas Lopes, the economic minister and lifelong friend of Juscelino Kubitschek, rural extension "did not exist before ACAR. ACAR introduced the very idea."[95] According to Roberto Campos, head of the National Bank for Economic Development under Kubitschek, "What little rural extension we have is dated there." The same observation was made by William Nicholls in his on-site analysis of Brazilian agriculture for the Ford Foundation in 1960. Nicholls

92. "The ACAR Program in Minas Gerais, Brazil," in *Subsistence Agriculture and Economic Development*, ed. Clifton Wharton, Jr. (Chicago: Aldine, 1969), 434–35.

93. Eliseu Roberto de Andrade Alves, "An Economic Evaluation of an Extension Program, Minas Gerais, Brazil" (M.A. thesis, Purdue University, 1968), cited in Ribeiro and Wharton, "The ACAR Program," 435.

94. Ribeiro and Wharton, "The ACAR Program," 432.

95. Interview with Lucas Lopes, Rio de Janeiro, October 10, 1986.

noted that while the São Paulo fomento had begun considering plans for rural extension as early as 1943, it actually developed them only in the late 1950s. "Hence," Nicholls concluded, "most of the credit for the recent rapid development of agricultural extension services in Brazil must go to the impetus given by the . . . American International Association."[96] ACAR and ABCAR were also successful in popularizing agricultural extension, with the result that within two decades it was an accepted, if limited, practice throughout the fifth largest nation in the world. By 1960, extension services reached nearly 12 percent of the country's municipalities, and between 1960 and the mid-1970s, low-interest agricultural loans as a percentage of total credit rose from 11 percent to 25 percent.[97] Other results were an increase in the prestige of agronomists and the introduction of extension courses into the curricula of Brazilian agricultural schools. As one agricultural economist noted, "In the formulation of agricultural policy, at both the state and federal level, the influence of the extension service is substantial."[98]

AIA succeeded in one of its highest goals. In 1960 a Ford Foundation researcher observed that ACAR had "approached the status of an indigenous Brazilian (rather than foreign) institution."[99] After 1961, when the federal and state governments took over the last vestiges of AIA control, the CAR organizations were no more American than *feijoada*, the traditional Saturday midday meal of black beans, dried beef, sausage, and oranges. ABCAR continued to operate until 1974, making loans primarily to small farmers and coordinating all rural extension in Brazil; that year it was reorganized and incorporated into a new division of the Ministry of Agriculture called Empresa Brasileira de Assistência Téchnica e Extensão Rural.[100] Its functions continue today.

Of course, like any other major development, Brazilianization had its pluses and minuses. The most important plus, far outweighing any drawback, was its autonomy. As a spokesperson from the Ministry of Agriculture told a largely American audience in Rio in 1967, "Do you know what is the best thing AIA ever did? It was to get out. When Nelson Rockefeller first came to Brazil and he and his colleagues set up AIA they all said that the goal was to get a program well-started, train people to do

96. Interview with Roberto Campos. Nicholls, "Brazilian Agricultural Economics," 15.
97. Baer, *The Brazilian Economy*, 327–28.
98. Schuh, *Agricultural Development of Brazil*, 244.
99. Nicholls, "Brazilian Agricultural Economics," 18.
100. *Cadastro da Administração Federal*, Brazilian National Archives, Section 43, p. 39. Empresa Brasileira de Assistência Téchnica e Extensão Rural absorbed ABCAR on November 6, 1974, under Law 6.126.

it, and then get out. And they have kept their promise."[101] The satisfaction appears to have been mutual. Rodman Rockefeller, son of Nelson, privately noted after a trip to Minas Gerais in 1972 that the autonomy of ACAR made for "an atmosphere free of colonial hangups." In ACAR, he wrote, "the Mineiros have made a monument to accomplishment out of a small stone planted 24 years ago. They did it and they know it—generosity mixes well with pride after true achievement and they were generous in their remarks about father."[102]

The negative side of Brazilianization was that ABCAR became subject to the vicissitudes of national politics. Whereas before ABCAR had enjoyed a special status giving it a measure of autonomy and insulation from the political process, as one more federal agency it was subject to the normal range of pork barrel politics. Into the mid and late sixties the traditional fomentos, which served larger fazendas, still received the bulk of funds for agricultural services, with the result that the number of farmers reached by extension in each state was still small in proportion to the total rural population. The underfunding of extension continued to be one of the remaining major bottlenecks in Brazilian agriculture in the 1970s.[103] Although this was a problem inherited from an earlier period, after 1961 ABCAR no longer had a unique, nongovernmental base from which to lobby for change. Also, by the late 1970s, farmers had pressured the Banco do Brasil, a prime source for extension loans, to relax the lending criteria which had been the basis of supervised credit.[104] These are the kinds of problems with which any government program has to deal, however, and they in no way obviated either the accomplishment of Brazilianization or the overall positive outcomes of the AIA-ABCAR program.

Yet not all observers have viewed the work of AIA and the CAR system with approval. Echoing some of the criticisms that were made of FSA during the New Deal, at least one American economist criticized CAR for its limited impact on overall agricultural productivity because of its emphasis on small farmers. "If the goal of the program had been social welfare, this would have been a valid form of action," Edward Schuh wrote in a book undertaken with Ford Foundation sponsorship in 1970. "However, if the goal was to increase agricultural production, which

101. Dalrymple, The AIA Story, 30.
102. "Notes: IBEC Brazilian Trip—January 17 through January 29, 1972," p. 10. RAC, IBEC, Box 62, Folder: "IBEC-Brazil-Planning-Expansion."
103. Schuh, Agricultural Development of Brazil, 340.
104. Interview with Roberto Campos.

could result in a broader base for the distribution of the gains from development, this approach had serious limitations."[105]

Schuh's recommendation that ABCAR work more with larger farmers must be taken in the context of the general debate on foreign assistance and economic development, which has long raged over the question of whether macroeconomic development paves the way for microeconomic development or vice versa. The massive projects of the World Bank and the Alliance for Progress in the 1950s and 1960s to build infrastructure (roads, ports, railways) were based on the idea that aggregate increases in productivity would create a bigger pie for Latin Americans to share. Critics in the 1960s and 1970s pointed out that Latin American elites and foreign corporations reaped most of the benefits from these projects, keeping all but a sliver of the pie for themselves. Complex, billion-dollar projects have also been criticized as more appropriate to the scale of development in the United States and Europe than to the scale of development in locales where a simple plow and a safe well can strengthen isolated village communities. In recent years, the debate has tended to come out in favor of small-scale, microeconomic projects to improve the daily lives of "real" (meaning, poor) people.[106] According to these criteria, AIA and its CARs hold up well.

Two notable Brazilian critics of ACAR and ABCAR and of the wartime programs out of which they grew are historians Gerson and Margarida Maria Moura. According to the Mouras, the programs were both ethnocentric and self-serving from the point of view of American interests. Rockefeller's efforts complemented an overall U.S. strategy of promoting North American civilization as "superior," which also reinforced the tendency of Brazilian elites to view "the farmer as an ignorant hillbilly,

105. *Agricultural Development of Brazil*, 242.
106. These criticisms of macroeconomic development have been raised so widely by both liberals and radicals in Latin America and the United States that it is hard to cite a completely representative sampling of sources. Some useful works are Sylvia Hewlett, *The Cruel Dilemmas of Development*, and Irma Adelman and Cynthia Taft Morris, *Economic Growth and Social Equity in Developing Countries* (Stanford: Stanford University Press, 1973). For criticisms from the perspective of the Dependency school of thought see Andre Gunder Frank, "On the Mechanisms of Imperialism: The Case of Brazil," in *Imperialism and Underdevelopment*, ed. Robert I. Rhodes (London: Monthly Review Press, 1970), 89–100. In 1970 the U.S. Congress created a new grantmaking institution, the Inter-American Foundation, specifically for the purpose of giving aid to small Latin American community groups to better life and promote economic development at the grassroots level. The impetus, according to the foundation's vice president, was a basic dissatisfaction with "classical macroeconomic growth models that left aside questions of who gained and in what ways." Robert Mashek, *The Inter-American Foundation in the Making* (Washington: Inter-American Foundation, undated), 5.

the countryside as a place forgotten by the politics of the State," and rural life as "a primitivism which impedes change, which is an obstacle to the growth of the country."[107] The Americans presented a model of agricultural modernity which was essentially a paradigm of rural practices in the United States and thus, the Mouras imply, inappropriate to Brazil. However, as should be evident from the history described above, the tenor of the CAR programs was anything but denigrating of the role of the small farmer. In the AIA (and FSA) view, the small farmer was the honest farmer, the man who deserved an economic break and a political voice, the bedrock of society and progress. And although there is no doubt that Nelson Rockefeller viewed American agricultural methods as superior to Brazilian and that he sought to foster a liking and admiration for American culture among Brazilians, these facts do not support a jump to the conclusion that he sought to bring Brazil under the sway of the United States by destroying the national culture. Such a claim also ignores the indigenous efforts of people like Milton Campos, whose agricultural reform programs predated Rockefeller's arrival in Minas Gerais by at least two years.

The Mouras view the wartime Food Supply Program and the later efforts of ACAR and ABCAR as a continuity and as fundamentally a reflection of American rather than Brazilian needs. They assert that a major purpose of the wartime effort was to conduct "a careful survey of Brazilian productive potential with a view to North American industrial and consumer needs in the post-war period," while the later programs actually implemented the goal of increasing "the productivity of Brazilian agriculture, especially the production of foods and strategic raw materials (rubber, vegetable oils, babassu, cotton, cocoa, Brazil nuts, and medicinal plants)."[108] Again, the facts belie these assertions. Although the Board of Economic Warfare was interested in the production of these materials during the war and encouraged their further development as exports to the U.S., AIA was concerned almost exclusively with domestic consumption. A more appropriate list of agricultural products would include milk, citrus fruits, green vegetables, and corn—none of which the United States exported to or imported from Brazil. Nor did AIA promote the use of American tractors, seeds, or fertilizers.

A final point the Mouras make is that another major purpose of the

107. "A Modernização dos Anos 40: A Agricultura Brasileira Pensada 'a Americana," unpublished paper (Rio de Janeiro: CPDOC Library, October 1983), 10, 14. Also see Gerson Moura's criticisms of Rockefeller's wartime programs in Brazil, in *Tio Sam Chega ao Brasil: A Penetração Cultural Americana*, 4th ed. (São Paulo: Brasiliense, 1986).
108. "Agricultura Brasileira," 3, 7.

U.S. and Rockefeller agricultural programs was to circumvent social unrest in Brazilian society through the "neutralization of social tensions."[109] Although comments to this effect appear from time to time in the documents of the OIAA and the Institute of Inter-American Affairs food programs (as in almost all government documentation from this period), references to communism or leftist movements or social unrest are notably rare, in fact almost nonexistent, in the internal documents of the AIA between 1946 and 1968. In twenty-two years, during the height of the Cold War, only one AIA document contained any sustained reference to social unrest and AIA's potential role in containing it. This document was Walter Crawford's original draft of a proposal for land reform based on resettlement in the campos cerrados, written in 1961. In the draft, Crawford included a section on the revolutionary "mood" of the Brazilian peasantry in describing the need for change. Yet two facts are of note: first, that it was the draft of a grant proposal to the ICA and thus had a government audience in mind; and second, that New York (AIA headquarters) told Crawford that the section would have to be cut from the final draft, indicating the organizational belief that politics should be kept separate from development.[110]

Another important indication of AIA's essentially nonpolitical stance can be found in the AIA response to a questionnaire of the U.S. Congress in 1964 to gather information on private, nonprofit organizations engaged in international assistance. Since the anonymity of the respondents was guaranteed, there seems to be no reason to doubt the candor of the answers. When given nine objectives and asked to rank them in terms of AIA's organizational priorities, AIA listed "Promote voluntary self-help in economic development . . . ," "Further mutual understanding . . . ," and "Foster a sense of interdependence among peoples" as its first three priorities, in that order. It rated the option "Combat Communist distortions, doctrines and propaganda" as its last priority.[111] Not only do the Mouras assertions seem unfounded, but AIA appears remarkably free of the anti-Communist preoccupation which dominated the government in this period.

On the Brazilian side of this question, the Mouras provide no information on the rural social tensions or movements which AIA supposedly

109. Ibid., 3.
110. Walter L. Crawford, "Agriculture in Brazil: The Mood, the Reality, and the Promise," January 1961. RAC, AIA, Box 7, Folder 58.
111. "Committee on Foreign Affairs, Questionnaire for Private, Non-Profit Organizations Engaged in International Programs, 1964," Copy of AIA's answers, part II, p. 6. RAC, AIA, Box 10, Folder 83.

tried to or actually did neutralize. Although the period 1945–60 was one of activism and conflict in Brazilian politics, accompanied by a substantial growth in the electorate and the trade union movement, these primarily urban phenomena had little effect on the quiescent rhythm of rural life. Even within the rapidly growing cities the spirit was decidedly reformist rather than revolutionary. The strong pressure for social change which surfaced from time to time in industrial strikes flowed into traditional trade unionism and electoral politics before 1960, not into radical, grassroots organizing. The Brazilian Communist Party itself had a reformist strategy of working through the democratically elected congress.[112] As John Humphrey notes, the political populism of both Vargas and Kubitschek was "constructed around labor support for a policy of national capitalist development."[113] AIA and its Brazilian affiliates, as rural organizations, were removed from the scene both of urban social conflict and political activism. Not until the creation of Francisco Julião's "peasant leagues" in the northeast at the opening of the 1960s did North Americans become aware of leftist organizing in rural Brazil. If Rockefeller's primary goal had been to neutralize social tensions, he could have picked several areas far more logical and central to this purpose than the farming communities of Minas Gerais in 1949.

In the United States the effect of AIA's efforts is less simple to ascertain than it is in Brazil. Clearly, Rockefeller sought to convince other Americans that individuals and private organizations could have a strong role in promoting international cooperation and economic development. The point of AIA, in the United States, was to agitate for greater private interest in Latin America and world interdependence generally. "Fundamentally, [AIA] is a recognition of the interdependence of nations," an evaluation commissioned by Rockefeller stated in 1951. "In pioneering a type of project specifically designed to implement this concept, and in stimulating public awareness and acceptance of this concept both at home and abroad, the sponsors of AIA have made a contribution to our national interest which will be of ever-widening significance."[114] Appropriately for a Rockefeller project, AIA was also a kind of celebration of private enterprise but imbued with a Roosevelt-New Deal internationalism. "The AIA approach . . . illustrate[s] problems and opportunity for

112. For a brief overview of the political history of this period see Flynn, *Brazil: A Political Analysis*, 134–43.

113. *Capitalist Control and Worker's Struggle in the Brazilian Automobile Industry* (Princeton: Princeton University Press, 1982), 19.

114. John French and Arthur Jones, "AIA—Appraisal of Major Programs," May 1951, Part One, p. 73. RAC, AIA, Box 2, Folder 10.

philanthropic enterprise and embodies pioneering experience in seeking workable mechanisms of international cooperation through private initiative."[115]

By the early 1960s, interest in private economic development projects had grown to notable proportions in the United States. The Cuban Revolution and the resulting Alliance for Progress woke Americans to the existence of a whole continent of countries to the south, and government officials entered the Kennedy era with a predisposition more favorable to private contractors. The President's Committee on Private Contracting by AID declared in 1961 that previous government attitudes toward working with private organizations to provide technical assistance missed the point. Such contracts were important, the committee stated, not as a fallback when government staff had too much work, but as a channel to "marshall the mutual efforts of the whole broad spectrum of the American economy." The involvement of private organizations in foreign assistance was a testament to the difference between liberal America and the statism of Communist countries. "The very fact that the society and economy of the United States is not a centrally organized and monolithic structure, but is a rich pluralism of public and private institutions . . . ," the committee reported, "argues eloquently for employing a cross-section of this great pluralistic structure in the major tasks that the President has defined for the Decade of Development."[116]

The Congress meanwhile formed its own committee on private initiatives in 1962 under Congressman Dante Fascell. Congressman Fascell, along with others, was later instrumental in forming the Inter-American Foundation, which gave aid funds *only* to private efforts. As the vice president of the foundation later documented, "Through the 1960s, there was strong official fascination with the use of private organizations to carry out foreign affairs programs."[117] From a tiny group of organizations working in Latin America in the 1950s, the number of U.S. non-profit groups involved in development activities increased to over eight hundred by the end of the 1960s.[118] AIA, as a prominent pioneer in private economic aid, was on the leading edge of this movement—its organizational efforts in the fifties confirmed by the individual activism of the sixties.

115. Robert W. Hudgens, Director of AIA, "Opportunity Abroad for Philanthropic Enterprise," ca. 1952, p. 4. RAC, R.G. 2, P.R., Box 1, Folder 12.
116. "Positive Contracting for AID," President's Task Force on Foreign Assistance, Working Group on Contracting, August 15, 1961, p. 9. RAC, AIA, Box 8, Folder 69.
117. Mashek, *The Inter-American Foundation*, 17.
118. Ibid., 12.

But Nelson Rockefeller's concern with turning American attention southward was by no means limited to leaders of the private, nonprofit sector. All of the commissions cosponsored with Brazil by the United States during the 1940s and 1950s (the Cooke, Abbink, and joint commissions), in addition to the Point Four advisory board which Rockefeller headed from 1950 to 1951, had emphasized the need for government to encourage American *companies* to take a more active and supportive role in developing Latin American economies, in particular Brazil's. As John Abbink had stated to Secretary of State Acheson at the conclusion of his mission in 1949, "The American members of the Joint Commission . . . are fully persuaded that our present policy of reiterating our faith in the willingness of private capital to move into countries like Brazil, while taking no active steps to foster a larger movement, is not adding to United States prestige abroad."[119] This challenge also intrigued Nelson Rockefeller when he left government at the end of World War II. It was to become the raison d'etre of the second major organization he sponsored in Brazil: the International Basic Economy Corporation.

119. *FRUS*, 1949, 2:557.

Chapter 4

"Good Works at a Profit":
The International Basic
Economy Corporation

I n the middle-class neighborhood of Fla-
mengo, located between the wealth of
Ipanema's white beaches in the Southern Zone of
Rio de Janeiro and the grimy brick *favelas* which
climb the hills and sprawl through the valleys of
Rio's Northern Zone, vendors attend steaming
vats of water filled with corn on the cob. Hungry
customers exit from a nearby Metro station and
line up to buy a quick snack before catching a
bus for the next leg of their trip home. They
watch as the vendor reaches with a tong into the
hot, milky looking water and takes out a fresh
ear of corn, ready to be salted and eaten. The
sight is a familiar one in Rio, where corn on the
cob is cheap, popular, and as traditional as pret-
zels on the streets of New York.

Since World War II, corn has become an increasingly important cereal crop in Brazil. Government price controls, larger tracts of land planted in corn, and better harvests actually lowered the cost of corn to the consumer (adjusted for inflation) by over one-fourth between 1945 and 1971.[1] Between 1980 and 1990, Brazil further increased its corn production by 40 percent with only a 2 percent increase in the area of cultivation.[2] Increased production has resulted largely from the use of more productive hybrid corn seed. These seeds help farmers double or even triple the size of their yields when used along with commercial fertilizers, and even without improved farming methods the superior productivity of the seeds gives them an edge over common corn seed. The use of corn hybrids is one of the few major agricultural innovations of the postwar period that farmers have adopted extensively throughout Brazil, where many technical improvements have been limited to specific crops in specific regions.[3]

Before World War II, two Brazilian agronomists started developing the tropical strains of hybrid corn seed which made this possible. The International Basic Economy Corporation (IBEC) sponsored their work, which became the cornerstone of the first, and perhaps most successful, IBEC subsidiary. The two largest business projects started in Brazil by Nelson Rockefeller through IBEC were the hybrid seed corn company Sementes Agroceres, Sociedade Anónima (SASA), founded in 1947, and Brazil's first stock market mutual fund, Fundo Crescinco (*Crescimento industrial e comercial,* Industrial and commercial growth), created ten years later.[4]

From the start, the path of IBEC was much less clear-cut than that of AIA. There were some precedents of nonprofit organizations doing good works abroad, like the Rockefeller Foundation in the field of health, for example, but there were none of avowedly capitalistic enterprises trying to promote the greater economic good of foreign countries while turning

1. John P. M. Higgins, "Impact Study: Sementes Agroceres, S.A.," p. 33. RAC, IBEC, Box 75, Folder: "SASA . . . Impact Study."
2. Interview with Ney Bittencourt de Araújo, Sao Paulo, August 24, 1990.
3. According to Schuh, "The relative importance of corn among the cereals [rice, corn, and wheat] has tended to increase [since 1954]." Corn has also been an exception to the general rule that agricultural improvements tend to remain local and crop-specific. Although farmers have been slow to adopt commercial fertilizers, and most rural units still did not have electricity as of the late 1960s, hybrid seeds were one of the few modern innovations used by small and big farmers throughout Brazil. Schuh, *Agricultural Development of Brazil,* 117, 168–69.
4. The letters "S.A." after the name of a Brazilian corporation have the same meaning as "Inc." after the name of an American corporation. In Portuguese, S.A. stands for *Sociedade Anónima.*

a profit for themselves. In fact, just the opposite was the rule; most companies never looked beyond their own profits, and some quite consciously exploited weak nations and peoples. Nelson Rockefeller realized that American capital generally went abroad for one of two reasons: for raw materials or to protect a privileged position in foreign markets.[5] Yet this was precisely the behavior which Rockefeller hoped to change. As the idea for IBEC grew, it veered from the path of demonstrating what the U.S. *government* and other nonprofit organizations should do for Latin America (as AIA was attempting) and styled itself as a model for what American *business* should do for Latin America. AIA would be the exemplar of American aid; IBEC the exemplar of American capitalism. "In the last century," Rockefeller told a reporter for *Newsweek,* "capital went wherever it could make the greatest profit. In this century it must go where it can render the greatest service."[6]

The concept of a profit-making corporation evolved gradually. At first Rockefeller envisioned a complex of activities which would continue the wartime cooperation of governments on a private, nonprofit basis. It was out of this notion that he fashioned AIA. But almost immediately, friends and associates began counseling Rockefeller to create a separate corporation for projects which might eventually make a profit. Attorney John Lockwood questioned the legality of combining nonprofit and for-profit activities and urged Rockefeller to distinguish "Sunday" charity from work-week business. Perhaps even more important, Rockefeller's Brazilian acquaintances questioned the viability of combining philanthropy with enterprise. After all, if Brazilians were to continue the projects Rockefeller helped to start, the ventures would eventually have to generate an income independent of the (possibly temporary) largesse of one, rather unusual, North American. In other words, philanthropy did not seem the route to self-sufficiency. "One phase of our [initial] plans left the Brazilians completely cold," Rockefeller later recalled. "Brazilians saw clearly . . . that if the development projects started in Brazil were to be sound and enduring, they would have to be financed and managed on a strictly businesslike basis, and their success measured by the standard yardstick of profits on money invested."[7]

5. Rockefeller made this observation in an oral history interview conducted by Wayne Broehl for a book on IBEC, July, 12, 1965, p. 1. RAC, Wayne Broehl Papers, Box 18, Folder: "Interview-NAR."
6. *Newsweek,* March 15, 1948, 62.
7. Quoted in "The Origins of AIA," by Ed Stuntz (AIA: December 1953), p. 12. RAC, R.G. 2, P.R.—AIA, Box 1, Folder 6. Rodman Rockefeller, who became president of IBEC in 1968, later said, "It became reasonably obvious that voluntary, non-profit, charitable

Rockefeller soon came to see advantages in a profit-making corporation. Although he apparently did not intend, at least initially, to profit financially from IBEC, he clearly saw it as presenting an opportunity to shape history.[8] Just as his grandfather had wrought nineteenth-century competitive capitalism into corporate capitalism, and his father had pioneered in the creation of welfare capitalism, Nelson set for himself the task of transforming the indifferent, exploitative U.S. business presence overseas into an enlightened capitalism which would show both Uncle Sam and the American system in a good light and preserve the capitalist system itself. As Rockefeller would explain his position to a Latin American audience a year or so later, he saw "the necessity of making wise adjustments of the capitalist system within the structure of political democracy in order to counteract those influences which, in their bitter haste to abolish the abuses of capitalistic organization, would, knowingly or unknowingly, destroy democracy."[9] Rockefeller's audience at the time was enthusiastic, according to a State Department official who was present, and was especially pleased to hear a North American who acknowledged that laissez-faire capitalism had to be brought into the twentieth century not just in the United States but also in Latin America. As to that necessity, Rockefeller intended to educate both North Americans and Latin Americans. U.S. businessmen would learn that it could be profitable to invest in basic development (not just raw materials extraction) and that such investment could be managed in ways consistent with local interests. Latin Americans would learn that cooperation with U.S. business could facilitate their national development, not simply stunt it. In the process, Nelson Rockefeller would establish himself as the leading light of foreign economic expansion and development, thereby building a domestic following in both business and politics.

And so IBEC itself became a kind of hybrid. When Rockefeller and a few associates filed the incorporation papers for IBEC in New York on January 9, 1947 (six months after the incorporation of AIA), they insisted

---

activities were not pertinent." According to Rodman, it made sense to distribute food and build houses on a charitable basis for the poor, but once IBEC began to direct its activities toward the middle class his father realized there was the opportunity to provide such services "at a profit—which is a regenerative activity which in effect creates its own replacements." Interview with Rodman C. Rockefeller, New York City, August 4, 1987.

8. A memorandum of 1946 made it clear that, although IBEC intended to make a profit, none of it was to "accrue to Mr. Rockefeller." Memo to "All Personnel" from J. W. Hisle, November 27, 1946, p. 1. RAC, R.G. 2, P.R.-AIA, Box 1, Folder 8.

9. Paraphrased quote reported by Frank P. Corrigan, U.S. Embassy (Caracas), to the Department of State, January 29, 1947, p. 1. NA, R.G. 59, Decimal File 811.503131/1–2947 (1945–49).

on the inclusion of a high-minded statement of principle. The goals of "the undersigned," the preamble stated, were "to promote the economic development of various parts of the world, to increase the production and availability of goods, things and services useful to the lives or livelihood of their peoples, and thus to better their standards of living."[10]

The deputy secretary of the State of New York challenged the unusual statement, maintaining that the Stock Corporation Law did not permit such a preamble, that the preamble confused the distinctions between nonprofit and for-profit, and that it might mislead the public by suggesting that IBEC was a charity instead of a business. In other words, he questioned not only whether the business-philanthropy hybrid would work, but whether it was legally consistent with American capitalism. The deputy secretary's consternation was not unexpected, considering that American courts had not yet established the legality even of corporate donations to unaffiliated, domestic nonprofit organizations. (This would not happen until the A. P. Smith case of 1951, in which stockholders unsuccessfully sued their board of directors for making a donation to Princeton University out of company profits.)[11] Lawyers for IBEC successfully countered the New York deputy secretary's initial objections, convincing him that IBEC was a special case which justified the "novel provision." They argued that since Latin Americans "tended to fear Yankee imperialism," a preamble was necessary to make clear the "social purposes" of IBEC. The lawyers pointed out that the articles would be translated into the languages of the host countries and that there was nothing in the preamble inherently inconsistent "with a profit-making enterprise."[12]

Rockefeller realized, however, that coherence between IBEC's social purposes and its profit-making mandate would have to be engineered. The small planning group which had created AIA and whose names were

10. "Certificate of Incorporation," IBEC, p.1. RAC, R.G. 2, P.R.-IBEC, Box 4, Folder: "Certificate of Incorporation."
11. Richard Eells, *Corporation Giving in a Free Society* (New York: Harper and Brothers, 1956), 16.
12. Quoted in Wayne Broehl, *United States Business Performance Abroad: A Case Study of the International Basic Economy Corporation* (Washington: National Planning Association, 1968), 9–10. Broehl's book, written with the full cooperation of IBEC, is currently the only published history of the corporation. Although it was completed too early to report on the last decade or so of IBEC's operations, it is useful for an overview of the corporation's beginnings in Brazil and Venezuela and its later investments throughout Latin America and other parts of the world. In the course of writing the book, Broehl assembled a large collection of original IBEC documents, which he later donated to the Rockefeller Archive Center. Since both the IBEC and Broehl collections are as yet unprocessed they are essential complements to one another in sorting through the welter of random files and reports.

on the IBEC Articles of Incorporation also elaborated a set of business goals and policies which one newspaper reporter at the time wrote "might alter the shape of postwar capitalism."[13] An early document outlined "certain fundamental policies . . . which the founders of IBEC believe are essential." The primary goal of IBEC, the document read, was to identify and break "economic bottlenecks" holding back development. In doing this it would be IBEC policy to "encourage financial participation by nationals" and to "employ local nationals to the greatest practicable extent and train nationals for technical and managerial posts."[14]

Yet it was one thing to articulate such principles and another to reconcile them with the imperatives of making a profit. And profit was essential, if Rockefeller was to prove his own leadership qualities as well as his premise that both U.S. companies and Latin American nations could benefit from economic development ventures. He hoped to set a precedent which other U.S. businessmen would follow, and to do so he needed to establish a profit incentive. Otherwise, as one newsmagazine in the U.S. observed, "it would be merely another charity limited by the Rockefeller purse."[15]

One of the most complex issues that Rockefeller and IBEC would struggle with in the ensuing years arose from the original IBEC commitment to "encourage financial participation by nationals." As a Rockefeller, Nelson hesitated to involve nationals in risky propositions which might fail and for which his family might then be blamed. On the other hand, why should partners who assumed none of the risks share equally in potential profits? Also, how could IBEC foster eventual local ownership of its successful businesses without giving away its own investment (a form of charity) and in the process dealing itself out of business? One reason why such questions never troubled the operation of projects like ACAR was that the Rockefeller contributions were straight-out donations. But in 1947 Nelson Rockefeller had not yet confronted the questions which would complicate his business transactions, and IBEC was launched with great optimism.

The press in both the United States and Brazil responded enthusiastically to the unveiling of Rockefeller's plans at press conferences he gave in

13. *Time*, November 25, 1946, 42. The signatories on the IBEC incorporation papers were Nelson Rockefeller, Berent Friele, Wallace Harrison, Francis Jamieson, and John Lockwood.
14. "Major Aims and Objectives" (undated but found in a collection of documents from early 1947), p. 2. RAC, R.G. 2, P.R.-IBEC, Box 8, Folder: "Public Relations—IBEC Projects—General."
15. *Newsweek*, March 15, 1948, 62.

Rio de Janeiro. *Time* magazine called the plans "good works at a profit" and "enlightened capitalism." If the plans worked, *Time* noted, "living standards would be raised, an extensive middle class would come into existence, and there would be an end to talk of [the] U.S. and exploitation." Rio's *Correio da Manha* said, "The American continent cannot survive while one part is strong and prosperous and the other poor and weak. Nelson Rockefeller was one of the first to realize this truth." *Diario da Noite* ran an editorial with the simple headline "Nelson," which commented, "He returns to encourage the development of our land resources in the generous and disinterested desire to improve the lot of the great masses of Latin America."[16] *Correio da Noite* was enthusiastic too: "A young, educated millionaire like Nelson A. Rockefeller could lead an adventurous and idle life. But he prefers to found companies, distribute wealth, and feed whole generations. And all this he does simply, without a trace of haughtiness."[17]

Inasmuch as IBEC had been an offshoot of AIA, the two organizations initially had a common, coordinated purpose: to foster development of Brazil's agricultural resources, with an emphasis on food for domestic consumption. But while AIA focused on improving the welfare and livelihood of the individual farming family, IBEC concentrated on projects to enhance Brazilian agricultural productivity in general. One reason for this was Rockefeller's recognition that as migrants to the cities swelled Brazil's industrial working class, the remaining agricultural workers would have to become more productive in order to provide the food which the rapidly growing nation required. "Our own situation in the U.S. is a good example of a balanced development in agriculture supplementing the industrial evolution of our country," Rockefeller told Brazilian officials.[18] The original plans, written by Kenneth Kadow, included projects to promote food canning and preservation, the use of fertilizers, development of hybrid seed, and the fishing industry. "Industrialization of Brazil's basic resources is the key to Brazil's successful future," Kadow wrote. "The proper development of these resources would go a long way toward evolving the Brazil of greatest economic and political interest to America."[19]

Project number one in Kadow's plan was a hybrid seed corn company. The idea resulted in part from Kadow's experience as head of the wartime

16. Quoted in *Time*, November 25, 1946, 42. Also see issue for September 27, 1948, 36.
17. Quoted in Dalrymple, *The AIA Story*, 31.
18. Speech at Itamaraty Palace, Rio de Janeiro, November 1946, p. 6. RAC, R.G. 2, Economic Interests, Box 1, Folder 6.
19. Kenneth Kadow to Nelson Rockefeller, May 17, 1946, pp. 15. RAC, R.G. 2, P.R.-AIA, Box 1, Folder: "AIA-General."

Food Supply Program for OIAA in Brazil. In 1943, OIAA imported vegetable seeds into Brazil, and the local people started over two million home gardens as a result. "We had three times the requests we could fill," Kadow recounted. Although by 1946 the Brazilian government and one small private company had experiments under way to test and improve seed varieties, they lacked the financing to produce a "cheap, good, reliable" source of seeds in the near future. "Cheap seeds in the hands of the poor makes [sic] possible food they can get in no other way," Kadow noted in his report to Rockefeller. "Even buying food at low prices is not as effective. They can always grow a little garden but they can't always buy food. . . . Millions of people would benefit."[20]

The idea for the project can also be traced to the influence of Henry Wallace, with whom Rockefeller had worked closely and continuously during the war. Corn hybrids were first developed in the United States at the beginning of the twentieth century, coming into wide use during the New Deal. In barely more than a decade, between 1933 and 1944, hybrid corn seed use in the United States increased from 0.1 percent of all acreage planted to 57 percent.[21] Wallace, a geneticist and the third-generation editor of *Wallace's Farmer* before coming into the posts of secretary of agriculture, secretary of commerce, and vice-president of the United States, had pioneered the breeding of these hybrids. His strains were some of the first to be adopted extensively. Wallace's home state of Iowa led in the use of hybrid seed, with 99 percent of all corn acreage planted with hybrids by the end of this period. As both a scientist and one of the architects of the FSA, Wallace quickly saw the potential of agricultural research to solve the intransigent problems of poverty and hunger, not just in the United States but worldwide. In this respect he led a generation of plant geneticists whose discoveries would increasingly affect world agriculture. In 1941 Wallace gave the Rockefeller Foundation the idea for its Mexican hybrid seed corn project, which helped to start the famous Green Revolution that the foundation exported (with mixed results) to India and elsewhere in the 1960s. Wallace also impressed on Nelson Rockefeller how much more productive hybrids were than common corn.[22] According to an interview in 1946, "Nelson Rockefeller never forgot."[23]

20. Ibid., p. 6.
21. Information taken from "Draft of a Hybrid Seed Corn Project," July 1946, p. 2. RAC, Broehl Papers, Box 17, Folder: "SASA (Brazil) I.
22. Information from a speech by Henry Wallace at the Ninth Meeting of the Central American Cooperative Corn Improvement Program, El Salvador, March 12, 1963, p. 1. RAC, Rockefeller Foundation Archives, R.G. 1.2, 200-D, Wallace, Henry A., Box 248, Folder 2399. Also see Raymond B. Fosdick, *The Story of the Rockefeller Foundation* (New York: Harper and Brothers, 1952), 148–85.
23. *Time*, November 25, 1946, 42.

In the first few years of IBEC's existence, Rockefeller and his team developed several commercial projects. The hybrid seed corn company was always at the top of the list, but other opportunities beckoned as well. Rockefeller convinced Cargill, the American agricultural firm, to cooperate with IBEC in building and operating two grain storage elevators, one in the outback of São Paulo state and the other in the state of Paraná.[24] IBEC also started a small company which provided helicopter crop dusting services and yet another firm which provided tractors on a contract basis for clearing land and cultivating crops. Another early IBEC venture was a hog production company which operated model farms to demonstrate how pigs could best be bred and raised.

All of the Brazilian companies, including SASA at first, were small and operated in only one or two states. From the start, Rockefeller and his associates distinguished between undertaking massive food development in the country and acting as a catalyst for such development. Because of Brazil's immense size, Rockefeller conceived of projects there as operating at the periphery of the economy, offering services and models which would encourage existing producers to be even more productive. Simultaneously, IBEC was starting companies in Venezuela under a subsidiary called the Venezuelan Basic Economy Corporation (VBEC), but there the intent was to affect the entire national economy by actually producing and distributing food on a major scale. Such a plan was conceivable not only because Venezuela was a much smaller country than Brazil, having a population of less than four million versus Brazil's forty-six million, but also because the oil companies, with their enormous profits, could be tapped for large sums for VBEC and AIA projects.[25] In its early years, Rockefeller's Venezuelan corporation operated four large farms that produced beef, sugar, milk, rice, fruit, chickens, and a variety of vegetables; a fishing company which built freezing units on shore and provided local fishermen with iceboxes and new motors for their boats in exchange for a

---

24. According to a vice president of IBEC, Rockefeller went personally to Cargill's Minneapolis headquarters to persuade them to undertake the Brazilian venture. Cargill officials apparently "saw many problems" with trying to work in Brazil, but "of course," the IBEC official added, "Nelson is not one to take no too lightly." From an interview conducted with IBEC Vice President W. D. Bradford by Wayne Broehl (undated), p. 81. RAC, Broehl Papers, Box 18, Folder: "Interview-Bradford."

25. AIA budgets between 1947 and 1949 reflect the fact that the preponderance of funds came from the American oil companies in Venezuela and thus had to be spent in that country. As of December 31, 1949, AIA had spent three times as much money in Venezuela as in Brazil, even though AIA (and IBEC) got a slightly later start there. By the end of 1949, AIA had only $44,045 in its account for Brazil, while it had $819,634 in its Venezuela account. "AIA Annual Report," 1949 (dated May 29, 1950), p. 4 of synopsis. RAC, AIA, Box 1, Folder 2.

portion of the catch; a chain of small supermarkets to lower food retail costs; and a milk company.

The experience of the company in Venezuela provided a contrast to the more modest efforts in Brazil and eventually proved an important lesson about the value of starting on a smaller scale with less visibility. The Venezuela projects had at least as many failures as successes, and in the end a sizable portion of the original investment was lost. After a five-year shakedown period, only the supermarkets and the milk company remained in business, enjoying a modest profit. The oil companies had invested and lost just over $8.6 million, and VBEC's parent corporation, IBEC, had lost about $1.2 million. The Venezuelan presidential administration of Rómulo Betancourt had strongly supported IBEC's efforts because of Rockefeller's acknowledgment to officials that "drastic adjustments and modifications in the structure of capitalistic organization in Venezuela [were necessary] if democracy is to be preserved and strengthened."[26]

But as the IBEC projects failed, criticism from both the right and the left caused the government to cool toward VBEC. When Betancourt was overthrown by a coup, the incoming regime indicated it wished to sever ties with the Rockefeller company. Since the government had subscribed to 50 percent of VBEC stock, Rockefeller negotiated a settlement which allowed the responsible government agency to withdraw without any financial loss. Still, the VBEC projects were widely criticized as fronts for oil company exploitation and American interference. Nearly $10 million later, it was clear that experimental operations on an extensive scale brought overexposure, from both a financial and public relations standpoint. VBEC continued as an IBEC subsidiary, but on a much smaller basis.[27]

26. Quote from U.S. embassy officer Frank P. Corrigan (in Caracas) describing Rockefeller's perspective as well as that of other "men of broad vision." Rockefeller explained his position to the Betancourt government in 1947 during a well-received, hour-long discourse in Spanish. According to Corrigan, Rockefeller's comments contrasted favorably with the attitude conveyed by most U.S. businessmen in Latin America, who usually opposed "any variation of the existing pattern of capitalistic organization." Rockefeller's flexibility was "a note which strikes sympathy in the minds of the current leaders of Venezuela and gives the people a new concept of capital's functions," Corrigan told the Department of State. Frank P. Corrigan, U.S. Embassy (Caracas), to the Department of State, January 29, 1947, p. 2. NA, R.G. 59, Decimal File 811.503131/1–2947 (1945–49).
27. See Broehl, *U.S. Business Performance Abroad*, 12–45, for an account of VBEC's early years in Venezuela. The government agency which Betancourt had assigned to work with VBEC was the Corporación Venezolana de Fomento. The agency contributed 50 percent of the initial venture capital, and Rockefeller committed VBEC to sell its remaining 50 percent interest to Venezuelans at the end of ten years. Because of the companies' various problems,

In Brazil, however, the absence of oil companies meant that a high level of investment was never an option, and Rockefeller never attempted it. IBEC could not possibly afford to buy enough farms or start enough fishing operations to increase the food supply of Brazil noticeably. Rather than become a major producer, then, the corporation aimed to work with Brazilian producers. As in Venezuela, the early projects in Brazil met with varied success, some—the model hog farms, for one—closing down within a few years because of organizational problems or bad luck with disease and pests, others struggling along under the burden of Brazil's inadequate system of transportation. For example, corn shipments from IBEC's grain elevators to São Paulo competed constantly with the more lucrative coffee crop for limited space on trains. IBEC sometimes had to wait days, even weeks, to get a railroad car.[28] But IBEC's first, largest, and undoubtedly most important subsidiary in Brazil was headed toward a different kind of future.

Sementes Agroceres, S.A.

Sementes Agroceres took its name from the Greek and Roman goddess of agriculture, Ceres.[29] The homage was appropriately paid. One might say the gods had been generous to Brazil. In 1946, through the use of tools not much more modern than the hoe, Brazil was already one of the most prolific agricultural nations on earth. Although Brazil depended on a modified monoculture for much of its export earnings, coffee was not the only crop grown extensively. Corn was actually the biggest crop in the country, and although Brazil's production was only one-tenth of the United States', it was fourth in the world. Cotton had also been a major export (in addition to coffee) in the prewar and wartime years, and Brazil had the world's third largest crop. The rice harvest was not large by Asian standards, but it was the largest in the western hemisphere. Of the major crops, only wheat had to be imported.

Brazil had diversification and volume, but it had problems with productivity and distribution. Lack of crop rotation and infrequent use of

---

however (some of which had to do with natural disasters, pests, and the lack of consumer acceptance of items such as frozen fish), the Venezuelans not only did not wish to exercise this option, but sold their entire portfolio back to IBEC.

28. Interview with IBEC Vice President W. D. Bradford by Wayne Broehl (undated), p. 83. RAC, Broehl Papers, Box 18, Folder: "Interview-Bradford."

29. From an interview with Ney Bittencourt de Araújo, president of SASA, *O Estado de São Paulo*, October 22, 1986, Agriculture Supplement, p. 8. *Sementes* is the Portuguese word for "seeds."

fertilizers rapidly depleted cultivated land, and the new lands being brought under cultivation to the west were of poor quality. Freight and storage space was so inadequate that many crops simply rotted. Over 70 percent of the Brazilian labor force worked in agriculture, yet their methods of cultivation were so primitive and land distribution was so skewed toward the wealthy that the average caloric intake was well below that of Argentina and barely above India's.[30]

Corn was used widely in Brazil both as animal feed and as food for humans. Brazilians frequently ate it fresh, on the cob, but also ground it into meal as the base for many traditional dishes and desserts known as *comida de caipira de milho* (country folk food made from corn). Even though Brazilians extensively planted and used corn, however, productivity was low by North American standards. At the end of World War II, the yield in the United States averaged thirty-four bushels an acre and Canada had almost forty. Brazil's yield was comparable to other third world countries: Mexico grew about eleven bushels of corn per acre, Brazil nineteen, and China twenty.

One of IBEC's first steps in Brazil was to approach two Brazilian geneticists, António Secundino and Gladstone Drummond, who were working at the agricultural college of Viçosa in Minas Gerais. Secundino and Drummond had spent several growing seasons developing strains of corn which would flourish under Brazilian conditions. Both had received advanced degrees in corn hybridization from Iowa State College in the United States, and Secundino had been an official in the Brazilian wartime Food Supply Program. As a result, he not only knew Rockefeller, but was friends with the agricultural experts whom Rockefeller had called on to start AIA. Secundino and Drummond, together with a couple of American partners from the wartime program, had founded a small company in 1945 called Agroceres Limitada, but they lacked both capital to expand production and marketing experience. IBEC wanted hybrid seed corn to become widely available to Brazilian farmers as soon as possible and proposed a joint effort between the geneticists and IBEC. The result was a new company called Sementes Agroceres, S.A.[31]

IBEC contracted with Secundino and Gladstone through Agroceres Limitada to provide management services to SASA and to share the results of their work in hybrids. The Brazilian-owned Agroceres was

30. Information cited in Broehl, *U.S. Business Performance Abroad*, 46–48.
31. The only work to date on the history of SASA is Ana Célia Castro, "Crescimento da Firma e Diversificação Productiva: O Caso Agroceres" (Diss., Universidade Estadual de Campinas, 1988).

given the option to buy up to 49 percent of the stock of SASA over a ten-year period, at the end of which the Agroceres owners could purchase additional shares to secure a majority holding. IBEC would become the minority stockholder. The price of these shares would be the original issue price plus simple interest at the rate of 5 percent.[32] In effect, Rockefeller signed up to take almost all of the initial risks of the company's first decade, after which he would sell ownership to the Brazilians—at an unchanging base price unaffected by inflation or company growth—if they thought the company sufficiently successful to be worth buying. In the meantime, Agroceres was free to build up its own seed business, on its own farm in Minas Gerais. SASA bought a farm in the small town of Jacarezinho, in the state of Paraná.

Rockefeller and his colleagues in IBEC were especially concerned about not appearing to monopolize the production of hybrid seed corn, which was one reason for keeping the businesses of SASA and Agroceres Limitada separate. Another condition of the contract, included on IBEC's insistence, was that Agroceres had to sell its pure hybrid lines to competing companies upon request, on an acceptable royalty basis. Neither IBEC nor Agroceres would be able to hold back important discoveries from use by other Brazilian scientists. "The [IBEC] Board was quite emphatic about this," Kenneth Kadow wrote to another Rockefeller staff member who was helping to negotiate the contract with Agroceres, "as they do not wish to be accused of supporting the development of a new monopoly."[33]

SASA's first two years were extremely promising. Because the cost of the hybrid seed corn was significantly higher than that of regular seed, SASA's representatives had to convince each farmer individually to take the risk. But they found customers and ended up selling every bit of the first small crop (36 tons of seed). Because of start-up costs, SASA still lost money that year, but successful sales convinced the company to increase production to 230 tons in 1949. It was a good call. "Clear skies, a hot drying sun, and dusty roads" gave evidence of a drought that hit central Brazil that year, with great injury to crops throughout the region.[34] Farmers who had yielded to SASA's salesmen and planted their fields with hybrid corn came out of the drought with good harvests. SASA had so many requests for hybrid seeds from its 1949 crop that António Secun-

32. Broehl, *U.S. Business Performance Abroad*, 51.
33. Kenneth Kadow to Dee W. Jackson, September 19, 1946, p. 1. RAC, Broehl Papers, Box 17, Folder: "SASA (Brazil) I.
34. John B. Griffing to SASA Board of Directors, February 7, 1949, p. 1. RAC, Broehl Papers, Box 17, Folder: "SASA (Brazil) I."

dino had to ration the seeds to customers. The company made its first profit.

SASA began to think about expanding further. When Nelson Rockefeller visited Brazil in 1950, he suggested to Secundino that the company plant for a larger harvest. Secundino was not convinced that he could market a larger crop, but Rockefeller said, "I prefer to sit on a batch of corn rather than rationing it."[35] Other members of SASA's and IBEC's boards also began analyzing the potential for expansion. Rockefeller's staff in Brazil was always somewhat more alert to the profit potential of SASA than he or his colleagues in New York. When the original contract with Agroceres was devised, Kenneth Kadow and other staff on location in Brazil wrote to the New York office that IBEC might want to agree to sell its majority position at some point, but as for themselves, they recommended "strongly" that "New York retain these shares as a splendid high return investment which will give an excellent income."[36]

At the beginning of 1950, when Secundino was rationing seeds from the previous successful harvest, the head of IBEC in Brazil, Arthur Vandenberg, Jr., son of the U.S. senator, began lobbying New York to consider a merger with Agroceres. SASA was IBEC's most successful operation to date, in Brazil or Venezuela, and was the venture that most warranted expanding. Yet the original agreement with Agroceres presented several obstacles to growth. First of all, expansion could be accomplished only with additional capital, but the Agroceres partners were not in a financial position to bring more money into the firm. In addition, what extra funds they could put together they intended to use to increase their holdings of the initial stock. If IBEC funneled more money into the company, it would be increasing SASA's worth while remaining obligated to sell the company to the Agroceres partners within a few years on the basis of its original value (plus 5 percent interest). Vandenberg wrote the attorney John Lockwood, "Even in the broadest concept of 'contributing to the welfare of the people', we could not be expected to build up an operation worth, let us say, CR$10.000.000,00 [ten million], and let it go at the end of seven years for 51% of SASA's present capital of CR$3.000.000,00 [three million]."[37] Furthermore, even though IBEC

35. Interview with António Secundino by Wayne Broehl, July 2, 1964, pp. 55–56. RAC, Broehl Papers, Box 18, Folder: "Interview-Jofre, et al." Also see Castro, "Crescimento da Firma," 65–66.

36. Kenneth Kadow et al. to Nelson Rockefeller et al., November 22, 1946, p. 1. RAC, Broehl Papers, Box 17, Folder: "SASA (Brazil) I."

37. Arthur Vandenberg, Jr., to John Lockwood, April 15, 1950, p. 1. RAC, Broehl Papers, Box 17, Folder: "SASA (Brazil) II."

was technically free to expand its seed operations without going through the subsidiary SASA (just as Agroceres was free to continue its separate operations in Minas Gerais), Vandenberg felt that from "a moral viewpoint," any expansion had to take place in partnership with Agroceres. But if IBEC did fund expansion in the important corn states through SASA, whatever market inroads they developed would "be for the ultimate account of others" who would then buy the company at a bargain.[38]

A final problem, which struck at the heart of IBEC's conflicting impulses to make a profit while encouraging Brazilian ownership, was that once the Agroceres partners exercised their option to buy control of the company, IBEC would have to sell its chance to play a major role in the most exciting development field it had yet entered, and one of its few opportunities to own the kind of profitable venture which was supposed to be its raison d'etre as an enlightened capitalist company. Once it controlled less than 50.1 percent of SASA, IBEC could no longer claim the subsidiary's assets or sales on its own profit and loss statements. IBEC had no desire to appear to be simply a holding company, and in any case Nelson Rockefeller was not constitutionally inclined to take such a backseat role. "Nelson likes to feel that he is managing," IBEC vice president W. D. Bradford noted.[39]

Even so, Rockefeller and his New York associates at first resisted the idea of merging the two companies. Lockwood agreed with Vandenberg that the contract with Agroceres should be changed since it distorted "normal development" by limiting capital expansion, but initially he ruled out the merger idea, stating, "We have thought it desirable to avoid, if possible, a single, Brazil-wide hybrid seed company on the ground of seeming close to a monopoly of this vital industry."[40] As arguments in favor of the merger piled up, however, Vandenberg was given authority to negotiate a merger with Agroceres Limitada. Over a period of a few months, Vandenberg and Secundino hammered out a new agreement which put the management of the company completely in the hands of Agroceres and gave the Agroceres shareholders the first option to buy control of SASA *if* IBEC ever chose to sell its controlling interest. IBEC was no longer committed to selling majority ownership within ten years,

38. W. D. Bradford to John Lockwood, June 2, 1950, p. 1. RAC, IBEC, Microfilm Roll J-16.
39. Interview with IBEC Vice President W. D. Bradford by Wayne Broehl (undated), p. 9. RAC, Broehl Papers, Box 18, Folder: "Interview-Bradford." Rodman Rockefeller provided information on the "very important corporate problem" of IBEC's profit and loss statement in the author's interview with him.
40. Lockwood to Vandenberg, April 24, 1950, p. 1. RAC, Broehl Papers, Box 17, Folder "SASA (Brazil) II."

and the Agroceres partners accepted a smaller total percentage (approximately 36 percent) of a larger, more valuable company.[41]

The strengthening of the company's resources came none too soon. The expansion which Rockefeller had encouraged Secundino to undertake produced a yield of 1,078 tons of seed in 1950, five times the previous year's harvest. The overall Brazilian harvest was also good that year, but because of Brazil's perennially inadequate storage facilities, the abundance quickly became overabundance. The price of corn dropped swiftly, and farmers stopped buying hybrid seed. SASA sold less than half of the seed it had grown, and over the next year and a half lost nearly $3 million cruzeiros—practically the entire value of the company before the merger. The relative inexperience of SASA's sales organization contributed somewhat to the problem, as did the general lack of trust among Brazilian farmers for agricultural innovations. Also, it was especially difficult to convince farmers to use corn hybrids because the seed had to be purchased anew each year. Unlike hybrid wheat seeds, which are self-pollinating and reproduce themselves unchanged, corn is an open pollinated plant which produces inferior seeds in the next generation.

As sales sunk lower and lower, so did the morale of the SASA staff and especially the Brazilian partners, who had put all of their life savings into the struggling company. Antônio Secundino had to borrow money from his father-in-law to meet expenses, and IBEC officials were seriously worried that he might just "throw in the sponge." John Griffing, an AIA extension organizer and SASA board member who was an old friend of Secundino, commented, "I have never seen a person more discouraged. . . . The item which really depresses Secundino is the dim outlook for the future." Another IBEC official relayed the information that "at his age and in his financial circumstances, Tony thinks the time has come to decide whether to go on or to establish himself in some other position, such as teaching, where he will have security."[42]

But Secundino was not a person to give up easily. His aggressiveness in fighting for the company and for the interests of its smaller partners never flagged. Coming from a large and well-respected family in Minas Gerais, he had a strong sense of what SASA would accomplish for Brazil if the company could survive. He was also determined that the agronomists and other staff whom he had persuaded to buy shares in SASA would not

41. See the text of the merger agreement between SASA and Agroceres, "Outline of Basic Points," September 20, 1950. RAC, IBEC, Microfilm Roll J-16.
42. See John Griffing to Arthur Vandenberg, Jr., October 30, 1951, p. 1; and Robert Fulton, Jr., to W. D. Bradford, December 5, 1951, p. 1. RAC, IBEC, Microfilm Roll J-14.

lose their investment. Secundino kept local IBEC representatives constantly informed of his concerns, and these individuals directed a steady stream of mail back to New York advising low-interest loans and other assistance from the parent company. IBEC came through with loans, and Nelson Rockefeller purchased one of SASA's farms (at a higher price than Secundino requested) in order to provide the company with working capital. The farm was leased back to the company until SASA was able to repurchase it.[43]

Within a few months, SASA pulled out of the crisis. In 1952, the company grew more corn than it had during the bumper crop of 1950, but this time sold its entire tonnage. Farmers were becoming familiar with the seed and were less likely to drop it in a panic. It still had to be rationed occasionally as demand grew. The seed was popular not only because it was prolific and resistant to environmental problems, but also because it produced a kind of corn that had a softer kernel. Semitropical strains of corn tended to have large, hard kernels, and Gladstone Drummond, SASA's chief geneticist, had developed a variety that was more appealing. Consequently, SASA was strongly competitive with the only other source of hybrid seed in Brazil, the São Paulo Department of Agriculture. Although the São Paulo hybrid was heavily subsidized by the state, both paulistas and farmers in Paraná and Minas Gerais were frequently willing to pay considerably more for the soft hybrid.

SASA's customers remained faithful even when the state dropped its price from 3.60 cruzeiros per kilo to 2 cruzeiros, following the election in 1950 of nationalist candidates at the state and federal levels. SASA kept its price at 5 cruzeiros as long as possible but finally had to raise it in 1951 to 6 cruzeiros (approximately 33 cents) to keep up with expenses, which were approaching 5.73 cruzeiros per kilo. At this point Secundino went to the governor of São Paulo to try to convince him to raise the state's prices even a little to reflect real costs. The bureaucracy yielded slightly, and the state's price went to 3 cruzeiros. When SASA had to raise prices once more in 1952, farmers again demonstrated their willingness to pay more than double for a better product. SASA charged 7 cruzeiros to the state's 3 and still sold more corn than it had in previous years. Although SASA made a policy of not claiming its seed was the best (in order to avoid

---

43. See Broehl's interview with Secundino, July 2, 1964, p. 56. Rockefeller paid $350,000 cruzeiros above the $6 million cruzeiros which Secundino asked for the farm, when an independent appraiser told Rockefeller that it was worth the higher price. Secundino recalled that he was "very impressed" by Rockefeller's honesty. RAC, Broehl Papers, Box 18, Folder: "Interview-Jofre, et al."

friction), newspapers in São Paulo openly called the IBEC variety superior.[44]

From 1952 on, SASA made profits every year and steadily increased the size of its crop and the number of employees. It still had to contend with the boom and bust cycle of Brazilian agriculture which resulted from occasional overproduction and lack of storage facilities throughout the country, but the company was now strong enough to withstand such fluctuations. In 1954, another slow year as a result of another glutted corn market, SASA made a profit of $3.5 million cruzeiros, contrasted with the $3 million cruzeiros it had lost only several years earlier in the previous down cycle. Annual dividends ranged from 10 percent to 18 percent throughout the 1950s and 1960s, and several recapitalizations allowed the company to expand. But instead of growing all of the seed corn itself, SASA contracted increasingly with farmers in São Paulo, Minas Gerais, and Paraná to grow seed under the supervision of company geneticists, thereby enlarging the number of farmers directly associated with the company's good fortunes.

The morale of the company's employees, who represented the bulk of SASA's Brazilian shareholders, grew along with the firm's reputation in Brazil. SASA's product was now doing so well that it sometimes seemed more like popcorn than seed corn. When António Secundino visited one mineiro farmer in 1952 to whom he had sold seeds the previous year, he was shocked to see corn lying all over the farmer's yard. Secundino scolded the farmer for not taking better care of the harvest resulting from SASA's good seeds and pointed out that corn should not be left out in the open to rot. The farmer replied, "It is all your fault. Entirely your fault. Last year all the corn I harvested from my place did not fill that corn crib, but with your seed, the crib is filled, my house is filled, and I had no place to put the rest."[45] Within ten years, 10 percent of all corn planted in Brazil was from SASA seed. By 1962, SASA's profits had zoomed to $60 million cruzeiros a year, and the seed was so popular it was being black-

---

44. *Folha da Manha*, São Paulo, November 11, 1951; *O Estado de São Paulo*, April 27, 1954. Found, respectively, in RAC, IBEC, Microfilm J-14; and the Broehl Papers, Box 17, Folder: "SASA (Brazil) II," Henry Bagley to Francis Jamieson, April 27, 1954. Also see Broehl, *U.S. Business Performance Abroad*, 54–55, for a discussion of SASA's problems with state competition.

45. Reported by W. D. Bradford (in São Paulo) to Robert Fulton, Jr. (New York), October 12, 1952, p. 1. RAC, Broehl Papers, Box 17 Folder: "SASA (Brazil) II." For an account of SASA's tonnage and net profits and losses over the period 1948 to 1954 see "For Annual Report: SASA-Sementes Agroceres, S.A.," June 2, 1955, p. 1–2. RAC, IBEC, Microfilm J-14. This microfilm roll also contains general correspondence through the 1960s documenting SASA's ongoing profitability.

marketed in areas where there was a shortage.[46] Secundino reported "with satisfaction" to the board in 1964 that even the state of São Paulo finally acknowledged the superior accomplishments of SASA's geneticists and had started selling the SASA hybrid through its Farm Bureau offices.[47] It has continued to do so into the 1990s.

But with success came conflicts over control and ownership of the company. From the beginning, António Secundino and Gladstone Drummond, both from families whose histories in Brazil stretched back hundreds of years, saw the company as Brazilian and as theirs. They had developed the hybrids, started Agroceres Limitada, and turned SASA into a national success story. Of course, they had both learned corn hybridization techniques at Iowa State College, and the money on which they had built was American. Because of this, they trusted Rockefeller and initially appreciated the participation of IBEC; but, as Secundino's son (who became president of SASA) bluntly recounted years later, "We readily accepted the investment of IBEC because it was our only way of surviving."[48] In 1951, during the merger of SASA and Agroceres, Secundino had willingly traded the option to purchase control of SASA in ten years for a smaller share of a larger, more stable company. Lacking resources to undertake capital expansion himself, it probably seemed best. But Secundino was never very happy with having lost the option and continued to view the eventual Brazilianization of the company as Rockefeller's moral obligation.[49]

It was a question both of money and control. Secundino chafed under IBEC's reporting requirements and the parent company's desire to hold onto SASA's stocks and the dividends they yielded. "Tony felt the pressure of IBEC," a close friend of António's recalled. "It was hard for him to live with some other entity that was associated with him when he was the one running the show and knew how to run things in Brazil."[50] Secundino needed IBEC's resources, however, and was willing to work with the hope of regaining control someday. In the meantime, he pushed for more for "his" company. In both 1954 and 1956 he successfully lobbied IBEC officials to increase SASA's capitalization. To prevent the Brazilian shareholders' participation from declining relative to IBEC's he argued for new issues of a special kind of stock, called *partes beneficiarias*, which em-

46. Marek Lubomirski to David Haweeli, August 27, 1962, p. 1. RAC, Broehl Papers, Box 17, "SASA (Brazil) II."
47. SASA Board Minutes, May 6, 1964, p. 2. RAC, IBEC, Microfilm J-15.
48. Quote of Ney Bittencourt de Araújo, *O Estado de São Paulo*, October 22, 1986, Agriculture Supplement, p. 8.
49. Interview with Aldrich. Also see Broehl's interview with Secundino, July 2, 1964, p. 57. RAC, Broehl Papers, Box 18, Folder: "Interview-Jofre, et al."
50. Interview with Henry Bagley, New York City, August 5, 1987.

ployees were entitled to buy and pressured IBEC into providing financing so that employees could afford to do so. When Brazilian banks did not have the cash to make short-term farm loans to SASA for its 1954 harvest, Secundino got a loan from IBEC. He even dropped the hint to an IBEC representative that the loan should be at a rate lower than that normally charged by the banks, though IBEC stuck to its policy of not giving a bargain loan to a company of which it did not own 100 percent.

Two years later, in 1956, when IBEC seemed to be stalling on issuing more stock which company employees could buy to retain their ownership percentage, Secundino voiced the concern that IBEC had allowed "the profit motive" to become "overly dominant." That is, he questioned why IBEC insisted on retaining a high percentage of SASA's profitable stocks when it seemed willing to gamble so much money on other development projects which were "heavy losers." An IBEC staffer reported that Secundino seemed to imply that "we are willing to take advantage of our good friends to make some doubtful bets." A few years later, in 1964, when SASA decided to repurchase the farm at Jacarezinho which it had mortgaged to Nelson Rockefeller during the financial crisis of 1951, Secundino negotiated tenaciously for the best price, threatening to resign if it was not low enough and arguing that the original crisis was all Rockefeller's fault anyway, since he had encouraged overproduction.[51]

IBEC officials recognized that Secundino was the key to the company's success as well as a person of dedication and vision, and they cooperated with him consistently. Nevertheless, IBEC representatives became increasingly cautious over the years in dealing with Secundino, who sometimes seemed autonomous to the point of being obstreperous. Vice President Bradford expressed his feeling at one point that Secundino and his colleagues did not seem to recognize the ways in which IBEC had contributed to the company or made it possible for the Brazilians to maintain ownership through the financing of their stock purchases. "We want to be fair with Tony, and I don't have to tell you that we want him and his men happy," Bradford wrote in a confidential letter to another colleague. "Why, however," he questioned, "is it necessary for IBEC always to have to contribute or give up something in order to keep good morale?"[52]

From a business point of view, it made eminently good sense to hold

51. See memos from António Secundino to Richard Greenbaum, September 20, 1956; W. D. Bradford to Richard Greenebaum, January 22, 1957; and F. A. Jamieson to W. B. Stroud, December 13, 1956 (RAC, IBEC, J 16). Also see Marek Lubomirski to Richard Aldrich, September 30, 1964 (RAC, Broehl Papers, Box 17, "SASA, Brazil, I") and Henry Bagley to Francis Jamieson, October 6, 1954 (RAC, R.G. 2, P.R., Box 4, Folder: "SASA-Brazil").
52. W. D. Bradford to Richard W. Greenebaum, January 22, 1957, p. 1. RAC, IBEC, Microfilm J-16.

onto a strong company, when so many of the development projects IBEC had entered into elsewhere had a hit-and-miss record. In addition to its projects in Brazil, IBEC had by the late 1950s expanded operations throughout much of the rest of Latin America and even into Spain and Italy. Since projects in these countries were frequently a risky proposition, IBEC started buying companies in the United States which generated strong profits in order to stabilize its own operations and cover its high research and development costs. IBEC officials saw the profits they made from these U.S. companies and from SASA as a fair return on investment, not as an example of "taking advantage of good friends." Indeed, only with profits could IBEC hope to set an example to other American companies or generate the income necessary to carry development to other countries or other parts of Brazil. Expansion involved "substantial cash requirements," as Rockefeller put it to one staff member in Brazil, "and one of the most important sources of cash is dividends from the successful operating companies like . . . SASA."[53]

But holding onto SASA beyond the time it became a success also meant violating the spirit of the original agreement with the Brazilian partners as well as IBEC's own principles. According to IBEC vice-president Richard Aldrich, Nelson Rockefeller's first cousin and the head of IBEC in Brazil during the mid-1950s, it was "a fundamental mistake" which eventually cost SASA some of its dynamism as a company. In his later view, IBEC should either have offered to buy out Secundino and Drummond at "a price which represented their blood, sweat, and tears over the years" or sold the company in its entirety to the Brazilians. But at the time, Aldrich and other managers responsible for IBEC operations in Brazil could not bring themselves to recommend selling off their best asset, and they were not ready either to embrace completely the business-first approach of buying out the local partners. Perhaps if other IBEC ventures had been more successful, as originally envisioned, they would have suggested to Rockefeller that he sell majority control. As it was, says Aldrich, "we sort of sat on our hands for awhile."[54]

By the mid-1960s, Aldrich was concerned enough about SASA's "vulnerability" and autonomy to appoint a young American as a special assistant to Secundino, "to draw SASA closer to the IBEC organization." Somewhat earlier Aldrich had conveyed to another representative of IBEC in Brazil his fear that any overt attempts "to step in and make management changes *could* result in the deliberate miscrossing of [ge-

53. Nelson Rockefeller to Richard Greenebaum (São Paulo), May 28, 1956, p. 1. RAC, Broehl Papers, Box 17, "SASA (Brazil) II."
54. Interview with Richard Aldrich.

netic] matrices" by SASA's agronomists. He noted, though, that the Brazilians stood to lose almost as much from sabotaging the company as the Americans: "A determent to such a move is the fact that many of the managers are shareholders of SASA and any such move or moves would hit them right in the pocketbook."[55] Nevertheless, Aldrich recognized, as he later recalled, "there was a point in time when those boys were ready to do about anything that would enable them to get the company back— and properly so. They had an expectation!"[56]

What mistrust there was of Secundino's staff did not seem to extend to him personally, however. While there had been numerous tough negotiations and sore points over the years, including bitterness over the question of ownership, the years gave depth and stability to the relationship between SASA and IBEC, which at root was a reflection of the relationship between Nelson Rockefeller and António Secundino. Rockefeller had left the presidency of IBEC in 1958, when he won the governorship of New York. He entrusted most day-to-day and even major policy decisions to younger men, such as Richard Aldrich, whom he felt he had indoctrinated sufficiently in the IBEC philosophy. But it was still Nelson whom António saw as the ultimate recourse. According to Aldrich, whenever Rockefeller visited Brazil, Secundino "would never let him forget" the original IBEC agreement to sell majority ownership to the Brazilians. Rockefeller would then inquire of Aldrich and others what was being done about the problem, and whether or not it was yet possible to honor the original arrangement. When Secundino was in a position to propose a buy-out of SASA by Brazilians in 1968, it was to Nelson he appealed, as a friend, harking back to their very first meeting at the Copacabana Hotel in 1946.[57] But business was one thing, and friendship another. SASA was just not for sale—yet.

Fundo Crescinco

At a congressional hearing in the early 1940s, a representative asked Nelson Rockefeller, "What does South America need?" Rockefeller responded, "I think it needs a great middle class of people such as we have in the United States."[58] To Rockefeller, as to many North Americans,

55. Richard Aldrich to Hans Horch, June 23, 1966, p. 1, and June 22, 1967, p. 1. RAC, IBEC, Microfilm J-16.
56. Interview with Richard Aldrich.
57. António Secundino to Nelson Rockefeller, March 31, 1968. RAC, Friele Papers, Box 2, Folder: "Rodman Rockefeller."
58. Quote cited in Hearings Before the House Committee on Foreign Affairs, *International Cooperation Act of 1949 ("Point IV" Program)*, (Washington: GPO, 1950) 91. This section on Fundo Crescinco first appeared in *Business History Review* 63, no. 1, 88–121.

the class structure in Latin America in the early twentieth century must have seemed nearly feudal. In Brazil as elsewhere in Latin America, land barons held most of the wealth of the country, dominated politics, and frequently had little interest in making agricultural improvements on the vast hereditary lands over which they ruled and on which succeeding peasant generations eked out a meager living for themselves and a comfortable living for their masters. Rockefeller, like much of the development-minded Brazilian elite, believed that the solution to Latin American economic problems was an enlightened (corporatist) capitalism. But a capitalist system required a capitalist class structure, not a feudal one.

In the 1940s, IBEC developed projects designed, in part, to foster the agricultural basis for an industrial working class through increased farm productivity. Greater productivity would enable fewer workers to produce adequate food for growing urban populations and ease the strains caused by rural folk migrating to the cities to find industrial wage labor. In the 1950s, IBEC would turn its attention toward the development of the middle class, the symbol and bulwark, as Rockefeller had noted, of North American capitalism. In Brazil, through a stock mutual fund called Fundo Crescinco, IBEC sought to create opportunities for the growth of middle-class wealth and the stimulation of middle-class interest in Brazil's economic development.

Fundo Crescinco's objectives reflected several key points in Brazilian and American thinking about development at the time, both in university and government circles. As an academic topic, "development economics" came into its own in the 1950s, spurred on by the creation of international planning groups such as the United States Economic Commission on Latin America and in the United States by the experience of the Marshall Plan and Point Four. In the resulting discussions about development, U.S. social scientists of the eminence of W. W. Rostow, Max Millikan, Seymour Martin Lipset, and Gabriel Almond and historians such as Louis Hartz, David Potter, and Carl Degler debated the applicability of American economic and political experience to the third world. As Robert Packenham has shown in *Liberal America and the Third World*, their debates, even when they concluded that the American experience was too exceptional to be a useful model, profoundly influenced the assumptions and design of American foreign aid.[59]

Among these assumptions was the notion that democracy is not a matter of will (laws and formal constitutions) but a matter of money

59. See esp. 4–5, 199–218.

(wealth and industrialization); that is, that economic development is the first building block of a stable, free society, both because a large middle class represents the spreading of abundance throughout the social structure and because the middle class has historically been the strongest supporter of liberal, democratic principles. Fundo Crescinco was conceived as a perfect way of putting these ideas into action by strengthening the middle class and harnessing local resources for economic development. Thus, for Rockefeller, democratization and social reform were not tangential to business and development, but resulted from them.

Fundo Crescinco's objectives were also linked to government policy discussions. A part of all conversations between U.S. and Brazilian officials revolved around how Brazil could raise local funds to match public loans or private investments coming from the United States. Although officials usually could not agree on how much money should be forthcoming from the United States, they unanimously accepted that Brazilians themselves would have to provide a major portion of the financing for development (especially the portion which could be paid for in local currency). Yet not all of the necessary funds could come from the Brazilian government, any more than all of it could come from the U.S. government. In both countries, private resources far outweighed government resources, and practicality as well as capitalist ideology dictated that private savings would have to be mobilized.

As chairman of President Truman's advisory committee on Point Four, Rockefeller was well aware of the difficulties in raising local capital. He was also a participant in exploring solutions at both the private and public levels. The Point Four report, issued by Rockefeller's committee in March 1951, took Brazil as its example of an underdeveloped country in which local savings were not well utilized. Of the $13 domestic savings per capita in 1947, only $6 went into genuinely productive investment, "as against $90 for Norway, $50 for the United Kingdom, and $35 for France and the Low Countries." In most underdeveloped countries, the report noted, "the bulk of savings traditionally finds its way into land holdings, buildings, or hoardings."[60]

At the governmental level, methods for raising local capital were a central concern of the Joint Brazil-U.S. Economic Development Commission. The commission's projects had been designed with the understanding that they would be financed equally by the Brazilian government and the World Bank and to a lesser extent Eximbank. The Brazilian section of the commission, working with Finance Minister Horácio Lafer, devised a

60. *Partners in Progress*, p. 84.

plan for raising income taxes by 15 percent for individuals in the highest income brackets for a period of five years. The revenue generated would go to create the BNDE, which in turn would provide local currency loans for the commission's projects. On December 5, 1951, after much partisan debate, the Brazilian congress passed the Lafer Plan.[61]

At the same time that Lafer and the joint commission were searching for ways to fill government coffers for development, Nelson Rockefeller and IBEC were exploring new ways to channel private resources. David Rockefeller, head of the Chase National Bank and Nelson's youngest brother, had the idea of creating an investment banking firm which would underwrite and sell stocks in Brazilian companies. The overwhelming majority of Brazilian corporations at the time were family owned and allowed for limited or no equity participation by outsiders. So few stocks were available to the general public that the Rio and São Paulo exchanges scheduled only thirty minutes a day for trading in corporate stocks and bonds. Securities in about one hundred companies, out of several thousand listed, were actually traded, of which only twenty to fifty were active. The only venture in which a small investor could hold shares was real estate deals: apartment houses, office buildings, and plots of land held for speculation.

David Rockefeller's idea, which Nelson and the staff of IBEC quickly embraced, was to encourage businesses to take their shares public by setting up an investment banking company to sell the stocks. Corporations which could contribute to development would gain new resources; the small investor would have new opportunities for nonspeculative earnings in productive enterprises; and Brazil would have the beginnings of a domestic money market. Of course, if the scheme was successful, Chase National Bank and IBEC would be in on the ground floor of a new, highly profitable business which they could expect to dominate at least for awhile. But Brazil would benefit, too, and so the firm would fulfill IBEC's dual goals of profit for its owners and progress for the host country. As Arthur Vandenberg, Jr., expressed to Francis Jamieson, "The establishment of a capital market would give the same advantages to Brazil that have been basic in the economic progress of the United States." In addition, Vandenberg noted, "the availability of reliable securities . . . will encourage the man of moderate income to save his money."[62]

61. *Diccionário Histórico-Biográfico Brasileiro*, 1735.
62. Arthur Vandenberg, Jr., to Francis Jamieson, July 6, 1951, p. 2. Also see Howard N. Knowles to Francis Jamieson, December 14, 1950, p. 1. The second letter attributes the inspiration for the investment firm to David Rockefeller, who, Knowles said, was "depend-

In 1951, David Rockefeller, who had been to South America before in Nelson's company, traveled to Brazil to launch the Interamerican Finance and Investment Corporation. IBEC and Chase National Bank took 52 percent of the stock of Interamericana, and fourteen Brazilian banks owned the remaining 48 percent. Interamericana was capitalized at $2.7 million at the official exchange rate, with IBEC and Chase purchasing their share of the stock in dollars. Consistent with its goal of serving as a model of American behavior for both Latin American and U.S. audiences, IBEC issued a press release tying Interamericana to general U.S. support for Brazilian development: "This is . . . in accord with the policies of the United States Government for promoting international development, including participation in the joint U.S.-Brazil Commission for Economic Development . . . [and will] contribute to the expanding economic strength of the Western Hemisphere."[63]

But Interamericana's contributions were cut short by a lack of success. Although it made a nominal profit in two of its first three years, in the fourth year it lost nearly $16 million cruzeiros (US $808,000) and had to be reorganized. A few months later it was disbanded. The problems which overwhelmed Interamericana were in essence the same ones it had set out to solve. Small investors had little experience with securities and had to be convinced not only of the merits of each stock or bond, but of the rationality of investing in securities at all. Brazil experienced marked, if typical, financial instability during this period (1951–55), and investors were apt to sell at the slightest indication of a downturn. Interamericana also had difficulty finding enough companies interested in selling new issues of their stock. New stock issues sold slowly because of the low demand for securities, and this was disconcerting for the company offering the stock. Brazilian law did not help, since it required that capital increases be declared null and void if not every share was sold. Interamericana's business was based on selling new stock issues, and there were just not enough of them to sustain the company. Within two years, as a vice president of IBEC later recalled, Interamericana "had gotten all [the stock] that was readily available and so at this point losses began to develop purely because of lack of securities to distribute."[64]

---

ing on NAR to go along with him." RAC, R.G. 2, P.R., Box 4, Folder: "IBEC-Chase National Bank." For the background to Fundo Crescinco see Broehl, *U.S. Business Performance Abroad*, 160–66.

63. July 18, 1951, p. 2. RAC, R.G. 2, P.R., Box 4, Folder: "IBEC-Chase National Bank."
64. Interview with W. D. Bradford by Wayne Broehl, p. 115. RAC, Broehl Papers, Box 18, Folder: "Interview-Bradford."

According to Richard Aldrich, however, Interamericana's downfall re-sulted mainly from a weakness built into the organization itself. As a wholesaler of securities, the investment company did not have its own sales staff and was thus dependent on the local banks that were its part-ners to sell the stocks and bonds to their customers. But for the banks this represented an inherent and natural conflict of interest, since banks are designed to funnel customer deposits not into securities, but into savings, which the bank can then use to make profitable loans. As Aldrich put it, selling securities for Interamericana placed a bank in the position of "competing with itself, in a certain sense, in a side of the business which is probably not as beneficial to it as is the use of those depositors' money to create higher profits for the bank."[65]

In 1956 IBEC staff began studying the possibility of reorganizing Inter-americana's resources into an open-ended mutual fund. Mutual funds had emerged as popular financial institutions in the United States during World War II, appealing especially to small investors who, having experi-enced the Great Depression, were looking for financial stability. U.S. experts hailed mutual funds as "a cure-all for our present [domestic] equity and venture capital problem, a strong bulwark against encroach-ing socialism, and the one bright hope on the dim financial horizon for awakening mass interest in securities. . . . creating [thereby] hundreds of thousands of new capitalists among the broader segment of the public . . . who previously were not investors in securities."[66] Remarkably, these domestic goals were almost identical to IBEC's international goals: that is, stimulating the accumulation of venture capital, reinforcing capital-ism, and building middle-class participation in stock ownership. IBEC's consideration of a mutual fund model for Brazil shows how short an interval there was between innovations in the United States (rural exten-sion, corn hybridization, and mutual funds) and the Rockefellers' appli-cation of them abroad.

In Brazil, the mutual fund would have several advantages over the investment company. It would not only employ its own sales representa-tives, but by its very nature would absorb some of the burden of making the complex investment decisions which Interamericana had expected the unsophisticated Brazilian investor to make. Whereas Interamericana had offered stock in a variety of corporations, the mutual fund would offer only one kind of share: its own. Small investors would not have to decide which corporations provided the best income at the least risk. They

65. Interview with Aldrich.
66. William D. Carter, "Mutual Investment Funds," *Harvard Business Review* (November 1949): 716.

would also have instant liquidity for their assets. Instead of buying corporate stocks which they might or might not be able to resell quickly (since demand was sluggish), they could buy shares in a mutual fund which the fund itself would redeem on demand.[67]

The fund could then purchase or sell securities in a wide variety of Brazilian companies, thereby stimulating development of the Brazilian stock market while earning dividends for its investors. Also, unlike Interamericana, the mutual fund would not concentrate on new stock issues alone and would thus have more investment options as well as provide a stimulus to the trading of existing issues. Both the fund and the individual investor would be supporting the development of the private sector as a whole, not just individual companies.

Before the mutual fund could be organized, the losses of Interamericana had to be accounted for. Chase made it clear that the bank was not interested in another gamble, so IBEC acquired all of Chase's shares in Interamericana, the two corporations sharing the capital losses in proportion to their original holdings. Nelson and David Rockefeller agreed that IBEC and Chase National Bank would absorb all of the cruzeiro losses of the fourteen participating Brazilian banks and offered either a cash repayment equal to the original investment or an equivalent holding in shares of the new mutual fund. To the Rockefellers' relief, twelve of the fourteen banks agreed to accept shares in the fund and to hold them for at least one year. Still, it remained a point of honor with Nelson Rockefeller that IBEC was "willing always to pay back to anyone any amount of investment on demand of the person."[68] It was a generous policy, although from a business point of view one perhaps better suited to an American bank with insured deposits than to a development company trying to introduce new ideas, methods, and products into a foreign country. From a political point of view, the policy ensured that Brazilians always saw Nelson Rockefeller as a benefactor first and a businessman second, if they saw him as a businessman at all.

By February 1957, the initial $30-million-cruzeiro fund (US $465,000) consisting of IBEC's and the banks' shares had been invested in a portfolio of Brazilian stocks, and Crescinco was ready to sell shares to the public. IBEC managed the fund through a wholly owned subsidiary called Empreendimentos (undertakings), which was to make money for IBEC by

67. At least one Brazilian warned Nelson Rockefeller that Interamaricana had been operating "in too sophisticated a manner for the Brazilian market." Interview with Jayme Bastian Pinto by Wayne Broehl, Rio de Janeiro, July 7, 1964, p. 107. RAC, Broehl Papers, Box 18, Folder: "Interview with Jofre, et al."
68. Interview with Nelson Rockefeller by Wayne Broehl, July 12, 1965, p. 7. RAC, Broehl Papers, Box 18, "Interview-NAR."

charging an annual management fee of 2 percent of the fund's total value. To hire a sales staff and lease an office for Empreendimentos, IBEC put up an additional $25,000 in new venture capital.[69]

Since Brazilian law, based on Napoleonic Code, did not specifically allow for such a thing as a mutual fund, Fundo Crescinco itself was unincorporated. Empreendimentos used a Brazilian legal device called the *condomínio* to undertake an individual contract with each purchaser of the shares. The contract allowed Empreendimentos to add the investor's assets to those of the other shareholders and to invest the funds. The condomínio arrangement prevented double taxation of the fund and the investor. Shareholders were taxed individually and, as in a real estate condominium, could sell their assets at will, without consulting the other shareholders.[70] To ensure that Crescinco would not take over the weak capital market or control major industries, IBEC promised the government it would not put more than 10 percent of its total assets in any one company or buy more than 22 percent of the voting stock of any corporation.

Rockefeller's public relations staff worried about possible reactions to the fund. Although the reception of Interamericana had been positive overall, IBEC had nonetheless had to weather some resistance and opposition arising from the linking of the Rockefeller name with foreign banking. *Ultima Hora,* a moderate nationalist paper close to President Vargas, had initially opposed the investment program in 1951, and Rio's *Emancipação*, a newspaper published by military officers favoring the nationalization of Brazil's oil, had called Interamericana "a powerful weapon set up in our country by the American monopolies, which will complete the action of the Bohan Mission [the joint commission]." Let Brazilians take heed, *Emancipação* editorialized, "for the enemy loses no time and is closing his tentacles."[71]

Opposition to Interamericana died down, but those paid to protect the Rockefeller name expressed reservations about opening the mutual fund to public participation. One IBEC official wrote to the chief public relations man, Francis Jamieson, that the risks seemed "unusually large" and that Nelson might expose himself to criticisms from unhappy shareholders as well as to "accusations from nationalist elements and the left as using an indirect device to extend his influence over basic Brazilian industries." Henry Bagley, Rockefeller's chief publicist in Brazil, said that even

69. Author's telephone conversation with Richard Aldrich, October 4, 1988 (hereafter, conversation with Aldrich).
70. Broehl, *U.S. Business Performance Abroad,* 166–67.
71. Quotes from *Emancipação*, translated by Henry Bagley for Francis Jamieson, August 21, 1951, p. 3. Also see p. 1 of Bagley's August 13, 1951, letter to Jamieson, recounting the

he "had a hard time swallowing this as something that was going to be of benefit to Brazil" and not simply an opportunity to bet on the stock market. Following discussions with IBEC's leaders, however, Bagley and others became convinced that the fund "would bring a lot of money— unproductive money because it was in the mattress or it was in the teapot—into circulation for the benefit of those who were holding it in the mattress or the teapot." And so the publicists set to work.[72]

Crescinco was launched with "very good propaganda—American style," Finance Minister Lucas Lopes later said, recalling colorful banners which lined the streets of Rio de Janeiro.[73] Advertisements in the major newspapers ran a picture of a smiling Brazilian holding a Crescinco certificate alongside text which explained that the investor would go forward with Brazilian business, industry, and agriculture. Response to the news was favorable, especially considering that Rockefeller would not allow his publicity staff to pay for coverage by the media (a common practice at the time), with the exception of advertising. In a summary of AIA and IBEC press coverage by Brazilian newspapers in the month preceding the opening of sales, Henry Bagley noted sixty-four mentions of the various Rockefeller projects, of which thirty-six were emphatically favorable, twenty-one neutral, and only seven unfavorable. Even the unfavorable mentions were rarely harsh or damning; they simply reported downturns in IBEC's businesses. The launching of Crescinco had evidently not damaged the Rockefeller name, and the Rockefeller name had not damaged the mutual fund's chances with the Brazilian public.[74]

The shares sold slowly but steadily to a cross section of the public. IBEC found over three hundred small-time entrepreneurs (from the manager of the steambath at Rio's Hotel Gloria to prostitutes in Recife) to take the shares almost door to door. Shares were priced at $100 cruzeiros per unit, which at the free market rate of 64.5 cruzeiros to the dollar cost approximately $1.55. To obtain the maximum number of investors possible, IBEC initially allowed investors to purchase as few as ten shares at a time, at a cost of $1,000 cruzeiros ($15.50). Because the cost of processing such small units was relatively high, however, IBEC soon raised the minimum initial purchase to $20,000 cruzeiros ($310) and the minimum

opposition of the newspaper *Ultima Hora* and its editor, Samuel Wainer. RAC, R.G. 2, P.R., Box 4, Folder: "IBEC-Chase National Bank."

72. Fred Gardner to Francis Jamieson, June 19, 1956, p. 1. The next day, Jamieson passed the letter to Rockefeller for his personal consideration. RAC, R.G. 2, P.R., Box 4, "Interamericana Finance and Investment Company." Quotes from Bagley taken from author's interview.

73. Interview with Lucas Lopes.

74. Bagley to Jamieson, January 30, 1957. RAC, R.G. 2, P.R., Box 12, Folder: "Bagley, Jan.-Dec. 1957."

reinvestment to $5,000 cruzeiros ($77.50). After eight months, in September 1957, Crescinco distributed its first dividend, $2 cruzeiros per share. Over 75 percent of the 925 shareholders decided to reinvest, and by the end of the year almost 1,400 people held stock in Crescinco. The value of the fund had increased from $30 million cruzeiros to $90 million. After this, the number of investors and the value of the fund grew steadily. In 1965, IBEC reported its success to USAID in the following terms:

At 12/31	Investors	Cruzeiros
1957	1400	90,000,000
1959	8,400	983,000,000
1960	14,400	2,561,000,000
1962	27,700	12,282,000,000
1963	44,800	23,090,000,000[75]

The fund's popularity was enhanced by two factors. First, it contributed to the development of Brazilian-owned enterprises. As of 1962, 85 percent of Crescinco's securities portfolio was invested in Brazilian companies, with 77 percent in industrial, mining, and utilities stocks and 8 percent in Brazilian bank stocks. The remainder of the fund's assets were in cash and government bonds (10 percent) and in U.S. companies which owned subsidiaries or did significant business in Brazil (5 percent). In order to purchase foreign securities, IBEC set up a separate corporation in the United States, Crescinco Investments, Inc., which was wholly owned by the Brazilian fund. Although IBEC officials were sensitive about complaints that a portion of the funds was going to capitalize U.S. businesses, they pointed out that the only way Brazilians could participate in the earnings of companies which made money through foreign subsidiaries was to buy stock of the parent company. So, for example, Crescinco purchased stock in Sears Roebuck and General Motors, which had manufacturing plants in Brazil, and in Studebaker-Packard, which sold cars there.[76]

But the primary reason why Crescinco placed a small percentage of its resources in U.S. investments was to stabilize the overall performance of the fund. In Brazil's highly inflationary economy, it was a constant struggle for the fund to earn enough dividends to stay ahead of monetary

75. Data selected from letter of Richard S. Aldrich to Philip Glaessner, March 17, 1965, p. 2 of appendix. RAC, IBEC, Box 79, Folder: "U.S. Government-Agency for International Development."
76. Richard Greenebaum to Philip Bauer, Jr., November 12, 1959, p. 1–2. RAC, Broehl Papers, Box 7, Folder: "Funds-Brazil, 2."

depreciation and actually make a profit. Since investments made in the United States were in dollars, the value of the stocks tended to climb steadily. That is, dividends were not constantly diminished by falls in the value of the currency, as in Brazil. The U.S. securities could be resold easily, unlike Brazilian stocks, so they also provided liquidity for Crescinco. Considering that investments in Latin America are frequently assumed to yield high profits, it is ironic that Crescinco's managers found the U.S. investments to be "the best part of the Fund as far as performance is concerned."[77]

According to Richard Aldrich, IBEC officials would have liked to put even more than 5 percent of the fund into U.S. securities, but they knew such a move would cause an uproar among Brazilians. Although to do so would have undercut Crescinco's claim to be financing the development of Brazilian companies, it would have increased dividend checks to Crescinco's middle-class investors.[78] Nevertheless, as it was, the overwhelming majority of the fund's investments were in Brazilian enterprises, and IBEC could substantiate its claim of fostering development, especially in industry. During the eleven-year period that IBEC managed the fund (1957–67), the investment pattern was roughly as follows:

Fund Investments (sample years):	1957	1962	1967
(Top four investments by industry by year:)			
Industrial Stocks:	55%	46%	55%
Metallurgy	7.7%	5.5%	11.3%
Electronics	6.6%	0	7.6%
Steel and Iron	4.7%	14.9%	0
Cement	0	4.1%	9%
Textiles	0	7.6%	7.2%
Autos	6.5%		
Food/Beverages:	3%	17%	7%
Retail/Commerce:	6%	14%	14%
Banks	8%	8%	12%
Totals	72%	85%	88%

(The remainder of the portfolio was held in cash, Brazilian government bonds, and U.S. securities. This was especially true during 1957, when the fund was yet to be fully invested.)[79]

77. Ibid., p. 1.
78. Interview with Aldrich.
79. RAC, IBEC, Microfiche Drawer 12, Crescinco Brazil, Annual Reports, 1402–20–01. Information drawn from the first, sixth, and eleventh annual reports.

The second and probably most important factor contributing to Crescinco's growing popularity was the fund's steady earnings. To provide some measure by which Crescinco's performance could be evaluated as well as to educate investors about the workings of capitalism, Crescinco published frequent reports comparing increases in the value of shares to increases in the cost of living, the value of the cruzeiro against the dollar, and even the Dow Jones Index in New York. Using 1957 as its base year, Crescinco reported both the cruzeiro earnings of its shares and the value of the earnings once they had been deflated for the rising cost of living. By applying the inflation estimates of the Fundação Getúlio Vargas in Rio de Janeiro, Crescinco was able to show that people who had invested in the fund stayed ahead of the rate of inflation every year between 1957 and 1960 and increased the real cruzeiro value of their holdings. For example, in the first two years, if reinvestment was sustained, a share would have increased in value from $100 cruzeiros to $148, representing a gross profit of 48 percent. Inflation in those years increased the cost of living by 28 percent, resulting in a net profit of 20 percent over two years.[80]

Gross profits for shareholders for the years 1957 to 1962 were as follows:

Year	Without Reinvestment	With Reinvestment
1957	18%	19%
1958	27%	29%
1959	32%	34%
1960	33%	35%
1961	26%	27%
1962	30%	31%[81]

From 1960 to 1965, Crescinco weathered a series of crises arising from political instability in Brazil. As one worried IBEC official wrote to New York, "The market is very instable and weak, reacting violently to rumors of political nature. The investment climate is poor and investors are

80. Broehl, *U.S. Business Performance Abroad*, 168–70. In 1962, IBEC officials estimated conservatively that the average annual return on shares in Crescinco, when all earnings were reinvested, was 29.06 percent. This figure did not reflect the adjustment for inflation, however. José Augusto Ferreira to Richard Aldrich et al., August 24, 1962. RAC, Broehl Papers, box 7, folder: "Fund-Brazil-3."
81. José Augusto Ferreira to Richard Aldrich et al., August 24, 1962. RAC, Broehl Papers, box 7, folder: "Fund-Brazil-3." Also see *Journal of Commerce*, March 10, 1959.

becoming noticeably disinterested in securities."[82] In the face of soaring inflation, the real earnings of shares diminished. By the end of Goulart's presidency, the annual inflation rate was 91 percent, and shares in Crescinco had lost nearly 35 percent of their value as gauged by the cost of living. A thriving, semilegal parallel market in speculative short-term loans (*letras de cambio*) provided heavy competition for Crescinco, which reported all investor earnings for taxation and could not compete, in the highly inflationary market, with the profit rates on loans for which the borrowers were paying interest of 60–100 percent. When a military coup threatened and finally overthrew the chaotic but democratically elected government of João Goulart in 1964, the fund went through its greatest crisis.

Between December 1963 and July 1965, redemptions of Crescinco shares outnumbered purchases two to one. Total sales for the twenty months were $8,116 million cruzeiros, with redemptions totaling $15,195 million cruzeiros. The decline was not straight down, however, as the fund repeatedly gained and then slipped in the market. To survive, Crescinco borrowed money to cover redemptions, selectively sold some of its less interesting stocks and, toward the end of the crisis, reluctantly allowed its sales staff to trade letras de cambio in order to keep a core of people working. At one point IBEC officials seriously considered suspending redemptions, but in the end managed to hold on a little longer. The fund squeaked by on a narrow margin.

Crescinco began to turn around in July 1965, when it registered its last negative balance and when the military government passed a series of amendments to the banking laws. At the beginning of 1965, IBEC vice-president Richard Aldrich and the president of Empreendimentos, Humberto Monteiro, had written to President Humberto Castelo Branco protesting the unfair advantages of letras de cambio and suggesting greater regulation. They pointed out that since the letras were in "bearer form," the investor purchasing them could remain anonymous and thereby evade income taxes on the high profits earned. In March a group of businessmen suggested to Marek Lubomirski, the financial representative of IBEC in Brazil, that the time was propitious to approach the government again about changes in the laws. The government would listen, it was suggested confidentially, because the military regime was "very much under the influence of U.S. financial and economic advisors and . . . their recommendations are usually taken seriously and fol-

82. Marek Lubomirski to Richard Aldrich, January 22, 1964, p. 1. RAC, Broehl Papers, Box 7, "Fund-Brazil, 3."

lowed." Lubomirski noted that any communication would have to come from experts in the United States, since suggestions from IBEC representatives in Brazil would be seen as self-interested. Aldrich, then based in New York, responded with a letter to Roberto Campos, minister of development. The letras, he emphasized, contributed not only to income tax evasion, but also to Brazil's exorbitant domestic interest rates. The "inflationary effects" could not "be helpful to the objectives which I know you are seeking," Aldrich wrote diplomatically.[83]

Finance companies which routinely handled letras de cambio mounted a vocal but ultimately unsuccessful opposition to any reform. IBEC cooperated with other fledgling mutual funds (formed after Fundo Crescinco) to counteract the lobbying of the finance companies and coordinated its campaign with blue chip companies on the stock exchange that were also concerned about the undermining of the securities market.

When the new banking law was passed it could not have fit Crescinco's needs more closely. Tax incentives were established for companies which offered their stock to the public instead of maintaining a closed ownership and for the people who invested in them; stamp taxes were eliminated on the transfer of shares to facilitate legal trade, as opposed to sales under the table; and all letras had to be registered so that their owners could not evade taxes. A Fundo Crescinco official wrote to IBEC's New York headquarters with some satisfaction, "I will say that we have contributed substantially to the drafting of this law. We worked through the Association of Credit and Investment Companies, the so-called Working Group of Mutual Funds, and directly as Crescinco, IBEC, etc. We talked to ministers, government officials and anyone else who would listen to us, and what the government would not agree to put in the law we managed to have included via various senators who agreed to submit amendments suggested by us."[84] The fund regained its prosperity under the rulings, and by 1968 Fundo Crescinco was the largest mutual fund outside of the United States and Europe.

The goal of the Brazilian middle and upper classes was to become a modern capitalist nation, and in this light the new laws made sense for the country as well as for Crescinco. As for the judgment of history and Rockefeller's goal of furthering an enlightened capitalist democracy, it

83. Richard Aldrich and Humberto Monteiro to Marshall Humberto de Castello Branco, January 18, 1965; Marek Lubomirski to Richard Aldrich, March 5, 1965, p. 1; Richard Aldrich to Roberto Campos, March 9, 1965, p. 2. RAC, Broehl Papers, Box 7, "Fund-Brazil, 3."
84. Marek Lubomirski to Robert Purcell, July 6, 1965. RAC, Broehl Papers, box 7, folder: "Fund-Brazil-3." Also see Lubomirski to Aldrich, April 1, 1965, same folder.

was ironic that these advances were associated with a military dictatorship. But Rockefeller, like most U.S. businessmen, made it a policy to deal with whomever was in power without regard to their party or how they came to power. For this reason, the Rockefeller projects obtained political support from all administrations in the democratic period from 1946 to 1964. What is most relevant for this analysis is that the laws which were passed were patently not of a type which only a military government could force on the market. One can easily imagine them as part of the kind of clean sweep of corruption campaign waged by President Jânio Quadros in 1960.

Interestingly, IBEC's records only rarely mention Brazilian politics or politicians, and IBEC's responses to the instability were above all businesslike. This may have been a matter of practicality rather than philosophy, however, at least on the part of some IBEC officials. According to Aldrich, any kind of participation by the corporation in the coup of 1964 would have placed it in a position of extreme vulnerability. Like other U.S. companies of this era, IBEC maintained an officially neutral stance toward changes in regime as the price of economic security in a nationalist environment. There is no evidence in IBEC's existing records or from IBEC's Brazilian partners of political improprieties or even of substantial political concerns on the part of the corporation—in fact quite the opposite is true, a circumstance no doubt influenced by Rockefeller's insistence on maintaining good relations across the spectrum of Brazilian politics.[85]

The Brazilian Response, Profits, and the End of IBEC

At the end of IBEC's first year, Francis Jamieson had assured Nelson Rockefeller that "our projects themselves, the course they take, and their success will naturally be the most effective method of answering the criticism both of the past and that to come."[86] But the name *Nelson*

---

85. There is one important fact which should be mentioned as a possible caveat to the assertion that IBEC did not intervene in politics. Richard Aldrich claims to have worked for the Central Intelligence Agency (CIA) at points in his career, although not in Brazil. In his vice-presidential confirmation hearings, Nelson Rockefeller alluded to his cousin's CIA connection. Unfortunately, the classified status of CIA personnel records does not permit an investigation either of Aldrich's status or of its relevance to Brazil. Interview with Aldrich; see also Hearings, Senate Committee on Rules and Administration, *Nomination of Nelson A. Rockefeller of New York to be Vice-President of the United States* (Washington, D.C.: GPO, 1974), 544.

86. Francis Jamieson to Nelson Rockefeller, November 21, 1947, p. 2. RAC, R.G. 2, P.R., Box 4, "IBEC-General."

Rockefeller loomed so large in the public mind that the projects were frequently overshadowed by responses to the person and persona behind them. Brazilians who were aware of Rockefeller could be divided into two categories: those who thought of him as "Nelson" (as one Rio newspaper, in the tradition of calling popular Brazilian leaders by their first name, put it) and those who thought of him as "Rockefeller." Henry Bagley found when he went to work as a publicist for AIA and IBEC in 1950 that he had to contend frequently with Rockefeller as "a big money, business, exploitive name—John D. Rockefeller, Sr., having set that pattern." The problem for Bagley was that because the grandfather was known as one of the robber barons "it was assumed that all Rockefellers were therefore robber barons."[87]

Nevertheless, in the 1940s and 1950s, during the twenty-year period that Nelson Rockefeller was personally most active in affairs in Brazil (before the governorship of New York and national political aspirations led him to focus on interests elsewhere), he was well liked and much respected. As appeals to nationalist sentiments became an increasingly important tactic during the late 1950s for discrediting political opponents, who in turn proclaimed themselves more nationalistic yet, *Rockefeller* became a convenient synonym for *North American imperialism*. "The name Rockefeller is known to practically every voter, so it is a fine one to attack," Bagley reported to the New York headquarters. Yet Bagley also noted in the same letter that a prominent politician who had recently criticized Rockefeller in the newspapers was actually not opposed to either Nelson or his work.[88] In 1958, a São Paulo state assemblyman demanded an explanation from Governor Jânio Quadros of his relationship with Nelson and David Rockefeller but withdrew the request for information the next day after it had gotten attention in the newspapers.

On a few occasions Rockefeller was accused of such improbable plots as trying to smuggle coffee seedlings out of Brazil to start a competitive business in neighboring Paraguay and building grain elevators in São Paulo to stockpile food "for use if the U.S. should run out of corn" in an emergency. But the tempests were invariably short-lived. Considering Brazilian nationalism and the connotations of the Rockefeller name, reac-

---

87. Interview with Bagley.
88. Bagley to Jamieson, November 11, 1957, p. 2. RAC, R.G. 2, P.R., Box 12, "Bagley, Jan.-Dec. 1957." The politician Bagley was writing about was Adhemar de Barros, the former populist governor of São Paulo who was then campaigning (unsuccessfully, as it turned out) to regain his position. Barros was famous in Brazilian politics for his opportunism. Among his supporters an unofficial slogan was "Rouba más faz" (He steals, but he gets things done). Skidmore, *Politics in Brazil*, 68.

tion against IBEC and AIA was remarkably mild. Rockefeller's publicity specialists were ever alert for any unfavorable press (they wanted details only on the bad news, Jamieson once reminded Bagley), but during a trip Rockefeller made to Brazil in 1958, Bagley found only 14 unfavorable reports in the press compared with 309 favorable or neutral ones. This was the same year that Vice President Richard Nixon was stoned in Venezuela and hounded in Peru.[89]

Among the many Brazilians who thought of him as *Nelson*, Rockefeller had made an immensely favorable impression from the start. He was "very popular, extremely *simpático*," recalled mineiro Lucas Lopes.[90] At first he was respected as the special emissary of the much-admired Franklin D. Roosevelt. But when Rockefeller came back after the World War II, in spite of the fact that he had lost his position under Truman, he was respected as a man who kept his word and seen as an intermediary between Brazil and the fickle American government. When President Truman named Rockefeller head of the special task force on Point Four, Getúlio Vargas praised the choice and called it "a satisfying demonstration of the interest in neighbor countries which is being shown by the great northern nation." In an editorial criticizing the inadequacies of Point Four, one São Paulo paper made a careful distinction between imperialistic America and Nelson Rockefeller: "As is known, the former Coordinator of Interamerican Affairs in Brazil always was decidedly in favor of many of the solutions suggested by our country, but hiding his disagreement with the narrow and intransigent viewpoint of the State Department and certain groups of American bankers and industrialists who systematically have taken a stand against plans for industrialization not only in Brazil but also in other South American countries."[91]

Brazilians' interest in and affection for Nelson Rockefeller was especially evident in 1959, when it became clear that he was a potential

89. Bagley to Jamieson, January 26, 1959, p. 1. RAC, R.G. 2, P.R., Box 12, folder for 1959. Also see Bagley to Jamieson, February 4, 1958, p. 2, regarding the assemblyman's demands (same record group, Folder: "Bagley-Iron Ore . . . 1958"); Bagley to Jamieson, May 31, 1951, p. 1, regarding grain silos (Folder: "Bagley, Jan.-June 1951); and Bagley to Jamieson, December 26, 1957, p. 1, regarding smuggling accusations (Folder: "Bagley-Coffee").
90. Interview. Alzira Vargas seconded this impression, stating in an interview with the author that Rockefeller "left in the society of Rio very good impressions. Everybody loved Nelson. . . . They trusted Nelson, not the name of Rockefeller." Interview.
91. The Vargas quote was in an interview with Brazilian newspaperman Samuel Wainer and reported to Francis Jamieson by Henry Bagley. Bagley to Jamieson, December 19, 1950, p. 1. Bagley also sent Jamieson the translation of the article on Point Four in *Diário Popular*, along with other clippings criticizing Point Four in *Estado de São Paulo* and *Diário de São Paulo*. Bagley to Jamieson, April 16, 1951, p. 1. RAC, R.G. 2, P.R., Box 12. The letters can be found in Bagley's general files for 1950 and January–June 1951, respectively.

presidential candidate. Newspapers in Brazil followed the Nixon-Rockefeller competition closely. "Brazilians always looked to Nelson as a possible president of America. . . . We always cheered for Nelson," according to Walther Moreira Salles, a business partner and close friend of Rockefeller as well as three-time ambassador to the United States.[92] Even outside of Brazil there was evidence of support for Rockefeller among those concerned with the southern hemisphere, who recognized that his regional bias would likely shift American foreign policy in a direction more favorable to Latin America if he became president. In Venezuela, where IBEC was constantly under suspicion for its connections with the oil companies, an IBEC representative reported that even the Communist press was being "quite discreet" and that no one had criticized Rockefeller's candidacy. "The Venezuelan newspapermen showed clearly their preference for nomination of their 'friend' Nelson and not for Nixon."[93] One well-known North American critic of U.S. policy, Simon Hanson, unexpectedly commented on the potential positive outcomes if Jânio Quadros, who was expected to win the Brazilian presidency, assumed office at the same time that Nelson Rockefeller became the next president of the United States. "If the Quadros-Rockefeller situation develops, as is expected," Hanson wrote, "we shall see economic developments in Brazil at a pace never dreamed of before."[94]

When Rockefeller stepped aside in recognition of Nixon's greater support within the Republican party, Brazilian disappointment was noticeable. One newspaper chain ran an editorial in their Rio, São Paulo, and Belo Horizonte editions which lamented, "Nelson Rockefeller represented, for his country as well as for Latin America and for this moment of history that we are living, a new breath of air, if not a new epoch in American politics. Despite his name, seemingly connected with the old oil capitalism, the present governor of New York represented, on the contrary . . . a consciousness of the new forces in action in the modern world and of the responsibility of the United States, in hemisphere and world policy."[95] A few months later a group of students at the law school of Juiz de Fora in Minas Gerais circulated a petition among the graduat-

92. Interview with Walther Moreira Salles, Rio de Janeiro, November 19, 1986.
93. Bernardo Jofre to Francis Jamieson, May 21, 1959. RAC, IBEC, Microfilm J-6.
94. *Latin American Letter*, August 15, 1959.
95. Editorial by Alceu de Amoroso Lima, printed in *Folha da Manha* (São Paulo), *Diário de Noticias* (Rio), and *O Diário* (Belo). Translated and transmitted to Francis Jamieson by Harry Bagley, January 28, 1960, p. 1. RAC, R.G. 2, P.R., Box 12, "Bagley, Jan.-June 1960." Bagley noted that the author was "a highly regarded writer, particularly respected in Roman Catholic circles."

ing class to name Rockefeller their "sponsor." Although the majority voted to give the honor to one of their professors, spokesmen for the group noted that it was not for "any lack of consideration for Mr. Nelson Rockefeller."[96]

The one reputation which Rockefeller may never have earned in Brazil was that of a businessman. IBEC's whole purpose was to show how American business, American capitalism, could work in harmony with the needs of Latin America. Yet IBEC's choice of projects, particularly in agriculture, and its practice of shielding nationals from economic risk undermined its image as a real business. IBEC was "a curious mixture of business and altruism," according to Roberto Campos. Rockefeller "had certainly business motivation," Campos observed years later, "but he could have picked a good many more quick profit-making operations. . . . Agricultural research is really a long-term proposition which is of doubtful profitability." Oswaldo Gudolle Aranha, son of the statesman and an entrepreneur, simply dismissed Rockefeller as a businessman. "IBEC was something extraordinary. . . . They had a tremendous presence and value in Brazil," Aranha said. "But from my point of view it was never really a business proposition. . . . Nelson never came in profit-minded. IBEC was an exact picture of that. It could never be successful or flourish."[97]

Yet at least some of IBEC's projects did flourish, most notably SASA and Fundo Crescinco. For the first decade, Crescinco appears to have been only a moderate moneymaker for the parent corporation. Since IBEC's shares in the fund barely kept pace with the dollars the company had used to purchase them, most of the profit came from management fees earned by the IBEC-owned Empreendimentos. The business historian Wayne Broehl has conservatively estimated that IBEC earned only $150,000 from the management of Fundo Crescinco between 1957 and 1966.[98] But this figure seems low both to Richard Aldrich and to Rodman Rockefeller, Nelson's oldest son, who became president of IBEC in 1968 and chairman in 1972. They point out that the management company's annual fee, 2 percent of the fund's total value, would have yielded profits higher than this, considering that by 1963 the fund was worth more than $23 billion cruzeiros.[99] At the 1963 exchange rate of 600

96. Bagley to Martha Dalrymple, April 1 and 8, 1960. RAC, R.G. 2, P.R., Box 12, "Bagley, Jan.-June 1960."
97. Interview with Roberto Campos; interview with Oswaldo Gudolle Aranha, November 14, 1986, Rio de Janeiro.
98. U.S. Business Performance Abroad, 201.
99. Conversation with Aldrich; conversation with Rodman Rockefeller, October 4, 1988.

cruzeiros to the dollar, the dollar value of the fund at that time was thus $38 million, which that year alone should have yielded a management fee of $760,000 (2 percent) before payment of commissions to the sales staff and other overhead costs.

The losses incurred by the management company during the worst years of the redemption crisis (1963–65), along with overhead costs, may account for the low net profit figure of $150,000 for the first decade. Unfortunately, the disarray of IBEC's records makes it impossible to assess the validity of Broehl's estimate, which was based on documentation readily available to him at the time of his study in 1968. In any case, it is clear that IBEC did realize some profits through management of the fund, and as the fund stabilized in the late 1960s these profits must have been increasingly substantial. The reality of higher profits, at least after 1966, is ultimately demonstrated by the high price for which IBEC was to sell the management company in 1972.

SASA also provided steady dividends, while its stock became increasingly prized. Throughout the 1960s and 1970s, IBEC received "on the average four to five requests a year" from Brazilians, Americans, and Europeans to sell its position in SASA, which was on its way to becoming one of the largest seed companies in the world and certainly the largest in the third world.[100] Yet IBEC's success in Brazil was unique and had much to do with the acumen and resilience of its Brazilian partners. António Secundino *was* SASA, and Fundo Crescinco had long had the strong support of the Brazilian banking community, most notably of Banco Moreira Salles (now Unibanco). In fact, in 1968 the Crescinco management company, Empreendimentos, was reorganized into a corporation called Banco de Investimento do Brasil, of which Walther Moreira Salles owned more shares than IBEC. As controlling partner, Moreira Salles took over the running of Crescinco in 1968, with ongoing board participation by IBEC. Moreira Salles also sat on the New York board of IBEC. He was one of only two non-Americans on the thirty-member board. The other was, surprisingly, not a Hispanic South American, but an Italian.[101]

The active involvement of Walther Moreira Salles in IBEC and in Fundo Crescinco was indicative of Rockefeller's intention of grounding

100. Rodman Rockefeller to Jorge Jamio, October 11, 1976, p. 2. RAC, IBEC, Box 74, Folder: "SASA-Sementes Agroceres, S.A., 1971 . . . 1973."

101. Information from IBEC's "preliminary prospectus" for the sale of common stock, "Registration Statement under the Securities Act of 1933," Securities and Exchange Commission, Washington, D.C., January 1970, pp. 17, 20, and 24. Copy obtained from Walther Moreira Salles.

his experimental projects in the bedrock of the most powerful and development-oriented segments of Brazilian society. Beginning in 1940, Moreira Salles and his father, aided by the government's nationalization of some foreign banks, rapidly expanded a small statewide bank into a national conglomerate. As a result of Moreira Salles's increasing prominence, he was asked to serve in diplomatic or financial capacities by every administration from 1945 to 1964. He was ambassador to the United States from 1952 to 1953 under Getúlio Vargas and from 1959 to 1960 under Juscelino Kubitschek, and he served as João Goulart's minister of finance. After the coup of 1964, Moreira Salles left government service and devoted himself to business activities, including IBEC. His long partnership and warm personal friendship with Nelson Rockefeller ("I miss him very much," Moreira Salles said seven years after Rockefeller's death) undoubtedly lent considerable strength and credibility to IBEC from the point of view of Brazilians.[102]

Outside Brazil, IBEC did not fare nearly so well. It was much harder to find committed local partners in countries like Venezuela, according to IBEC vice-president W. D. Bradford, and financial and political instability had a more negative effect there on ventures which were based on business confidence, such as stock mutual funds. For reasons Bradford was unable to pinpoint, financial shocks in Brazil failed to produce runs on the mutual fund to the extent they did elsewhere.[103] Whereas Fundo Crescinco managed to weather its redemption crisis and make at the least a small profit of $150,000, similar funds which IBEC started in Colombia (1959), Argentina (1960), and Chile (1961) had repeated crises and ended up losing more than $2 million during the same period of time.[104]

Rodman Rockefeller attributed at least part of the difference in performance to the greater tolerance for inflation and more optimistic approach to business risks of Brazilians compared to people in the Spanish-speaking countries. "I have never met a despondent Brazilian," Rockefeller reflected, noting that the Brazilians in his business experience always had a sense there would be a *jeito* for dealing with any crisis. Translated loosely, *jeito* means "a clever way of resolving some obstacle."[105] In Brazil, finding jeitos is considered something of a national pastime and symbol of the national character. It might be compared with

---

102. *Diccionário Histórico-Biográfico Brasileiro*, 3046–48. Quote from interview with Walther Moreira Salles.
103. Broehl interview with Bradford, pp. 7–8. RAC, Broehl Papers, Box 18, Folder: "Interview-Bradford."
104. Financial estimates calculated by Broehl, *U.S. Business Performance Abroad*, 201.
105. Interview with Rodman Rockefeller.

the spirit captured by the American phrase "can do." For IBEC at least, it was one respect in which Brazilian and American business styles resonated with one another.

By the end of the 1960s IBEC had expanded into thirty-eight countries, was managing several dozen companies, and had over a hundred subsidiaries whose activities ranged from the construction of middle-class housing to the growing of coconuts to the manufacture of automobile parts to the breeding of chickens. The corporation made literally everything from soup to nuts—and was greatly overextended. IBEC's overhead was tremendous. Since it made a point of entering fields which other corporations thought too risky or not sufficiently profitable, it was constantly breaking new ground and paying the price in research and development costs. In addition, IBEC tried to develop simple models which others could learn from, in effect fostering competition. As Broehl noted in his study of IBEC for the National Planning Association, "The nature of the businesses in which IBEC has been innovator typically has allowed ease of entry by others. IBEC has pioneered not in high-capital efforts—steel mills, manufacturing plants, mines—but in processing and distribution businesses where, once the ground was broken, emulators could easily enter."[106] This approach presented a curious dilemma for a family whose fortune had been made by an oil monopoly that, basing itself on Andrew Carnegie's homespun axiom "Pioneering don't pay," specialized in taking over the successful ventures of others.[107]

IBEC's strongest profits came in the late 1950s, when it reported a return of approximately 11 percent on investment, but during the 1960s overall profits frequently dropped well below 9 percent.[108] The companies which performed best were usually not those in developing countries, but those in Europe or the United States. But even its investments in U.S. manufacturing plants began to weaken as heavy industry there started to decline. IBEC was simply too diversified to run all of its enterprises efficiently or with cost effectiveness. When the oil crises of the 1970s hit, the corporation was not prepared either for the shift in the balance of payments or for the shift in power relations which would lead many "host countries" to question the presence of even so "nice" an American company as IBEC. Rodman Rockefeller recounted, "It was very clear that we were going to have to start undoing what we had spent the last fifteen years doing."[109] Although IBEC officials hoped they could

106. *U.S. Business Performance Abroad*, 283.
107. Collier and Horowitz, *The Rockefellers*, 35.
108. Broehl, *U.S. Business Performance Abroad*, 285.
109. Interview with Rodman Rockefeller.

save the company by selling off most of the subsidiaries and narrowing its scope to agribusiness alone, it was essentially too late to turn it around.

The oil crisis was especially pertinent in IBEC's reconsideration of its investments in Venezuela and Brazil, where the corporation had gotten its start. In oil-rich Venezuela, the successes of the Organization of Petroleum Exporting, Countries resulted in the country's "becoming increasingly nationalistic and . . . impossible to live with," according to Rodman Rockefeller. In Brazil it was "difficult to operate on a dollar basis," as the oil-importing nation became "increasingly damaged by the balance of payments problem with the result of a substantial increase in inflation."[110] Brazil also had its share of nationalism, which had grown stronger under the military dictatorship.

From the late 1960s on, the government pressured SASA to find a way to become Brazilian-owned. SASA needed agricultural credit to operate its farms, and the government frequently denied or threatened to deny to SASA the subsidized loans which were available to other companies. SASA officials complained to IBEC that they were being penalized for their association with the American corporation and by 1976 had "come to the conclusion that IBEC's major ownership of the Agroceres equity could sooner than later seriously damage the company."[111] According to Rodman Rockefeller, the Brazilian government also wanted IBEC to sell its interest in the Banco de Investimento do Brasil (that is, in Empreendimentos/Fundo Crescinco) and had suggested that Walther Moreira Salles make an offer.

The combination of IBEC's corporate problems and Brazilian complications finally brought the outcome that Nelson Rockefeller had desired from the beginning, but that had been stymied over the years by IBEC's inability to develop enough profitable ventures: namely, Brazilian private control of important national enterprises. In 1972, IBEC sold its remaining shares in the mutual fund management to Unibanco (Moreira Salles) for $10 million.[112] Again, the state of IBEC's records does not permit an accurate estimate of the amount that Moreira Salles paid before 1972 to increase marginally his position in the company, and the recollections of Rodman Rockefeller and Richard Aldrich differ on this point. But the final payment of $10 million alone would have represented a handsome profit on the $25,000 cash that IBEC advanced in 1957 to hire a

110. Ibid.
111. See António Secundino to Nelson Rockefeller, March 31, 1968 (RAC, Friele Papers, Box 2, Folder: "Rodman Rockefeller") and Jorge Gamio to Rodman Rockefeller, October 1, 1976, p. 2, RAC, IBEC, Box 74, Folder: "SASA-Sementes Agroceres, S.A., 1971 . . . 1973."
112. Conversations with Rockefeller and Aldrich.

aff for Empreendimentos. In addition, between 1980 and 1985, IBEC sold all of its shares in SASA for another $9 million. A syndicate headed by the Secundino family obtained 51 percent of the stocks of the corporation, with the National Development Bank acquiring the majority of the remaining shares, which they then sold to the Brazilian public.[113]

In the end IBEC had made a good profit in Brazil, and the Brazilians had acquired two extremely valuable corporations—both of which still exist. In 1986, Ney Bittencourt de Araújo, son of António Secundino and current president of SASA, was named Agronomist of the Year in Brazil, and Fundo Crescinco is now one of several mutual funds listed on the Brazilian stock exchange, some of which are even larger than the pioneer. The thirty-year delay (1955–85) in achieving complete Brazilian control and ownership of SASA represented a significant conflict with IBEC's stated goals. But the outcome matched Rockefeller's original intent.

In spite of the capital gains IBEC received from SASA and Fundo Crescinco, the Rockefeller family had meanwhile decided to disinvest in the corporation, which was seen as a losing proposition overall. Holders of IBEC's common stock were given a chance to sell their shares back to the corporation at the original price, even though the stock's value was much less. In 1980, little more than a year after Nelson Rockefeller died, the family sold operating control of IBEC to a British corporation named Booker, and in 1985 IBEC was merged into Booker and out of existence. Its remaining shares in SASA were the last thing which IBEC sold.[114]

The impact of SASA and Fundo Crescinco on the economic development of Brazil is difficult to measure but nonetheless eminently observable. The economist Werner Baer estimates that corn productivity nationwide grew from 1,256 kilos per hectare to 1,479 between 1947 and 1980—an increase of 18 percent. In São Paulo state, where SASA was based and where there is an active department of agriculture, productivity increased by 65 percent over the same period.[115] Between 1980 and 1990, the increase in productivity jumped again, to nearly 40 percent. SASA agronomists further estimate that even in locales where hybrid seed did not dramatically expand yields it stemmed declines in productivity resulting from farmers' widespread failure to use fertilizers, even though all the fertilizers needed to grow corn (with the exception of potassium) are produced within the country. In 1971, SASA calculated that if *common* corn had been continuously planted in this manner, overall yields

113. *O Estado de São Paulo*, October 22, 1986, Agriculture Supplement, p. 8.
114. Timeline provided by the office of Rodman Rockefeller.
115. Baer, *The Brazilian Economy: Growth and Development*, 322–23.

would have dropped from the 1945-47 average by 33 percent. These estimates were substantiated by conditions in the impoverished northeastern state of Bahia, where without hybrids productivity did decline by 35 percent between World War II and the mid-1960s. An analysis by SASA of its invoices also showed that 80 percent of the farmers who had previously bought hybrid seed became regular users and that customers, on the average, were planting only twenty hectares of corn—indicating that SASA was reaching small to middle-size farms.[116] One U.S. agricultural expert examining Brazilian development in 1970 concluded that Sementes Agroceres was one of the five strongest agricultural research organizations in the nation and listed SASA and IRI as two of the three important nongovernmental agencies doing research.[117]

SASA flourished even further once it was completely nationalized. Its equity went from $18 million in 1980 to $60 million in 1990, at which time it controlled 57 percent of the corn seed market in Brazil and exported seed to Bolivia and Paraguay. Interestingly, it also fulfilled some of IBEC's earliest visions, which the American company had been unable to realize. Recalling the failed IBEC hog farms, in the 1980s SASA diversified into breeding stocks in swine and chickens, which they sold in Brazil as well as in Bolivia, Paraguay, Uruguay, and Argentina. They also adopted the IBEC model of joint ventures with host foreign nationals, starting subsidiaries in Colombia, Venezuela, and Ecuador. Yet another new SASA division, meanwhile, began hybridizing and exporting vegetable seeds (other than corn) throughout Central and South America.[118]

Fundo Crescinco has been most useful as a model for the creation of other mutual funds and as a stimulant to the trade in securities. "Fundo Crescinco was very good because it was the first open investment fund based on Brazilian shares," according to Lucas Lopes. "We learned a lot about the stock market from it." Paulo Pereira Lira, president of the Banco Central do Brasil in the 1970s, commented, "This was one of the first experiments in setting up an organization to mobilize savings and gear them toward the stock market. They had all the expertise from abroad, and apparently were quite successful."[119]

The first competitors of Fundo Crescinco emerged in 1960, three years after IBEC's venture into mutual funds. That year, three new mutual

116. *Impact Study: Sementes Agroceres, S.A.*, John P. M. Higgins, April 1971, pp. 28–30. RAC, IBEC, Box 75, "SASA . . . Brazil-Publicity-Impact Study."
117. Schuh, *Agricultural Development of Brazil*, 236–38.
118. Interview with Bittencourt.
119. Interview with Lucas Lopes; interview with Paulo Pereira Lira, Rio de Janeiro, October 27, 1986.

funds appeared, "copying ipsis verbis the Crescinco regulation," an IBEC staff member ruefully noted—conscious of the irony that the successful replication would eventually lead to diminished market share and profits for IBEC. But Crescinco's head start and significantly larger resources built up over time ensured it a continued strong position in the market. In addition, IBEC recognized that such competition fitted with its goals as originally defined by Rockefeller and was ultimately "beneficial to the development of the capital market in this country." The example set by Fundo Crescinco and its competitors was subsequently followed by the government, which established its own fund (called FINAME) in 1965 through BNDE.[120]

The changes in the Brazilian banking laws that IBEC, Fundo Crescinco, and other mutual funds had supported in 1965 also affected the development of the capital market. According to the economist Stefan Robock, the resulting incentives for firms to go public and for investors to buy shares instead of letras "stimulated a fantastic boom in the Brazilian stock market, which began in 1966 and culminated in June 1971, when the average *real* capital gain on shares acquired a year earlier amounted to 427 percent. The number of shares traded on the Rio de Janeiro and São Paulo exchanges increased fourfold from 1968 to 1971."[121] Although local financing for long-term development is still inadequate in Brazil, and the government's endemic funding problems continue to strain the capital market there, contemporary economists conclude that the stock market has gradually but unmistakably improved as a source of development funds over the past few decades. In 1987, two to three hundred companies made regular use of the stock market for financing, compared to only twenty to fifty when Nelson and David Rockefeller first investigated the market.[122] By its own model and by promoting reforms in the banking law, Fundo Crescinco helped bring about change.

At the end of the 1980s, other mutual funds competed successfully with the Brazilian-owned Fundo Crescinco. Their success demonstrates the extent to which IBEC officials were able to transfer their methods and expertise to Brazil, and the equally important extent to which Brazilians were able to make these methods their own. Interestingly, mutual funds with social development or other ideological goals also became popular

120. Hans Horch to Richard Aldrich, August 20, 1960, and B. David Lanes to Hans Horch and Marek Lubomirski, March 25, 1965. RAC, Broehl Papers, box 7, folders (respectively): "Fund-Brazil-2" and "Fund-Brazil-3."
121. *Brazil: A Study in Development Progress* (Lexington, Mass.: D. C. Heath, 1975), 122.
122. The Economist Intelligence Unit, *Country Profile: Brazil, 1987–88* (London: The Economist, 1987), 44–45.

in the United States in the 1980s, perhaps unwittingly inspired by much earlier efforts such as Fundo Crescinco.[123]

SASA and Fundo Crescinco are also notable as model projects designed with a concern for the distributive aspects of development. As a capitalist and extremely wealthy man, Nelson Rockefeller was comfortable cooperating with the powerful Brazilian elite, whom he hoped to enlist in promoting the economic advancement of the entire nation. Rockefeller clearly accepted such people as the nation's leaders and believed, from his own experience perhaps, that robber barons could become progressive capitalists who recognized worker welfare as a measure of their own security. Yet Rockefeller also believed in going directly to other classes of society, rather than simply relying on the upper class to pass on the benefits of development, whether that meant creating seed for small farmers or financial opportunities for the urban middle class. IBEC's choice of business partners in Brazil, middle-class António Secundino and banking magnate Walther Moreira Salles, demonstrates this eclecticism.

But had Nelson Rockefeller met his own career and political goal of creating an exemplar of postwar capitalism? It seems clear that IBEC demonstrated that U.S. business could, if it so desired, cooperate with Latin American development, even if it did not fulfill every promise. This alone was a signal accomplishment, considering the many occasions on which the goals of the two have been so diametrically opposed (for example, in the stripping of Latin American natural resources for the benefit of American mining companies or in the exorbitant remittances of profits from manufacturing). But IBEC's accomplishments were not simply symbolic; they were also concrete. IBEC had pioneered in the creation of a viable stock market and had foreshortened by a decade or more the dissemination of appropriate agricultural technology by encouraging and financing the work of Brazilian geneticists.

Yet for other corporations to learn from IBEC it had to be seen as something other than an oddball hybrid of altruism and enterprise. In this respect, IBEC was much less successful. Although the Rockefeller publicity machine obtained wide press coverage for IBEC over the years, and the corporation's profits and accomplishments were regularly heralded in *Business Week* magazine, IBEC never entirely shook the reputation of

123. See, for example, the New Alternatives Fund, the Pax World Fund, and the Dreyfus Third Century Fund. According to the columnist David Horowitz, mutual funds wield "tremendous power" in financial markets which many "investors want to see used to promote peace, protect the environment and enhance the quality of life." *San Diego Union*, January 12, 1987, D-3.

being a do-good enterprise whose calculations were based on something other than a strong business sense.[124] As one banker quoted in a *Business Week* article put it, attempts to mix profit making with economic development were examples of the "IBEC syndrome."[125] Even Rockefeller's family questioned the wisdom of the ambitious directions in which Nelson took IBEC. When John D., Jr., responded to a request from his son for additional funds in 1950, he told Nelson he personally "would have started with fewer enterprises in fewer countries in a smaller way and on a more conservative financial basis, extending the operations only with earnings from successful companies and on the basis of the proved success not only of the principle, but of each specific undertaking."[126]

Brazilians too viewed IBEC as something other than an example of what the typical American corporation could do or would do for their country. Although SASA and Fundo Crescinco were tremendous financial successes, Rockefeller also started five smaller companies in Brazil, and four of them had indifferent or disastrous financial outcomes. Brazilians as well as Americans tended to remember IBEC's financial losses more than its successes, perhaps partly because the failed businesses were more numerous.[127] Brazilians joked that IBEC was "Papai Noel mais dois por cento" (Santa Claus plus two percent) because of IBEC's policy of assuming all the risks of its joint ventures and offering to buy out local partners when an enterprise failed, as in the case of Interamericana.[128] IBEC's strong association with agriculture at a time when most people equated economic progress with industrial growth also compromised the image IBEC tried to project as a firm on the forefront of development efforts.

Brazilians who knew Rockefeller recalled him with fondness, but they described him always as an "idealist" or a "humanitarian" or a "friend of Brazil." For a man with his eye on high political office in the United States, it certainly made more sense to err on the side of philanthropy than to risk being called an exploiter. As Oswaldo G. Aranha said, "Nobody ever talked against Nelson. He was never a 'businessman' in Brazil."[129] It was a two-edged compliment for a man who sought to set a standard for American capitalism but an understandable one. Rockefeller moved too frequently between government, philanthropy, and business to be seen

124. See *Business Week*, September 10, 1955, April 27, 1957, and February 4, 1967.
125. Cited by Broehl, *U.S. Business Performance Abroad*, 277.
126. John D. Rockefeller, Jr., to Nelson Rockefeller, February 24, 1950, p. 1. RAC, R.G. 2, Economic Interests, IBEC, Box 2, Folder 8.
127. Broehl, *U.S. Business Performance Abraod*, 57–74.
128. Interview with Aldrich.
129. Interview.

clearly through the prism of any one sector and perhaps too frequently to be fully successful in any one sector.

Despite Rockefeller's exceptionalism, his beliefs and practices were consistent with the ideology of developmentalism as espoused by the liberal academic community at the time and consistent also with the increasing interest of business in finding an accommodation with the foreign demands for reciprocity in investment which began to emerge in the 1950s. Rockefeller's activities also followed the express policy of the U.S. government in the 1950s and 1960s, which was to promote Latin American development. His most successful projects, however, had a staying power and earned a local acceptance that often eluded bureaucratic, conflict-ridden government aid programs.

But innovations rarely have an unmixed success: they generate unforeseen dynamics of their own, even as they must continue to cope with the difficult problems they were designed to solve. SASA's very success, for example, made it difficult to part with when other projects failed to generate new revenue for IBEC's ongoing growth. What is more, a variety of events, including the coup d'état in Brazil in 1964 and the near collapse of the "Brazilian miracle" in the wake of the 1980s debt crisis, have shown that economic growth does not always produce enduring prosperity and that the middle class is not always the bulwark for democracy that Nelson Rockefeller and many liberal Americans, Europeans, and Latin Americans assumed it would be. The astronomical profits of banks and the stock market during Brazil's 1,000 percent inflation in the late 1980s show that a profitable, diversified money market can paradoxically coexist with deepening poverty, industrial shutdowns, and city bankruptcy, as in the case of Rio de Janeiro. Yet Rockefeller's role in the development of the Brazilian stock market cannot be blamed for the inflation and debt crisis of the eighties. Although his assumptions about the middle class may have been naive, they represented a benign logic about the connections among economic development, income distribution, and political democracy. Still, it would take other Americans to convince even some Brazilians that real business could be compatible with real development.

Chapter 5

Business Looks Abroad:

Postwar Capitalism and

Willys-Overland do Brasil

For American industrial statesmanship this is an opportunity of historic significance. Our managerial capitalism has the *power* to frustrate the Kremlin's strategy by energizing the economic development of the former colonial nations. But market and profit incentives can never do the job alone. There must be a higher motivation. Our industry overseas must become the symbol and carrier not of a dollar imperium but of human values and of hope to peoples emerging into a chaotic world from centuries of colonialism.

—J. Anthony Panuch,

"A Businessman's Philosophy for Foreign Affairs"

If World War II and its consequences brought unprecedented opportunities for the U.S. government to exert influence in the world, it equally widened the horizons of American business. Political turmoil and economic devastation in Europe, combined with the occupation of Japan and Germany, produced a vacuum of leadership in the Western bloc and in much of Asia that the United States rushed to fill. Similarly, the disruption of British and German economic dominance in South America, followed in subsequent years by the gradual decolonization of Africa and Asia, effectively wiped clean the slate of world economic relationships in a way that represented for American business as much of a break with the past as the nation's rejection of its own colonial status. For the first time in American history, most of the world was open and ripe for the plucking.

Yet opportunity is one thing and seizing it another. During the first years after the war, American business turned its attention to the reconversion of industry and then to the practically boundless opportunities for profit right in the United States. As measured by indices of trade and investment, American businessmen seemed to have only moderate interest in the rest of the world. By 1950, exports and imports as a percentage of gross national product dropped to an all-time low of 3.6 percent and 3.1 percent, respectively.[1] Long-term direct foreign investment grew at a healthy but unspectacular rate of 5 percent a year throughout the 1950s, although it varied widely by region of the world.[2] Business publications reflected the domestic preoccupation of most companies. A national index of business and economic research for 1950–56 listed twice as many studies of Arkansas as of the world outside the United States. Among the hundreds of listings there were no subject headings for "exports" or "international trade."[3] Leading journals like *Harvard Business Review* ran at most a handful of articles on international topics each year, many of which, notably, were devoted to exhorting businessmen to look beyond the hypnotic delights of the domestic market to the pressing needs and opportunities of foreign economies.[4] According to a State Department

1. *Historical Statistics of the United States*, part 2 (Washington: GPO, 1975), 887. Exports and imports have always been a relatively small percentage of U.S. gross national product, especially in the twentieth century. For most of this century, however, exports have averaged somewhat over 4 percent and imports over 3 percent.
2. Ibid., 870. From 1950 to 1960 (inclusive), private direct foreign investment grew by 170 percent, which amounts roughly to a 5.5 percent annual rate compounded annually.
3. *Index of Publications of Bureaus of Business and Economic Research, 1950–1956* (Eugene, Ore.: Bureau of Business Research, 1957).
4. See, for example, the following, all in *Harvard Business Review*: Panuch, "A Businessman's Philosophy for Foreign Affairs" (March-April 1957), 41–53; H. J. Dernburg, "Prospects for Long-Term Foreign Investment" (July 1950): 41–51; M. C. Conick, "Stimulating Private Investment" (November-December 1953): 104–12; W. Jack Butler, "Public Relations for Industry in Underdeveloped Countries" (September-October 1952): 63–71; idem, "Fighting Communism Overseas" (July-August 1956): 96–104; and Clifton R. Wharton,

report of 1952, there was "very little general purpose or portfolio investment except in Canadian securities and in obligations of the World Bank."[5] Profits at home, the instability and hazards of the outside world, the productivity of American labor, the affluence of American consumers, and the continuing abundance of many raw materials all combined to make investments abroad seem to many corporations simply not worth the trouble. As one writer in *Harvard Business Review* summarized the problems of overseas enterprises, "The hazards are great, the headaches many, and the opportunities at home are substantial."[6]

In light of this, many of the articles written by proponents of foreign investment naturally drew more of their warmth from ideological arguments than from economic ones, asserting that U.S. business had not only an opportunity to invest, but, more important, a responsibility. Yet the notion of any kind of social responsibility associated with business, whether domestic or international, was itself part of a larger question: namely, what role was business to play in postwar America and in the postwar world?

Although it is debatable to what extent the policies of the New Deal were incompatible with the aims of business, it is clear that businessmen and indeed capitalism itself had been on the defensive since the Great Depression. Domestically, this meant a transfer of power from Wall Street to Washington in the wake of the New Deal; internationally, it meant that the U.S. government took the leadership in running the world economic system. As Emily Rosenberg notes, after World War II, "governmental or intergovernmental agencies such as IMF, IBRD, GATT, AID, USIA, and other technical-assistance agencies assumed functions previously conducted by private citizens."[7] Economic recovery and the critical contributions of industry to the war effort helped rehabilitate business in the public estimation, yet questions remained about how business could shore up its reputation for being responsible and at the same time defend the threatened influence of the private sector in American life, which seemed to be diminishing as the role of the government expanded.

Businesses' arguments in favor of a strong private sector were plainly

---

Jr., "Aiding the Community: A New Philosophy for Foreign Operations" (March-April 1954): 64–72. Also see "Foreign Aid Without Tax Dollars," *Nation's Business* (July 1957): 82–88.

5. August Maffry, "Program for Increasing Private Investment in Foreign Countries" (December 18, 1952, mimeographed), cited by Conick, "Stimulating Private Investment," 108.
6. Butler, "Fighting Communism Overseas," 99.
7. *Spreading the American Dream: American Economic and Cultural Expansion, 1890–1945* (New York: Hill and Wang, 1982), 231.

self-serving but also went beyond that. Since Alexis de Tocqueville it has been a cultural axiom that American democracy is based on a plurality of public, private, and voluntary associations shifting and sharing power among themselves. While producing material benefits for a number of Americans, from recipients of welfare to recipients of military contracts, big government has nonetheless produced new anxieties about the concentration of power in postwar America. Whereas in the late nineteenth and early twentieth centuries the monopolies bore the brunt of social criticism for their bigness and power, since World War II it is government which has felt the sting of popular suspicions.

To a small but important segment of businessmen, foreign investment represented an exceptional opportunity on two accounts: first, as a way of responding creatively to the growing force of nationalism in host countries which were increasingly critical and demanding of foreign investors; and second, as a way of reasserting the central role of business in the American "mission" as the bearer of techniques and opportunities for economic—and thus political—development abroad. Or, as a writer for *Harvard Business Review* stated it, "Our leadership in world politics has created a concomitant role for industry."[8] Internationalist businessmen saw that to seize this opportunity corporations would have to find ways to respond—superficially if not substantially—to the demand for development in order to ensure both the willingness of foreign governments to accept direct investment and the recognition of the U.S. government that such investments were consistent with the national interest.

The Business Advisory Council's Committee on Latin America, organized by the U.S. Department of Commerce, was one of the most important conduits of business opinion to the Department of State. Top representatives of the biggest U.S. companies in Latin America participated actively: David Rockefeller of Chase National Bank, Leo Welch of Standard Oil of New Jersey, Sam Baggett of United Fruit Company, H. W. Balgooyen of the American and Foreign Power Company, and H. A. Davies of International Harvester, among others. (Although Nelson Rockefeller never sat on this committee, his influence was undoubtedly felt through his brother David and close friend Assistant Secretary of State Edward Miller.) In response to a memorandum on U.S. Latin American policy written by Miller in 1952, committee members made it clear that in their opinion government had assigned to business too limited a role in the shaping of the postwar world and particularly in the development of the poorer countries. Just as government social programs threat-

8. Butler, "Public Relations for Industry," 63.

ened to swallow up private charity at home, so foreign aid programs appeared to threaten the traditional role of business as the main source of financing for development abroad.[9]

Committee members complained almost to a man that members of the State Department were either suspicious and distrustful of business or at best not especially persuasive as advocates for "free, private, competitive enterprise as the system which has made our country strong and prosperous."[10] David Rockefeller, in a statement that echoed those of other committee members, wrote Miller that the government did not seem "genuinely convinced that foreign investment is desirable and in the best interests of the United States." The foreign policy result, Rockefeller said, was "an unbalanced program that has given almost exclusive emphasis to government aid and actually discouraged private initiative."[11] While there is no evidence that the government discouraged private investment and much evidence that business opinion on Latin American questions helped shape national policy, the chaotic decision-making process of government and ideological divisions within the business community itself at times hampered coordination and even consistent cooperation.[12] In addition, the expansion of government authority, whether over domestic industry or foreign aid, consistently provoked a defensive response by businessmen, who often felt they had to defend the free enterprise system.

Indeed, to the internationally oriented fraternity of American businessmen who represented what Michael Hogan calls the "New Deal synthesis," including Nelson and David Rockefeller, the struggle to extend the hegemony of the American Way throughout the world was quite clearly, even explicitly, synonymous with the need to extend capitalism in its highly developed, corporatist American form. Although government appeared to them to tend on occasion toward an anticapitalist mentality, they held to the point of view that the triumph of the American system was the triumph of capitalism and that no one was better suited to fight

9. During this same period other business leaders were developing rationales for domestic corporate philanthropy, based on the need ."to defend and preserve" the role of the private sector in educational, scientific, and welfare activities. Eells, *Corporation Giving*, 10–11.
10. H. W. Balgooyen to Edward Miller, May 20, 1952, p. 5. NA, R.G. 59, Lot File 53D26, Office Files of the Assistant Secretary of State for Latin America, 1949–53, Box 3, Folder: "Business Advisory Council."
11. "Comments Submitted by Mr. David Rockefeller on . . . U.S. Relations with Latin America" (undated), 4–5. Found with written comments by other committee members, from May 1952, in NA, R.G. 59, Lot File 53D26, Office Files of the Assistant Secretary of State for Latin America, 1949–53, Box 3, Folder: "Business Advisory Council."
12. Wagner, *U.S. Policy Toward Latin America*, 117–19, 132.

that battle than business.[13] As a writer for *Harvard Business Review* stated in the mid-1950s, "For the American businessman, communism . . . must be seen . . . as the supreme competitive test: freedom versus the totalitarian Soviet brand of state-managed existence."[14] As Nelson Rockefeller once put it, the United States must prove that its system held out the most hope to Latin America and "must frankly call it capitalism."[15]

On the surface, this point of view fit perfectly with the policy of the Eisenhower administration. Dwight D. Eisenhower assumed office in 1953 with a predisposition to form military alliances as the basis for relations with Latin America and a distaste for aid to promote economic development. Secretary of the Treasury George Humphrey had one of the strongest voices in the Cabinet, and his unequivocal opposition both to grants and soft loans for Latin America set the tone for the first years of the administration's policy. Humphrey made his stand on the premise that economic development was going to happen through business dealings or not at all and that there was no way that government was going to subsidize the development of foreign industry which might eventually compete against American.[16] Milton Eisenhower, the president's brother and special emissary to Latin America, stated the new approach to aid more gently but with equal clarity when he opened an inter-American conference in 1955 whose purpose was "to boost future U.S. investment in Latin America through a partnership of businessmen instead of governments."[17]

Secretary of State John Foster Dulles, with Eisenhower's support, ran a foreign economic policy based on free trade for industrial products, development through private investment, and minimal government-to-government assistance. When the American ambassador to Brazil tried to convince Dulles that Brazil's status as a major ally and "coming role in the world" entitled it to special consideration beyond these policy guidelines, Dulles listened with skepticism, commenting dryly that "mere size of population [does] not connote world power, even when coupled with

13. Panuch, "A Businessman's Philosophy," 52: "Government people (outside the military procurement agencies) haven't the faintest idea how modern industry works. They have a tendency to what von Mises calls 'the anti-capitalist mentality.' "
14. Butler, "Fighting Communism Overseas," 104.
15. Morris, p. 240.
16. *Fortune*, November 1953, 114. For a clear discussion of Humphrey's role also see Rabe, *Eisenhower and Latin America*, 64–83.
17. *Time*, March 14, 1955, 95.

abundant natural resources." Dulles compared Brazil to India and China, which also had large populations but which had not, as of the midfifties, "exerted the necessary energy and skills or followed the right policies to develop a status equal to their size."[18] Dulles had a show me attitude about Brazil's importance.

In the larger strategic scheme, both Dulles and Eisenhower lacked interest in Latin America and believed, as Eisenhower expressed it in a letter to his brother, that as a region not "directly open to assault" it did not merit grant aid for economic development.[19] Eisenhower's perspective on the Cold War in Latin America would change in mid-1958, but for the better part of his administration he saw no reason to reprioritize U.S. aid programs to give greater assistance to the western hemisphere. Whatever external or internal threat Communism posed in Latin America could be best handled by a strengthening of Latin American police forces, thought Eisenhower, who initiated the first U.S.-sponsored program to do just that, using monies earmarked for economic development projects.[20] Because the economic status quo in Latin America presented no problem for the United States and because whatever problems the status quo presented for the poor of Latin American could presumably be handled by their police, relying on business to produce trickle-down development was perfectly consistent with the administration's political realism.

But while the Eisenhower administration publicly pronounced its confidence in the ability of foreign investment to produce economic develop-

18. Memorandum of Conversation, John Foster Dulles and Ellis O. Briggs, August 28, 1957. NA, R.G. 59, 1955–59, Decimal file 611.32/8–2857.
19. Dwight Eisenhower to Milton Eisenhower, December 1, 1954, p. 1. FGV, CPDOC, Eisenhower Library Documents, Code 3, 54.12.01.
20. Eisenhower used discretionary technical assistance funds provided by the Mutual Security Act of 1954 to start a Public Safety Program for training foreign police forces in order "to maintain internal security and to destroy the effectiveness of the communist apparatus in the Western Hemisphere." ("U.S. Policy Toward Latin America," National Security Council, August 20, 1956, 16. Found in *Declassified Documents Reference System* [Carrollton Press, 1982], 333-B.) When the National Security Council established a new operating plan with regard to Latin America in 1956 (NSC 5613), the Public Safety Program became the core component in the new Overseas Internal Security Program. Although Congress attempted to undercut the administration's support for repressive regimes by ruling in 1958 that "internal security requirements shall not normally be the basis for military assistance programs to American Republics," Eisenhower could legitimately claim that no *military* funds were being used for such purposes since the necessary funds were being taken from economic programs instead. For an account of Eisenhower's initiative in suggesting the police program see A. J. Langguth, *Hidden Terrors* (New York: Pantheon Books, 1978) 48. For the congressional ruling on internal security programs see the *Mutual Security Act of 1959*, U.S. Senate Committee on Foreign Relations (Washington: GPO, 1959), 708.

ment, the government consistently ruled out proposals for major tax concessions to encourage such investment and made virtually no attempt to educate businessmen about their supposed responsibilities. In 1951, Nelson Rockefeller's report to Truman on Point Four had outlined a comprehensive proposal for offering incentives to U.S. business investment in underdeveloped areas. These recommendations formed the basis for a series of tax reform proposals made over the next nine years, none of which, however, was strongly endorsed by the supposedly probusiness Eisenhower administration. According to Burton Kaufman, the White House, in spite of its rhetoric about relying on U.S. business to produce economic development, "had never been enthusiastic about any of the provisions for encouraging private investment abroad."[21]

During the better part of Eisenhower's two terms in office—from 1955 to 1960—foreign direct investment in Latin American grew less quickly than at any point in the thirty-year period from 1940 to 1970. While American investments in Western Europe and Canada increased in the second half of the 1950s by 123 percent and 65 percent, respectively, investments in Latin America increased by only 24 percent.[22] Oddly, Eisenhower and his advisers failed to anticipate that the private investment on which they based their foreign economic policies would not materialize—perhaps because they were simply slow to take Latin American development questions seriously. They focused on nonstatist solutions to development as much to avoid these questions as to affirm the role of the private sector. U.S. corporations, and their Latin American partners, were on their own.

Notably, the few foreign aid and investment initiatives that the administration did put forward in the 1950s drew some of their strongest support from business. Repeatedly arguing against the stands taken by Treasury Secretary George Humphrey, corporate executives turned out in force first to protest the dismantling of the Eximbank in 1954 and then to support the creation of the International Finance Corporation (first proposed by Nelson Rockefeller's Point Four Committee). Business also continued to support the government's limited technical assistance programs, held over from the Truman era.[23]

American trade journals occasionally reflected an awareness of the role

21. *Trade and Aid*, 158. Also see 4–6, 46–47 for an overview of the Rockefeller recommendations.
22. Percentages based on investment data for 1955 and 1960 in *Historical Statistics of the United States*, part 2, p. 870. For further data see Kaufman, *Trade and Aid*, 162.
23. Wagner, *U.S. Policy Toward Latin America*, 114–15, 118, 132.

assigned to business by the Eisenhower administration, with relevant articles tending to fall into one of two categories: those that proclaimed *all* American ventures abroad to be a form of foreign aid, regardless of how or for what purposes the particular businesses were organized, and those that encouraged taking a harder look at how American business could fit itself into the postwar environment of developing countries. One of the best examples of the first type, from *The Magazine of Wall Street* in 1958, called America's total overseas investment "a gigantic Point Four program . . . which eclipses in scope and magnitude the more publicized achievements of U.S. and U.N. projects." As evidence of the "silent revolution in living standards" brought about by these investments, the author noted that from billboards the world over "Colgate dentifrice smiles its bright assurance of sparkling teeth" and "Palmolive soap caresses with cosmopolitan impartiality the complexions of dusky Nubian maidens, porcelain Japanese Geishas and alabaster Swedish beauties."[24] Other articles on the automobile and food refining industries made similar claims to private Point Four programs based on little more than the sheer presence of American capital.[25] In spirit, these articles matched the empty assertions of the Eisenhower government, which was equally vague about what American investments would actually accomplish in the way of development.

In contrast, articles which encouraged American businessmen to take up the development challenge tended to raise substantive questions concerning the ways in which corporations conducted themselves abroad. The business analyst Clifton Wharton, Jr., who had written his doctoral dissertation for the University of Chicago on Rockefeller's ACAR, argued that companies had to initiate specific programs to bring about development and cited examples of companies which had started projects to "grapple with the basic problems of health, disease, and hunger." Without these programs, he admitted, foreign countries were frequently justified in charging that American business was simply opportunistic. Wharton quoted the president of Costa Rica as saying, "We resent the pretense of speculators who assert that their motive in investing money abroad is to foster the development of our countries. . . . The sole objective in most cases is to make money, and our economic development is only a doubtful consequence." Wharton concluded that it was "up to the executives of

24. A. W. Zanzi, "$32 Billion Overseas Investment—Capital With a Mission," *The Magazine of Wall Street*, January 4, 1958, 442.
25. See "Corn Products Refining: Old Line Company in New Growth Phase," *The Magazine of Wall Street*, October 26, 1957, 152, and *Automobile Facts*, February-March 1955, 8.

foreign subsidiaries to show . . . that privately financed aid and assistance are not a new form of colonialism and exploitation."[26]

Wharton's statements complemented the ideas of other proponents of foreign investment, notably the members of the Business Advisory Council's Committee on Latin America. This committee reflected a growing awareness among certain men that business could not afford to ignore development questions to the extent that perhaps the U.S. government could, if business wanted to protect its long-term role. Since the advent of the Good Neighbor policy and, most specifically, the nationalization of Mexican oil in 1938, the U.S. government had put business on notice that it would use force to defend corporate interests only when the executive branch saw fit for broader security reasons, as in the so-called turn of Guatemala to communism in 1954. Since business confidence is predicated on the reliability and predictability of environmental factors over years if not decades, the on-again, off-again interventionism of the U.S. government began to force business to find its own accommodation with local regimes. It was an accommodation that would increasingly trade security of investments for, among other things, neutrality on local political questions and concessions to the development goals of foreign countries. Specifically, in the early 1950s, the Business Advisory Council began discussing the idea of elaborating an informal standard of conduct for business abroad—discussions that would later inform the founding of organizations such as the Council of the Americas.[27]

The first references to a possible standard of conduct can be found in the responses of the Business Advisory Council to Edward Miller's statement in 1952 on U.S. relations with Latin America. At the end of his analysis, Miller raised the question of whether or not American business leaders could arrive at a "common standard of conduct" in Latin America as a way of improving their position. Although some of the respondents answered that it would be "hardly possible to have a common standard of conduct at the level of details," most agreed that American businessmen should adhere to a general set of principles modeled on the practices of responsible business in the United States—practices, of course, which were the hallmark of regulatory, corporatist America.[28]

26. "Aiding the Community," 65, 72.
27. For a fuller treatment of this subject see Cobbs, "U.S. Business: Self-Interest and Neutrality."
28. Quote taken from letter of H. A. Davies to Edward Miller, May 12, 1952, p. 4. Also see letter of H. W. Balgooyen, May 20, 1952, p. 6. From NA, R.G. 59, Lot File 53D26, Office Files of the Assistant Secretary of State for Latin America, 1949–53, Box 3, Folder: "Business Advisory Council."

Not only should companies investing in Latin America "conduct their business on the same high standard of conduct and efficiency as they would at home," as one representative phrased it, but they should also, as another executive wrote, "treat labor fairly, train and develop local people into positions of responsibility, [and] refrain strictly from meddling in the foreign country's politics."[29] Other executives stressed that companies could ensure good relations only by "recognizing and respecting legitimate local rights and aspirations and by scrupulously avoiding any political action" and that businessmen should "learn more about Latin America . . . study the languages, comprehend the national aspirations of the people and learn to see the parallel between the development of those countries in this century and our own in the 19th century."[30]

While it is highly debatable to what extent American companies followed these guidelines, it is clear that at least on an intellectual level some business thinkers had begun to apply notions of corporate responsibility to foreign investments by the early and mid-1950s. The Rockefeller influence was not the only one, but it was unmistakably important: aside from Nelson's participation on the Point Four commission and David's participation on the Business Advisory Council, writers on foreign investment used the Rockefeller projects and companies as models of corporate social responsibility abroad.[31] But *social responsibility* failed to address the major concern of Latin Americans, which was how to change the basic relationship of foreign nationals to American subsidiaries: from that of employees to that of owners.

Latin Americans had long criticized U.S. firms for refusing to share the profits of foreign operations through sales of common stock. U.S. government reports noted as early as 1942 that American firms were resented for

29. A. Thomas Taylor to Miller, May 19, 1952, p. 3, and F. T. Magennis to George Wythe, p. 4. NA, R.G. 59, Lot File 53D26, Office Files of the Assistant Secretary of State for Latin America, 1949–53, Box 3, Folder: "Business Advisory Council."

30. Quotes, respectively, from Theodore Weiker, Jr., to Miller, May 12, 1952, p. 6, and H. A. Davies to Miller, May 12, 1952, p. 4. NA, R.G. 59, Lot File 53D26, Office Files of the Assistant Secretary of State for Latin America, 1949–53, Box 3, Folder: "Business Advisory Council."

31. Butler, "Public Relations for Industry," 66, writes about VBEC; Wharton, "Aiding the Community," 68, calls the AIA "the most outstanding project of all in the field of corporate giving abroad"; see also Saville Davis et al., "The Struggle for Men's Minds Abroad," *Harvard Business Review* (July-August 1952): 129, in which Nelson Rockefeller is called "the most far-sighted businessman who has gone into Latin America . . . since the war." In his widely read *Manual of Corporate Giving* (Washington: National Planning Association, 1952), Beardsley Ruml characterized the Rockefeller projects as the best example of "5% programs" abroad. The one article in the book on corporate philanthropy abroad focused on the work of the American International Association.

withholding stock participation from foreign nationals.[32] Yet the wholly owned subsidiary was nearly the rule for American investments abroad, both in Europe and Latin America, and few of the most active proponents of foreign investment suggested any change.[33] Although the various IBEC businesses usually incorporated some local participation in ownership (frequently less than 50 percent), they focused more on conducting useful development projects and encouraging other Americans to invest abroad than on the issue of stock participation per se. The first large American corporation actually to make stock participation a major issue—and thereby to advance the discussion of U.S. investment in the postwar world—was the Kaiser Corporation, headquartered in Oakland, California, and run by one of the leaders of development in the western United States, Henry J. Kaiser.

Jeeps for the Jungle, Sedans for São Paulo: Willys-Overland do Brasil

On top of precipitous Corcovado, standing under the monumental figure of Christ, tourists of all nationalities look out on the shimmering panorama of Rio de Janeiro's white beaches fringing the vast, azure Bay of Guanabara, encircling the giant lake of Rodrigo de Freitas, stretching out along the endless Atlantic coast. But the real drama of Rio de Janeiro is behind the spectators, in the naked granite mountains which soar up from the sands, crowned with emerald jungle and masking the wild hinterland of Brazil. For as far as the eye can see, the strangely shaped peaks stretch away, forming a wall behind the populous coastal strip. The wall is part of a geological escarpment which runs nearly the entire length of Brazil and which, until recent years, limited settlement of the valleys and plains of the interior. Only explorers, like the famous *Bandeirantes* of São Paulo, dared leave the exotic but gentle coast for the rigors of the mountain jungles. In the early 1950s, the rebellion of Brazilians against the natural barriers blocking access to most of their nation coincided with the business difficulties of Henry Kaiser and his son Edgar Kaiser in the United States. Facing away from the alluring coast and sea, Brazilians determined to find and develop the interior. Presidents Getúlio Vargas and Juscelino Kubitschek led the way. With the cooperation of Henry Kaiser, one result was a jeep industry for Brazil.

<hr />

32. See Green, *Containment of Latin America*, 191.
33. For example, between 1946 and 1959, none of the *Harvard Business Review* articles on the need to increase and improve foreign investments suggested local stock participation as a way to enhance the long-term standing of American business abroad.

The jeep captured the imagination of the world in World War II. General George C. Marshall called it America's greatest contribution to modern warfare. It was everywhere and went anywhere, from the Sahara to the Alps. For members of the Brazilian Expeditionary Force stationed in Italy, it was a revelation. "The jeep was part of my life from then on," Oswaldo G. Aranha, son of the Brazil's foreign minister, later said of his experience as a young soldier in Italy. "I kept driving jeeps, seeing jeeps do this, do that. I saw that we should have here this car . . . to come into the interior, to develop the interior, to *find* the interior."[34] Another Brazilian impressed with the jeep's potential was a prominent naval officer who became an admiral, Lúcio Meira. Meira was an early disciple of Roberto Simonsen, the business leader who first articulated the developmentalist school of thought in opposition to those Brazilian economists, like Eugênio Gudin, who still held to the validity of an international division of labor. Following the war, military officers were frequently the strongest supporters of developmentalism, and Meira was squarely within that tradition. But while Lúcio Meira saw in the ubiquitous wartime jeep a bridge to the interior, he foresaw as well the need for an automobile industry capable of producing vehicles for all of Brazil, rural and urban. For the young Aranha, the burning question became how to get jeeps to Brazil. Meira asked the question of how Brazil was to build an entire industry.[35]

In 1950, the onset of the Korean War and the return of Getúlio Vargas to the presidency brought a new urgency to the need to establish an automobile industry. By 1947 Brazil had exhausted the foreign exchange reserves created by the World War. Suddenly, a new war loomed and Brazil was in the position of competing for vehicles in high demand. The Aranha family's personal adviser and representative in the United States warned that any profits the war might bring Brazil would be nullified by the high price of imports. "We should try and get ready to assemble Jeeps in Brazil as well as some of the agricultural implements which go with the Jeeps," he advised.[36]

At the time there were no automobile manufacturing plants in Brazil, only assemblers of "completely knocked down" vehicles imported from other countries, mainly the United States. For the most part, even the assembly operations were wholly owned subsidiaries of foreign firms,

34. Interview.
35. Interview with Admiral Lúcio Meira, Rio de Janeiro, November 12, 1986.
36. John Thompson to Oswaldo Aranha (senior), August 30, 1950, p. 2. FGV, CPDOC, OA 50.08.30/1.

such as Ford Motors do Brazil and General Motors do Brazil. Since the
Aranhas owned a car distributorship and repair business in Rio de Janeiro, the natural first step was to negotiate for an assembly contract with
Willys-Overland Export Corporation, the Toledo, Ohio, owner and manufacturer of Jeep. With the assistance of their American point man and the
financial participation of a wealthy Brazilian family headed by Theodoro
Quartim Barbosa, a financial associate and friend of Nelson Rockefeller,
the Aranhas concluded the deal with Willys and began assembling jeeps
in 1953 under the corporate name of Willys-Overland do Brazil (WOB).
Although the Aranha-Barbosa group was majority owner of the WOB
plant, Willys-Overland Export Corporation retained an interest in the
operation.[37]

The Aranhas and Barbosas soon experienced the difficulties confront-
ing all producers reliant on imported parts: no matter what the costs
saved by local assembly, the foreign currency needed to import completely knocked down packages was still not adequate. In 1953, the
government of Brazil implemented a foreign currency auction system in
which importers had to bid with cruzeiros for a limited number of dollars
to make foreign purchases. While Willys of Toledo pressured the Aranha-
Barbosa group to take on more and more unassembled units, the WOB
owners struggled constantly to obtain the expensive currency necessary
to meet their original commitments. Meanwhile, throughout Brazil, the
assembly of cars from completely knocked down imports declined
rapidly. From a high of more than one hundred thousand in 1951, the
number of locally assembled vehicles tumbled to barely twenty-five thousand in 1953 and then to less than twenty thousand in 1955.[38] The
population was multiplying, urbanization was proceeding apace, the
economy was poised on the brink of massive expansion, and yet transportation resources were diminishing.

The Vargas government responded by stepping up its efforts to foster a
domestic automobile industry which could manufacture more and more
of the parts then imported. When Vargas formed a national Commission
on Industrial Development in 1951, Lúcio Meira joined it as the representative of the navy and soon assumed responsibility for a Subcommission on Jeeps, Tractors, Trucks, and Automobiles. Under Meira's single-
minded leadership, the subcommission went to work creating a series of

37. Interview with O. G. Aranha.
38. Lincoln Gordon and Engelbert L. Grommers, *United States Manufacturing in Brazil:
The Impact of Brazilian Government Policies, 1946–1960* (Boston: Harvard University
Press, 1962), 47. (From official Brazilian import statistics.)

new import laws which protected the small Brazilian parts industry and severely limited importation of any parts produced in the country. With the objective of gradually achieving total nationalization (meaning 100 percent production on Brazilian soil, but by private domestic or foreign companies), the subcommission got the export-import authority of Brazil to pass another regulation in 1953, one which required that cars be imported unassembled only, minus the parts produced and available in Brazil.[39]

Meira traveled to the United States at the invitation of the Ford Motor Company. His goal was to convince the conglomerate to convert from assembling to manufacturing in Brazil, and he hoped that the invitation expressed a willingness to listen. But Henry Ford II, after hosting the Brazilian officer for a month at the huge Michigan plant, turned the tables by trying to convince Meira that it was both uneconomical and infeasible to manufacture cars in Brazil because of the lack of iron, steel, trained workers, parts, markets, and even roads. (As Oswaldo G. Aranha later described Brazil's state at that time, "We were an island where you had to bring in a screw to do anything.")[40] But Meira's resolve was only strengthened. He argued that even if the Americans could build cars more economically, Brazilians simply did not have the currency to purchase them and yet desperately needed transportation in order to build the economy. "We wanted an industry, economical or not," he later recalled.[41] Reporting to the elder Oswaldo Aranha, who had rejoined the Vargas government as minister of finance in 1953, Meira recommended the creation of an executive council with broad administrative powers to draw and implement plans for the founding of a complete automotive industry. In June 1954, two months before the government came to an untimely end with the suicide of President Vargas, the executive council was formed.[42]

The Brazilians were not the only ones finding it difficult to break into the auto industry. In the United States, surrounded by all the resources of the eminent world power, Henry J. Kaiser was taking the first (and only) serious licking in his illustrious entrepreneurial career. Kaiser was a developer par excellence. A booming, bustling, gregarious man with a wide smile and a gaze as bright and direct as a hawk's, he had a mind that was

39. Interview with Lúcio Meira.
40. Interview, Rio de Janeiro, August 23, 1990.
41. Ibid.
42. For Meira's reports to Aranha (senior), see the archives of Getúlio Vargas: FGV, CPDOC, GV 54.01.06/8. Also see the *Dicionário Histórico-Biográfico Brasileiro*, entry on Lúcio Meira, 2175.

always racing ahead to the next detail, the next project, the next industry. He worked tirelessly, not hesitating to call a staff member in the middle of the night to plunge into an important business problem. He demanded and got speed, accuracy, thoroughness, and total commitment from every top employee. He also radiated and expected from others a "can do" attitude. "Problems," he once said during an intense negotiation between union representatives and management, "are only opportunities in work clothes." When the negotiators emerged later that evening, bone-tired from the day's work, Kaiser asked what had happened and was told, "We've just finished solving our opportunities."[43]

Born the son of German immigrant parents in a small farmhouse in upstate New York in 1882, Kaiser began a series of odd jobs at the age of thirteen. While working as a clerk in a dry goods store for $1.50 a week, he found an after-hours job taking photographs at a nearby studio. He was so successful at increasing business that he bought out the proprietor, eventually owning and operating three studios on the Atlantic coast soon after the turn of the century. On the storefronts he placed the sign "Meet the Man with a Smile." In 1906, at age twenty-four, Kaiser left the East for good, determined to make his fortune out West. He soon became intrigued by the construction business, and especially by road building. Within a few years he created one of the largest construction firms in the region, with contracts in Washington, Oregon, and California. With only two full-time employees initially, Kaiser would take jobs anywhere, consistently underbidding his competitors and hiring local labor for the construction work. Kaiser's first job in California was in the town of Redding. Since the train slowed down near Redding but did not stop there (as Kaiser's associates liked to tell the story), Kaiser simply jumped off the moving cars, rolling in the dust and coming to land under a tree, suitcase in hand.

Kaiser's success lay in his willingness to adopt new methods: he was the first road builder to substitute motor-driven tractors systematically for hand and mule labor, and he pioneered the use of diesel engines for land-moving equipment, replacing gas engines with diesel ones himself, since the manufacturers would neither provide diesel models nor sell the equipment with the gas engines left out. In the early 1930s, Kaiser learned other lessons invaluable to the company's growth and to its later involvement in Brazil: the benefits of the joint venture and the importance of having good relations with government. Kaiser's first big contracts came through joint ventures with other American companies: to build roads in

43. *The Kaiser Story* (Oakland: Kaiser Industries Corp., 1968), 62.

Cuba (1927) and then to construct the huge dams built during the Great Depression—Hoover, Bonneville, and the Grand Coulee (1931–43). Kaiser was a partner in Six Companies, Inc., which pooled the resources of major Western construction companies to undertake the massive public works projects. Throughout the 1930s, Kaiser built one public works project after another in combination with other companies: the San Francisco-Oakland Bay Bridge, tunnels in Colorado and Maryland, dry docks at Pearl Harbor and Mare Island, aqueducts in New York.

On the first of the great dams, the Kaiser organization prepared the sand and gravel, while Henry Kaiser himself was elected chairman of the executive committee of Six Companies in recognition of his organizational abilities. Kaiser also took charge of relations with government, becoming a one-man whirlwind lobby in Washington when Congress balked at appropriations for the projects. Over time, the Kaiser Company became one of the largest recipients of funds from the Reconstruction Finance Corporation. According to an article in the London *Economist* in 1949, the envious alleged that "the Kaiser magic lies as much in government relations as industrial technique."[44] When Kaiser entered the war effort and an entirely new field of industry by launching Liberty ships at the rate of one a day, he became a national hero. He broke all records by building the ships in four days. According to Franklin D. Roosevelt's biographer, the president even considered Kaiser as a possible vice presidential running mate in 1944.[45] But in the early postwar period, the Kaiser magic seemed to falter: when it came to the auto industry, Kaiser just could not pull the rabbit out of his hat.

The Kaiser-Frazer Corporation was another joint operation, but unlike Kaiser's other ventures it was fatally undercapitalized. Although the company started out in 1946 with $54 million from shares sold to an enthusiastic public, this amounted to very little in an industry where other companies could set aside hundreds of millions just to retool for new models. Supply shortages at the end of the war, inadequate links to car dealerships, a glutted market in the early 1950s, and the constant demand for new models compounded the problems of inadequate capital, with the result that after only a few marginally profitable years Kaiser-Frazer withdrew in defeat from the American auto industry. Two years before going under, however, Kaiser moved to diminish his mounting losses by pur-

44. *The Economist*, December 3, 1949, 1240.
45. James MacGregor Burns, *Roosevelt: The Soldier of Freedom* (New York: Harcourt, Brace, Jovanovich, 1970), 504. Also see Mark S. Foster, "Giant of the West: Henry J. Kaiser and Regional Industrialization, 1930–1950," *Business History Review* (Spring 1985): 1–23.

chasing Willys-Overland Motors, Inc., and its profitable Jeep line in 1953.[46] The jeep business promised to lend stability to the volatile fortunes of Kaiser Motors, while offering the possibility of success in a line of specialty vehicles which would not have to compete head-on with the Big Three in passenger car production. It was another "opportunity in work clothes."[47]

Kaiser also began looking for other ways of cutting what looked to become more than $100 million worth of losses as Kaiser-Frazer went under. The solvency and credibility of the larger Kaiser operation were at stake. DeLesseps Morrison, then mayor of New Orleans, a promoter of inter-American trade and a friend of the Kaiser family, proposed a solution. At a meeting with Henry Kaiser and his eldest son, Edgar, who had headed the auto operation, Morrison suggested that Kaiser transfer his factories, tools, and trained personnel to Latin America and set up a manufacturing operation there. Kaiser resisted the idea. Having built a two-hundred-mile highway in Cuba nearly thirty years earlier, Kaiser had found that local officials expected bribes at every turn in the road, literally. The practice infuriated Kaiser, who refused to pay and whose operation was shut down at one point. He had not taken a foreign contract since then and was reluctant to go abroad again if it meant doing business under those conditions. But Morrison's assurances that it was possible to get cooperation without bribes, and the pressure of the debt, prevailed.[48] In August 1954, Henry J. Kaiser went on a twenty-seven-day tour of Latin America, with stops in Mexico, Colombia, Brazil, Argentina, Ecuador, and Peru. In Brazil, Oswaldo G. Aranha of WOB acted as host.

Aranha, like Lúcio Meira, had already begun investigating ways of developing an automobile manufacturing capability in Brazil. Unbeknownst to Kaiser, Aranha had traveled to Toledo earlier in the year to tour the Willys-Overland Motors plant.[49] One step ahead of his American guest, Aranha knew the requirements of the jeep operation and had

46. *Time*, April 6, 1953, 96. The purchase of Willys made Kaiser Motors the fourth largest U.S. auto manufacturer.

47. See *The Kaiser Story*, as well as Mimi Stein, *A Special Difference: A History of Kaiser Aluminum and Chemical Corporation* (Oakland: Kaiser Aluminum and Chemical Corp., 1980). Although commissioned and published by the Kaiser companies, these works are nonetheless useful guides to basic facts about Kaiser. Also very important is Mark S. Foster, *Henry J. Kaiser: Builder in the Modern American West* (Austin: University of Texas Press, 1989).

48. Stein, *A Special Difference*, 95–96; also see deLesseps Morrison, *Latin American Mission* (New York: Simon and Schuster, 1965), 205–06.

49. First interview with O. G. Aranha. Also see letter from Oswaldo G. Aranha to Hickman Price, August 30, 1954, p. 2. Copy provided by Dr. Aranha.

already thought about how they could be met in Brazil. As far as Aranha was concerned, what remained to be seen were the terms. True to his character, Kaiser arrived with very definite ideas about what those should be.

Aside from some strong reservations about the ready availability of steel in Brazil, Kaiser had two main ideas: he wanted to establish an industry which could produce cars as well as jeeps, and he wanted to begin in a country where local partners would have sufficient money and entrepreneurial spark to assume majority ownership. Since Kaiser needed to dispose of the tools and dies for both passenger cars and jeeps, he had important financial reasons for wanting to set up an operation abroad which would produce both kinds of vehicles. Selling off the assets of Kaiser Motors to diminish the debt was his number one priority. But Kaiser's propensity to look for the development implications of his projects framed these financial considerations. He had long since viewed himself as a developer in the broadest sense of the word. During the Depression he had had a vision of helping to industrialize the western United States to create more jobs—something which he in fact did. He was for "the development of the West by any industrialist who is passionately and primarily devoted to its interest," and he knew what it felt like to have outsiders (in this case, easterners) come in and snap up local opportunities.[50] During his trip to Brazil, most of the businessmen Kaiser spoke to emphasized their interest in the manufacture of jeeps alone. But Kaiser envisioned a broader, bigger industry which would not only produce jeeps for Brazil, but foster the development of other basic industries, including auto parts, and might even export cars that could challenge U.S. manufacturers on their own turf. "This would be building a country—not just making a contract to sell some equipment," he told the young Aranha.[51] A shrewd salesman, Kaiser must have recognized that this was a hard argument for a Brazilian to resist.

Kaiser also had good reason, from a financial point of view, to seek out local participation in ownership. The company's debt burden in the United States would have made it difficult for Kaiser to set up a wholly owned subsidiary even if he had wanted to. He had little cash to contribute to a new enterprise, and he needed payment for the used equipment. With his genius at tapping into government resources, Kaiser must have realized that a backdoor bailout of his domestic operation lay in finding Brazilian partners who could apply for loans to the Eximbank to

50. Quote of Henry Kaiser cited by Mark Foster in "Giant of the West," 18–19 (also see 7).
51. Henry J. Kaiser and Robert C. Elliott to Edgar F. Kaiser and E. E. Trefethen, Jr., August 18, 1954, p. 2. BL, HJK Papers, carton 162, file: "SA-Automobiles-Brazil, 1 of 2."

purchase the idled equipment. Kaiser would be able to have his cake (cash to pay off debts) and eat it, too (continued participation in the automobile business through shares in the new operation).

There were other precedents for a joint venture as well. Not only did Kaiser have extensive experience with such partnerships, but it was also increasingly common practice after 1945 for U.S. companies to enter into joint venture relationships with Brazilian partners in order to gain a foothold in protected industries. The Brazilian government imposed high import taxes on any items that directly competed with goods manufactured in the country. As soon as a company in Brazil could demonstrate that it was producing an item in sufficient quantity, steep taxes would go into effect to protect the young industry. Some U.S. companies which exported to Brazil began manufacturing operations simply to avoid having markets closed off to them. As industrialization began to snowball in the early 1950s, companies found themselves hurrying into new activities and taking on local partners in order to move into a market as quickly as possible.[52] Although the lack of any existing or imminent auto manufacturing in Brazil ruled out this incentive in Kaiser's case, the growing number of companies resorting to local partnerships meant that he was not alone in adopting this technique.[53]

But Kaiser's approach was nonetheless unique. Kaiser insisted on a minimum of 51 percent ownership by Brazilians. No other American company operating in Brazil in the 1950s, including IBEC, had a similar policy. The overwhelming majority of American companies operating in joint ventures retained majority ownership, and in the rare cases in which the Brazilian partners were dominant, the American investors had other, more sizable ventures in which they exercised control.[54] In a brief interview that President Getúlio Vargas granted the famous American busi-

---

52. Gordon and Grommers, U.S. Manufacturing in Brazil, 22–27, 140–41.

53. Before 1956, there was no auto manufacturing in Brazil, except for parts. Even the government owned Fábrica Nacional de Motores was still only assembling vehicles (trucks) under license from the Italian firm Alpha Romeo. Dicionário Histórico-Biográfico Brasileiro, 1211.

54. Gordon and Grommers, U.S. Manufacturing in Brazil, 138–39. Gordon and Grommers's survey of U.S. manufacturers in Brazil was based on interviews with the thirty-six top American companies in Brazil, as identified by the prominent Brazilian-American investment firm Deltec, S.A. The authors found that as of 1961 approximately one-third of these companies were involved in some type of joint venture with local capital. Of the companies surveyed, none had joint venture arrangements before World War II, most partnerships having been established only in the early 1950s. Only three of the thirty-six U.S. companies were minority partners in joint ventures, and two of these companies had larger ventures which they controlled. I am assuming, since Kaiser corporation was one of the participants in the survey, that Kaiser is the company the authors referred to when they indicated that there was only one company whose major operation in Brazil was primarily locally owned.

nessman on August 20, 1954, Henry Kaiser explained that if he decided to locate a manufacturing plant in Brazil "we would want the Brazilians to own the majority of stock in our company."[55] Vargas responded warmly, noting that he had already read about Kaiser as a "great industrialist, great adventurer, great leader of men." The president, rather an adventurer himself, seemed to take to Kaiser. Puffing happily on his cigar, Vargas apparently enjoyed discussing Brazil's industrialization with the American entrepreneur.[56]

Kaiser's modus operandi was based on what he considered both fair and prudent: he thought it was fair for the foreign country to benefit and prudent for an American company to make sure that it did. Over the years, Henry Kaiser had demonstrated in dealings with labor and the public his awareness of the value of making sure that everyone felt invested in the success of a given operation. Kaiser consistently settled labor negotiations with the United Steel Workers before the rest of the industry and in 1946 chided other steel producers for being stingy with workers at the expense of the nation. This, combined with his experiments with prepaid health care, earned him the epithet "socialist" from conservative businessmen.[57] "Welfare capitalist" or "corporatist innovator" would have been more appropriate.

Over the years Kaiser had also come to see the value of public participation in his companies through ownership of common stock. At first he had taken his companies public only under duress from financial advisers and the banks. As the Great Depression had shown, business was inherently risky and, in the words of one of his top assistants, "Henry Kaiser didn't want anybody to lose any money off of him."[58] Kaiser soon found that public participation had many benefits, however, not the least of which were publicity and good will. The experience convinced him that, when he went abroad, the local people should make some money out of the venture.

Kaiser calculated his own interests very closely but in broad terms. Like

---

55. Morrison, *Latin American Mission*, 207.

56. Henry Kaiser and Robert Elliott to Edgar Kaiser and E. E. Trefethen, August 17, 1954, p. 5. BL, HJK Papers, carton 162, file: "SA-Automobiles-Brazil, 1 of 2."

57. Foster, "Giant of the West," 19.

58. Interview with E. E. Trefethen, Oakland, California, January 15, 1987. According to Trefethen, Henry Kaiser was finally pushed into going public by Bank of America, which could no longer handle 100 percent of the company's need for capital. Trefethen shared the leadership of Kaiser Company with Henry's son Edgar as the founder approached retirement age, eventually becoming vice chairman of the board of Kaiser Industries. Edgar was chairman. Kaiser once said, "He is as much my son as Edgar." Quote cited by Stein, *A Special Difference*, 158.

Rockefeller, he viewed capitalism not as a zero-sum game that only the rich or only Americans could win, but as a system which depended for its legitimacy and vitality on its ability to increase the absolute wealth of all participants. Kaiser genuinely believed that for his own venture to thrive in Brazil, it had to create wealth for all concerned, not just for the American partners; otherwise, it ran the risk of being resented by the public and harassed by the government. Kaiser never expressed any concerns about Brazilian nationalism or political turmoil, yet he apparently regarded local ownership as an essential stabilizing factor.[59]

Kaiser was also alert to the ways in which his project could serve the national interests of both the United States and Brazil and thus deepen goodwill toward the company. "Brazil is of such importance to the United States and has such a record of cooperation with our country in international affairs that the assumption is that Washington would look favorably upon an auto industry project of benefit to Brazil," Henry Kaiser wrote to Edgar from Brazil.[60] Undoubtedly, Kaiser recognized that this special relationship would give an edge to Brazilian partners in seeking Eximbank loans for the project. Before leaving on his trip Kaiser had also conceived the idea of tying the new project to a revitalization of the Good Neighbor policy. He asked his staff to work into a promotional brochure the statement "It is our conviction that the Good Neighbor policy can be and should be quickened, re-energized and re-vitalized into definite *Better Neighbor* actions and cooperation that can bring to realization enormous benefits and accomplishments."[61]

But Henry Kaiser's statements about U.S.-Brazil relations at times had an edge of advocacy—he publicly criticized the U.S. government for not taking a more active interest in Brazil's development—and his reasons for promoting majority Brazilian ownership do not seem to have been only opportunistic.[62] He could have achieved his public relations objectives and reaped the benefits of an influx of Brazilian capital while keeping local ownership well below 49 percent. He could also have applied the principle of local ownership only to Brazil, which had a strong entrepreneurial elite and incentives for nationalization. Instead, Kaiser and his

59. Interview with E. E. Trefethen.
60. Henry Kaiser and Robert Elliott to Edgar Kaiser and E. E. Trefethen, August 17, 1954, p. 2. BL, HJK Papers, carton 162, file: "SA-Automobiles-Brazil, 1 of 2."
61. Telegram from Robert Elliott to Chad Calhoun, July 23, 1954. BL, HJK Papers, carton 161, file: "SA-Automobiles-general."
62. See *Diário de São Paulo*, August 20, 1954, 11, for an example of Kaiser's criticisms, and Kaiser's press release from September 9, 1954, p. 6. BL, HJK Papers, carton 164, file: "South America-Mr. Kaiser Sees Opportunities."

successors made 50 percent local ownership a company goal in all the other countries they were to enter after Brazil: Argentina, India, England, Spain, Ghana. Although Kaiser never articulated an explicit political philosophy, a strong belief in the tenets of modern corporatist capitalism is evident in all his actions, from joint ventures under government sponsorship to cooperation with unions to the development of one of the United States' largest employee health programs, Kaiser Permanente. Kaiser's entire U.S. operation was a reflection of the corporatist model of business restraint and self-regulation to achieve societal harmony within a framework of reasonable profits. For Kaiser, this had proved a winning formula, and so it was logical that he took it abroad. His additional innovation was to decide that, in a foreign context, social harmony and reasonable profits were best achieved by keeping American participation below the highly symbolic line of 50 percent.

Partial local ownership would have been simply prudent; majority local ownership was an expression of what Kaiser considered a fair acknowledgment of national sovereignty. Kaiser's recognition that foreign investment was intimately connected to questions of sovereignty placed him at the forefront of those seeking to build stronger relations between American business and the postwar developing world.

Kaiser spent the first few days of his trip to Rio de Janeiro in August 1954 talking with both American and Brazilian officials and businessmen. One of his meetings was with George Washburne, the head of Interamericana, the investment firm that Chase and IBEC had set up with twelve Brazilian banks. Washburne impressed him enough that he sent a report of the meeting to Edgar. Familiar with the extreme difficulties of selling securities in Brazil's small financial market, Washburne counseled Kaiser against public participation in such a massive project, suggesting that he instead find partners among wealthy Brazilian families. Washburne also suggested that Kaiser keep majority ownership: "I would not go into it, if I were you, unless I had well over 50% interest at this stage. I'd be darn sure to keep control to make sure it has the chance to succeed." He further warned Kaiser not to "believe any promises that anyone gives you here, such as promises they will make steel available," without having the company's very best technical people carefully evaluate each claim.[63]

Although he urged caution, Washburne was nonetheless enthusiastic about Kaiser's proposed entry into Brazil and recommended to Kaiser

---

63. "George Washburne (on Financing Auto Industry)," August 16, 1954, p. 2. BL, HJK Papers, carton 162, file: "SA-Automobiles-Brazil, 1 of 2."

some local experts. Washburne was especially taken with Kaiser's idea that, with its lower labor costs, Brazil might eventually export cars back to the United States. ("It's staggering," he said. ". . . I won't be able to sleep tonight.")[64] The other businessmen to whom Kaiser spoke echoed Washburne's enthusiasm, with the result that at the end of a few days Kaiser had concluded that Brazil had the "No. 1 market potentials in South America" and was "the place where a maximum feasible disposition of Kaiser-Willys . . . could be made." Kaiser saw as particularly advantageous the low labor costs, the fast-growing population and urban market, the natural resources of iron, the protectionism which would be granted a new producer of auto parts, and Brazil's size and importance to the United States. He also favorably noted the determination of Brazilians themselves to develop their "own full-fledged auto industry."[65] Kaiser was especially impressed by an article Lúcio Meira had written on the need for such an industry in Brazil and collected a copy to take home.[66]

An official of Willys-Overland Export Corporation had asked Oswaldo G. Aranha to host Kaiser during his stay in Rio. Aranha made sure Kaiser was comfortable with the accommodations at the Copacabana Palace and took care to introduce him to the elite of the capital city, including the president himself. But while businessmen on all sides pressed Kaiser to take an interest in various propositions, Aranha hung back, awaiting the right moment. Finally, on the second evening of his visit, Kaiser indicated his surprise that Aranha had not yet brought up the possible expansion of WOB. Aranha continued to play it cool, answering that Kaiser was a guest and should feel free to do whatever he wanted without feeling pressed by his host's business interests. The next day, while driving through the vestiges of the tropical high forest on the way to the national steel plant of Volta Redonda some hours distant from Rio, the explosive, expressive American finally lost patience with Aranha's gracious delays. "Look, stop this car immediately! I want to get out," he told his surprised companion. "If you do not start talking to me about business in Brazil, I will get out immediately!"[67] Not wanting to see his guest tromp off into nowhere, Aranha began.

Without disclosing the fact of his earlier visit to the Willys plant in

64. Ibid., p. 3.
65. Henry Kaiser and Robert Elliott to Edgar Kaiser and E. E. Trefethen, August 17, 1954, p. 2. BL, HJK Papers, carton 162, file: "SA-Automobiles-Brazil, 1 of 2."
66. Robert Elliott to Henry Kaiser, November 8, 1954, pp. 1–3. BL, HJK Papers, carton 162, file: "SA-Automobiles-Brazil, 1 of 2." (Article from *Rodovia*, May 1954.)
67. First interview with O. G. Aranha. Also see letter of Aranha to Hickman Price, Jr., August 30, 1954, p. 2. Copy provided by Dr. Aranha.

Toledo, Aranha outlined his ideas for setting up an automobile industry in Brazil. Kaiser immediately challenged the feasibility of Aranha's conception, emphatically stating that he "would not enter the auto industry in Brazil without making sure of adequate and sound sources of steel and of other factors to assure low-cost auto production."[68] Aranha tried to convince Kaiser that there was adequate steel production in the country to start with, but Kaiser clung stubbornly to his objections until the party reached Volta Redonda. There, engineers were able to convince him that the integrated steel plant had the capacity to supply an auto industry. After this the outlook "brightened considerably," Kaiser reported to Oakland headquarters.[69] A few days later, Kaiser left Brazil with the rudimentary outlines of a business deal with Aranha.

Kaiser continued his trip southward, spending a few days in Argentina, where, after overcoming a strong reluctance to do business with the dictator Juan Perón, he eventually concluded another deal to start an additional auto manufacturing plant there.[70] Leaving Argentina on August 24, Kaiser made a stopover in Rio de Janeiro. Disembarking, he and the members of his party found the airport in an uproar. "Vargas has killed himself," a dazed policeman blurted out in response to their inquiries. Soon after dawn that morning, following an immense political crisis of several weeks sparked by the attempted assassination of one of the president's political opponents, Vargas had responded to an army ultimatum that he resign by placing a gun to his heart and firing once. The Aranha family, at the president's side through the midnight hours until he excused himself to go to his bedroom, rushed into the room. The elder Oswaldo Aranha, Brazil's great statesman and Vargas's comrade through war and revolution since 1930, wept.[71]

The younger Aranha wrote to Kaiser a few days later explaining why he had been unable to greet Kaiser at the airport after that "horrible night . . . that ended so tragically" and asked Kaiser to wait a few weeks before sending his engineers to make a study of production requirements. Poli-

68. Henry Kaiser and Robert Elliott to Edgar Kaiser and E. E. Trefethen, August 18, 1954, p. 1. BL, HJK Papers, carton 162, file: "SA-Automobiles-Brazil, 1 of 2."
69. Ibid.
70. According to New Orleans Mayor deLesseps Morrison, who was a companion on the South American trip, Kaiser almost canceled the Argentine leg of the journey a couple of times and initially refused to attend the events in his honor in Buenos Aires. Kaiser was finally persuaded by Morrison to talk with Perón but then abruptly left his meeting with the president after a Perón aide hinted that a bribe might be in order. By the time the Americans reached their hotel, Perón had left an urgent message to reopen negotiations. Kaiser was able to conclude the deal without resorting to bribery. Morrison *Latin American Mission*, 208–15.
71. Skidmore, *Politics in Brazil*, 141–42.

tics and business had come to a standstill, and Aranha wanted to make sure Kaiser's representatives got "an exact idea of my country and its possibilities, without suffering the influence of the turmoil in which we now live."[72] Over the next few months, Aranha and the Kaisers hammered out the precise terms of an agreement, Edgar Kaiser gradually taking over the negotiations from his father. For awhile the Kaisers considered signing a deal with a different Brazilian group also interested in development of the auto industry, but the Aranha-Barbosa group's willingness to take on cars as well as jeeps and the considerable stature of the Aranhas and Barbosas in banking and politics (the Barbosa family was closely associated with Fundo Crescinco and Nelson Rockefeller) finally won over the Americans.[73] In February 1955, Edgar Kaiser signed a contract with Oswaldo G. Aranha and Theodoro Quartim Barbosa for the development of an auto industry in Brazil.

Under the agreement, Edgar Kaiser promised to sell half of the jeep equipment to the Aranha-Barbosa group for the cash equivalent of its "definitive fair value" as calculated by an independent engineering firm and mutually agreed upon. To purchase the equipment, Aranha and Barbosa would apply to the Eximbank of the United States for loans. Once the Brazilians owned 50 percent of the equipment, both parties were to sell their half of the machinery to a reorganized WOB for an equal number of shares in exchange. In addition, both parties were to sell other physical assets such as the assembly plant in Brazil and the Kaiser passenger car equipment to the venture, again in exchange for shares, and the Aranha-Barbosa group agreed to make additional subscriptions to the company's common stock in order to provide the capital necessary for expansion of WOB's plant and facilities. As a result of these transactions Kaiser would own approximately 45 percent of the reorganized WOB and the Brazilian group 55 percent. Representation on the company's board of directors and voting control of the corporation would be "proportionate to their respective holdings of common stock."[74] The docu-

72. Oswaldo G. Aranha to Henry Kaiser, August 30, 1954, p. 1. Copy provided by Dr. Aranha. Also found in BL, HJK Papers, carton 161, file: "South America-'A' Misc."
73. Memorandum from Webb Wilson to E. E. Trefethen, January 12, 1955, p. 7. BL, HJK Papers, carton 162, "Automobiles-Brazil, 2 of 2." The American lawyer who consulted for the Kaisers in their Brazilian negotiations was Edward G. Miller, Jr., a friend of Nelson Rockefeller and the former assistant secretary of state under Truman who had been responsible for setting up the Joint Brazil-U.S. Economic Development Commission.
74. Agreement between Theodoro Quartim Barbosa, Oswaldo G. Aranha, and Kaiser Motors Corporation, February 17, 1955, p. 8. Copy provided by Dr. Aranha. A November 1954 draft of the agreement can also be found in BL, HJK Papers, carton 162, file: "SA-Automobiles-Brazil, 1 of 2."

ment was "beautiful," Aranha later said, but, unfortunately, it was a plan never to be implemented.[75]

After the death of Vargas, a caretaker government held power until the election and inauguration of Juscelino Kubitschek a year and a half later. The interim government, headed by former Vice President Café Filho, had neither as strong a commitment to industrialization as the Vargas government nor as much influence in implementing its own policies. The interim president chose as finance minister the fiscal conservative Eugênio Gudin, who had little sympathy with the WOB plan and its particular Brazilian backers. The Aranha family was heavily identified with the fallen Vargas regime and with the policies of accelerated industrialization against which Gudin had spoken for years. In a meeting with Gudin shortly after Café Filho came into power, Henry Kaiser pointed out that an automotive factory would save the country up to $65 million a year in foreign exchange, reducing or eliminating the need to import completely knocked down vehicles. Gudin responded that he realized this and "wanted to help" but could not approve the use of Brazil's limited foreign reserves for such a project.[76] Kaiser's arguments that an auto industry would reduce imports and broaden the nation's general industrial capacity fell on deaf ears.

The Café Filho government, meanwhile, was crafting the legislation that would be its primary legacy to the future of Brazil: SUMOC Instruction 113. This was a new regulation of the Superintendency of Money and Credit (SUMOC) which gave significant incentives to foreigners for investment in Brazil. The policy, adopted in January 1955, affected the Kaiser-Aranha-Barbosa relationship in two important ways: first, it granted import licenses to Brazilians only for *new* equipment while allowing foreigners to import both new and old equipment, and second, in exchange for important tax concessions and currency privileges, it prevented foreign investors from receiving cash or deferred payments from Brazilians for imported equipment. That is, when Americans brought certain kinds of equipment into Brazil, they were allowed to receive only shares in the enterprise which imported the goods, rather than direct payment.[77] The idea was that this would increase the amount of foreign investment based on risk capital instead of Brazilian debt. With the adoption of SUMOC Instruction 113, key aspects of the Kaiser-Aranha-

75. First interview with O. G. Aranha.
76. Memorandum of Conference with Eugênio Gudin, November 5, 1954, p. 3. BL, HJK Papers, carton 162, file: "SA-Automobiles-Brazil, 1 of 2."
77. Gordon and Grommers, *U.S. Manufacturing in Brazil*, 19–20, 160. Also, interview with Sydney Latini (Confederation of Commercial Associations of Brazil), Rio de Janeiro, November 7, 1986.

Barbosa agreement were effectively abrogated: the Brazilian partners were prohibited from purchasing the used American equipment which they had planned to sell to the reorganized company in order to establish themselves as full partners, and the Kaisers were prohibited from receiving payment for the equipment from their Brazilian partners.

Oswaldo G. Aranha, like many Brazilian businessmen, vehemently protested the new regulation to Eugênio Gudin, claiming it would have the overall effect (as it did) of increasing foreign equity in Brazilian companies.[78] Conceivably, the Aranha-Barbosa group could have used cash to purchase additional shares of the reorganized WOB to achieve the goal of 55 percent majority ownership. But that meant doing so without financing from the U.S. Eximbank, which lent money only for the purchase of American equipment, and without the machinery as collateral, from the point of view of Brazilian banks. It simply was not possible, in the tight Brazilian money market of the 1950s, to obtain loans just for the risky purchase of common stock.[79] The Aranhas and Barbosas, like most Brazilians, could not keep up with wealthier American investors when business was put on a pay-as-you-go basis.

A few days after Instruction 113 was announced, a discouraged Aranha wrote to Edgar Kaiser, "As you can see, the Instruction closed all doors for us to go in with you in our program. The amazing part of it Edgar is that a foreigner can bring into Brazil industrial equipment and invest but for the Brazilians, if they want to bring in something big and helpful for the future progress of the country, this Instruction has denied them this right." Aranha called the government's announcement "a blow to our plans."[80]

Nevertheless, the Kaisers and Aranhas persisted in trying to find a way around Instruction 113 throughout the spring of 1955, until one bureaucratic stumbling block after another finally led Oswaldo G. Aranha to suggest that the joint venture agreement be terminated so that the Kaisers could pursue development of the auto industry on their own, free of "any legal or moral commitment" to the Aranha-Barbosa group and without being hindered by the difficulties of the Brazilian partners.[81] Edgar Kaiser accepted Aranha's proposal but expressed confidence that

78. First interview with O. G. Aranha. Also see Gordon and Grommers, *U.S. Manufacturing in Brazil*, 40–44, 137.
79. Second interview with Oswaldo G. Aranha, Rio de Janeiro, November 14, 1986.
80. Oswaldo G. Aranha to Edgar Kaiser, January 11, 1955, p. 1. BL, HJK Papers, carton 161, file: "SA-Automobiles-Argentina, 4 of 4."
81. Memorandum initialed by Edgar Kaiser, Oswaldo Gudolle Aranha, and Theodoro Quartim Barbosa, June 14, 1955, p. 1. Attached to a letter from Edward Miller to Edgar Kaiser, July 5, 1955. BL, HJK Papers, carton 162, file "SA-Automobiles-Brazil, 2 of 2."

at some point the joint venture would succeed, even though "just when and the details are not clear at this time." Certainly, Kaiser added, "we could have no finer partners."[82] Aranha and the younger Kaiser continued to correspond regularly, sharing news of their wives and children as well as information concerning Brazilian politics, Willys-Overland, and the Kaiser ventures elsewhere in Latin America.[83]

Yet neither the Aranhas nor the Kaisers were ready to give up on the idea of majority Brazilian ownership and at least significant Brazilian control in whatever manufacturing venture eventually got off the ground. Although greatly disappointed, Oswaldo G. Aranha later commented that "by heart" the Brazilian group felt themselves equal partners with Kaiser and that Edgar Kaiser himself always acted in that spirit.[84] "Edgar persisted in the idea that we should be treated as equals, but in reality it didn't come out that way," Aranha commented. "Business takes you into new roads that you don't even want to go down."[85] The solution that Kaiser and the Aranha-Barbosa group eventually worked out was to create Brazilian majority ownership through sales of stock to the general public rather than through a partnership. Although diffuse stock sales would effectively give Kaiser, as the largest minority shareholder, much more control of the corporation than had been anticipated under the original plan, members of the Aranha and Barbosa families would stay on the board of directors of WOB to ensure Brazilian participation in decision making, if and when the company could expand into manufacturing.

But in spite of the new government incentives for foreign investment, cooperation was still lacking from the Café Filho government, which had slipped further into lame duck ineffectuality. The break came in October 1955 with the election of Juscelino Kubitschek. Kubitschek brought charisma, optimism, and a passionate belief in economic development to the presidency. Childhood experiences, including his father's early death,

82. Edgar Kaiser to Oswaldo G. Aranha, June 17, 1955, p. 2. Copy provided by Dr. Aranha.
83. In Argentina, with Perón's support, Kaiser was able to implement plans for an auto plant much sooner than in unstable Brazil. Even after Perón was ousted in 1955, the Kaiser company (Industrias Kaiser Argentina) continued its work virtually uninterrupted and was the first of seventy-two foreign companies taken off the black list of the new government, which investigated all ventures set up by Perón for corruption. Because of the large participation of the government in the joint venture along with local private investors, the Kaisers owned only about one-third of the Argentine company, instead of the one-half projected in Brazil. Business Week, June 21, 1958, 108. Also see September 29, 1955, memorandum of conversation between Edgar Kaiser and President Leonardi following the overthrow of Perón. BL, HJK Papers, carton 161, file: "Argentina-Autos, 2 of 4."
84. First interview with O. G. Aranha.
85. Second interview with O. G. Aranha.

shaped his outlook. As Miriam Cardoso notes, Kubitschek must have felt that "if an orphan boy, left at a tender age in the world with only his mother, a simple teacher in the interior of Minas, could arrive at the Presidency of the Republic—why could not a nation, no more lacking in resources than he had been, become rich and powerful?"[86] Kubitschek also had a politician's sensitivity to the changing requirements of vote-getting in populist Brazil. Celso Lafer credits Brazilian politicians' growing commitment to development in the 1950s to the expansion of electoral participation in the same period and the need thereby to satisfy an increasingly vocal and heterogeneous electorate.[87] Certainly, Kubitschek tied development to democratization, the achievement of social equality, and the maintenance of social harmony, arguing that "underdeveloped zones are zones open to the penetration of antidemocratic ideology."[88] Most important, for people like Kaiser and Rockefeller, Kubitschek also brought with him a confidence that Brazilians could collaborate with American investors to their nation's advantage. "The collaboration of foreign capital is not a subject for emotional debate; it is a technical necessity," Kubitschek wrote the year he assumed office. "To reject foreign capital without having the technical or economic capacity to replace the rejected investments is not nationalism: it is weakness and timidity."[89]

Within weeks of being elected, Kubitschek named Lúcio Meira the new minister of transportation and public works. During the period of turmoil following Vargas's suicide, Meira had maintained his commitment to developing an automobile industry, publishing numerous articles on the need for such an industry and strengthening his personal ties with Kubitschek.[90] Even before the president-elect's inaugural, Meira contacted Oswaldo G. Aranha to ask him to renew his efforts to bring the jeep factory to Brazil. Aranha excitedly wrote Edgar Kaiser, "Over night the picture changes from a government that did not even have the good will to examine our propositions to a new and eager government that shows that [it] is going to help in every way possible any plans with regard to the establishment of this type of industry."[91]

86. *Ideologia do Desenvolvimento*, 98.
87. "O Planejamento no Brasil: Observações sôbre o Plano de Metas (1956–1961)," in *Planejamento no Brasil*, ed. Betty Mindlin Lafer (São Paulo: Editora Perspectiva, 1975), 31–37.
88. Quoted in Cardoso, *Ideologia do Desenvolvimento*, 134.
89. Quoted in ibid., 170.
90. *Dicionário Histórico-Biográfico Brasileiro*, p. 2175. Interview with Lúcio Meira.
91. Oswaldo G. Aranha to Edgar Kaiser, December 16, 1955, p. 1. Copy provided by Dr. Aranha. Copy also available in BL, EFK Papers, carton 289, Folder 2a.

Kubitschek had identified the creation of an automobile industry as one of the foremost goals in his famous program of *Metas* (targets), and indeed the industry eventually became the leading sector in Brazilian industrialization. Lúcio Meira, along with Roberto Campos as head of the BNDE, recommended to the president that he appoint a working group responsible only to the chief executive to expedite the effort; it was to be modeled after the kind of commission that Meira had recommended to Vargas. In June 1956 Meira's commission, the Executive Group for the Automobile Industry (GEIA), began work. It was the first and ultimately one of the most successful of a series of presidential working groups which Kubitschek created to implement the metas program. As Celso Lafer has pointed out, in trying to overcome the Byzantine inefficiencies of the federal bureaucracy "the Government did not opt for the total reform of the administrative system, but for the alternative of a parallel administration."[92] Franklin D. Roosevelt had followed the same executive strategy twenty years earlier during the New Deal.

With a presidential mandate and a clear path through the normally congested bureaucracy, GEIA quickly laid out the basis for a national automotive industry. Under the leadership of Lúcio Meira and his assistant for the automotive program, a young, energetic Brazilian named Sydney Latini, GEIA decreed that a variety of highly advantageous privileges would be given for a limited time to a limited number of automobile manufacturers, based on their ability to show how they could comply with certain requirements set up by GEIA. The incentives were automatic inclusion under SUMOC Instruction 113 (bringing substantial tax and currency benefits), exemption from import taxes on all manufacturing machinery brought into the country regardless of value, and extremely favorable tax rates on the subsequent importation of car parts not yet produced in Brazil. Given that the value of automotive manufacturing machinery was in the many millions of dollars, the savings on import taxes alone would be enormous. But GEIA's requirements were also high: companies had to demonstrate how they would achieve nationalization within five years. Each year, vehicles would have to come a certain number of percentage points closer to complete local manufacture, as measured by the total weight of the truck, jeep, or car. Jeeps and trucks, deemed more essential than passenger cars, were granted the most favor-

92. "O Planejamento no Brasil," 40. Also see Lucas Lopes, "JK e o Programa de Metas, Palestra do Ministro Lucas Lopes," speech given in Brasília, May 14, 1986, 24–26. (Copy provided by Dr. Lopes.) ABCAR would be another good example of the Kubitschek propensity for working around a given bureaucracy (in this case the Ministry of Agriculture) rather than attempting to change its *fomento* program.

able tax rates and had to comply with the most rigorous nationalization schedules.[93]

GEIA established a strict deadline for the submission of plans. Companies such as the wholly owned subsidiaries of Ford and General Motors that imported finished cars or assembled completely knocked down packages had to get in on the program immediately or not only forfeit the GEIA incentives but lose access to the Brazilian market forever. Once Brazil was manufacturing its own cars, licenses would not be granted for foreign imports. General Motors submitted plans fairly readily, but Ford resisted the program, complaining about its infeasibility and filing an application on the day of the deadline. But the American-affiliated company which jumped into the program as soon as it was announced and which became the first manufacturer of gasoline engines in Brazil was Willys-Overland. Sydney Latini later said that "some companies considered the plans very ambitious—too ambitious when the means of nationalization were the utilization of national parts fabricated in Brazil. But Willys was exactly that company out of all the others which believed in the law." According to Latini, Willys was the one American-affiliated company which, to use a Brazilian soccer metaphor, always wore the shirt of the local team.[94]

The first WOB vehicles rolled off the line in early 1957 while the factory was still being built. By the end of that year Willys had produced more than nine thousand jeeps and Aerowillys sedans, 60 percent of which by weight had been manufactured in Brazil.[95] To accomplish this, WOB management had to arrange for contracts with Brazilian parts producers to obtain those pieces of the vehicles which WOB could not yet produce. The goal of GEIA in insisting on the speed of nationalization was to foster an auto industry that was organized horizontally, with hundreds of companies contributing to production and benefiting from economic growth, rather than one organized vertically, with two or three giants manufacturing all components. For example, at one point WOB had contracts with more than fourteen hundred parts producers, all Brazilian.[96] If no Brazilian companies were capable of producing a necessary part, such as the transmission, Willys would persuade an American parts manufacturer to

93. Interview with Latini; *Dicionário Histórico-Biográfico Brasileiro*, 2176; Gordon and Grommers, *U.S. Manufacturing in Brazil*, 48–53.
94. In Latini's words, Willys "vestiu a camisa." Interview with Sydney Latini.
95. *Quem Controla O Que: O Capital Estrangeiro No Brasil* (São Paulo: Editôra Banas, 1961), 1:341. Gordon and Grommers, *U.S. Manufacturing in Brazil*, 49.
96. Interview with Max Pearce (general manager and then president of WOB), Orinda, California, January 14, 1987.

set up a joint venture with Brazilian investors. According to Euclydes Aranha Netto, the brother of Oswaldo G. Aranha and later a director of WOB, finding and assisting nascent auto parts producers required extraordinary time and effort. "It was a war," he later recalled, but "a beautiful war with very interesting battles."[97] Although the other three U.S. automakers, Ford, General Motors, and International Harvester, also purchased parts from Brazilian manufacturers and helped facilitate joint ventures, Willys was, according to Latini, always the "most aggressive, most advanced" company, utilizing a far greater number of nationally produced parts than the others. It was "the pioneer."[98]

At the beginning, the top personnel in Willys were Americans, but Kaiser's technical assistance policy allowed foreign nationals to stay in the host country for only two years. During that time they had to train at least one and preferably two or three Brazilians to take over their jobs. By the end of the 1950s only a few Americans, among them the head of WOB, Max Pearce, remained in the company, and there was one American on the board of directors. Five of the seven board members were Brazilians and included Euclydes Aranha, Oswaldo's brother, and Paulo Barbosa, the son of Theodoro Quartim. An advisory executive council which included Theodoro Quartim Barbosa himself had no representation from Kaiser.[99]

Nevertheless, because the provisions of SUMOC Instruction 113 had left Kaiser corporation as the largest single stockholder, the Americans continued to have decisive influence on questions of consequence. The most telling example of this was the firing in 1959 of Hickman Price, Jr., the American who headed the company before Pearce, Price's top American assistant, took over. Price was extremely well liked by the Aranhas and Barbosas and by Lúcio Meira and Sydney Latini of the Brazilian government.[100] Price spoke Portuguese fluently, had an outgoing, dynamic personality, and was an intense advocate for the development of a Brazilian-owned parts industry. But according to Pearce, who supported Price's leadership, Price was also "a bit slippery," not above offering a bribe to a petty official if it meant getting a shipment or two processed a bit faster. "His morals weren't all up to their [the Kaisers'] standards," Pearce remembered. Price's enormous self-confidence also had a ten-

97. Interview, Rio de Janeiro, August 14, 1990.
98. Interview.
99. Interview with Max Pearce.
100. Interviews with Aranha, Meira, and Latini.

dency to bubble over into an arrogant attitude toward Edgar Kaiser as a minority stockholder, whom Price at one time called "that boy."[101]

Edgar Kaiser was more mild-mannered than his ebullient father but equally determined and steely-nerved. When Edgar Kaiser arrived at the Rio airport and told Max Pearce that he had come to fire Hickman, Pearce commented that in light of Price's strong Brazilian support "it's going to take some doing." Edgar Kaiser did not respond but spent the rest of the day in meetings with Oswaldo Aranha, Theodoro Quartim Barbosa, and Lúcio Meira explaining his objections to Price and making the point that it was the Kaisers who had arranged for the financing to set up the company and supported the project from the beginning. Max Pearce commented later, "I had a great lesson in international finance and power. . . . It was all over, just like that, in one day. . . . This was Kaiser of the Kaiser empire. Hickman's support just disappeared."[102]

Under Hickman Price and Max Pearce, the labor policies of Willys-Overland were much like those implemented by other American car manufacturers in Brazil although, again, the role of WOB was particularly important since it was the first manufacturer to get under way. Auto companies generally offered higher wages than those of older Brazilian manufacturers, such as those in the textile industry; moreover, they offered benefits including stability of employment, medical care for workers and their families, educational assistance, and low-priced food in worker cafeterias.[103]

The effect was to increase competition among employers for workers and to establish a precedent for improved working conditions which other industries eventually had to match. By the mid-1970s, other industrial sectors had raised their wages to attract workers, and other non-monetary benefits and services had, according to one labor analyst, "become commonplace among large employers."[104] From 1949 to 1959, employment in auto manufacturing grew more quickly than in any other

101. Interview with Pearce.
102. Interview with Pearce.
103. Interviews with Latini and Pearce. Also see Willys Anuário de Progresso, 1956–57, 23, which described employee ownership of company stock. BL, HJK Papers, carton 162, file: "Automobiles-Brazil Brochure." In the mid-1960s Willys began plans for a complete Social Center for employees which would be attached to a model community including residences for 1,620 families, a school, a hospital, stores, a cultural center, a pool, tennis courts, and a lake with a picnic ground. The plans, calling for an expenditure of over $11 million, were never implemented, presumably because the company was sold before they could be. BL, EFK Papers, Carton 249, Item 7L, "Social Center, WOB," January 1964.
104. Humphrey, Capitalist Control and Worker's Struggle, 81.

industry in the nation, increasing by over 318 percent in ten years.[105] According to Latini, it was "without doubt" the turning point in "the modernization of relations between employees and employers, bosses and employees." In addition, the grouping of workers in large numbers promoted unionization, lending support to the Brazilian Workers Party (Partido Trabalhista Brasileiro), headed by the political descendants of Getúlio Vargas.[106] After the coup of 1964 severely curtailed all political parties, the workers of the auto industry became an important force and ultimately helped pressure the dictatorship into relinquishing power.[107]

Although the Aranhas and Barbosas retained stock in WOB and served on the board of directors, Brazilian ownership of the company after 1956 consisted mainly of shares in the hands of the general public. Kaiser chose Deltec, the only investment banking firm underwriting stock after Interamericana went under, to handle the stock issue on a commission basis. Because the Brazilian stock market was still so undeveloped (Fundo Crescinco was just getting organized), Deltec scattered two hundred sales representatives throughout the country, sending caravans of bright yellow jeeps into remote areas. In the cities, salesmen took WOB stock almost door to door, making an average of five calls a day, five to six days a week. To ensure the widest possible sales to Brazilians at all economic levels, purchasers were allowed to buy the stock on an installment plan. As a special incentive, anyone purchasing more than five hundred shares was given a 10 percent discount on the purchase of a Willys car or jeep if he or she held onto the stock for at least a year and a half. Willys kept in touch with its stockholders through a glossy annual report, published in Portuguese, which emphasized its "program of nationalization."[108] Borrowing a page, perhaps, from the effective public relations techniques used by Rockefeller's projects, the annual reports featured colorful center foldouts that showed graphically the progress being made toward complete local manufacture. By 1959, WOB had thirty thousand Brazilian shareholders who owned 52 percent of the company. Aside from one Brazilian bank, it was the largest publicly held company in the entire nation.

Because of the heroic efforts required to market stocks in Brazil, it was an expensive process. Willys's first stock issue cost the company over 20

105. Schuh, *Agricultural Development of Brazil*, 11.
106. Interview with Latini.
107. Humphrey, *Capitalist Control and Worker's Struggle*, 3–11.
108. *Quem Controla O Que: O Capital Estrangeiro no Brasil*, 1:341. For a description of Deltec's sales strategies see Gordon and Grommers, *U.S. Manufacturing in Brazil*, 106, and S. R. Pemberton to file, July 27, 1959, p. 2. RAC, IBEC Microfilm, Roll 45. A copy of Willys's first annual report is in BL, HJK Papers, carton 162, file: "SA-Automobiles-Brazil."

percent of the capital raised. To most companies, such costs were a discouragement against sales of stock to the public. For this reason, among others, those American companies which chose to undertake joint ventures usually formed partnerships or sold stock in large blocks to the very wealthy.[109]

In addition to stock subscriptions, financing for WOB came through American bank loans obtained and guaranteed by the Kaiser corporation for a 3 percent fee. "In those days, no way could you borrow money from an American bank," Max Pearce later said about the loans routed through Kaiser. In spite of the 3 percent charge, "I was happy as hell to get the money," Pearce added.[110] WOB also received some American loans directly through Chase National Bank and the various financing operations run by IBEC. The American Overseas Finance Corporation, a wholly owned subsidiary of IBEC, lent several million dollars to Willys to set up operations and later to develop the Willys station wagon. Fundo Crescinco also got in on the Willys operation, holding a substantial number of shares on behalf of the mutual fund's Brazilian investors.[111]

IBEC representatives in Brazil were impressed by the work of Willys and especially by the extent to which Kaiser had successfully maintained the Brazilian character of the firm. "WOB has already gained many advantages from being thought of essentially as a Brazilian company and it will undoubtedly continue to benefit from this in the future," the vice president of the American Overseas Finance Corporation noted in an internal memorandum. "WOB is undoubtedly extremely widely known in Brazil. Having some 30,000 Brazilian shareholders, it is thought of generally with great nationalistic pride." Richard Aldrich, then head of IBEC in Brazil, took special note of the fact that WOB's financial stability and leading position in the auto industry enabled it to weather with minimal damage the recurrent Brazilian economic and political tur-

109. Gordon and Grommers, *U.S. Manufacturing in Brazil*, 106.
110. Interview with Pearce. As owner of Willys-Overland Export Corporation, Kaiser also charged WOB a 3 percent royalty on manufacture of the jeep, although this went down to 1 percent on the jeep station wagon, since it was designed in Brazil, and on the Aerowillys car, after the model was discontinued in the United States. These were reasonable rates even by later standards. In the 1960s, when legislation on royalties became more stringent in Brazil, foreign companies were told they could charge royalties only when they owned less than 50 percent of a firm and that royalty payments could not exceed 5 percent of gross sales (Baer, *The Brazilian Economy*, 187–89). Kaiser met both of these requirements in the midfifties, without government prompting.
111. See Hickman Price, Jr., et al., to Norbert A. Bogdan, July 2, 1956, and Press Release No. 16, July 11, 1958, regarding "Investment in Willys-Overland do Brasil S.A." RAC, IBEC Microfilm, Roll 45.

moil.[112] Hans Horch, another top IBEC official, considered Willys the only company in Brazil which had had long-term success in the field of public financing.[113] Willys represented precisely the kind of American investment that IBEC and Nelson Rockefeller had hoped to encourage in Brazil.

Willys Overland and the U.S. Business Community

A number of other Americans also considered the Kaiser participation in WOB a model of effective foreign investment. Businesses' concerns about the standing of American companies in Latin America were growing through the late 1950s and into the 1960s. Although no formal corporate code of conduct had yet evolved, it was becoming clearer that the exploitative behavior of some corporations threatened the reputations—and foreign assets—of all. The behavior modifications frequently suggested included better treatment of workers, political neutrality toward regime changes, improved public relations, and at least moderate profit-sharing through tax payments or joint ventures.

Indeed, there is evidence that, after Eisenhower's relative neglect of Latin America until almost 1959, many segments of the business community welcomed John F. Kennedy's activist proposals. The intent of the Alliance for Progress to promote economic development fit well with businesses' concerns about finding ways of proving to Latin American nationalists that private investment could be responsible and beneficial. Especially welcome were indications that Kennedy's approach might include new tax incentives for foreign investment—incentives Eisenhower's advisers had ruled out. U.S. investment in Latin America, slow under Eisenhower, showed an even sharper downward trend as the sixties began. Meanwhile, criticism of business exploitation was becoming noticeably bitter abroad, especially in the wake of the Cuban Revolution, and some well-publicized expropriations resulted.[114]

112. S. R. Pemberton to file, July 27, 1959, pp. 1–2. RAC, IBEC Microfilm, Roll 45.
113. Interview with Hans Horch by Wayne Broehl, July 3, 1964, p. 83. RAC, Broehl Papers, Box 18, file: "Interview-Jofre, et al."
114. Literature on the Alliance for Progress has often suggested a basic antagonism between its goals and the interests of U.S. businessmen. However, my research indicates that much of this antagonism came from government, not business. For a fuller elaboration of this thesis see Cobbs, "U.S. Business: Self-Interest and Neutrality." For a discussion of the opposite thesis see Abraham F. Lowenthal, "United States Policy toward Latin America: 'Liberal,' 'Radical,' and 'Bureaucratic' Perspectives," *Latin American Research Review* 8 (Fall 1973): 3–25; and Ruth Leacock, "JFK, Business, and Brazil," *Hispanic American Historical Review* 8, no. 4 (1979): 636–73.

The fears businesses had about these trends evidenced themselves in several ways. First was the increasingly active discussion of the concept and possibility of joint ventures with Latin American businessmen as a way of promoting at least partial local ownership and circumventing nationalist criticisms. Four or five years after Henry Kaiser first went to Brazil, joint ventures became a topic of interest to the broader American business community. As *Time* magazine put it, "The joint venture helps to give Latin America the outside capital it needs while giving the outside capitalist the security he wants." The same article cited WOB as the prime example of the "fastest-growing kind of foreign investment in Latin America." In Mexico, *Time* noted, joint ventures accounted for 11 percent of North American investment at the end of 1959, while in Brazil joint ventures accounted for twenty-three of the top fifty-six stocks on the Rio and São Paulo exchanges.[115]

Willys drew the special attention of business writers. An article in *Harpers* described the Kaiser technique of "offering a local stock issue to the people of the host country" as the most promising development in the future of inter-American economic relations. Citing the Kaiser company in Argentina, which operated on the same principles of local share participation and 100 percent local manufacture as did WOB, the writer noted that "it places the American company in the position of inviting the host country to participate in the free-enterprise system rather than mouthing platitudes about it while closely guarding corporate ownership." The article also commended Willys for its use of "the stockholder-relations techniques developed in the United States, mostly new abroad, which include progress reports, quarterly statements, and the full-bloom type of annual report now expected by stockholders big and little."[116]

From the mid-1950s through the early 1960s, Henry and Edgar Kaiser and many of the executives who worked for them seem to have had an increasingly strong sense of their work as charting a new direction for American business in the developing world. By having Brazilians participate not only in the operation but, even more important, in the ownership of the auto industry, Willys demonstrated, as Henry Kaiser wrote in notes on the development of the industry, "how it is possible in the business and

115. December 14, 1959, 37.

116. Thomas Aitken, Jr., "The Double Image of American Business Abroad," *Harpers*, August 1960, 22. The Kaiser corporation was also praised, especially in 1954, for its decision to invest in Latin America at all and for its role as a "recruiter" of foreign capital and technical assistance. See *Business Week*, October 9, 1954, 162, and the *Washington Post*, October 10, 1954, editorial. In 1958, *Business Week* called Industrias Kaiser Argentina "a barometer of relations between the Argentina government and U.S. companies." *Business Week*, June 21, 1958, 108.

economic world to extend cooperation in tangible symbolism of the 'good partner-good neighbor' policy."[117] At the annual meeting of the National Industrial Conference Board in New York City in 1959, J. C. Delaplain, senior vice president of Willys-Overland Export Corporation, the U.S. subsidiary of Kaiser, explicitly advocated joint ventures as the best development tool at the disposal of business. "We have a standard policy of limiting the American ownership to fifty per cent of a foreign company," he told the delegates, adding, "it's usually less." The policy, Delaplain explained, was "vital to the local company's maintenance of its national identity and flavor." Although many businessmen tended to look at nationalism as "a nasty word," the Willys official told his listeners, "It might behoove every one of us to remember that until about the turn of the century, here in our own country we were a heavy debtor nation. We took a very dim view of anyone who tried to push us around."[118]

Of course, most joint ventures fell short of the Kaiser model, and in many ways were simply sops to public opinion. Touches which made a company seem more Brazilian created a nicer appearance in the eyes of the general public, an American representative of Burroughs do Brasil told one State Department official.[119] Most companies never allowed locals to attain majority ownership of the venture, and it was the exceedingly rare company which actually sold shares to the general public. The economist Lincoln Gordon, ambassador to Brazil under John Kennedy, argued in *Harvard Business Review* in 1959 for the long-term advantages of joint ventures "not only as a means of promoting economic development but also as a safeguard for corporate survival in the country concerned."[120] But he also noted that the question of joint ventures was still hotly disputed, and a couple of years later, in Brazil, Gordon sent a confidential report to the State Department detailing the spirited opposition he had encountered among American companies to allowing Brazilian ownership of shares.[121] Still, the climate of opinion had shifted

---

117. "HJK Notes of Development of Automobile Industry in Brazil," 2. Although this document is undated, I assume it was written around 1957, since later in his notes Kaiser refers to ten thousand Brazilian stockholders, and by 1958 Willys had already around fifteen thousand. BL, HJK Papers, carton 162, file: "SA-Automobiles-Brazil, 1 of 2."
118. J. C. Delaplain, "Joint Ventures Overseas . . . Setting Up A Workable Partnership," May 21, 1959, pp. 5–6, 8. BL, EFK Papers, carton 250.
119. Despatch from U.S. embassy in Rio, October 22, 1959, p. 1. NA, R.G. 59,1955–59, Decimal file 832.053/10–2259, EMW.
120. "Private Enterprise and International Development," *Harvard Business Review* (July-August 1960): 138.
121. Airgram from Lincoln Gordon (US-AID Office in Rio) to Department of State, June 5, 1962, regarding "Participation Private Enterprise in Alliance for Progress Program," p. 2. FGV, CPDOC, CDA, BJK 62.06.05.

enough so that, by the third year of the Alliance for Progress, business executives would support a U.S. government vote in favor of an Economic Commission for Latin America resolution encouraging joint enterprises.[122]

Businesses' concern about political trends also manifested itself in continued discussions about appropriate codes of conduct and ways in which businesses could improve their public relations through advertising, more thorough financial disclosures abroad, training and promotion of foreign nationals, and contributions to community improvement projects in host countries. Beginning in the early 1950s the National Planning Association published a volume every one to two years in which, by applying essentially these criteria, it analyzed the impact of foreign corporations on host economies. Interestingly, one of the first companies analyzed in the series (by Nelson Rockefeller's associate Stacy May and friend Galo Plaza in 1958) was United Fruit, and it was treated as something of an errant sheep returned to the fold. Although the volume clearly aimed at rehabilitating the company in the public eye, it also distinguished "modern," responsible business practices from the historically "paternalistic" labor policies of United Fruit and from the "shortcomings and ineptitudes" of its relations with host governments.[123] To Latin Americans this account was little more than a whitewash, yet within the context of the multinational business community the book signaled an early attempt at corporate self-regulation through peer pressure. Notably, IBEC was one of the last companies featured in the series, in a highly positive account by Wayne Broehl.

The issue of corporate conduct grew even more pressing in the 1960s. Business groups held conferences on the subject, articles were written, and business and Department of Commerce officials activated under the Alliance for Progress discussed how business could build trust with local communities. This decade saw the proliferation of private groups devoted in one way or another to coping with the foreign crisis of confidence in U.S. business; among these were the Business Council for International Understanding, the Latin American Information Committee, and the Latin American Business Committee. Edgar Kaiser himself, becoming personally interested in questions of third world development, joined a variety of committees including the Pan American Society, the Inter-American Council of Commerce and Production, and the Business Group

122. Edwin Martin to Lincoln Gordon, August 8, 1963, p. 1. John F. Kennedy Library, Jack Behrman Papers (hereafter JFK, Behrman Papers), box 1, file: "AID and Private Investment Correspondence, 9/63–12/63."
123. Stacy May and Galo Plaza, *The United Fruit Company in Latin America* (Washington: National Planning Association, 1958), 209, 240.

for Latin America. Kaiser was one of thirty-three charter members of this last organization, which later became the Council for Latin America under David Rockefeller's leadership. Criticisms from nationalist governments abroad, the left in the United States, the development committees of the United Nations, and even the American government prompted the council to spend "most of the sixties" formulating guidelines for corporate conduct in Latin America.[124] Although the Kaisers had not participated in the practices which had generated most of these criticisms, Edgar was nonetheless deeply concerned about the preservation of American business abroad and contributed heavily of his money and time to efforts, especially those of David Rockefeller, aimed at encouraging companies to examine their policies and public relations.[125]

As a model foreign investor, Kaiser was called upon at times to venture beyond Latin America. In 1958, through an introduction arranged by the State Department, Kaiser made the acquaintance of Kwame Nkrumah, with whom he quickly developed a working friendship characterized by an unusually high level of trust. While State Department and Eximbank officials parried with Nkrumah over questions of nationalism, communism, and imperialism, Kaiser and Nkrumah quietly carried out negotiations for Ghana's first hydroelectric dam and aluminum smelter. The state-owned dam on the Volta River was important because it would increase the nation's electric power more than twenty-two times, providing power to both rural and urban areas, while the privately owned aluminum smelting plant would use up the excess electricity generated by the dam. The aluminum company (owned 90 percent by Kaiser, 10 percent by Reynolds) would pay for the power in dollars, thereby providing hard currency to meet the foreign debt on the hydroelectric project. In Ghana no local investors had sufficient capital to invest substantially in the project at the time it was established. But three years after the plant began producing, Kaiser Aluminum approximated the effects of local ownership when it set up a special fund to which it committed 50 percent of annual pretax profits. Today, a Ghanian board of directors administers the fund, which receives millions each year and is used to address various social, medical, and educational priorities.[126]

124. Testimony of Enno Hobbing, "Multinational Corporations and United States Foreign Policy, Hearings on the International Telephone and Telegraph Company and Chile, 1970–1971," U.S. Senate Committee on Foreign Relations (Washington: GPO, 1973), pt. 1, p. 382.
125. Telegram from Edgar Kaiser to Max Pearce, February 28, 1963, p. 1. BL, EFK Papers, carton 379, Folder 21b; Inter-Office Memorandum from Edgar Kaiser suggesting a $5,000 contribution to David Rockefeller's organizational efforts, September 29, 1964, p. 1. BL, EFK Papers, carton 385, Folder 1.
126. Interview with E. E. Trefethen, with additional information offered by Bob Irelan, vice

Conclusion: Profits and Losses

Meanwhile, in Brazil, WOB had grown and prospered. In 1959 Willys produced the first vehicles to be exported from Brazil: 25 jeeps sold to Chile.[127] Between 1957 and 1965, the company averaged cash dividends of 8 to 12 percent (in good years 18 percent) annually on stock and sold over 325,000 cars and jeeps. Although Willys had to import certain parts unobtainable in Brazil before 1965 at a cost of $44 million in foreign exchange, the company estimated that by producing most of the vehicle in Brazil it had saved $641 million in foreign exchange over the ten years.[128] But in spite of these accomplishments, by the second half of the 1960s the challenges facing the young Brazilian company seemed to mount.

Throughout the fifties, Willys dominated not only the jeep market but also the car market in Brazil. But the Willys car was a six-cylinder model, and so it was quickly overtaken in popularity by the less expensive four-cylinder Volkswagen once the German company began manufacturing in Brazil. Still, in the sedan division, Willys retained a solid lead on the Ford and General Motors subsidiaries, which had entered manufacturing primarily with the intent to hold a place under the GEIA system. In the midsixties, the two companies began to move into the country in a more substantial way, bringing with them the considerable engineering and financial resources of the parent corporations. Also, market demand in Brazil began to shift away from trucks and jeeps toward passenger vehicles.[129] In 1965, for the first time, Ford announced that it would begin manufacturing a car in Brazil, namely, the Ford Galaxie. Up to that time, the company had produced only trucks and tractors.

Although Willys had developed its own engineering division and had introduced new models, its strength was in jeeps, not cars. WOB did not have the resources or the world-famous passenger models to compete with the American giants (or with the German Volkswagen) once they decided to enter the market in a big way. The company had always

---

president for public relations, who was present during the interview. See also Stein, *A Special Difference*, 116–17, and Philip Reno's references to the Kaiser Volta River Project in "Aluminum Profits and Caribbean People," in *Imperialism and Underdevelopment*, ed. Rhodes, 86.

127. Despatch from U.S. embassy in Rio to Department of State, February 27, 1959, pp. 2–3. NA, R.G. 59, 1955–59, Decimal file 832.00/2–2759.

128. Willys-Overland do Brasil, Public Relations Division, Undated press statement, p. 5. BL, EFK Papers, carton 249, Folder 3. Also see interview with Jerome Hough by Wayne Broehl, Treasurer, WOB, July 8, 1964, pp. 105–06. RAC, Broehl Papers, Box 18, file: "Interview-Jofre, et al."

129. Humphrey, *Capitalist Control and Worker's Struggle*, 49.

struggled to sustain adequate financing, between stock sales to an un-sophisticated public, loans guaranteed by Kaiser, and funds wrestled from the tight Brazilian and foreign money markets. This left little sur-plus for long-term research and development. "The combination of Kaiser and the Brazilian capital was much weaker than Ford and General Motors," the economist Roberto Campos later noted.[130] There were simply no deep pockets to draw from, and deep pockets were necessary if WOB was to develop the kinds of engines that could compete with top American and European machinery. According to Euclydes Aranha, in 1967 such technology was at least five years away for WOB.[131] Other auto manufacturers felt the pinch as well: in the 1960s, six of the smaller companies were to be taken over by the giant firms of Ford, Volkswagen, and Fiat.[132]

The situation in many ways repeated the experience of the under-capitalized Kaiser-Frazer venture but with a crucial difference: this time, the Kaiser corporation was dealing with its reverses from a position of strength rather than of weakness. In 1967, when Ford approached Kaiser about selling its interest in Willys, Kaiser had a very valuable property to offer. When the deal closed, Kaiser sold its equity in WOB to Ford, along with its equity in Industrias Kaiser Argentina to Renault, for a combined total of $40 million.[133] The profits were large enough to clear Kaiser corporation of its long-term debt and the losses on the disastrous automobile investments in the United States. "What we finally figured out, after looking back at the whole Kaiser-Frazer affair, is that overall we did not lose money in the automotive industry," the financially conservative Eugene Trefethen later commented.[134]

The Ford Corporation, meanwhile, began buying up whatever stock it could from the Brazilian owners, with the intent of creating a wholly owned subsidiary to the extent possible. Given Kaiser's substantial chunk of the company, a complete takeover of ownership and control was only a matter of time for a company with Ford's assets and policies. Offering a price somewhat above the current trading value, the corporation was successful in getting Brazilians to sell most of their stock. Since the value of the shares had been declining somewhat, some of the small investors made money (if they had bought at a previous low), others lost, others broke even. It had been an average, not especially profitable investment,

130. Interviews with Campos, Trefethen, and Pearce.
131. Interview with Euclydes Aranha.
132. Humphrey, *Capitalist Control and Worker's Struggle*, 49.
133. *Kaiser Facts 1969* (Oakland: Kaiser Inter-company Communication Service, 1969), 23.
134. Interview with Trefethen.

according to Aranha and Pearce.[135] In 1983, when 11 percent of the stock was still in Brazilian hands, Ford made another public offer, bringing in yet more shares. Today, only 3 percent of Ford Brasil, S.A. is owned by Brazilian investors, one of whom is Euclydes Aranha.[136] They are the original shares of Willys-Overland, some of them, undoubtedly, the same ones sold out of the back of the bright yellow jeeps which had climbed through the tropical high forest leading out of Rio de Janeiro.

For Oswaldo and Euclydes Aranha, it was the end to a bittersweet story of pride in bringing to Brazil the beginnings of an auto industry, of respect and admiration for the Americans who had helped make it possible, of sadness that the laws the Brazilian government had passed to encourage foreign investment had stymied the one deal which promised an equal partnership between Brazilians and Americans (based on a united rather than dispersed Brazilian ownership), and of disappointment in the policies which had led Ford to throw away the effort and cost of building a stockholdership of forty-five thousand Brazilians, all of them advocates for the company. In all, Willys represented a mixed victory, but a victory nonetheless for Brazilian-American relations on the level of private diplomacy.

Willys had contributed a technologically appropriate product to a country in need of basic industry, while making provisions for local ownership. Willys had also been a leader in attaining Juscelino Kubitschek's Meta of an automobile industry in five years, showing those who had doubted that 100 percent local production could be done. The automobile industry would also have important implications for attempts like those of SASA to bring the Green Revolution to Brazil, since mechanized farm equipment was a central by-product of jeep and truck production. And, finally, Willys had demonstrated to Brazilians that under some circumstances it was possible, working with certain Americans, to further the aims of business as well as the goals of development.

To corporations in the United States, the company had demonstrated a variety of methods by which American multinationals could enhance

135. Interviews with Aranha and Pearce. According to the head of Kaiser public relations, Bob Irelan, the corporation has never been a "blockbuster" stock even in the United States. The reason he gives is that the company has operated on the philosophy that its constituency is larger than its shareholders and includes the communities and countries in which the firm operates. (Conversation with Bob Irelan, Oakland, California, January 15, 1987.) Of course, this represents precisely the point of view (and consequences for shareholders) that opponents of corporate philanthropy, such as the stockholders of the A. P. Smith Company of New Jersey, found so objectionable in the early 1950s. Eells, *Corporation Giving*, 16.
136. Information provided by Scott T. Fenstermaker, Senior Attorney, Ford Motor Company.

both the appearance and the reality of contributing to development in the postwar world. It had also shown that development could be fully consistent with the profit motive. It was a point the Eisenhower administration would have appreciated, even though it had made little attempt to encourage this process. As Sydney Latini put it, looking back, "Many times the performance of American citizens has been far more important than that of the U.S. government."[137] Or, as Euclydes Aranha would later phrase it, reflecting on the lack of U.S. support for Brazil's economic development under a democratic government in the 1940s and 1950s and its support for the establishment of a brutal military dictatorship in the 1960s, "The mistakes made in Brazil . . . were [made] by the American government, not by American citizens."[138]

137. Interview.
138. Interview.

Chapter 6

The Rockefeller-Kaiser

Legacy: Corporatist Ideology,

Pluralistic Practice

> The manifold and intricate quality of modern free society—its richness in the fields of non-governmental group activity, of economic and cultural interests—thus gives to foreign policy a scope that goes far beyond the activities of small groups of officials or well-publicized negotiations. . . . We must never forget that the opportunities for effective action and influence are wide—far wider than the official channels through which a government's influence is exerted.
>
> —Rockefeller Brothers Fund,
> *Prospect for America*

> For we must remember that in this country there is a free enterprise of philanthropy and voluntary service as well as a free enterprise based on profit and loss.
>
> —Nelson Rockefeller,
> *Future of Federalism*

The study of foreign relations has come a long way since the days when scholars looked almost exclusively to diplomatic notes to discover the progression and meaning of international events. But the increasing sophistication of foreign relations studies reflects much more than simply the maturing of the historical profession. It reflects as well the growing complexity of the international scene in the postwar period and the need of historians to understand the variety of actors now crowding the stage of foreign relations, many of whom are not diplomats or other government officials.

The corporatist model of international relations helps to explain how many of these actors cooperated in the postwar era, and specifically how the United States sought to export its political and economic systems to Europe and Asia through the mechanisms of reconstruction. But this model is too coherent to describe U.S. policy toward Latin America. By definition, the decisions of the corporatist state are guided by a long-range strategy. It coordinates with banks, corporations, academia, and foundations to expand the sphere of U.S. influence through the promise and delivery of substantial economic growth. Corporatism makes most sense as a model of U.S. foreign policy when applied to geographical regions in which security and economic interests combined to give greater focus and consistency to government actions.

In Latin America, the corporatist model fits only if one subtracts the element of the U.S. government role. Certain North Americans did seek to export corporatist ideology and methodology, but they were frequently private citizens, not diplomats. The model of complex interdependence, which takes a more freewheeling and contingent view of politics, may better describe U.S. government actions toward regions whose position of low priority meant that government policy followed the crisis of the moment rather than a clear long-range plan, and where the private sector had a correspondingly greater role.[1]

As Robert Keohane and Joseph Nye stated in 1977, "A number of scholars see our era as one in which the territorial state, which has been dominant in world politics for the four centuries since feudal times ended, is being eclipsed by nonterritorial actors such as multinational corporations, transnational social movements, and international organiza-

---

1. See Wagner, *U.S. Policy Toward Latin America,* 166–67 (the role of crises in decision making) and 130–53 (the role of the private sector).

tions."[2] It is possible to see in the activities of Rockefeller and Kaiser an early working recognition of the three tenets of the emerging world system which Keohane and Nye would label complex interdependence: first, the existence of multiple channels for influencing relations between nations; second, the reorienting of the foreign affairs agenda in ways which allow, at times, the low politics of economic and social affairs to vie for priority with the high politics of military security; and third, the diminishing applicability of military force as a tool for obtaining economic and political goals.[3]

Nelson Rockefeller and Henry Kaiser shared a belief in the economic interdependence of nation-states in the postwar world. They were not alone in this belief but rather represented the continuation of a trend in thinking since the Great Depression which encompassed the free trade passion of Cordell Hull, the developmentalism of Henry Wallace, and the internationalism of Wendell Willkie's *One World*.[4] Rockefeller's and Kaiser's approach to business and international relations recognized not only that the traditional colonial system was dying, but that the unregulated free trade system which produced few observable benefits for less developed countries was dysfunctional as well and created the potential for political and economic instability which could threaten the interests of the United States. As Assistant Secretary of State Adolf Berle articulated this outlook at a U.S.-Canadian conference in mid-1941, "We are both morally and economically better off as the American nations strengthen their economic position. Any rise in their standard of living we consider a direct benefit to our economy and to our hemispheric security."[5] Yet while Rockefeller and Kaiser may have shared ideas, their backgrounds and reasons for adopting this perspective differed.

Rich Neighbors

Nelson Rockefeller was first and foremost a political operator. He fell in love with the drama and power of politics in his early thirties, and as the

2. *Power and Interdependence: World Politics in Transition* (Boston: Little, Brown, 1977),
3. Another excellent work in this same tradition, which posits, among other things, that state power and wealth have been diminished by the increasing power and wealth of multinationals, is Robert Gilpin, *U.S. Power and the Multinational Corporation* (New York: Basic Books, 1975).
3. See Keohane and Nye, *Power and Interdependence*, 23–37.
4. For descriptions of Willkie's and Wallace's views see John Morton Blum, *V Was for Victory: Politics and American Culture During World War II* (New York: Harcourt, Brace, Jovanovich, 1976), 265–67, 281–83.
5. Green, *Containment of Latin America*, 78–79.

heir to redundant millions became entranced with what he could accomplish by virtue of his own authoritative voice, charismatic personality, and strong will—that is, what he could accomplish by virtue of the personal attributes that money could neither buy nor create. Experimental ventures in Latin America meant little to him in terms of personal financial gain: the high profits from his sizable investment in Venezuela's Creole Petroleum would have rolled in regardless. He did not think it necessary for U.S. companies to withdraw from extractive enterprises in Latin America in order to accomplish development there, and this notion clearly served his financial interests. But there was nonetheless no compelling economic reason for him to concern himself personally with Latin development. Political ambitions offer the only reasonable explanation for his intense interest in Latin America, which far exceeded the level of interest that might have been prompted by an attraction to the cultures and people of a given region.

Rockefeller shared Franklin D. Roosevelt's vision of North American penetration and control of Latin America through a system of alliances rather than outright military control. Roosevelt based his Good Neighbor policy on a recognition of the diminishing returns of military intervention in Latin America: not only did such intervention have high domestic and international political costs, but the post–World War I diminution of the British economic presence created new opportunities for the United States to strengthen its influence abroad in other ways. In another era, Rockefeller would undoubtedly have approved of more direct methods of control (such as those employed by President Theodore Roosevelt), and he unhesitatingly accepted alliances with dictators from Perón in 1945 to Castelo Branco in 1964. But the United States'urgent need to have cooperative, as opposed to recalcitrant, allies in the interwar years—as expressed in the Good Neighbor commitment not to intervene militarily in Latin America—had made force the last rather than the customary first recourse of U.S. Latin American policy. For the first time in U.S.–Latin American relations, the United States had to bargain for what it wanted, since it had foresworn the right simply to take it. Although force had never been a component of U.S. relations with South America to the extent that it had been in the Caribbean, the renunciation of force during the 1930s and 1940s removed a distant threat and gave new negotiating strength to all countries of the region.

One result of the about-face was that Latin Americans effectively managed to elevate the low politics of economic development to a status which competed with the high politics of collective security in international negotiations. Before and during World War II, Latin American countries, Brazil above all others, used the desire of the U.S. government for a strong alliance to push the United States toward a commitment to development of the hemisphere. Such a commitment included expanding the role of the Eximbank and creating multilateral committees and bilateral joint commissions for the explicit purpose of undertaking development studies. After the war, Brazil successfully negotiated more economic assistance, even though the removal of the Nazi threat meant that the aid it received fell short of expectations. During the Korean War Brazil again played on wartime anxieties, this time to strengthen the U.S. commitment to the Joint Economic Development Commission. Latin American nations made economic issues the cause célèbre of every hemispheric meeting from the Chapultepec Conference of 1945 to the Punta del Este Conference of 1961.

Although Latin America never got the Marshall Plan it sought, its clamors and, most especially, the Cuban Revolution eventually did bring about an Alliance for Progress. The United States had far much more to bargain with than any country of Latin America and also a variety of covert means at its disposal for being nasty when discussions took an unfavorable turn. Yet Latin Americans had increased their political options vis-à-vis the northern giant. As Edward Miller, assistant secretary of state for Latin America, noted about the "changed bargaining position of the U.S.", "The old Latin American fear of the United States resulting from the use of its superior power in Mexico, Cuba, Panama and elsewhere has, during the last two decades, gradually been replaced by a feeling that our adherence to the non-intervention and other doctrines of the inter-American system . . . puts them in a position secure from the arbitrary use of United States strength."[6] Just as the traditions of late medieval chivalric love had made women into objects to be wooed instead of hit over the head and dragged along, so the Good Neighbor policy did not change unequal power relations but instead helped to modify the rules for obtaining a given goal. The bouquet of roses with which Nelson Rockefeller hoped to gain Latin American fidelity and a spot in the limelight of postwar American politics was economic development.

Henry J. Kaiser, on the other hand, was primarily a businessman, an entrepreneur in the grand style with a genius for manipulating the New Deal and postwar corporatist connections among government, business, and labor. He was the prototype for a new kind of industrialist whose

---

6. "United States Relations with Latin America," May 1952, p. 13. NA, R.G. 59, Lot 53D26, Office Files of the Assistant Secretary of State for Latin America, 1949–53, File: "Business Advisory Council."

success lay in his embracing rather than resisting the expanded role of government in the private economy. John Blum notes that Kaiser's wartime relations with government broke the molds of traditional entrepreneurship and classic free enterprise: "Energy, ability, ambition, those things Kaiser had; but government supplied his capital, furnished his market, and guaranteed his solvency on the cost-plus formula—and so spared him the need for cost efficiency, rewarded speed at any price, and came close to guaranteeing his profits."[7] Kaiser knew where government resources were concentrated and how to develop the projects which would gain public favor. He went abroad to further, perhaps even to save, his own business empire, but he did so with a strong sense of a new way in which foreign empires had to be built to stand the test of time: on multinational ownership, good public relations, and the manufacture of strongly marketable, hence broadly useful products.

Kaiser operated at the forefront of a group of business leaders who recognized that the U.S. government was not as ready as it had been before the Good Neighbor policy to defend American corporations with open force and that business would have to watch out for itself in the future. This understanding, combined with a trend toward increased direct investments abroad, led some business thinkers to place new emphasis on the importance of peaceful, nonantagonistic relations with host countries. "Granting that the use of physical force is out," as one member of the Business Advisory Council said in 1952, it was essential, in the words of another committee member, "to build up and cement a great deal closer relationship and understanding with these countries."[8] Kaiser provided a model for how this could be achieved. Focusing on development became a primary means of currying political favor and enhancing the corporate reputation both with foreign governments and influential observers in the United States. For his efforts, as we have seen, newspapers and business journals throughout the United States pointed to Kaiser as the leader of enlightened foreign investment. Along with David Rockefeller, Kaiser's son Edgar also became a leader in the 1960s of businesses' attempts to cope with the rising demands of developing countries through joint ventures, employee benefit programs, and sophisticated public relations techniques.

But in spite of the differences which led Nelson Rockefeller to emphasize politics and Henry Kaiser to emphasize business, they had an impor-

7. *V Was for Victory*, 115.
8. H. A. Davies to Edward Miller, May 12, 1952, p. 3; and A. Thomas Taylor to Edward Miller, May 19, 1952, p. 1. NA, R.G. 59, Lot 53D26, Office Files of the Assistant Secretary of State for Latin America, 1949–53, Box 3, File: "Business Advisory Council."

tant common outlook. In addition to the fact that a focus on economic development served their own particular purposes, they also genuinely believed in the inherent value of such development. The experience of the Great Depression and World War II had convinced them as well as a number of their contemporaries that strengthening the economies of at least some of the poorer countries was in the direct interest of the international system over which the United States was attempting to assume mastery.

The Ideology of Interdependence and Its Practical Applications

Much of the rhetoric of interdependence which peppered the public and private statements of midcentury American leaders from Roosevelt to Rockefeller to Rostow was overblown and disingenuous. Hopeless poverty in Bolivia may have occasionally disturbed the sentiments of well-fed Americans but certainly never their Sunday supper. And yet for some, protestations of economic interdependence were more than wartime propaganda. The Great Depression had demonstrated the catastrophic effects of depressed demand brought on by diminished purchasing power. For the first time, economists were able to make arguments which caught the attention of capitalists for the necessity of higher wages in order to increase the purchasing power of workers. Corporatist cooperation among business, government, and labor to achieve growth made political as well as economic sense. It took no great leap of imagination to extend the argument to the international system: just as low wages for workers helped to trigger domestic depression, so low incomes for less developed countries acted as a brake on the international trading system. By the early 1950s it was clear that falling demand for raw materials and consequently falling prices seriously compromised the ability of economically midsize countries like Brazil to purchase imports and otherwise participate in the world trading system. The economic distress of Latin American countries was not just a "poor advertisement" for the United States as a regional leader, as Edward Miller put it. It also created economic complications for U.S. exporters, who had trouble collecting payments, and fostered Latin American reliance on the U.S. government for bailout loans such as those given in 1951 to Argentina and in 1953 to Brazil for the payment of short-term debt.[9]

Going beyond simple maintenance of the trading system, the world-

9. Edward Miller, "United States Relations with Latin America," May 1952, p. 3. NA, R.G. 59, Lot 53D26, Office Files of the Assistant Secretary of State for Latin America, 1949–53, File: "Business Advisory Council."

wide economic expansion of the United States also depended on development to some extent. For investors like Kaiser, who desperately needed
the opportunities provided by foreign ventures, expansion into Latin
American manufacturing was possible only to the extent that internal
markets were strong enough to support absorption of new products, local
investors had the resources and interest to cooperate with such development, and the national infrastructure was sufficient for the needs of industry. For these reasons Kaiser based his industries in Brazil and Argentina,
which already led in industrial development and market size.

Lloyd Gardner has shown that during World War II a number of private
leaders and high officials, including Sumner Welles, Spruille Braden, Adolf Berle, and Nelson Rockefeller, had accepted the need for at least
moderate industrialization in Latin America. They "had not failed to
notice that trade developed more rapidly and more completely with nations like Canada, where the production of semi-finished and finished
manufactures was encouraged . . . than in places where the standard of
living stayed mired around the subsistence level." [10] Although these men
envisioned a "neo–Adam Smith" division of labor in which Latin America would focus on light industry and the United States on heavy industry,
they also believed that strict laissez-faire was not adequate to bring such
development about and that the U.S. government should undertake to
promote and direct it.

Yet the war's end shifted attention away from Latin America. The parts
of the world economy which became of greatest concern to government
officials were the developed nations of Europe and those parts of Asia at
risk of Communist influence. So when the Allies negotiated the General
Agreement on Tariffs and Trade (GATT) in Geneva in 1947, the tariff cuts
and other actions they took to promote free trade applied almost exclusively to industrialized goods. As Burton Kaufman observes, GATT
"largely ignored issues that concerned the predominantly agricultural
and commodity-exporting countries of the Third World, such as the negotiation of commodity agreements and the removal of restrictions on agricultural imports." [11] Indeed, as has been widely noted, the United States
not only ignored the trade problems of Latin America, but actually fixed
terms to its unilateral advantage in the 1950s. [12] The Marshall Plan, like

10. Lloyd C. Gardner, *Economic Aspects of New Deal Diplomacy* (Madison: University of
Wisconsin Press, 1964), 195
11. *Trade and Aid*, 2.
12. Wagner, *U.S. Policy Toward Latin America*, 57; Walter LaFeber, *Inevitable Revolutions: The United States and Central America* (New York: W. W. Norton, 1983), 90;
Kaufman, *Trade and Aid*, 8.

GATT, underscored the fact that the primary locus of U.S. concern and international experimentation was Europe and that most U.S. officials were more dedicated to shoring up traditional trading partners than to bringing new countries into the system. The mere threat of economic dislocation was not enough to prompt government to undertake the activism characteristic of its role in a corporatist system. U.S. leaders also had to be convinced that this dislocation took place in a so-called important part of the world and had implications for national security. On neither account did Latin America measure up. And so, as Gardner notes, the New Deal's model of inter-American cooperation and economic development was "never fully tried,"[13] even though it resurfaced briefly in the ill-fated Joint Brazil-U.S. Economic Development Commission.

At least, we can add now, it was never fully tried by *government* before 1960. Nelson Rockefeller remained committed to promoting Latin American development, and Henry Kaiser recognized benefits to his own enterprise as well as to Brazil and Argentina in the development of stronger economies and stronger markets. Neither man appears to have approached postwar investments abroad with the idea of fostering development only within certain noncompetitive limits. The U.S. government being unwilling to take substantial leadership on Latin American development issues in the decade and a half following World War II, private individuals and groups filled the vacuum, supporting efforts to broaden economic cooperation, introduce modern capitalist management practices, and implement the corporatist promise of reduced social conflict through economic development. Along with international organizations like the United Nations Economic Commission for Latin America and academics like Walt Rostow and Max Millikan, Rockefeller and Kaiser contributed substantially to the development debate in the 1950s and helped lay the basis for a stronger U.S. government response to development in the early 1960s.

Motivations: Personal and Political

But the story of Rockefeller's and Kaiser's activities does not simply underscore the critical role of nongovernmental actors. It also points to the variety of motivations behind initiatives in international relations, beyond simple economic calculations. In addition to the economic benefits of development in making the world capitalist system go, Rockefeller, Kaiser, and like-minded business and government figures of the time clearly

13. *Economic Aspects of New Deal*, 213, 216.

saw development efforts as supporting the unique claim of the United States to political leadership of the postwar world. What other nation was in a position to rebuild the economies of defeated enemies and devastated allies as well as to promise (if not necessarily deliver) a golden age for all, even the underdeveloped countries, in the foreseeable future? The Truman Doctrine, the Marshall Plan, and Point Four represented a new, nonmilitary kind of mobilization—backed up, of course, by alliances such as the Organization of American States and the North Atlantic Treaty Organization—which reinforced the U.S. presence front and center on the stage of world politics. Reconstruction and development increased the international prestige of the United States while giving it enormous influence over the countries which it helped. In terms of maintaining Pan-American solidarity, in particular, the carrot of economic aid would continue to prove useful. Although in 1954 the Central Intelligence Agency covertly trained and supplied the local troops which overthrew the elected government of Jacobo Arbenz in Guatemala, it was the promise of a continued advantageous economic association with the United States (in addition to their own anticommunism) which helped convince the greater number of Latin American governments to pass the U.S.-sponsored anti-Communist manifesto which laid the basis for the coup. According to Stephen Rabe, judicious "horse-trading" by John Foster Dulles on economic issues went a long way toward rallying support.[14]

The development debate had vital domestic implications as well, becoming an important area in which to stake a claim to leadership. Rockefeller and Kaiser were as conscious of their national audience as they were of the foreign audience. The ventures in South America enhanced the corporate image of the Kaiser companies and, as Mark Foster comments, "induced financiers, who for years had dismissed Kaiser as the federal government's welfare child, to sit up and take notice."[15] Similarly, the wide publicity Rockefeller gained for his activities and proposals redounded to his credibility as a presidential aspirant. Both men saw nongovernmental leadership in questions of development as strengthening the position of the private sector in American life. Businesses' marked interest in development enhanced their reputation for responsibility, staved off government encroachment on areas that were traditionally their prerogative, and increased corporate access to government sources of financing such as the Eximbank.

14. *Eisenhower and Latin America*, 52. Also see Wagner, *U.S. Policy Toward Latin America*, 63–64.
15. *Henry J. Kaiser*, 175, 294.

Gestures made toward the economic development of poor countries also helped to keep the shine on the American self-image of moral superiority. As Mark Foster, Henry Kaiser's biographer, has noted, the industrialist expressed optimism throughout his life that Americans would never succumb to "godless materialism" and that capitalism could and would make possible worldwide utopian abundance by the year 2000.[16] Nelson Rockefeller was less optimistic that such things would happen more or less automatically but equally eager for Americans to set such goals for themselves. He was especially worried in the mid-1950s, as perhaps only someone with a personal knowledge of immense hereditary wealth and privilege could be, about the corrupting effects in the United States of "a prosperity unknown in world history" existing in contrast with great poverty in other parts of the world.[17] In other words, how would the rich neighbor coexist with the poor neighborhood?

Rockefeller jotted in abbreviated notes to Henry Kissinger in 1957, "In my opinion unless this nation dedicates itself to something bigger than itself & its own selfish interests their [sic] is real danger of the development of a national guilt complex & a turning away from a belief and a faith in our own system of values—this it seems to me will be particularly true among the young people and the intellectuals. On the other hand coop. [cooperation] in the eco. [economic] and social field with other peoples throughout the world gives us a tangible [sic] outlet & expression for our feelings and sense of values & lays the base for a world order based on love and the brotherhood of man."[18] If he had had a crystal ball, Rockefeller could not have better characterized the crisis of faith that "young people and the intellectuals" underwent ten years later or better anticipated some of the enormously popular outlets—the Peace Corps, for example—created by policymakers for the "expression [of] our feelings and sense of values." Essentially, Rockefeller's concern for his country mirrored his parents' concern for the Rockefeller progeny: that they find a way to live comfortably with wealth and power, neither abusing it nor relinquishing it. For Americans, this meant finding ways to believe, in spite of postwar dominance and a largely exploitative relationship with Latin America, that the

16. Ibid., 276.
17. Handwritten notes of Nelson Rockefeller to Henry Kissinger on the draft of the report (dated July 18, 1957) of "Subpanel III—U.S. International Economic and Social Objectives and Strategy," p. 1. RAC, RBF Special Studies Project, Series 10, Box 63. This report was one among many which Nelson Rockefeller reviewed and wrote detailed comments on as part of his participation on the special Rockefeller Brothers Fund that drafted Prospect for America.
18. Ibid.

nation was different from corrupt and fallen empires of the past. Programs that promoted economic development, Rockefeller foresaw, could provide the focal point for a rallying of American public spirit. John Kennedy would later claim the technique for his own.

For various reasons, then, individuals such as Nelson Rockefeller and Henry Kaiser found that balanced economic development in Latin America, within a capitalist context, could actually be in their nation's and their own best interest. The way they went about constructing projects that fostered such development reflected their own skill in manipulating the postwar ties among business, philanthropy, and government. For Rockefeller, this meant lobbying for his point of view in a variety of governmental forums—including confidential meetings with the president and State Department, participation on Truman's Point Four commission, and testimonials before Congress—while using private funds to create model projects and maintain strong relationships with foreign dignitaries. Lacking an ongoing government appointment between 1946 and 1953 and being at odds with other members of the Eisenhower administration after that, Rockefeller engaged in private diplomacy to maintain a high profile in U.S.–Latin American relations and to build domestic recognition for his expertise on questions of foreign economic development. At the same time, in Latin America, Rockefeller's continued identification with the U.S. government lent credibility to his efforts. Brazilians looked to Rockefeller, even out of government, as their connection to North American power.

Henry Kaiser stayed clear of most foreign policy debates, but he was as adept as Rockefeller at exploiting the connections between government policy and private opportunity. Kaiser entered Kubitschek's Targets program with the same gusto that he had brought to the public works of the New Deal, with equal success in building broad popular support and obtaining government concessions. Meanwhile, in Washington, Kaiser stayed in close communication with officials of the State Department, Eximbank, World Bank, and other agencies, using a variety of occasions and forums to emphasize the compatibility of his investments with the professed goals of U.S. foreign economic policy.

And in important respects the activities of Rockefeller and Kaiser accorded with government policy. Truman and Eisenhower clearly linked Latin American economic development with private American investment not to create optimal conditions for rapid economic growth (otherwise they would have established another Marshall Plan), but instead to reassert the primary role of the private sector in foreign economic relations with Latin America. By denying to Latin American countries the foreign aid which the United States was bestowing on other parts of the world, policymakers forced the southern republics to rely on private investment even though that investment was often not forthcoming. Those investments which were made and which actually resulted in development lent credibility to the U.S. policy. And when such activities made profits they acted as an advertisement to induce other U.S. companies to venture abroad and thereby extend American influence.

Rockefeller set up the AIA as a model, hoping by force of example to lead the way to greater government involvement in development. He believed strongly in the value of private nonprofit efforts, but he saw them as complements, not alternatives, to government action. While Rockefeller envisioned distinct public and private sectors, sturdy and pluralistic, he did not see them as being at odds with each another. Indeed, if his own activities are any indication, he saw their interests and work as being enmeshed. Kaiser, similarly, saw the value of collaboration between government and the private sector, which in his case translated into dollars and cents.

Corporatism and Consequences

In some respects, the Kaiser-Rockefeller story confirms the corporatist analysis of American foreign relations which has become an important part of historical literature in recent years.[19] Certainly, this story supports one aspect of global corporatism as Thomas McCormick defines it: the postwar attempt to manage conflict not through force but through "a collaborative consensus on the imperatives of growth."[20] Kaiser and Rockefeller subscribed to the necessity of developing semiperipheral countries in order to enhance them as markets for U.S. goods and to increase their social stability through a prosperity based on "productionism," or "expanding the pie." In addition, Kaiser and Rockefeller were leaders in a larger movement within the business community that aimed at encouraging better self-regulation to avoid abuses which threatened the reputation of all U.S. multinationals and at implementing wage and

---

19. See Thomas McCormick, "Drift or Mastery? A Corporatist Synthesis for American Diplomatic History," in *The Promise of American History: Progress and Prospects,* ed. Stanley J. Kutler and Stanley N. Katz (Baltimore: Johns Hopkins University Press, 1982), and the articles by John Lewis Gaddis ("The Corporatist Synthesis: A Skeptical View") and Michael J. Hogan ("Corporatism: A Positive Appraisal") in *Diplomatic History* 10, no. 4 (Fall 1986): 357–77.

20. "Drift or Mastery?" 326–27.

profit-sharing policies that increased the stake of host countries in the success of foreign investors.

But this story conflicts fundamentally with aspects of the corporatist analysis which attempt to explain how elites in the public and private sectors collaborated in a coherent system. In the case of Rockefeller—for all his power, influence, and initiative—one is struck more by his difficulties in achieving cooperation with the foreign policy administration of the U.S. government than by his successes. Kaiser, on the other hand, obviously benefited from government connections. Yet his practices abroad seem the result more of his own foresight than of attempts *by the state* "to facilitate self-regulation . . . by the private sector."[21]

In this case, business was ahead of government on questions concerning the proper role for business in the postwar world. The Truman and Eisenhower administrations evidenced little real interest in the subject. Aside from Assistant Secretary Miller's brief foray into a discussion of a "code of corporate conduct" in 1952, the U.S. government made almost no attempts to encourage business self-regulation in Latin America and, by refusing to consider tax incentives for direct foreign investment, showed little interest in actively fostering economic growth even based on the model of private initiative. Although Kaiser's and Rockefeller's activities complemented government policy—and certainly did not conflict with it—it would be hard to describe them as operating hand in glove, in the way a corporatist model would lead one to expect. The model of complex interdependence, which allows for a somewhat more autonomous role on the part of private and nonterritorial actors, may be more appropriate, at least in regard to U.S. relations with Latin America. Interestingly, the corporatist model makes more sense in Kaiser's and Rockefeller's collaborative relations with the Brazilian state.

Looking beyond Rockefeller's and Kaiser's roles as nongovernmental actors in foreign relations and beyond their motivations, one finds that the final relevant issue to examine is the consequences of their activities for American life, foreign policy, and relations with developing countries, specifically Brazil. In terms of American life, Rockefeller and Kaiser were well-known symbols of the kind of people-to-people assistance which appealed to the pluralistic, antistatist tendencies of national culture. The idea that individuals, not bureaucracies, make the difference would come into full bloom with the Peace Corps just a few years later. Youthful volunteers would venture out to do battle with poverty and other causes of social instability just as earlier American missionaries had done battle

21. Ibid., 328.

with heathenism. Nonprofit organizations concerned with foreign economic development would proliferate, asserting their right to represent the American "mission" abroad and frequently developing points of view critical of Washington's foreign policy. Rockefeller's emphasis on the wide channels for influencing foreign policy in a free society served not only to justify his own extragovernmental activities, but also to define in part what made democratic, capitalist societies different from communist ones.[22] The activities of Rockefeller and Kaiser helped to legitimize citizen diplomacy, adding new connections to the uncharted but intensely linked network of influence running between the public sector and the private sector in American life.

For better or worse, the Rockefeller and Kaiser companies also provided early models for effective multinational corporate expansion in the postwar period. They not only developed sophisticated approaches to the public relations problems of foreign direct investment in nationalist countries, but demonstrated the practicability of local capital participation and multinational boards of directors. Ironically, while testing new methods for the expansion of American business interests worldwide, they contributed to ideological rationalizations for multinational conglomerates operating not necessarily in the national interest, but in the broader interests of the corporation wherever it happened to find the best opportunities. According to Rockefeller's and Kaiser's lights, for overseas business to serve only American interests was positively un-American. One effect of enhancing multinational corporate strength, as Robert Gilpin argues, may have been to develop the "periphery" of the world economy at the expense of the "core," accelerating the loss of jobs (such as in the automobile and auto parts industry) to overseas workers and the stagnation of the American industrial base.[23] Although one can debate the extent to which Gilpin's general thesis is accurate, it nonetheless raises

22. Throughout the 1950s Rockefeller emphasized to the intellectuals whom he paid to advise him and to policymakers he knew that the United States had to make a convincing case regarding what it was for (democratic capitalism), not just what it was against (communism). This was one of Rockefeller's motivations in organizing the Rockefeller Brothers Fund Special Studies Project (culminating in *Prospect for America*), which Underwood and Daniels call a response to the "blandness of the Eisenhower years [which] had offended liberal Republicans as well as Democrats." Underwood and Daniels, *Governor Rockefeller in New York*, 5. Also see Berle, *Navigating the Rapids*, 645, 667.
23. *U.S. Power and the Multinational Corporation*, 77–78. Peter Evans also cites this as one of the disadvantages of what he calls "dependent development." He writes, "For the center, perhaps the most important consequence of dependent development is the creation of a split between the interests of center country states and their own multinationals." Peter Evans, *Dependent Development: The Alliance of Multinational, State, and Local Capital in Brazil* (Princeton: Princeton University Press, 1979), 321.

intriguing questions about the long-term consequences of growing corporate sophistication in the 1950s and 1960s.

Peter Evans's study of Brazilian industrialization offers substantial evidence of a continuing reluctance by multinationals to innovate in ways that benefit local economies; in this light, it is clear that the joint venture models offered by Henry Kaiser and Nelson Rockefeller were exceptional. They influenced corporate culture in some ways but not in others. Unlike the corporations described by Evans, those of Rockefeller and Kaiser were not forced to take on local Brazilian partners by political pressure or induced to consider expansion into new industries by state threats of exclusion under the laws of similars. In other words, they elected to innovate, rather than waiting until forced to do so.

Undoubtedly, a crucial aspect of the explanation is that both men owned the enterprises they commanded. They were not the managers of São Paulo subsidiaries who had to argue against a New York logic based on risk avoidance. Evans uses the concept of "bounded rationality" to describe the behavior of most multinational corporations in countries of the periphery. He argues that managers, basing their decisions on an imperfect knowledge of local conditions and on their responsibility for global profits, not simply local ones, tend *not* to seek out opportunities for maximizing profits through growth or innovation. "Bounded rationality," says Evans, "helps explain why foreign investors [in Brazil] did not spontaneously start manufacturing operations in the periphery during the earlier phase of imperialism. . . . Sometimes they may have been right not to invest. The point is that if and when they were wrong, they were likely to be wrong in the direction of overestimating the riskiness of investment on the periphery. The classic entrepreneur is just the opposite. When he is wrong, it is likely to be because he underestimates risk."[24]

Rockefeller and Kaiser extended themselves to local conditions, exploring for themselves the opportunities for innovation. If anything, in Evans's words, they constitutionally tended to underestimate risk. They were entrepreneurs who reflected the "big thinking" style of the Roosevelt and early postwar eras as well as the blithe utopianism that at times softened the arrogant, parochial assumptions of American liberalism. For Kaiser this meant worldwide abundance by the year 2000. For Rockefeller it meant a "Dream World of 1984—United States Style," in which nation-states would cede a portion of their sovereignty to regional coalitions under the United Nations which could achieve the "wide-spread dynamic economic growth . . . basic to individual opportunity and to the development of those social institutions which make possible the uni-

24. *Dependent Development,* 36.

versal aspirations for the dignity, freedom and well-being of the individual."[25]

In addition to furthering corporate awareness of development and good citizenship issues, Rockefeller and Kaiser had an important effect on U.S.-Brazil relations. Kaiser enhanced the image of American business by showing an eagerness to cooperate with Brazilian plans, while Rockefeller's close working relationship with a variety of Brazilians at the highest levels of government served to prolong Brazilian goodwill toward North America during the 1950s. Both men proposed projects consonant with Brazilian developmentalism at the time, and worked well with local politicians and businessmen who wanted to Brazilianize U.S. technology. Their efforts undoubtedly helped reinforce Brazilian perceptions (in accord with U.S. goals) that capitalism was the economic system to be preferred. As the list of grievances against the United States grew longer and longer in the late 1950s, eventually leading Kubitschek and his successors to recognize the bankruptcy of the special relationship and propose instead such multilateral solutions for economic development as Operation Pan America in 1958, the private activities of Rockefeller and Kaiser were counterweights to the worsening trend of official U.S.-Brazil relations. And to the extent that their activities did foster aspects of Brazil's development as a regional economic power—its agriculture, financial market, and heavy industry—Rockefeller and Kaiser furthered the traditional American policy of enhancing Brazilian prestige within the Latin American context in order to increase the southern nation's usefulness as a strategic ally in Pan-American questions.

Within the larger Latin American context, however, the Kaiser-Rockefeller activities could do little, limited as they were, to ameliorate the oppressiveness of the power imbalance between North and South. Given the wide disparity in resources of all kinds, the imbalance would have existed regardless of policy on either side, but it was made intolerable by the arrogance, continued interference, and deepening economic control of the United States, combined with the increasing nationalism of Latin American nations in the 1950s and 1960s. The failure of the Alliance for Progress to promote significant economic change revealed once and for all how tiny was the carrot that the United States offered to Latin Americans in return for their allegiance. At the same time, covert and overt intervention in Guatemala (1954), Cuba (1961), Brazil (1964), and the

25. Nelson Rockefeller, "Dream World of 1984—United States Style," 4. This statement is from a collection of handwritten and typewritten notes made by Rockefeller during the Special Studies Project. There is nothing to indicate that he ever showed it to anyone. RAC, RDF Special Studies Project, Series 10, Box 68, File. "Overall Panel—March 19 and 20, 1957."

Dominican Republic (1965) showed the narrow limits of the United States' willingness to negotiate conflicts before resorting to a stick.

The low point to which relations had declined as well as the limits of private diplomacy and personal goodwill was most clearly demonstrated in 1968. Nelson Rockefeller, acting as an official U.S. representative in Latin America for the first time since the inaugural of Getúlio Vargas in 1951, went on a fact-finding tour for President Richard M. Nixon, and his presence caused widespread student riots. Little did it matter what Nelson Rockefeller had done to promote food development, rural extension, and investment opportunities for the middle class. Angry young Latin Americans were either unaware of these efforts or simply unimpressed by them in light of Rockefeller investments in Venezuelan oil, which indeed were part and parcel of the old guard system of North American imperialism. To them the name Rockefeller, like that of the United States, symbolized above all the callous extraction of Latin American wealth.

Interestingly, many Latin Americans (and liberal U.S. academics) were also unimpressed by the report which resulted from Rockefeller's trip. In urging the government not to turn its back on Latin American dictatorships even though it should prefer democracies, the report essentially reiterated the nonintervention principle of the Good Neighbor policy. Indeed, twenty-three years earlier Rockefeller's intense negotiations to return Peronist Argentina to the inter-American fold over Cordell Hull's moral objections had been "a high point in the growth of the Good Neighbor policy," according to Bryce Wood.[26] But in 1968 such a stand would not wash. Following the dismantling of the policy in the previous decade, reformist and revolutionary Latin Americans no longer believed in the possibility of real nonintervention. The question was simply on whose side the United States would come down, and Rockefeller's report legitimized normal diplomatic and economic relations with dictatorships.

To historians, one of the most interesting legacies of these particular postwar ventures into private diplomacy, foreign philanthropy, and direct investment may be the extent to which they show that American-sponsored development did not lead *necessarily* to distorted, dependent, or exploitative development patterns under all conditions. As Robert Packenham notes, older analyses of Latin American dependency approached the problem "holistically," uniting, by definition, national dependency, exploitation, and internal inequality with expansive North

---

26. *The Dismantling of the Good Neighbor Policy* (Austin: University of Texas, 1985), 195.

American capitalism.[27] Case studies which show types of North American economic intervention that did not foster greater dependency are essential to reaching a more complex understanding both of the postwar relationship between North and South and of the strands of American ideology in the postwar period. Such studies may also enable scholars to separate analytically, as Nelson Rockefeller and Henry Kaiser tried to do practically, the existence of power disparities from exploitative practices.

In the three cases described here at length, AIA, IBEC, and WOB, the goods and services delivered were broadly useful to the Brazilian population, fit within the context of national goals set by the Brazilian government, and spread economic benefits in the form of wages, food, and stock ownership across a reasonably broad spectrum of society. In other words, they were a success, as defined by having been nationalized in one way or another, by contributing to significant (though, as is always the case, not untroubled) economic development, and by enduring for a number of decades. Brazilian involvement and control as well as the compatibility of Brazilian and American goals and cultural values and the sensitivity and mutual respect of the individuals involved made for this success.[28] Although these efforts were not characteristic of U.S. responses to Latin America at the time, or even now, they may point to better ways of designing development projects in the future.

Finally, these efforts underscore the extent to which the scholarly trend toward a broader definition of what counts as foreign relations is important and useful. While on some occasions a corporatist model of foreign relations may best fit the American case and on other occasions a pluralist model, it is clear that in this country both the public and private sectors play an important role in shaping relations with the rest of the world. Operating autonomously or in collaboration, their overlapping efforts give further texture to an increasingly complex, competitive, and interdependent world. With regard to Latin America from 1945 to 1960, that meant a private sector awakening to the necessity of corporatist compromises, a government largely dedicated to maintaining the status quo, and an opportunity for two individuals with the motive and nerve to reshape the foreign relations of U.S. capitalism.

27. "Trends in Brazilian National Dependency since 1964," in *Brazil in the Seventies*, ed. Riordan Roett (Washington, D.C.: American Enterprise Institute, 1976), 92. Also see Packenham, "Holistic Dependency and Analytic Dependency."
28. In the case of Willys, I use the word *nationalized* not in the sense of owned (that part of the experiment failed when Ford took over), but in the sense that Kubitschek's government used it: 100 percent local manufacture of automobiles.

Selected Bibliography

and Notes on Sources

Published Works and Other Secondary Sources

Adelman, Irma, and Cynthia Taft Morris. *Economic Growth and Social Equity in Developing Countries*. Stanford: Stanford University Press, 1973.

Aitken, Jr., Thomas. "The Double Image of American Business Abroad." *Harpers*, August 1960, 12–22.

Alsop, Stewart. *Nixon and Rockefeller: A Double Portrait*. Garden City, N.Y.: Doubleday, 1960.

Arnove, Robert F. *Philanthropy and Cultural Imperialism: The Foundations at Home and Abroad*. Boston: G. K. Hall, 1980.

Baer, Werner. *The Brazilian Economy: Growth and Development*. 2d ed. New York: Praeger, 1983.

———. *Industrialization and Economic Development in Brazil*. Homewood, Ill.: Richard D. Irwin, 1965.

Baldwin, David A. *Economic Development and American Foreign Policy: 1943–1962*. Chicago: University of Chicago Press, 1966.

Baldwin, Sidney. *Poverty and Politics: The Rise and Decline of the Farm Security Administration*. Chapel Hill: University of North Carolina Press, 1968.

Benjamin, Jules R. "The Framework of U.S. Relations with Latin America in the Twentieth Century: An Interpretive Essay." *Diplomatic History* 11, no. 2 (Spring 1987): 91–112.

Berle, Jr., Adolf A. *Navigating the Rapids, 1918–1971*. Edited by Beatrice Bishop Berle and Travis Beal Jacobs. New York: Harcourt, Brace, Jovanovich, 1973.

———, and Gardiner C. Means. *The Modern Corporation and Private Property*. New York: Macmillan, 1932.

Berman, Edward. *The Ideology of Philanthropy: The Influence of the Carnegie, Ford, and Rockefeller Foundations on American Foreign Policy*. Berkeley: University of California Press, 1983.

Blum, John Morton, ed. *The Price of Vision: The Diary of Henry A. Wallace*. Boston: Houghton Mifflin, 1973.

———. *V Was for Victory: Politics and American Culture During World War II*. New York: Harcourt, Brace, Jovanovich, 1976.

Bolling, Landrum R. *Private Foreign Aid: U.S. Philanthropy for Relief and Development*. Boulder: Westview Press, 1982.

Broehl, Wayne. *United States Business Performance Abroad: A Case Study of the International Basic Economy Corporation*. Washington: National Planning Association, 1968.

Brown, Richard. *Rockefeller Medicine Men: Medicine and Capitalism in America*. Berkeley: University of California Press, 1979.

Bullock, Mary Brown. *An American Transplant: The Rockefeller Foundation and Peking Union Medical College*. Berkeley: University of California Press, 1980.

Burns, E. Bradford. *The Unwritten Alliance: Rio Branco and Brazilian-American Relations.* New York: Columbia University Press, 1966.

Burns, James MacGregor. *Roosevelt: The Soldier of Freedom.* New York: Harcourt, Brace, Jovanovich, 1970.

Butler, W. Jack. "Fighting Communism Overseas." *Harvard Business Review* 34, no. 4 (July-August 1956): 96–104.

———. "Public Relations for Industry in Underdeveloped Countries." *Harvard Business Review* 30, no. 5 (September-October 1952): 63–71.

Cardoso, Fernando H., and Enzo Faletto. *Dependency and Development in Latin America.* Berkeley: University of California Press, 1979.

Cardoso, Miriam Limoeiro. *Ideologia do Desenvolvimento, Brasil: JK-JQ.* Rio de Janeiro: Paz e Terra, 1978.

Castro, Ana Célia. "Crescimento da Firma e Diversificação Productiva: O Caso Agroceres." Diss., Universidade Estadual de Campinas, 1988.

Collier, Peter, and David Horowitz. *The Rockefellers: An American Dynasty.* New York: Holt, Rinehart, and Winston, 1976.

Collins, Robert M. *The Business Response to Keynes, 1929–1964.* New York: Columbia University Press, 1981.

Conick, M. C. "Stimulating Private Investment." *Harvard Business Review* 31, no. 6 (November-December 1953): 104–12.

Connery, Robert H., and Gerald Benjamin. *Rockefeller of New York: Executive Power in the Statehouse.* Ithaca: Cornell University Press, 1979.

Curti, Merle. *American Philanthropy Abroad.* New Brunswick, N.J.: Rutgers University Press, 1963.

———, and Kendall Birr. *Prelude to Point Four: American Technical Missions Overseas, 1838–1938.* Madison: University of Wisconsin Press, 1954.

Daland, Robert. *Brazilian Planning: Development Politics and Administration.* Chapel Hill: University of North Carolina Press, 1967.

Dallek, Robert. *The American Style of Foreign Policy: Cultural Politics and Foreign Affairs.* New York: Oxford University Press, 1983.

———. *Franklin D. Roosevelt and American Foreign Policy, 1932–1945.* New York: Oxford University Press, 1979.

Dalrymple, Martha. *The AIA Story: Two Decades of International Cooperation.* New York: American International Association, 1968.

Davis, Saville, et al. "The Struggle for Men's Minds Abroad." *Harvard Business Review* 30, no. 4 (July-August 1952): 121–32.

DeConde, Alexander. *American Diplomatic History in Transformation.* Washington: American Historical Association, 1976.

Dernburg, H. J. "Prospects for Long-Term Foreign Investment." *Harvard Business Review* (July 1950): 104–12.

Desmond, James. *Nelson Rockefeller: A Political Biography.* New York: Macmillan, 1964.

Development of Brazil: Report of the Joint Brazil–United States Economic Development Commission. Washington: GPO, 1954.

Dicionário Histórico-Biográfico Brasileiro, 1930–1983. Rio de Janeiro: Forense-Universitária Ltda., 1984.

Eells, Richard. *Corporation Giving in a Free Society.* New York: Harper and Brothers, 1956.

Erb, Claude C. "Prelude to Point Four: The Institute of Inter-American Affairs." *Diplomatic History* 9, no. 3, 249–69.

Ettling, John. *The Germ of Laziness: Rockefeller Philanthropy and Public Health in the New South.* Cambridge: Harvard University Press, 1981.

Evans, Peter. *Dependent Development: The Alliance of Multinational, State, and Local Capital in Brazil.* Princeton: Princeton University Press, 1979.

Fitzgerald, Deborah. "Exporting American Agriculture: The Rockefeller Foundation in Mexico, 1943–53." *Social Studies of Science* 16 (1986): 457–83.

Flynn, Peter. *Brazil: A Political Analysis.* London: Ernest Benn Ltd., 1978.

Foreign Commerce Yearbook. Washington: GPO, by year before 1950.

Foreign Relations of the United States. Washington: GPO, by year.

Fosdick, Raymond B. *The Story of the Rockefeller Foundation.* New York: Harper and Brothers, 1952.

Foster, Mark S. "Giant of the West: Henry J. Kaiser and Regional Industrialization, 1930–1950." *Business History Review* 59, no. 1 (Spring 1985): 1–23.

———. *Henry J. Kaiser: Builder in the Modern American West.* Austin: University of Texas Press, 1989.

Frank, Andre Gunder. *Capitalism and Underdevelopment in Latin America: Historical Studies of Chile and Brazil.* New York: Monthly Review Press, 1967.

Fundação Getúlio Vargas. *Impasse na Democracia Brasileira, 1951–1955: Coletânea de Documentos.* Rio de Janeiro: Fundação Getúlio Vargas, 1983.

Fundação Getúlio Vargas, *Dicionário Histórico-Biográfico Brasileiro.* Rio de Janeiro: Forense—Universitária, 1985.

Gardner, Lloyd C. *Economic Aspects of New Deal Diplomacy.* Madison: University of Wisconsin Press, 1964.

Gellman, Irwin. *Good Neighbor Diplomacy.* Baltimore: Johns Hopkins University Press, 1979.

Gilpin, Robert. *U.S. Power and the Multinational Corporation.* New York: Basic Books, 1975.

Gordon, Lincoln. *New Deal for Latin America: The Alliance for Progress.* Cambridge: Harvard University Press, 1963.

———. "Private Enterprise and International Development." *Harvard Business Review* 38, no. 4 (July-August 1960): 134–38.

———, and Engelbert L. Grommers. *United States Manufacturing Investment in Brazil, 1946–1960.* Cambridge: Harvard University Press, 1962.

Gorman, Robert F. *Private Voluntary Organizations as Agents of Development.* Boulder: Westview Press, 1984.

Green, David. *The Containment of Latin America: A History of the Myths and Realities of the Good Neighbor Policy.* Chicago: Quadrangle Books, 1971.

Haines, Gerald K. *The Americanization of Brazil: A Study of U.S. Cold War Diplomacy in the Third World, 1945–1954.* Wilmington, Del.: Scholarly Resources, 1989.

Hartz, Louis. *The Liberal Tradition in America.* New York: Harcourt, Brace, and World, 1955.

Hawley, Ellis W. "The Corporate Ideal as Liberal Philosophy in the New Deal." In *The Roosevelt New Deal: A Program Assessment Fifty Years Later,* edited by Wilbur J. Cohen, 85–103. Austin: University of Texas Press, 1986.

Hess, Therese, et al. *The Disability of Wealth: An Inquiry into the Nomination of Nelson Rockefeller as Vice-President.* Washington: Institute for Policy Studies, 1974.

Hewlett, Sylvia. *The Cruel Dilemmas of Development.* New York: Basic Books, 1980.

Hilton, Stanley. *Brazil and the Great Powers, 1930–1939: The Politics of Trade Rivalry.* Austin: University of Texas Press, 1973.

————. "Brazilian Diplomacy and the Washington-Rio de Janiero 'Axis' during the World War II Era." *Hispanic American Historical Review* 59, no. 2 (May 1979): 201–31.

————. "The United States, Brazil, and the Cold War, 1945–1960: End of the Special Relationship." *Journal of American History* 68, no. 3 (December 1981): 599–624.

Hirschman, Albert O. *Getting Ahead Collectively: Grassroots Experiences in Latin America.* New York: Pergamon Press, 1984.

————. *The Strategy of Economic Development.* New Haven: Yale University Press, 1958.

Hogan, Michael J. *The Marshall Plan: America, Britain, and the Reconstruction of Europe, 1947–1952.* Cambridge: Cambridge University Press, 1987.

Humphrey, John. *Capitalist Control and Worker's Struggle in the Brazilian Auto Industry.* Princeton: Princeton University Press, 1982.

Kaiser Story, The. Oakland: Kaiser Industries Corporation, 1968.

Kaufman, Burton J. *Trade and Aid: Eisenhower's Foreign Economic Policy.* Baltimore: Johns Hopkins University Press, 1982.

Kennedy, David M. *Over Here: The First World War and American Society.* New York: Oxford University Press, 1980.

Keohane, Robert O., and Joseph S. Nye. *Power and Interdependence: World Politics in Transition.* Boston: Little, Brown, 1977.

Kesaris, Paul, ed. *O.S.S./State Department Intelligence and Research Reports, XIV, Latin America, 1941–1961.* Washington: University Publications of America, 1982.

Klarén, Peter F., and Thomas J. Bossert. *Promise of Development: Theories of Change in Latin America.* Boulder: Westview Press, 1986.

Kramer, Michael S., and Sam Roberts. *"I Never Wanted to Be Vice-President of Anything."* New York: Basic Books, 1976.

Kubitschek de Oliveira, Juscelino. *Diretrizes Gerais do Plano Nacional de Desenvolvimento.* Belo Horizonte, 1955.

Lafer, Betty Mindlin. *Planejamento no Brasil.* São Paulo: Editora Perspectiva, 1975.

Leacock, Ruth. "JFK, Business, and Brazil." *Hispanic American Historical Review* 59, no. 4 (1979): 636–73.

Leite, Cleantho de Paiva. "Vargas Foreign Policy, 1951–1954: An Inside View." *Occasional Papers in Latin American Studies.* Stanford: Stanford-Berkeley Joint Center for Latin American Studies, 1984.

Levinson, Jerome, and Juan de Onis. *The Alliance That Lost Its Way: A Critical Report on the Alliance for Progress.* Chicago: Quadrangle Books, 1970.

Little, George F. G. "Fazenda Cambuhy: A Case History of Social and Economic Development in the Interior of São Paulo." Ph.D. diss. University of Florida, 1960.

Lopes, Lucas. "JK e o Programa de Metas: Palestra do Ministro Lucas Lopes." Brasília. May 14, 1986.

Lowenthal, Abraham F. *Exporting Democracy: The United States and Latin America.* Baltimore: Johns Hopkins University Press, 1990.

————, and Albert Fishlow. *Latin America's Emergence: Toward a U.S. Response.* New York: Foreign Policy Association, 1979.

Luce, Henry R. *The American Century.* New York: Farrar and Rinehart, 1941.

Mashek, Robert W. *The Inter-American Foundation in the Making.* Washington: Inter-American Foundation, n.d.

McCann, Frank. "Brazil, the United States, and World War II: A Commentary." *Diplomatic History* 3, no. 1 (Winter 1979): 59–76.

————. *The Brazilian-American Alliance, 1937–1945.* Princeton: Princeton University Press, 1973.

McCormick, Thomas. "Drift or Mastery? A Corporatist Synthesis for American Diplomatic History." In *The Promise of American History: Progress and Prospects*, edited by Stanley J. Kutler and Stanley N. Katz, 318–30. Baltimore: Johns Hopkins University Press, 1982.

Millikan, Max F., and Walt W. Rostow. *A Proposal: Key to an Effective Foreign Policy*. New York: Harper, 1957.

Morris, Joe Alex. *Nelson Rockefeller: A Biography*. New York: Harper and Brothers, 1960.

Morrison, deLesseps. *Latin American Mission*. New York: Simon and Schuster, 1965.

Mosher, Arthur T. *Technical Cooperation in Latin American Agriculture*. Chicago: University of Chicago Press, 1957.

———. *Technical Cooperation in Latin America: A Case Study of the Agricultural Program of ACAR in Brazil*. Washington: National Planning Association, 1955.

Moura, Gerson, and Margarida Maria Moura. "A Modernizacão dos Anos 40: A Agricultura Brasileira Pensada 'a Americana." Unpublished paper. Rio de Janeiro, October 1983.

Moura, Gerson. "Brazilian Foreign Relations, 1939–1950: The Changing Nature of Brazil—United States Relations Before and After the Second World War." Diss. University College London, 1982.

———. *Tio Sam Chega ao Brasil: A Penetração Cultural Americana*. 4th ed. São Paulo: Brasiliense, 1986.

National Planning Association, *Technical Cooperation in Latin America*. Washington: National Planning Association, 1954.

Ninkovich, Frank. *The Diplomacy of Ideas*. Cambridge: Cambridge University Press, 1981.

———. "The Rockefeller Foundation, China, and Cultural Change." *Journal of American History* 70, no. 4 (March 1984): 799–820.

Packenham, Robert A. "Holistic Dependency and Analytic Dependency: Two Approaches to Dependency and Dependency Reversal." *Occasional Papers in Latin American Studies*, Number 6. Stanford: Stanford-Berkeley Joint Center for Latin American Studies, Winter 1984.

———. *Liberal America and the Third World: Political Development Ideas and Social Science*. Princeton: Princeton University Press, 1973.

———. "Trends in Brazilian National Dependency since 1964." In *Brazil in the Seventies*, edited by Riordan Roett, 89–115. Washington: American Enterprise Institute, 1976.

Panuch, J. Anthony. "A Businessman's Philosophy for Foreign Affairs." *Harvard Business Review* 35, no. 2 (March-April 1957): 41–53.

Parker, Phyllis. *Brazil: The Quiet Intervention, 1964*. Austin: University of Texas Press, 1979.

Partners in Progress: A Report to President Truman by the International Development Advisory Board. Foreword by Nelson A. Rockefeller. New York: Simon and Schuster, 1951.

Persico, Joseph E. *The Imperial Rockefeller: A Biography of Nelson A. Rockefeller*. New York: Simon and Schuster, 1982.

Potter, David M. *People of Plenty: Economic Abundance and the American Character*. Chicago: University of Chicago Press, 1954.

Quem Controla O Que: O Capital Estrangeiro No Brasil. São Paulo: Editôra Banas, 1961.

Rabe, Stephen G. *Eisenhower and Latin America: The Foreign Policy of Anti-Communism*. Chapel Hill: University of North Carolina Press, 1988.

Report of the American Technical Mission to Brazil. Washington: Board of Economic Warfare, December 1942.

Report of the Joint Brazil–United States Technical Commission. Washington: GPO, 1949.

Rhodes, Robert I., ed. *Imperialism and Underdevelopment.* London: Monthly Review Press, 1970.

Ribeiro, José Paulo, and Clifton R. Wharton, Jr. "The ACAR Program in Minas Gerais, Brazil." In *Subsistence Agriculture and Economic Development,* edited by Clifton Wharton, 424–38. Chicago: Aldine, 1969.

Rockefeller Brothers Fund. *Prospect for America.* New York: Doubleday, 1961.

Rockefeller, Nelson A. *The Future of Federalism: The Godkin Lectures.* Cambridge: Harvard University Press, 1962

———. *The Rockefeller Report on the Americas: The Official Report of a United States Presidential Mission.* Chicago: Quadrangle Books, 1969.

Roett, Riordan. *Brazil in the Sixties.* Nashville: Vanderbilt University Press, 1972.

———. *The Politics of Foreign Aid in the Brazilian Northeast.* Nashville: Vanderbilt University Press, 1972.

Rostow, Walt W. *Eisenhower, Kennedy, and Foreign Aid.* Austin: University of Texas Press, 1985.

Rowland, Donald W. *History of the Office of the Coordinator of Inter-American Affairs.* Washington: GPO, 1947.

Ruml, Beardsley, and Theodore Geiger, eds. *The Manual of Corporate Giving.* Washington: National Planning Association, 1952.

Schuh, G. Edward. *The Agricultural Development of Brazil.* New York: Praeger, 1970.

Skidmore, Thomas E. *Politics in Brazil, 1930–1964: An Experiment in Democracy.* New York: Oxford University Press, 1967.

Stein, Mimi. *A Special Difference: A History of Kaiser Aluminum and Chemical Corporation.* Oakland: Kaiser Aluminum and Chemical Corp., 1980.

Trask, Roger. "The Impact of the Cold War on United States–Latin American Relations, 1945–1949." *Diplomatic History* 1, no. 3 (Summer 1977): 272–73.

Tulchin, Joseph. *Problems in Latin American History.* New York: Harper and Row, 1973.

Turner, Michael. *The Vice-President as Policy Maker: Rockefeller in the Ford White House.* Westport, Ct.: Greenwood Press, 1982.

Underwood, James E., and William Daniels. *Governor Rockefeller in New York: The Apex of Pragmatic Liberalism in the United States.* Westport, Ct.: Greenwood Press, 1982.

United Nations, *Statistical Yearbooks.* New York: United Nations, by year.

U.S. Congress. House. Committee on Foreign Affairs. *Historical Series, Selected Executive Session Hearings of the Committee, 1951–1956.* Volume 16. Washington: GPO, 1980.

U.S. Congress. House. Committee on Foreign Affairs. Hearings. *International Cooperation Act of 1949 (Point Four Program).* Washington: GPO, 1950.

U.S. Congress. House. Committee on the Judiciary. *Debate on the Nomination of Nelson Rockefeller to be Vice-President of the United States.* Washington: GPO: 1975.

U.S. Congress. House. Committee on the Judiciary. *Nomination of Nelson A. Rockefeller to be Vice-President of the United States, Hearings.* Washington: GPO, 1974.

Wagner, R. Harrison. *United States Policy Toward Latin America.* Stanford: Stanford University Press, 1970.

Weis, W. Michael. "Roots of Estrangement: The United States and Brazil, 1950–1961." Ph.D. diss. Ohio State University 1987.

Welles, Sumner. *Where Are We Heading?* New York: Harper and Brothers, 1946.

Wharton, Clifton R., Jr. "Aiding the Community: A New Philosophy for Foreign Operations." *Harvard Business Review* 32, no. 2 (March-April 1954): 64–72.

Wills, Gary. *Nixon Agonistes*. Boston: Houghton Mifflin, 1970.
Wilson, Joan Hoff. *American Business and Foreign Policy, 1920–1933*. Lexington: University of Kentucky Press, 1971.
Wirth, John. *The Politics of Brazilian Development, 1930–1954*. Stanford: Stanford University Press, 1970.
Wood, Bryce. *The Dismantling of the Good Neighbor Policy*. Austin: University of Texas, 1985.
———. *The Making of the Good Neighbor Policy*. New York: Columbia University Press, 1961.
Zoumaris, Thomas. "Containing Castro: Promoting Homeownership in Peru, 1956–61." *Diplomatic History* 10, no. 2 (Spring 1986): 161–81.

Unpublished and Archival Materials

Rockefeller Archive Center, Pocantico Hills, North Tarrytown, New York: Berent Friele Papers (unprocessed); American International Association; International Basic Economy Corporation (unprocessed); John R. Camp Papers; Rockefeller Brothers Fund; Rockefeller Brothers Fund Special Studies Project (in process); Rockefeller Family; Rockefeller Foundation; Wayne Broehl Papers (unprocessed).
Bancroft Library, University of California, Berkeley: Edgar F. Kaiser and Henry J. Kaiser Papers.
Ford Foundation Archives, The Ford Foundation, New York: Unpublished staff reports and oral histories.
Fundação Getúlio Vargas, Centro de Pesquisa e Documentação de História Contemporânea do Brasil, Botofogo, Rio de Janiero, Brazil: Papers of Ernani Amaral Peixoto; Eugênio Gudin; Getúlio Vargas; and Oswaldo Aranha. Also, archives based on selected documents from the British Foreign Office; from the John F. Kennedy Library; from the Dwight D. Eisenhower Library; and from the Harry S Truman Library.
Itamaraty, Arquivos do Ministro das Relações Exteriores, Rio de Janeiro: Missões Diplomáticas Brasileira, Washington, Ofícios; Estados Unidos da America, Notas and Despachos.
National Archives of the United States, Washington: Records of the Department of State (Record Group 59), including: Decimal Files for 1945–59; Records of the Committee on Inter-American Economic Development (1944–45); Inter-American Economic Affairs Committee (1945–50); Office of American Republic Affairs (ARA); Office of Research and Intelligence, ARA; Office Files of the Assistant Secretaries of State for ARA, Edward G. Miller, Jr., John M. Cabot, Henry H. Holland; Records of the Officer-in-Charge of Brazilian Affairs, Sterling Cottrell.

Oral History Interviews (conducted by the author)

Richard S. Aldrich. Burlingame, California, January 8, 1988.
Euclydes Aranha Netto. Rio de Janeiro, August 14, 1990.
Oswaldo Gudolle Aranha. Rio de Janeiro, October 29, 1986, November 14, 1986, and August 23, 1990.
Henry W. Bagley. New York City, August 5, 1987.
Ney Bittencourt de Araújo. São Paulo, August 24, 1990.
Roberto Campos. Rio de Janeiro, October 13, 1986.

J. Burke Knapp. Portola Valley, California, April 1, 1985.
Sydney Latini. Rio de Janeiro, November 7, 1986.
Paulo Pereira Lira. Rio de Janeiro, October 27, 1986.
Cleantho de Paiva Leite. Rio de Janeiro, October 24 and November 4, 1986.
Lucas Lopes. Rio de Janeiro, October 16, 1986.
Admiral Lúcio Meira. Rio de Janeiro, November 12, 1986.
Max Pearce. Orinda, California, January 14, 1987.
David Rockefeller. New York City, June 14, 1989.
Rodman C. Rockefeller. New York City, August 4, 1987.
Walther Moreira Salles. Rio de Janeiro, November 19, 1986.
E. E. Trefethen. Oakland, California, January 15, 1987.
Alzira Vargas. Rio de Janeiro, November 18, 1986.

Notes on Sources

Because of the nature of the topic, this research is based on sources in both the United States and Brazil, public and private. In the United States I found the collections of the Rockefeller Archive Center, the Bancroft Library, and the National Archives in Washington, D.C., to be the most useful.

Many of the particular collections which I used at the Rockefeller Archive Center were either not yet processed or were just being processed. It is a testament to the flexibility and helpfulness of the archive's administration and staff that these papers were nonetheless readily made available. The large archives of the International Basic Economy Corporation and the papers of Wayne Broehl are the most disorganized of those collections still un-processed and can be frustrating to work with. Files are not chronological, boxes are not organized by subject, and papers sometimes stick out at all angles. On the other hand, the carefully and elegantly processed archives of the American International Association, the Rockefeller Foundation, the Rockefeller Family, and the John R. Camp papers are a compensation. One reason I used as many different collections as I did is that most of the papers of Nelson Rockefeller himself were not yet open, and so it was necessary to rely on the papers of his associates and on organizational collections for clues to his activities and ideas.

The University of California's Bancroft Library contains the complete papers of Henry J. Kaiser and Edgar F. Kaiser. Henry Kaiser's papers have been fully processed, while those of Edgar are still being completed. In this case as well, I found the archive's staff to be helpful and unfailingly generous in sharing collections as they were being processed. Each collection is organized by topic and date, and the papers of the two men tend to overlap, especially with regard to the early days in Brazil. Edgar Kaiser's archives contain considerable information about the later operations of WOB, while Henry Kaiser's papers are most helpful with regard to the early period. Use of the National Archives is essentially self-explanatory, due to its clear index and reference systems. I must admit, though, that I did not find extensive amounts of information there that would significantly alter the picture of U.S.-Brazil relations reflected in the condensed but comprehensive volumes of *Foreign Relations of the United States*. The collection that was most useful to me, and that offered the most new information, was the office files of Assistant Secretary of State Edward G. Miller, Jr. This collection was helpful both for its files on the Business Advisory Council and for correspondence with Nelson Rockefeller.

In Brazil I used the collections at two institutions. The first collections I used were at the Centro de Pesquisa e Documentação de História Contemporânea do Brasil (CPDOC), which is a part of the Fundação Getúlio Vargas in Rio de Janeiro. Both CPDOC and the foundation are relatively young institutions devoted to research on Brazil. CPDOC houses the papers of many of Brazil's leading politicians, most especially from before the overthrow of democracy in 1964. It is a relatively unusual institution in Latin America, where political figures frequently take their records with them when they leave office, and where organized archives are often not open except on a privileged basis. CPDOC welcomes all scholars, and its staff is efficient, friendly, and helpful. At the archives, documents must be ordered by number, using indexes provided in CPDOC's research room. This system operates efficiently in that archivists retrieve the documents quickly. But it represents a major drawback for researchers who, when browsing through whole boxes or cartons in other archives, often find that the most interesting file is in front of or behind the file which appeared most important in the index. In addition to the records of leading Brazilians, CPDOC also has a useful collection of duplicated documents from American and British archives brought back by historians who have done research in those countries.

I was also fortunate to be able to use the archives of Itamaraty (the Ministry of Foreign Relations) in Rio de Janeiro, where the pre-1959 records of the ministry (before its move to Brasília) are kept. I say fortunate because this is not a privilege that is uniformly given either to Brazilian or North American researchers. Although it took several weeks for my application to use the archives to be approved, it was. I have no explanation for why this courtesy was extended to me, but I am grateful for it. The collection is in many ways rather limited. I was told that there are only three types of records: notes from the American embassy in Rio to Itamaraty (Notas); correspondence from the Brazilian embassy in Washington to Itamaraty (Missões); and despatches from Itamaraty to the embassy in Washington (Despachos). There are no records available, or at least no records were made available to me, of internal correspondence or reports within the ministry. The Notas, Missões, and Despachos are pasted into scrapbooks, which makes them easy to handle but also, one would suspect, likely to deteriorate more quickly as the glue and paper interact over time. One also wonders which documents may have been selected out, if any.

Another extremely important source for this research was oral history interviews with a variety of Americans and Brazilians who were either leading political figures or participants in activities with Rockefeller and Kaiser. Every person whom I asked to participate in this study was good enough to do so, and I owe a great debt to them for their generosity and candor.

Index

Abbink, John, 69, 72–73; and postwar aid, 53–55; and Joint Commission, 75; and World Bank, 92; and American International Association, 124, 139

Acheson, Dean, 70; and postwar aid, 53–54; and Joint Commission, 76, 78; and World Bank, 83, 87; and American International Association, 139

Africa, and competitive coffee production, 70

Agency for International Development (AID), 121–23, 130, 138

Agriculture: and government–supported development, 8, 14; and American International Association, 100–05, 110–11, 113, 116–17; and ACAR, 106–12, 115; problems of, 118; reform, 119–20; and Abbink mission, 124; financing of, 125, 133; and CAR, 131; and ABCAR, 134; reform, 135–36; and IBEC, 140–41, 146–48, 179; and SASA, 150–61. *See also* Extension services

Agroceres Limitada, 151–55, 158, 183

Aldrich, Richard: and SASA, 160–61; and Fundo Crescinco, 166, 171, 173–75; and IBEC, 179, 183; and Willys-Overland do Brasil, 225

Alliance for Progress: basis of, 13, 97; and American International Association, 121–22, 130, 134, 138; and Willys-Overland do Brasil, 226, 229; and Cuba, 239; and corporatism, 251

Aluminum, 230

American International Association, 100–07, 109, 123; and postwar aid, 56–58, 60; and medical services, 107–08; in Venezuela, 110; development of, 110–19; and Kennedy, 121; and resettlement, 122; and State Department, 124; financing of, 125–26, 128–29; expansion of, 127; administration of, 130; impact of, 131–32, 134–38; and Brazilianization, 133; and interdependence, 137; and IBEC, 141–44, 146, 176–77; and SASA, 151, 155; and

Fundo Crescinco, 169; and economic development, 247; and corporatism, 253

American Overseas Finance Corporation, 225

American Republic Affairs, 92

Aranha, Euclydes, 222, 232–34

Aranha, Oswaldo, 59, 64–65, 69

Aranha, Oswaldo Gudolle: and IBEC, 179, 188; and Willys Overland do Brasil, 207–08, 213–18, 222–24, 233

Argentina, 62, 69–71; defense policy of, 35; in wartime, 44; and postwar aid, 52, and Eisenhower administration, 97, 99; and IBEC, 181, 185; and Kaiser automobiles, 214, 218n, 227; and interdependence, 241–43; and corporatism, 252

Associação Brasileiro de Crédito e Assistência Rural (ABCAR), 101, 105–08, 118, 127; funding of, 126, 128; outcomes of, 131–35

Associação de Crédito e Assistência Rural (ACAR): annual reports of, 109; and Brazilianization, 110, 133; history of, 111–12, 115–18, 120; and Kennedy, 121; and State Department, 124; financing of, 125–26, 128; outcomes of, 131–35; and IBEC, 145; and postwar capitalism, 198

Associação Nordestina de Crédito e Assistência Rural (ANCAR), 116

Automobile industry, 8; and Willys-Overland do Brasil, 206–07, 219–23; and labor, 223; and Brazilian politics, 224; and joint ventures, 227; profits, 231, 233

Bagley, Henry, 70, 109, 117, 168–69, 176–77

Bank loans, and ACAR, 106

Bank of Brazil, 117

Barbosa, Theodoro Quartim, and Willys-Overland do Brasil, 203, 215–18, 222–24